S0-AHN-658

ANOTHER FRANK CAPRA

RECENT BOOKS IN THE SERIES

Film at the Intersection of High and Mass Culture, by Paul Coates
Hollywood Censored: Morality Codes, Catholics, and the Movies, by Gregory Black
Inside Soviet Film Satire: Laughter with a Lash, Andrew Horton, editor
Melodrama and Asian Cinema, by Wimal Dissanayake
Russian Critics on the Cinema of Glasnost, Michael Brashinsky & Andrew Horton, editors

ANOTHER FRANK CAPRA

LELAND POAGUE

Iowa State University

Once again,
for Susan

Published by the Press Syndicate of the University of Cambridge
The Pitt Building, Trumpington Street, Cambridge CB2 1RP
40 West 20th Street, New York, NY 10011-4211, USA
10 Stamford Road, Oakleigh, Melbourne 3166, Australia

First published 1994

Printed in the United States of America

Library of Congress Cataloging-in-Publication Data
Poague, Leland A., 1948–
Another Frank Capra / Leland Poague.
p. cm. – (Cambridge studies in film)
Includes bibliographical references (p.).
ISBN 0-521-38066-9 (hardback). – ISBN 0-521-38978-X (paperback)
1. Capra, Frank, 1897–91 – Criticism and interpretation.
I. Title. II. Series.
PN1998.3.C36P63 1994
791.43'0233'092 – dc20 94-9603
CIP

A catalog record for this book is available from the British Library

ISBN 0-521-38066-9 hardback
0-521-38978-X paperback

Contents

List of Illustrations

In many ways Frank Capra is the most familiar of American filmmakers, the most familiarly *American* of the generation of Hollywood directors who got started in the silent era and came of artistic age in the heyday of the 1930s, Hollywood's Golden Age. On the basis of his autobiography, we can say that Capra's love affair with America began even before he emigrated to America from Sicily in May of 1903; the first chapter of *The Name above the Title* opens "It all began with a letter. A letter from America – when I was a big-eyed child of five."[1] Some would say that Capra never ceased to be that big-eyed child, for whom America never ceased to be a source of almost other-worldly hope and fascination; others would claim that Capra's status as a social outsider – as a rough-and-tumble immigrant street tough in turn-of-the-century Los Angeles, as a well-educated (B.S. Throop College) but unemployable chemical engineer bumming around the American Southwest after World War I, as the ace go-it-alone director of a Poverty Row film production company known as Columbia Pictures – gave him an imaginative fulcrum from which to thematically and stylistically lever apart the "pattern of sameness" of the standard Hollywood story.[2] We will have occasion to ponder these and other pictures of Capra at greater length in the chapters that follow.

"America's Love Affair with Frank Capra" is a different though obviously related story.[3] On most accounts *that* story begins with the release of *It Happened One Night* in February of 1934. The film received positive notices, though typically as an unexpectedly deft example of the "bus talkie" cycle that was already in its waning stages. Strikingly, many among the more enthusiastic reviewers neglected to mention Capra by name; others were caught more than slightly off guard by the film's box-office staying power. Otis Ferguson's *New Republic* column of May 9 admits that "it is a little late in the day for mention of *It Happened One Night*" but does so anyway because "the picture is still floating around the little houses."[4] Moreover, even *after* Capra's "bus picture" captured a fistful of awards – including five major Oscars – William Troy was moved to ponder the gratifyingly grass-roots aspect of *It Happened One Night*'s success:

> There had been a whole succession of pictures based on the picaresque aspects of the cross-country bus; neither Claudette Colbert nor Clark Gable was a reigning favorite with the great popular public; and Frank Capra was merely one of several better than average Hollywood directors. In brief, the wholly spontaneous response with which the picture was received could be traced to no novelty or originality in its component elements.

Only "something of a miracle – in the least sentimental sense of that word" – could explain "the particular quality which separates this film from the dozen or more substantially like it."[5]

After the success of *It Happened One Night,* of course, things changed, not always for the better. Capra's was "The Name above the Title"; "Capra film" soon became a freestanding generic category – and a tempting critical target. Contemporary reviewers were quick to condemn the political sermonizing of Capra's immensely successful "populist" trilogy, and hence condemn those very same audiences who had saved *It Happened One Night* from bus-picture obscurity. The "America" of Capra's industry peers was a little slower in its faultfinding, to judge by the fact that Capra received best directing Oscars for *Mr. Deeds Goes to Town* and *You Can't Take It with You.* However, Capra's failure to garner major Oscars for *Mr. Smith Goes to Washington* or *Meet John Doe* or *It's a Wonderful Life* is often taken as evidence of a career decline, especially so given the pressure Capra was under, as an independent producer-director, to score big or go broke with the latter two films.

America's "love affair" with Frank Capra is certainly far from over. Despite its initially disappointing box-office performance, *It's a Wonderful Life* has become over time such an intimate and intricate part of American culture that both Christmas and Frank Capra are unthinkable without it. This latter fact alone is worth dwelling on because it establishes what I take to be an insurmountable barrier between the experience we can and should have of Capra's films *now* and any experience that his original audiences might have had. Films that Capra took a lifetime to create – and contemporary viewers a lifetime to experience, and largely in the order of their initial release – are now simultaneously available for concerted viewing thanks (largely) to the preservation efforts of Kit Parker Films and to the rise of video (cable, VCR) technology. Few members of *It's a Wonderful Life*'s original audience were likely to have seen *any* other Capra film very recently save his *Why We Fight* documentaries; their sense of Capra would probably have been far too weak to inform very deeply their viewing of his latest effort. However, it is the rare film student these days whose first viewing of an early Capra film is not already deeply influenced by previous and repeated viewings of *It's a Wonderful Life* on television, an experience obviously unavailable to any member of Capra's audience prior to 1947.

Indeed, academic film study is largely a product of the last thirty years, though that brief span has proven time enough for scholarship to institutionalize a range of viewing strategies undreamt of during Capra's filmmaking lifetime. Beside me as I write is a long shelf of books devoted in whole or part to Capra's career – many of which are required reading in college seminars on Capra – yet it is a curious fact of that scholarly tradition that it persists in thinking of its task in deeply paradoxical terms, as the story of Capra's purported decline, repeated despite all the contrary evidence just cited, makes clear. Indeed, of the fourteen feature films Capra made between 1934 and 1961, only two – *Broadway Bill* and its remake, *Riding High* – fail to appear on various standard lists of top grossing films for the years in question.[6] So box office is less an issue than some would make it, even if, as Charles Maland reports, three times as many people saw *Mr. Smith* as saw *State of the Union*.[7] Rather, what people like Maland seem to have most clearly in mind is less Capra's commercial fate or his artistic capacity than a decline in his status as a cultural weathervane; Capra stopped winning Oscars for his theatrical films after 1938, and his postwar films are far less readily described as at the vanguard edge of cultural change or renewal – at which point the interest of historically minded film scholars is likely to wane.

On some accountings, that is, Capra's importance follows from the "pastness" of his films, from the cultural effects they *had* at the time of their original production and release. Thus Charles Maland can urge that Capra's films "portray an image of ideal American middle-class values" and can use the claim to describe both "the cultural power and significance" of Capra's films between 1932 and 1948 and the subsequent decline of that power:

> Though middle-class values, particularly those of individualism and the success ethic, were under siege in the darkest years of the Depression, the country emerged without significant redistribution of wealth and power in part because images like

Capra's portrayals of America helped recreate a faith in the system. After that faith had solidified, and Americans – anxious about the Soviet threat after World War II – began to take a much darker, more realistic, and more materialistic approach to human affairs, it is no surprise that Capra's fortunes as a filmmaker should decline.[8]

Actually, there are two kinds of pastness at work in Maland's approach to Capra's cultural value. One of these I would call "explanatory," or "deterministic." In his study's concluding chapter Maland cites the editors of *Cahiers du cinéma* to the effect that "*every film is political,* inasmuch as it is determined by the ideology which produces it," from which they (and he) conclude that it is the work of film criticism, by specifying how different filmmakers fit (differently) into the "very clear picture" that is ideology, to "help change the ideology which conditions them."[9] The goal here is evident and admirable: positive social change. The method, however, is problematically analogical and (as film criticism) self-defeating. The "unknown" factor in this formulation is the film at hand; the known, which both determines and explains the film, is "ideology." Implied is a distant hope that a sure enough grasp of the machinery of culture will allow us to shift the gears and change the product. The more pragmatic consequence of placing "the known" at some point external or anterior to a given film is to empower the critic-as-knower over and against the film and its (putatively) passive viewers/consumers. In a classroom situation this means that a context students are required effectively to take on faith, as a product of scholarly or textbook authority, always subsumes the experience of film viewing. The film-critical catch here is obvious, especially in cases where films are unabashedly taken as symptoms of some larger historical circumstance or dilemma – why bother with the films at all? More specifically or pertinently, why bother with the kind of close textual analysis that keys on features consumerist audiences are unlikely to register much less reflect upon?[10]

A second sense of pastness is at work in such a view of film criticism that follows from but also undermines the first. Despite the repeated claim that Capra's cultural influence went on the decline after 1948, Maland frequently shifts into a present tense mode, as if Capra were still very much with us, were nowhere near "past" enough. "When Capra most closely identifies sacred values with the symbols of America," writes Maland, "he is centrally within the American grain – and he tends to inhibit social change."[11] The unavoidable implication of the latter phrase, at least for those committed to the necessity of social progress, is that we need to get *past* Capra, to put his cultural "mass" so far behind us that the ideological force of his gravity can no longer delay or retard our progress. However, the way to this gravityless "utopia" too often involves a mode of historical accounting that is rhetorically explanatory but (as history) self-contradicting.

An exemplary case in point is Nick Browne's recent analysis of *Meet John Doe*. Despite Browne's laudable ambition to advance "a fully cogent paradigm of the film/society relationship" as "a condition of interpreting changes in the evolution and function of film forms," he does so in order to "(re-)construct the historical dimension of Capra's work in the late thirties," which requires him "to demonstrate the premises of the audience's place" in the cultural and textual economy of *Meet John Doe*.[12] Moreover, by audience Browne clearly means "the audience that Capra sought," "the film's intended audience," the audience "inscribed" in and by the "dialogue" sustained between the overt rhetoric of the film and the more covert "socio-historical subtext" that, though read off of the film, finally "links" up with "the historical record."[13] Though Browne is explicitly committed to modeling shifts in text-context relations, his reconstruction of context always moves *backward* in time, from the 1941 moment of *Meet John Doe*'s initial theatrical release to the anterior conditions and events that made the release of *Meet John Doe* possible and interpretable.

A happy result of this procedure is to demonstrate, once again, the complexity and contingency of cultural relations and representations. Browne's picture of *Meet John Doe* shows it to be deeply related to a particular cultural moment, a sense of connectedness that many find grievously lacking in our postmodern metaera; that moment, moreover, is clearly rife with institutional conflicts and oppositions that might have resulted in a different film and that we can take as figuring our own hopes for remaking or redirecting the story of our culture. Barely acknowledged, however, is the implication that *Meet John Doe* can be fully grasped only against the causal context of its genetic circumstances, the latter understood quite exclusively as the social and institutional events leading up to the film's initial distribution, which comes near to saying that people disinclined to follow Browne into the Warner Bros. corporate archive would be better off to defer to Browne's authority. Or worse, that we cannot see and think intelligently about a film until its production history is excavated and placed in the public domain. The promise of "explanation" here effectively threatens the endless deferral of experience, keeps most films buried in a past that will never likely be made present. What gets lost or elided in the process is any sense of subsequent "reconfigurations" of *Meet John Doe,* as if interpretation itself had no history, as if the fifty years between our present and *Meet John Doe*'s past hardly mattered, as if the shift of "exhibition" from cinema palaces to university lecture halls to living-room VCRs has made no appreciable difference. There is considerably more to the notion of context than is known in Browne's philosophy. No doubt Browne would counter by suggesting that his model of social formations could readily be extended to include subsequent construals of the film – his own, for instance. However, Browne's apparently contingent decision to limit his consideration of *Meet John Doe*'s reception chiefly to that of its initial theatrical run is certainly compatible with the hope that Capra's ongoing and explicitly baleful cultural influence can be cut back or eliminated. Moreover, that hope directly contradicts the notion that social context determines (hence explains) cultural function, unless one assumes that in nearly all relevant respects the context in which we understand *Meet John Doe* today is identical to that of the film's first audience.

The background question at issue here is finally the relation of history to interpretation and to interpretive authority; the kind of answer I give to that question goes a long way toward explaining the shape of the book that follows. What I find most objectionable about the familiar picture of Capra is its retrospective denial of the power of retrospection. That Capra's films are culturally powerful is usually taken as a given. Too often, however, purportedly explanatory appeals to history are (more or less) disguised attempts to deny that power by substituting historical reconstruction for interpretive analysis and by limiting history to "the past." An elementary version of this denial is that which seeks to domesticate Capra's strangeness by reference to his life story; this is clearly a favorite tactic of Capra's autobiography, in which the story of his rise and fall is told as if it were something out of Horatio Alger or Charles Dickens – or Frank Capra. However, that only repeats the problem; Capra's life was no less strange than his movies. A related tactic for making Capra less strange is that which seeks (like Browne) to tie Capra and his films to a "determinant" historical moment. This tactic too has its limits. To claim that *Meet John Doe* is significant to us because of the significance it had for audiences or circumstances circa 1941 effectively puts the relevance issue on perpetual hold by begging the question of why that audience and its circumstances are relevant to viewers fifty years later.

Of course, history is hardly avoidable; in the following pages I too will make reference to Capra's autobiography and to social and production history. However, the authority I want to claim in so doing is less a matter of historical accuracy than of rhetorical aptness, a matter of the conviction I can solicit on behalf of the interpretive pertinence of the data I cite and the claims I advance. Put another way, I am chiefly interested in the relevance of Capra *now*. Indeed, the history that best helps us to answer the "relevance now" question is *not* the history of the film's making but that of its subsequent reception through time, a tradition in which the present book will eventually take its place and be historicized in turn.

I want to be as clear as possible about my own interests in these matters. A revised version of my doctoral dissertation on Capra was published in 1975 as *The Cinema of Frank Capra: An Approach to Film Comedy*. My primary motive in writing the present volume has been to work out and put on record a view of Capra that seems (to me, at least) astonishingly different from the Capra I came to know in graduate school. A primary historical concern of the pages that follow is to specify how that change came about, a specification I take on philosophical and ethical grounds to be *internal* to the claim of any genuine film criticism. As will become plain, the chapters that follow are obviously indebted to the efforts of contemporary feminist film scholars; I am now convinced that an important element of Capra's ongoing claim to cultural attention is his status as a protofeminist director. Furthermore, *that* claim is deeply indebted, in turn, to a mode of close textual analysis that has only lately – thanks chiefly to the examples of David Bordwell and Kristin Thompson – become a standard practice among film critics.[14] Crucial here is the extent to which previously neglected textual data can be seen to adhere into patterns that profoundly displace lately accepted understandings. Indeed, an important measure of the value of criticism is exactly its capacity to bring new data and patterns to light in ways that deeply change the views we hold. I hope I have done that here, and accordingly that the Capra encountered by at least some future viewers will lead to very different cultural consequences than those anxiously foreseen by Charles Maland and many others.

In order to render the familiar Capra somewhat less familiar I have organized the present study so as to avoid certain otherwise obligatory topics. I do not discuss *It Happened One Night* at great length, for example, though references to it are frequent and I hope suggestive. Nor have I felt obliged to discuss the whole populist trilogy as an unbreakable set. What I have to say about *Meet John Doe,* for example, is said largely in the opening segment of Chapter 1, well in advance of more extended discussions of *Mr. Deeds Goes to Town* and *Mr. Smith Goes to Washington.* Indeed, discussion of the latter two films is interrupted by an extended analysis of *Lost Horizon,* a film generally considered extraneous to Capra's otherwise profoundly American cultural project. Despite the generally chronological progress of Chapters 2–6, Chapter 1 undertakes in various ways to examine the necessarily retrospective aspect of all film criticism, the sense in which every truly interesting reading of a film is a kind of rereading. The first part of Chapter 1 considers *Meet John Doe* as, in some ways, Capra's tendentious and troubled rereading of his own rise to national prominence, a view inspired in part by Capra's depiction of John Doe on the cover of *Time* magazine, a gesture any reader of *The Name above the Title* is likely to register as an explicit gesture of self-inscription in view of Capra's own appearance on *Time*'s cover in August of 1938. The second segment of "Picturing Capra," though intended primarily as an introduction of critical terms lately crucial to my own thinking about Capra, also provides a capsule summary of the main trends in Capra criticism over the last three decades. The last segment of "Picturing Capra" offers a retrospective analysis of *You Can't Take It with You,* a film oddly neglected by most Capra scholars in the populist rush to get from *Mr. Deeds* to *Mr. Smith.* Capra received his last theatrical Oscar for *You Can't Take It with You;* its production prompted *Time*'s decision to feature Capra on the cover. In view of their devotion to history, the general reluctance of contemporary Capra scholars to consider a film that by "cultural weathervane" standards was one of Capra's most successful and significant movies amounts to a form of cultural repression. Its very strangeness prompts returning to it. A similar strangeness, regarding Capra generally, prompts my entire project.

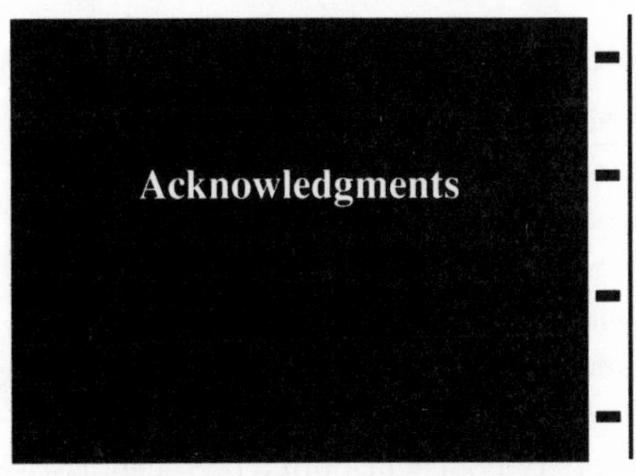

Acknowledgments

The first Capra film I explicitly remember seeing is *Pocketful of Miracles,* watched on a black and white television in the Sunnyvale, California, home of Robert and Leone Sanford while my wife and I were visiting over Christmas break in 1971. Later Susie and I saw *It Happened One Night* in one of William Cadbury's film classes at the University of Oregon, and then *Mr. Smith Goes to Washington* in the University of Oregon Film Society series. Soon thereafter I ran into Bill Cadbury at the reserve desk in the University of Oregon library. I told Bill I had chanced upon my dissertation topic. It turned out to be the chance of a lifetime.

So it is no easy thing to write acknowledgments some twenty years later as my second Capra book is going to press. Everyone thanked in *The Cinema of Frank Capra* deserves my thanks yet again; in many cases, thanks are due as much for love and support and encouragement in the years intervening as for kindness shown while I was researching my dissertation. Jon and Carol Sanford, William Cadbury, William Rothman, and Frank Capra are especially in my thoughts as I ponder my indebtedness on these accounts.

I am also deeply grateful to Raymond Carney for writing *American Vision: The Films of Frank Capra* and to Stanley Cavell for writing *Pursuits of Happiness: The Hollywood Comedy of Remarriage.* My specific debts to both are thoroughly documented in the chapters that follow. I have always taken Capra seriously, which means attending as carefully as possible to the human qualities his films embody and celebrate. From Cavell I learned how shallow my engagements had been, especially on questions of gender; from Carney I learned how important it was always to keep one eye on the surface of the text, to avoid premature immersion in the fable at the expense of cinematic detail. It was only after I had taught Capra under the sustained influence of Carney and Cavell that I realized I had something more to say, and found adequate terms for saying it. On these and other accounts I owe Ray Carney and Stanley Cavell more than a few words of thanks. I owe them a whole book's worth. Here is the book. (Special thanks are also due to Cambridge University Press for permission to quote at length from Carney's *American Vision* and Cavell's *Disowning Knowledge,* as well to Harvard University Press for allowing extensive quotation from Cavell's *Pursuits of Happiness*.)

A number of my Iowa State University colleagues offered crucial assistance when it came to securing support for my research efforts, among them Donald Benson, Carol Chapelle, and Frank Haggard. Most of this book was written while I was on Faculty Improvement Leave; thanks to Iowa State University for providing the time and the material assistance. (Thanks to Liz Beck of the ISU Honors College for helping to arrange screenings.) Colleagues who gave generously and helpfully of their time to read and comment upon portions of the manuscript included Joseph Kupfer, Dale Ross, Dan Green, Loring Silet, and Katherine Sotol. Many students contributed to the conversation of this book; in thanking Peter Koehn and Laura Lacasa I thank them all. I am profoundly grateful to Alan Lutkus, Richard Ness, and Arlene McMillen (not to mention Kit Parker) for helping me round up viewing prints of many of Capra's more obscure films. Without their efforts I would never have managed.

Several people read the entire manuscript and kept me going when there seemed no place to go; Ray Carney, Dennis and Diana Swanson, Beatrice Rehl, and William Rothman are to be thanked for their support and suggestions. (It was Diana Swanson who, at a crucial moment, suggested I read Jessica Benjamin's *The Bonds of Love*.) My ISU colleague and fellow Oregon graduate Susan Carlson read a late-generation draft with extraordinary care and diligence. Readers familiar with Professor Carlson's *Women and Comedy* may well imagine how intricate our exchanges on questions of gender and genre have been over the years, and how enlivening – at least for me. Nearly every page of *Another Frank Capra* has benefited from Susan Carlson's meet and happy counsel. Her commitment to the process and project of this book – if not always to its more controversial particulars – exemplifies criticism at its collegial and conversational best. I am forever in her debt. Editors Michael Gnat and Ernestine Franco are also to be thanked for their timely and valuable suggestions. Such lacks as remain – of grace, foresight, or cogency – are entirely my own to regret.

Though they did not play a direct role in the process of drafting and revising *Another Frank Capra,* a number of colleagues and friends deserve my thanks for helping to sustain the larger conversation of my career over the last decade, often as readers of manuscripts that, in retrospect, were obviously preparatory to the current effort. On this account I gratefully acknowledge Neil Nakadate, Don Benson, Charie Thralls, Thomas Kent, William McCarthy, Marian Keane, Phil Gentile, Darryl Fox, Mary Beth Haralovich, and Marshall Deutelbaum. Thanks are due to Charles Wolfe and Barry Kroll for bibliographical assistance – and to the infinitely patient and understanding staff of the Interlibrary Loan Department of Iowa State's Parks Library, especially Kathryn Patton. Thanks to Kathy Parsons of the Parks Library Reference Department are also long overdue. I am grateful to Patricia King Hanson and Alan Gevinson for providing a copy of *Meet Frank Capra: A Catalog of His Work,* which proved immensely helpful in thinking through the complexities of Capra's filmography.

Frame enlargements from *State of the Union* appear courtesy of Universal Studios, thanks especially to the efforts of Jennifer Sebree. Linda Robertson and Genevieve Pyle helped immensely in producing the illustrations, as did the crew at the Iowa State University Photo Service. Extended passages of dialogue from *Lost Horizon* and *Mr. Smith Goes to Washington* are reproduced with the permission of Columbia Pictures. Also reproduced by permission are frame enlargements from *Ladies of Leisure, Forbidden,* and *Lost Horizon.* Readers puzzled by the general dearth of illustrations are entitled to know that the primary decision regarding the use of frame enlargements in this book belonged (quite literally) to Columbia Pictures.

I dedicated *The Cinema of Frank Capra* to my wife, Susan. Our life together in the years intervening has traced a curiously Capraesque path – from Oregon to upstate New York, where place-name references to Rochester and Elmira took on added resonance, not to mention a moment after the birth of our first child when a younger brother arrived in a Christmas Eve snowstorm to help us celebrate that most familial of holidays, and then to Ames, Iowa, where that same prodigal brother showed up unexpectedly to help us refurbish a somewhat run-down old house whose address, in years gone by, at least, was 109 Sycamore Street. That brother and his wife are now the parents of a newborn. Susan and I are now parenting teenagers. (To Amy and Melissa I owe a father's abiding gratitude – for their patience, when they did not want to watch *It's a Wonderful Life* just one more time, and for their whole-hearted companionship when watching it again was exactly what the moment called for.) For all these miracles I am immensely grateful – and not least for the chance provided by *Another Frank Capra* to rededicate my work to Susan, in token of a lifetime's admiration and affection. Not all youth is wasted on the wrong people.

CHAPTER 1
Picturing Capra

The Preface sketches a strategy for "defamiliarizing" the films of Frank Capra on the premise that the currently familiar understandings of them are no longer intellectually satisfying. Along the line I take special note of Nick Browne's historical analysis of *Meet John Doe*. In a way, the project of Browne's essay is also one of defamiliarization. Though Browne repeatedly refers to Capra as a utopian "populist," he pointedly avoids the rags-to-Hollywood-riches version of the Capra story often cited to explain Capra's broad appeal to thirties audiences. In its place Browne puts two other pictures, one a panorama of the historical development of a monopolistic Hollywood as a social institution aligned against other such institutions (the family, the church, the schools, the government), the other a close-up of the contractual arrangements obtaining between Frank Capra Productions, the Bank of America, Warner Bros., and Vitagraph (Warner's distribution arm). Moreover, what Browne finds most fascinating about *Meet John Doe* is the way its story and mode of address reflexively confront the larger social dilemma figured by the Paramount antitrust case in which the government sued the studios on behalf of independent exhibitors and producers. Though Capra effectively allegorizes this conflict in *Meet John Doe* – with media mogul D. B. Norton standing for the studio system while John Doe (or, alternately, Ann Mitchell) stands for the Capraesque "independent" – the basic crux is finally that nothing short of a literal "miracle" would allow Capra to assert the value of expressive independence in the language of classical Hollywood without relying upon the monopolistic power of Warner Bros. to reach (or create) his audience.[1]

I will eventually consider the efficacy of *Meet John Doe*'s Christmas Eve conclusion, to which Browne's theological reference alludes. Here I want to register my somewhat anxious agreement with Browne's decision to avoid the more explicitly biographical mode of explanation that Capra scholars have been prone to invoke over the years, though my agreement does *not* entail any doubts on my part regarding the general reality of Capra's authorship. (Far from it.) I have accordingly organized this chapter so as to foreground the process of "intertextual" inference by which viewers and critics construct "Frank Capra" as an interpretive hypothesis on the basis of various "pictures." Primary among these are the "motion pictures" Capra is on record as directing; indeed, I will conclude this chapter with an analysis of *You Can't Take It with You* that understands Grandpa Vanderhof as an unjustly neglected self-portrait on Capra's part. But other pictures obviously play an important part in the drama of interpretation and appropriation, especially those that help to establish various "reading strategies" through which the films are necessarily understood in the first place. The second segment of this chapter will address two such frameworks, the concept of "genre" and the concept of "the classical narrative cinema." The chapter's first section, "Meet Frank Capra," undertakes to complicate the text–context relationship somewhat by considering how Capra himself incorporates a portion of the historical record into the extremely complex visual texture of *Meet John Doe*. Readers who desire a more conventional biographical introduction will find some satisfaction here.

Meet Frank Capra

Meet John Doe (1941) was the first (and only) film produced by the version of Frank Capra Productions incorporated by coowners Frank Capra and (screenwriter) Robert Riskin in July of 1939. Upon the success of *Meet John Doe* depended the immediate future of Capra's own company and also (according to Capra) the long-term prospects of the independent producer-director "one-man, one-film" school of moviemaking that Capra had publicly advocated in a series of magazine articles beginning in 1936.[2] Moreover, it was with *Meet John Doe* that Capra intended to answer charges that he was a cinematic Pollyanna, a purveyor of simpleminded fairy-tale "Capra-corn." Capra wrote of his hopes for the film in *The Name above the Title:* "Riskin and I would astonish the critics with contemporary realities: the ugly face of hate; the power of uniformed bigots in red, white, and blue shirts; the agony of disillusionment, and the wild dark passions of mobs." Thus Capra's "first completely independent film venture . . . was *aimed* at winning critical praises."[3]

Though written some thirty years after the fact, Capra's autobiographical account of the making of *Meet John Doe* confirms Nick Browne's picture of the film as deeply engaged in its historical and institutional moment, a moment characterized by a decisive shift from a Depression to a wartime economy, fascism displacing unemployment as a primary topic of ideological concern. More specifically, *Meet John Doe* represents Capra's very explicit and self-conscious attempt to "reconfigure" his own institutional status, most obviously by declaring his independence of Columbia Pictures, where he had worked since late 1927, after the release of *Mr. Smith Goes to Washington* in 1939. However, the institution that was the focus of Capra's deepest anxieties – both in making *Meet John Doe* and in the world of the film he made – was the press, most especially its "critical" arm. Capra's "independence," we might say, existed within limits; in seeking (and needing) the approval of "intellectual critics" Capra sought not only to confirm (by rewriting) his own status but to vindicate cinema as an art form. Put another way, though Capra's quarrels with Columbia's Harry Cohn and with the studio–producer system generally were already the stuff of fan-mag legend, Capra was now, more literally than ever before, his own producer, his own boss. In defending himself against charges of aesthetic irrelevancy, Capra was both required and inclined to defend the capacity of "classical Hollywood style" to make room for the individual voice, despite the charges of assembly-line "sameness" that Capra was himself prone to level at the studio system.

Given Capra's public status in the late 1930s – as president of the Academy of Motion Picture Arts and Sciences and of the Screen Directors Guild – it was inevitable that people (Capra among them!) would link Capra's dilemma as a spokesman for Hollywood with Long John Willoughby's as a spokesman for "All John Does Everywhere." Indeed, the Capra/Doe equation is frequently called upon to explain Capra's failure of "voice" when it came to concluding *Meet John Doe*. Long John's inability to speak the whole truth of his fantastic story when publishing magnate D. B. Norton's neofascist storm troopers cut the power of the ballfield amplification system can thus be seen as prefiguring (or postfiguring) Capra's well-publicized inability to provide *Meet John Doe* with a satisfyingly "Capra-esque" finale after Long John leaves the John Doe convention in disgrace. Capra and screenwriter Robert Riskin had plotted themselves "into a corner," as Capra recalled the incident in *The Name above the Title,* as if their story too could never be (told) whole.[4] Indeed, any number of critics have followed Richard Glatzer in taking the dilemma as betokening "a perverse sense of self-parody'' on Capra's part that links John Doe's renunciation of ''mass preaching'' (auto)biographically with Capra's growing doubts about ''social mythmaking'' at a time when Hollywood seemed to be out-preached and out-mythed by the likes of Goebbels and Hitler. A goodly number of biographical details can be adduced to confirm the ''self-parody'' notion. Glatzer cites the way ''Long John's accidental transformation from drifter to national figure parallels Capra's own early drifting experience and subsequent involvement in moviemaking'' as well as the way ''Willoughby's awakening to his power over the studio audience during the key scene of his first radio speech . . . parallels Capra's emotional and physical illness which followed the success of *It Happened One Night,* and his ultimate decision to create social myth in *Mr. Deeds Goes to Town.*''[5] In a like mood, Charles Maland notes that ''Doe's picture appears on the cover of *Time,* just as Capra's had in 1938. Both were getting recognition, and both wondered if they deserved it''[6] (Fig. 1).

Whether self-consciousness necessarily entails self-doubts of the sort attributed to Capra by Glatzer and Maland is an open question. Maland's mag-cover equation, nevertheless, bears crucially on the way I currently understand the film, however minor a detail the *Time* allusion may seem at first. (Capra repeatedly refers to the *Time* cover in his autobiography, and the cover photo, by itself or framed by the original mag-cover graphics, is one of the most widely circulated images of Capra to this day.)[7] At stake is the concept of personal authorship as it applies to the reputedly impersonal mechanisms of the classical Hollywood cinema. Moreover, the site where the debate takes place, on this accounting, is less the historical terrain mapped out by Nick Browne and others than the ''textual'' arena of *Meet John Doe* as described by Dudley Andrew and Raymond Carney. Both see *Meet John Doe* as staging a debate over film authorship – figured in the relationship between the film's three Slavko Vorkapich montage sequences and the more conventional dramatic passages they serve to punctuate – into which (on my understanding) Capra injects even more complexity by invoking his own status as cultural icon via the Cooper/Doe *Time* cover.

Most critics who make the connection read it negatively, like Glatzer and Maland; Doe is a fake, so maybe Capra is a fake as well. However, anyone who remembers the story accompanying Capra's *Time* cover might just as well decide to read the *Meet John Doe* allusion differently, as foreshadowing John's eventual (if also deeply problematic) declaration of independence of Norton and his schemes. Indeed, the basic substance of

Figure 1. His picture on the cover: *Meet John Doe.*

"Columbia's Gem" (as the original *Time* story was titled) involved the as-if inevitable Hollywood power struggle that went on between producers and directors, between "cinemanufacturers" and "craftsmen," with Capra cast as one of several successful exceptions that proved the rule, and it concluded with the prediction that Capra would eventually follow Riskin in leaving Columbia to join Sam Goldwyn.[8] How "independent" one could be in the Hollywood context was thus a constant Hollywood issue, of which Capra seemed far more painfully aware than most.

The issue is raised, on Dudley Andrew's reading of *Meet John Doe,* by the film's Slavko Vorkapich montage sequences. As a general Hollywood rule, montage sequences amounted to a holdover from the silent era and one of later Hollywood's few "concessions" to the artistic legacy of experimental filmmaking. Unlike the base-line "classical Hollywood" film, these montage "intrafilms" disobey the system's "rules concerning invisibility of technique, clarity of development, primacy of character, and most crucially, homogeneity of narration."[9] Here the filmmaker, instead of hiding behind a coherent cause–effect series of psychologically motivated actions, comes to the forefront, asserting the power of film to elide space and time in the creation of novel images and associations, as opposed to the rigorous subordination of image to narrative typical of the generic Hollywood film.

Nevertheless, in the Hollywood film generally, and in *Meet John Doe* particularly, this excess of stylistic energy is absorbed (on Andrew's reading) into "the standard logic of the Hollywood narrative voice."[10] Despite their frantic pace and literal layering of information, montage sequences serve chiefly as punctuation, as a concise means for telescoping time and recirculating the primary graphic and narrative motifs of the film. For example, *Meet John Doe*'s first Vorkapich montage, serving as prologue to John Doe's first inspirational radio address, tells (at least) two stories: the story of Ann Mitchell's series of "I Protest" articles, published under the name (and picture) of John Doe, and the story of the rising circulation of D. B. Norton's *New Bulletin* as depicted by newspapers and money changing hands (the hands nearly always in close-up, detached from faces and bodies). Supposedly free expression (Ann's, Vorkapich's) is thus appropriated and controlled by a larger system of expression (Norton's, Capra's).

A similar emphasis on the limits of personal expression, similarly focused via discussion of the role of montage sequences in *Meet John Doe,* marks Raymond Carney's discussion of the film in *American Vision: The Films of Frank Capra.* In Capra's earlier films, on Carney's reading, montage sequences are typically used to embody and represent systems of social communication that exist "in fierce competition with . . . the personal styles and tones of the chief characters in the films."[11] The catch, as Carney understands *Meet John Doe,* is that its chief characters are too unformed to compete with the newer technologies of experience that the montage sequences epitomize.

As Carney observes, "John Doe" himself is a nullity, a publicity stunt, a fiction; indeed, even the self who embodies that fiction, a minor-league baseball player known as "Long John" Willoughby, is himself always already a fiction, an entertainer, a "pitchman" (in Capra's play on the baseball–advertising analogy), whose first name, in its coincidence with the first name of the mythical "average American," only complicates matters. When Ann Mitchell tells John to "think of yourself as the real John Doe," the "self" referred to is thus a matter of constant deferment – which John? Nearly the same question can be asked of Ann herself in view of the schizophrenic split between the righteous personal anger of the woman who writes the "I Protest" columns and the dissociatedly elegant cynicism of the woman who gladly accepts the patronage of D. B. Norton; Stanwyck's Ann Mitchell is as much a creature in the making, in process, as the fictitious John Doe she urges people (herself among them) to meet.

This uncertainty, this ''deferral'' of identity, this schizophrenia, is taken by Carney to typify the entire film, especially given the fact that each of the film's major characters can be taken as standing in for an aspect of Capra's authorial self. I have already noted the link of Capra and John implicit in the *Time* magazine reference (to which I will return); we might observe here that Long John's wanderings as a musically inclined hobo, one willing to engage in fraud for the sake of a sore pitching arm and a meal, are an echo of the post–World War I years Capra spent, after his discharge from the army, as an itinerant laborer, musician, and storytelling, bookselling mountebank. Indeed, John and Capra are both rescued from (relative) obscurity by meeting up at a crucial juncture with a woman in the form of Barbara Stanwyck whose self-creation through dramatic actions is underwritten and directed by a man of wealth and power. This latter formulation suggests yet another equation linking Capra and an on-screen surrogate, D. B. Norton and Frank R. Capra, both of whom ''direct'' Barbara Stanwyck's actions in *Meet John Doe*. This equation authorizes Carney's claim that the ''broadcasting'' or deferral or ''cutting up'' of identity that typifies montage sequences earlier in Capra has expanded in *Meet John Doe* to account for the entire film, making it Capra's ''cinematic version of American cubism.''[12] It is to this multiplication and subsequent fracture of identity that Carney explicitly attributes Capra's inability to finish the film, or his need to finish it five times over.

The interpretive dispute here is finely tuned. Andrew emphasizes Capra's ultimate power and responsibility, his knowing *use* of montage sequences to solve narrative problems, which also entails Capra's blindness to the monolithic power of his medium despite his pretensions to one-man, one-film independence of the system that empowers him; Carney's Capra, far from being blind to the dilemma, openly fears being absorbed by the medium that made him: ''Capra sees that if his pet myth of personal freedom and independence from the mass market can be converted into a marketable commodity'' – as, for example, *Meet John Doe* – ''then none of our personal dreams and fantasies are safe from the threat of social, political, and institutional systematization and exploitation.''[13] Despite their differences on the matter of Capra's authorship, Andrew and Carney invoke alike a demonic, nightmarish either/or logic: Either Capra authors or the system authors. At a certain level *Meet John Doe* evinces a similar understanding of the technologies of expression, to the extent that authorship within the film is *contested,* as (at the end) between Long John and D. B. Norton. However, at another level – a level pointed to by the montage sequences that Carney and Andrew both enlist as evidence – an alternative model of authorship is offered. We might call it a matter of (a positive) ''difference.''

Both Carney and Andrew take the montage sequences of *Meet John Doe* as generally unitary in form and function. Carney makes no distinctions at all among them and only refers to Vorkapich in passing. Andrew is more definite in noting that there are three such sequences, all of them by Vorkapich, one coming in the middle of each of the three reels of the 16mm print. What both overlook is the presence of yet one other montage sequence, the one behind the opening credits, an oversight that allows a simplified picture of the Vorkapich material and (arguably) of the film's conclusion as well.

The credit montage differs from the other three in two important respects. Though all four sequences rely on graphics and dissolves or superimpositions to layer information, the graphics of the credit sequence are *not* a matter of newspaper headlines within the film world but of credits from the filmmaking world, an acknowledgment of responsibilities rather than a deceptive and irresponsible circulation of signifiers. Moreover, though many of the shots in all four sequences have human beings as their subject, only in the credit sequence is the shot scale routinely one that allows for complete representation of whole persons; the credit sequence does *not* give us anonymous hands edged out of the frame by newspapers or magazines or circulation graphs.

Indeed, the credit-sequence montage effectively ''personalizes'' the movie to follow, though in a decidedly complex and (at least in retrospect) ambivalent fashion. The credits themselves, for example, are in two different fonts, block letters for most purposes, a cursive (as if handwritten) script for others: *Presenting Gary* Cooper and *Barbara* Stanwyck in *Frank Capra's* ''Meet John Doe.'' Moreover, the ''people'' shots are of two sorts: extreme long-shots of crowds, ''the people'' literally diminished, ''little people,'' alternating with full and medium-shots of recognizable human figures, typically of workers, often women workers. Even the music reflects this complexity. The sound montage is built from pieces of various ''American'' tunes, but this general ''Americanness'' is qualified, even questioned, by their sequencing. The first tune we hear is Stephen Foster's "Hard Times, Come Again No More" (playing over a shot evoking the heroic style of 1930s documentary photography; the tune also accompanies Ann Mitchell's first reading of her father's diary). The last is "Take Me Out to the Ball Game," as if play or game might be a way "out" of "Hard Times."

Capra, we might say, is written all over the credit sequence. His devotion to America, his affection for the people, his playfulness, his insistence on his "name above the title" – all are there. However, so too is an awareness of potential conflict, the prospect that people will diminish themselves by crowding together; that play will replace work, will make times harder by diverting attention from the jobs at hand; that the personal quality of script will be replaced by the impersonality of block letters (as, in the first shots after the credits, the eccentrically calligraphic "Bulletin" sign is replaced by the streamlined sans-serif "New Bulletin" plaque). Capra inscribes himself into this ambivalence very directly – and twice over. The sign of his proprietary interest, the possessive "Frank Capra's" *Meet John Doe,* appears over the longest shot of the credit sequence (a city square or intersection, lines of pedestrians and cars); his "worker" credit as director appears over the closest shot of the sequence, a tight medium-shot of an infant in a hospital nursery (Fig. 2). Indeed, two shots are involved here, a conspicuously moving camera track along a row of newborns, followed via dissolve by a closer shot that reframes to center a particular infant, over which we hear the final strains of "Take Me Out to the Ball Game," the unsung last lines of which would be "Three strikes you're out, at the old ball game."

I read this last image–sound complex as a culmination of the credit sequence, as exemplifying its author's relationship to his images and his characters. *His* status as implicit character is denoted by the credit itself (*Directed by* Frank Capra) and by the obtrusive camera movement. Nevertheless, that camera movement picks a child out from a crowd of children, as if by chance; individuality is a possibility, not a certainty. Moreover, given black-and-white photography and the connection of women with work and the feminine connotations of "Doe," the name with which Ann Mitchell chooses to sign her "whole world's going to pot" protest letter, we might wonder about the uncertain gender of the child singled out, as if Capra the imageworker and Ann Mitchell the wordworker were each equatable with the baby in the hospital crib, hence with each other. Furthermore, the connection of Capra to Long John Willoughby is implicit in the pitchman character evoked by ''Take Me Out to the Ball Game.'' As the third film in Capra's populist trilogy, *Meet John Doe* might very well be taken as the third pitch, as Capra's last strike. But who, exactly, is the pitcher, who the batter?

This uncertainty or multiplicity of authorship is then picked up in the Vorkapich montage sequences that follow, the first of which we have already discussed. Like the first, the second Vorkapich montage also tracks the expanding influence and presence of John Doe, now a public speaker rather than a crusading amateur newspaper columnist, though Ann still writes the scripts, and Norton still ''produces'' them. Shots of Ann and John traveling from city to city alternate with signs denoting John Doe clubs or banners announcing a John Doe appearance or maps detailing the nationwide progress of the John Doe movement.

Unlike the first montage sequence, however, the second includes near the end a series of thirteen shots that shift from a primarily graphic to a more dramatic mode. We move from Wall Street to Washington, D.C., to the Capitol steps, to the Democratic Party Headquarters, to the Republican; and in each setting the same minidrama is played out, the same question (more or less) posed by one character to another: What do the John Does want? However, the shift of modes here is signaled, as if caused, by the insertion into the sequence of the edition of *Time* with Cooper/Doe on the cover as the ''Man of the Hour.'' His presence there obviously signals his importance to ''National Affairs'' (the magazine section where his story is purportedly elaborated). The use of *Time* here (rather than some other magazine) also amounts to a claim of authorship on Capra's part, a reference to his own appearance on the cover in 1938, an equation (also) of Capra, whose name appears ''above the title'' of *Meet John Doe,* with John Doe himself, whose name provides the title for the John Doe movement and is featured, like a marquee credit, in the many banners announcing his appearances.

This equation of Capra and Cooper/Doe, and with it our sense that the authorial function of *Meet John Doe* is becoming increasingly more personal yet (also) more tenuous, is confirmed by the last of the Vorkapich montage sequences. Like the first, it begins with newspaper headlines, this time announcing John a fake rather than a prophet. Cut to a shot of a John Doe flyer floating toward a curb side sewer grate, with walking feet (moving right to left) above it, feet we can take as John's given the next shot, a close-up of Willoughby walking toward the camera, superimposed over

Figure 2. Taking credit, a doubled-self.

concentric rings of water, as if John were flowing in or down the sewer, and as if the sewer, in some sense, were John's own consciousness, as subsequent superimposed shots, of people hurling accusations at the still visible image of John, would indicate.

Some of the "subjective" images in this sequence are new to the film, as if they emerged from John's own consciousness – an already *split* consciousness in the sense that the figures *in* it and the figure *of* it are equally present on the screen, and equally thinned out, watered down, by superimposition. However, when we get to the depths of John's consciousness, the images we see most are images from *Meet John Doe,* images in which John appears, but that he could not therefore have witnessed or remembered from the angles here presented (Fig. 3). These images are Capra's images, even if they are cut together by Slavko Vorkapich, even if the scenes they image were in some sense authored by Ann Mitchell and (behind her) D. B. Norton. John is thus a "screen" for Capra's projections, yet John is also, in a sense, Capra, as if Capra were screening himself.

There is a Freudian ambiguity in my use of "screen" that I take as complicating the view of *Meet John Doe* offered by Andrew and Carney. Both of them, I have argued, invoke a unitary notion of authorship. The picture of Capra's authorship I have sketched here, on the basis of only a few of the film's many frames, is by contrast of an authorship split in its essence, and from the very beginning. Capra puts himself on screen by staying off screen; the screen both reveals him (for supporting his images) and conceals him (on the model of a Freudian censor). Or maybe we should say that Capra genuinely needed some element of ignorance or blindness, something to hide behind – he began shooting *Meet John Doe,* after all, well before having a satisfactorily complete script in hand – in order to avoid the certainties of authorship that characterize his on-screen surrogates, especially D. B. Norton.

I spoke earlier of a positive difference as characterizing the authorial function of *Meet John Doe.* Partly this difference is the one just cited, Capra's from Norton. Partly, also, it is Capra's from Hollywood, from the Hollywood practice of having everything set out assembly-line fashion, literally scripted, in advance. Within the context of that system – a system embodied within the film by Norton's quasi-fascist combination of media and paramilitary organs – it makes some sense to describe Capra and Vorkapich as contesting with one another. However, the overall momentum of the film – as measured here by the analysis of its four primary montage

Figure 3. Screening identities in *Meet John Doe*.

sequences – is in the direction of a montage of authorships, as if no single voice alone is voice enough, as if voices must be replicated, duplicated, broadcast, directed, projected, in order to be sufficiently or effectively heard.

In this light we might cast a sidelong glance at the notorious ending of *Meet John Doe,* which even Capra partisans, Andrew and Carney among them, continue to find problematic. Again it is a matter of either/or – of a postmodernist technoworld in which selfhood (Doe's, Willoughby's, Ann Mitchell's, Frank Capra's) is *either* totally an effect of "the system," of "the machine," which "inscribes individuals within its own alternative 'intentional' structure, independent of their will or wishes," *or* is preserved by rejecting society altogether, as Walter Brennan's character apparently undertakes to do in his repeated sermonizing against the "heelots," his prophetic shorthand reference for nearly all social interaction.[14] In Andrew's words, the Colonel "is the fully unsocialized human" who represents the temptation "to exist outside narrative desire altogether."[15] Carney differs from Andrew chiefly in taking the Colonel's rejection of the system as effectively confirming the existence of Norton's inhuman technoworld: "A world full of figures like the Colonel would leave Norton undisturbed."[16] On both accounts Capra appears to have directed himself into a dramatic and ideological cul-de-sac from which he tries to escape by having it both ways, shifting narrative registers (with the aid of the last Vorkapich montage) from social narrative to religious parable. As a result, Capra effectively presents a Colonel-like escape – Capra's own escape from narrative logic, a logic that silenced John forever in the ballfield rally sequence – as a social solution, despite the film's overwhelming demonstration that "the social" is inescapably the problem. Carney calls this "symbolmongering," implying that Capra's invocation of Christ ("The first John Doe") – via the ending's snowy Christmas setting, church bells, Beethoven's "Ode to Joy" – is an insufficient response to a world where symbols are always already "mongered" beyond recovery.[17]

Part of the unhappiness here, it should be noted, involves the "predictive" aspect of the film's ending, especially Ann's hysterical prediction that the John Doe movement will "grow" and "grow big, because it'll be honest this time." Clearly Carney is right in suggesting that this prediction carries little conviction as it applies to the depicted world of the film. Indeed, Ann herself (Capra himself) quickly scales the prediction back to "keeping" the John Doe idea "alive." Furthermore, that idea, though couched in New Testament rhetoric, amounts to little more (though nothing less) than "Be a Better Neighbor," as one John Doe button describes it. In a world of expressive isolation – the world of John Doe, but also the world of Christ's exemplary "good Samaritan" who figures what it means to "love thy neighbor as thyself" – neighboring only takes two, the Samaritan and the man fallen by the roadside. We might call this (also) a matter of a positive difference, less either/or than both/and.

If we understand montage broadly, as an art of significant juxtaposition, we might say that the film's concluding sequence – in which Long John climbs to the roof of City Hall, intent on carrying out Ann's original suicide threat as token of his earnest commitment to John Doeism – is another instance of montage, and on several levels. For example, the film's concluding scene is implicitly in juxtaposition with, for being a remake of, the scene in the Millville City Hall when Ann and Norton cynically propose the lecture tour in support of the burgeoning John Doe movement, a proposal effectively if far less cynically seconded by Bert Hansen and his wife and the other members of the local John Doe Club who tell John their story in support of the view that John should *not* carry through with the suicide threat: "You can be mighty useful walking around for a while."

Already John is functioning as a kind of screen, as a support for an idea or an image (he is repeatedly framed, in this sequence, with portraits of Lincoln and Washington *mise-en-abîme* in the background; Fig. 4), an image understood quite explicitly (by Mrs. Hansen) as a living out of John Doe's first radio speech. However, the entire scene is explicitly presented under the sign of falsehood or disbelief. As Norton and Ann get out of his limousine at scene's beginning he tells her to "present it to him as a great cause for the common man." In the film's concluding moments John serves a similar function as screen or support, but in this case the scene is far less clearly scripted in advance; or better, the in-advance scripts do not survive the honesty of the moment, neither John's script for jumping nor Norton's script for covering up the suicide. Moreover, the "authorship" of the scene is far more thoroughly disseminated. Nearly everyone on the City Hall roof (including Norton, though not his minions) has an equal turn at dissuading John from suicide.

The most spectacular plea is Ann's; she throws herself into John's arms and finally collapses in spiritual exhaustion (Fig. 5), like Jefferson Smith, who also collapses into a kind of spiritual trance upon committing himself to fighting on for a "lost cause" in *Mr. Smith Goes to Washington.* How-

Figure 4. *Mise-en-abîme*: Honest Abe Lincoln and Long John Willoughby.

ever, as other characters speak – even the Colonel – the cutting of the sequence centers their remarks on the expressive blankness of Long John's face (repeatedly singled out as a token of believability). By contrast, John speaks not at all after telling Norton to "take a good look." The comments of the others come, literally then, "over" John's silent image, and the image they project there is of their own knowing grasp of the circumstances. Both Hansens still call John "Mr. Doe" – that part of the fiction still lives – but no longer under the illusion fostered by Ann's initial radio speech. In allowing himself to be looked at, in withstanding the knowing gaze of his audience, in knowingly becoming *their* audience, Long John finds an eloquence not possible in the speeches he is given to make. John most truly speaks himself when that self is spoken by and with (the right) others. It makes a difference.

The notion that John Doe "finds" himself as that self is represented to and by others helps us come to better grips with the problem of *Meet John Doe*'s conclusion. The complaint that Capra orchestrates religious symbolism so as "to hush all doubts" clearly does *not* address the circumstances of the characters within the film; their doubts are not hushed, nor are they

Figure 5. " . . . it isn't dead, or they wouldn't be here."

witness in the same way we are to the full specifics of that orchestration.[18] Clearly the doubts supposedly hushed here are those of Capra's audience, but in that case the "predictive" problem shifts from the depicted world of the film to the world of the film's viewer. Perhaps Doe's world is not one where symbols are any longer efficacious. In our world, however, questions of efficacy quite obviously matter, or else the entire dispute about the film's ending would never have arisen or been sustained. The efficacy of the film's closing scene therefore remains an open question, dependent on our projections, on our (critical) voice-overs. Seen this way, the end of the film is less an escape than an appeal, an especially open and openly vulnerable appeal to an ongoing social narrative.

The social narrative I have in mind here involves one last species of montage, the montage of those critical voices that have coauthored this brief account of *Meet John Doe* precisely in their differences from one another. I know for a fact that I could not have come to my present understanding of the film or of Capra's inscription therein without the collaboration of Raymond Carney and Dudley Andrew. The last time I wrote about the film I was amazingly insensitive to many aspects of film style; my chapter on the film in *The Cinema of Frank Capra* barely mentions the film's montage sequences, for example. Central to my willingness to undertake this project is the conviction that criticism is a matter of conversation, of critics with each other, of critics with the films they study. My purpose in deliberating at such length over a few moments in a single film is to assert the principle that the best way to "Meet Frank Capra" is to think as profoundly as possible about the films he made. That is where Frank Capra is still most alive to us; it is equally where we are most alive to him.

Before going on to a more thorough analysis of the generic and stylistic elements of Capra's authorship, I want to acknowledge an important consequence of this "conversational" view of films and of film criticism as it applies to *Meet John Doe,* especially so because the point to make anticipates a major focus of chapters to come. Not all films are equally alive to all audiences at all times. I can well imagine a contemporary feminist critique of *Meet John Doe,* for example, that rephrases the Andrew–Carney complaint about the film's conclusion.

Where Andrew reads the conclusion as sleight of hand that presents escape as resolution, a feminist critique might instead describe the conclusion as one that presents resolution as escape. Specifically, one could describe the film's social narrative as a contest between the overtly demonic patriarchy embodied in D. B. Norton and his fascist minions and the more benign version of patriarchy implicit in the biblical narrative represented by the Christ references and by Ann's absent father, who exists primarily in the form of a book that is re-presented, as it were, by a virgin daughter. However, if patriarchy is the problem, Christianity can hardly stand as a fully satisfying conclusion or resolution. Escaping to Christianity only repeats the problem in a different register. Or perhaps we should say that the degree to which the ending satisfies depends altogether on the extent to which a given viewer is willing to grant some metaphoric (as opposed to dogmatic) validity to Capra's use of Christian symbolism.

The metaphoric validity I wish to claim for the film's use of Christian symbols derives from a remark by Luce Irigaray to the effect that Christ is the "most feminine of all men."[19] I have already observed a feminist subtext alongside the film's autobiographical one. Key here is the equation of Capra and the Ann Mitchell character, which can be traced back to the film's credit montage. The point to be made is that John Doe too has a feminine side to him that provides additional thematic resonance to the film's depiction of difference. Especially interesting here is the implication

Figure 6. Capra's Pietà.

that Long John, in seeking to act out Ann's suicide threat, in becoming John "Doe" on her behalf, in her stead, is effectively taking on Ann's identity; just as she, in playing out Jefferson Smith's role, takes over as the Christ figure. In the final tableau John is the Mary figure in Capra's version of the Pietà, Ann the broken Christ in his/her arms (Fig. 6).

Another element of gender-role reversal or exchange can be elaborated by reference to the cover of *Time* magazine. That Cooper's image on the film-world cover evokes, as if by replacing, Capra's image on the real-world cover is usually taken to equate the two men. Indeed, the anxiety generated by the film's deeply troubled conclusion tends to throw the focus of the film's self-reflexivity into the masculine (Capra=Cooper) register; each is a frustrated "speaker" who risks actual or artistic suicide for the sake of confirming his moral/intellectual earnestness. Often lost in the anxiety is the degree to which Ann Mitchell's actions – inventing a character, and a story for him, both of which are nearly autobiographical; selling that story to the highest bidder; casting someone to enact the role; costuming and prompting the actor; telling photographers how and when to shoot the picture; scripting speeches that ring of ideological commitments far in excess of the initially mercenary context, though an excess quickly seized upon by audiences and exploited by financial powers – amount to nothing less than an explicit and detailed self-portrait of Capra's Hollywood career.[20]

The self-referential quality of the Ann/Capra analogy is confirmed by certain details of the *Meet John Doe–Time* magazine intertext. To begin with, it is Ann Mitchell – we learn from one of John's bodyguards in the scene immediately following the second Vorkapich montage – who is responsible for putting John's picture on the cover. An oddly similar relation between Capra and *Time*'s cover can be inferred from the historical record. *Capra's* picture on the August 8, 1938, cover of *Time* depicts him – via a caption: "His stories cannot match his story" – as both cause and effect, as the creator of stories and as a story in the making, the latest Capra hero. *Cooper's* March 3, 1941, appearance on *Time*'s cover only a week or two in advance of *Meet John Doe*'s initial release features a close-up of Cooper over the caption: "Gary Cooper – John Doe: He made the cover." Which character is which, or which cover is being alluded to, remains ambiguous. Unambiguous is the fact that Capra effectively put Cooper's image on *Time*'s cover, as Ann Mitchell put John Doe's on; each is a media wizard to be reckoned with, and in each case that wizardry is tied to the multiplication and distribution of images.[21]

One more intertextual connection is worth making here, if only to anticipate the discussion of *You Can't Take It with You* that concludes this chapter. The text of the *Time* story that accompanies Capra's cover photo begins with a backstage parable, the story of a Columbia prop man smoking a cigarette on the set of *You Can't Take It with You* and dropping a spark into a crate of firecrackers. Life here oddly imitates art, to the extent that a crucial event in both the stage and screen versions of *You Can't Take It with You* is a massive fireworks explosion occasioned by a police raid on the Vanderhof household; while the raid itself is sparked by government fears that Ed Carmichael's advertisements for fireworks amount to Red propaganda ("Watch for the Revolution"), the spark that ignites the basement fireworks factory is provided by Mr. DePinna's pipe, which police refuse to let him retrieve in their rush to round up suspects.

In the Kaufman–Hart play the fireworks factory is never seen, only referred to, and the explosion amounts to a scene stopper, a sonic eruption ex machina that brings the second act to a chaotic close. In the film, by contrast, the fireworks explosion amounts to a cinematic explosion, marking a wild and severe shift in film style, a shift from the comfortable and folksy light harmonies of screwball comedy to the dark imagery of urban film noir; lights go out, darkness is punctuated by bombs bursting strobelike in air, and the scene shifts from a domestic interior to a city street full of cops and squad cars and fire trucks and paddy wagons (shades of *Scarface!*). Indeed, just as the explosions begin, Capra shifts editing registers, from the sight-gag rhythm of Penny Sycamore peeking under a cop's coat to see his gun ("Just like a play, isn't it?") into a montage of shouting faces, each illuminated by the flash of exploding chemicals (as if in reply to Penny: This most emphatically is *not* a play).

In which case it can hardly be coincidental that Capra poses on *Time*'s cover in the act of lighting his pipe and looking directly into the camera, his face knowingly agrin as if on the verge of a punch line, a large book gripped in his left hand, a finger marking a place roughly two thirds of the way through the manuscript – the end of Act II, I imagine – a box of matches balanced between his second and third fingers. This man lights fires, the picture seems to say, talking fires that speak a language of flashing light. When Ann's new editor gives her the boot in the opening scene of *Meet John Doe,* he cites her "lavender and old lace" column as his reason. "What we need is fireworks," he goes on to say in explanation. Once Long John is cast as John Doe, moreover, the editor remarks gleefully that the fictitious character and byline will enable them to "blast [their] heads off" without regard for accuracy or accountability. The echo of Capra's own dilemma, as a Capra-corn director seeking to shake up the critical establishment, is hard to miss. Only a little harder to catch is the way the fireworks link equates Frank Capra and Ann Mitchell as political "gossip columnists." We will have more to say about Capra's status as the purveyor of "sentimental" or "melodramatic" fiction presently.

Critical Concepts

The Preface expresses certain reservations about film-critical historicism. However, I have just invoked what might seem a historically contingent if not ephemeral connection – that between some lines of dialogue in *Meet John Doe* and the August 8, 1938, cover of *Time* – to advance the view that Ann Mitchell is fully as much Capra's surrogate in *Meet John Doe* as Gary Cooper. By doing so I seek to acknowledge that interpretive hypotheses *depend* on prior experiences, among them the viewer's experience or knowledge of "history" and of other art forms and art works. (My complaint about Nick Browne's reading of *Meet John Doe* is chiefly that his notion of history is too restrictive.) Put another way, what a film *has* meant is always potentially a part of what it *can* mean. To the extent that human beings in our culture are perpetually reluctant to think about the forces that link their own lives to larger structures of power and privilege, the sort of historical reconstruction and analysis favored by orthodox Capra critics retains obvious pedagogical and heuristic value.

It must be remembered, however, that such linkages of text and context are almost inevitably a matter (in Kenneth Burke's happy phrase) of "prophecy after the event."[22] Thinking about the cover of *Time* and the various connections that can be made between the magazine story and *Meet John Doe* is most emphatically *not* a matter of explaining some unknown or uncertainly known phenomenon (the film) by cause–effect reference to some more clearly known background set (biography, history, industry); nor is it the recovery of some original meaning ham-handedly "covered up" by the film, as if the film were not the real object of our attention, something we would just as soon do without. There are knowns and unknowns on *both* sides of the text–context analogy. Which figures or illuminates which is nearly always an open question, however earnestly we might long for narrative or theoretical closure.

An important part of any even provisionally complete history of Frank Capra would be a survey of the terms or concepts by means of which Capra's films have been variously understood and encountered across the decades. In an earlier draft of this chapter I thought to acknowledge the importance of critical concepts after a limited fashion by confining my survey to those terms at work in the textbook Capra essays that routinely appear in standard university-press anthologies. For brevity's sake, I have limited my discussion of terms exclusively to those most "critical" to the understanding of Capra that my later chapters develop.

Two paradigms, or term-sets, are involved here: one by my lights too "familiar" to Capra criticism, one not familiar enough. I have already alluded to a historical anomaly in the reception of Frank Capra. Many intellectual critics in the later 1930s took exception to the increasingly political substance of Capra's films, thus setting the stage for Capra's subsequent attempt, with *Meet John Doe,* to garner highbrow praise. Still, it is Capra's populist legacy, especially in the *Deeds–Smith–Doe* trilogy, that latter-day film scholars most often cite to justify their critical interest in Capra's films. A result of this paradox has been a sustained debate about the film genre or genres Capra's films embody or reproduce. Is "Capra film" truly a genre unto itself, or are his films better understood by reference to formal or cultural models that preceded him. Recent critics have tended to take the latter view, and increasingly for the purpose of assessing the gender component of the Capra cinema as it relates to larger questions of ideology. The discussion of genre and ideology in the following section lays conceptual groundwork for engaging the gender question more fully in subsequent chapters.

By contrast, the debate over the status of the "classical narrative cinema" is far less clearly articulated. Given the equation of Capra and Hollywood, there is a tendency to construe Capra's film style as "transparent," or "invisible," in keeping with studio-style norms of the period. A key moment in the history of my own thinking about Capra was the recognition that Capra's editing patterns often avoid the standard shot/reverse-shot logic by which classical narration is typically rendered subservient to narrative. It is a guiding claim of the present study, hinted at in my remarks on *Meet John Doe* and elaborated more fully later, that Capra's narrational presence is overtly intrusive in ways criticism to date has barely acknowledged.

Genre and Ideology

According to Raymond Durgnat, "genre is a way of grouping films by parts of themselves – significant parts, but only parts. Thus, what is true of auteurism is true of genres (indeed, auteurism is a special form of genre – the 'John Ford' genre or the 'Greta Garbo' genre). We recognize a film as 'a film by *x*' or as 'an *x*-type film' by the presence of a sufficient number of traits typical of *x*, and not by the absence of anything which is non-*x*."[23] Durgnat's summary of the logic of genre does *not* dictate which *kind* of *x*-trait (or set of them) we might wish to use in a given instance. Moreover, it is clear from Durgnat's subsequent application of the genre concept that genre categories can be overlapping or coextensive; a given *x*-trait may belong to several genres or subgenres. However, it is certainly true of the current state of Capra scholarship that the traits most in question in defining the *kind* of movie made by Frank Capra are political or ideological traits. In Capra's case, at least, "genre" and "ideology" are effectively synonymous.

An index of the importance and the problem of ideological analysis as it applies to Capra is Jeffrey Richards's "Frank Capra and the Cinema of

Populism,'' without question the most influential piece of Capra criticism ever written. According to Richards, the basic conflict in American political life before the New Deal was between Federalist (big business, big government) and anti-Federalist (yeoman farmer) factions, the latter associated with ''two successive Populist reactions, Jeffersonian and Jacksonian Democracy,'' followed after the Civil War and the Industrial Revolution by a final ''revival of Populism, a last desperate bid to retain individualist values, the values of the old Revolution, in a society where Organization was inexorably taking over.''[24] And take over it did, on Richards's account, with the triumph of Roosevelt's New Deal. Shut out of history, then, the Populist impulse retreats into mythology where its individualist self-help doctrine, seriously if not fundamentally discredited by the experience of the Depression, can be tempered (in words partly borrowed from Richard Griffith) by '' 'the fantasy of goodwill', the genre which Capra so successfully translated into the cinema.''[25] In narrative terms this fantasy mimes ''the Log Cabin to White House success story'' typified by Jackson and Lincoln; in ideological terms the fantasy argues for equality of opportunity tempered by ''good neighbourliness'' whenever ''equality'' yields misery.[26] Richards quotes Lincoln to the effect that ''Republicans are for both the man and the dollar, but in the case of conflict, the man before the dollar.'' This is, Richards goes on, ''Capra in a nutshell.''[27]

A number of the historical inaccuracies in this account deserve brief notice. A political philosophy grounded in the lives and works of such autodidacts as Jefferson and Lincoln, for instance, is ill-described as anti-intellectual; few more learned men have ever held the presidency, however ''popular'' they eventually became. The only real evidence Richards provides that Populism in any form ever was anti-intellectual is Capra's send-up of the opera crowd and the psychiatrist in *Mr. Deeds Goes to Town,* though he fails to balance that against Longfellow's habit of quoting Henry David Thoreau, or against Longfellow's demonstration in the courtroom scene that the doctor's ''doodling'' goes as far to prove the latter's sanity and humanity as Longfellow's tuba playing proves his.

Far more serious charges against the Richards account of Populism have been lodged by Duncan Webster in *Looka Yonder!: The Imaginary America of Populist Culture.* According to Webster, the real Populist party in American history – the one American historians give the label to – began in the 1880s as the National Farmers' Alliance and became the People's Party in 1892 (shades of *Meet John Doe!*). Although the People's Party candidate in the presidential election of 1892, James B. Weaver of Iowa, was prone to cite Jefferson and Jackson ("The rugged utterances of these statesman," said Weaver during the 1892 campaign, "ring out today like a startling impeachment of our time"), this amounted, contra Richards, to "a strategic mobilization of the past rather than nostalgia."[28] Moreover, according to Webster, Richards's focus on self-help individualism as the essence of Populism egregiously "overlooks the co-operative ideals of the 1890s agrarian movement and also the farmers' [quite non-Jeffersonian] demands on the state," especially "for state regulation of the emergent corporate capitalism."[29] Indeed, that was exactly what Roosevelt's New Deal finally managed. As Webster remarks on this latter account, once again in direct reply to Richards: "The New Deal is not the death of populism but one of the significant sources of our images of rural poverty and protest."[30] So too, we might add, is Frank Capra.

Richards thus proposes to read Capra through a Populist matrix, when he just as often reads Populism through Capra – despite the fact that Capra's political vision was "sufficiently vague and rhetorical that a case could probably be made for Capra the liberal, the conservative, the Jeffersonian, the Populist, even the Popular Fronter."[31] In Durgnat's terms, generic ideological "parts" are being asked to stand in for a very elusive and (evidently) complex aesthetic whole, as if the goal were exactly to deny that complexity by means of a summary generic characterization.

A far more productive approach to the genre question as it bears on Capra is found in Robin Wood's "Ideology, Genre, Auteur." Here again ideology and genre are paired concepts; "American capitalist ideology" is roughly equatable with "the values and assumptions so insistently embodied in and reinforced by the classical Hollywood cinema."[32] Unlike Richards, however, Wood does not tell, as it were, a single populist fable that Capra can then be understood as unproblematically translating into the language(s) of cinema. Rather, Wood understands the ideology of genre as comprising any number of ethical and/or narrative tropes: capitalism, the work ethic, marriage, nature as agrarianism/nature as wilderness, progress, technology, the city, and so on. "The most striking fact about this list," Wood goes on to say, "is that it presents an ideology that, far from being monolithic, is *inherently* riddled with hopeless contradictions and unresolvable tensions" that it is the "function" of genre to "naturalize" or "deny."[33] Durgnat makes the same point in "Genre: Populism and Social Realism": "Genres, like ideologies, are a manner of concealing inner tensions.''[34] And the essentially Freudian catch for (in) both Durgnat and Wood is that these tensions are revealed in the very act of concealment; tensions must be expressed before they can be repressed. *Repression* is thus a form of *expression*. Accordingly, those forms and works are most interesting, on Wood's general account of the logic of genre, that ''contain'' (as both providing and restraining) the greatest number of such tensions, the greatest number of generic and ideological ''impurities.''

Wood's primary examples of generic complexity derive from detailed readings of Capra's *It's a Wonderful Life* and Hitchcock's *Shadow of a Doubt;* both are seen to mix elements of the western, small-town comedy, and film noir, though each in ways crucially inflected by the presence of a strong artistic personality. Chapter 6 presents an extended analysis of the former film. In the meanwhile we can exemplify something of the process and consequences of generic/ideological analysis by briefly contrasting two ''canonical'' interpretations of the generic component of *It Happened One Night.*

Like any number of critics before and since, Andrew Bergman describes *It Happened One Night* as the first instance and founding member of the ''screwball comedy'' genre. Like Wood, Bergman sees the business of genre as the resolution of ideological tensions: ''The overwhelming attractiveness of the screwball comedies . . . had to do with the effort they made at reconciling the irreconcilable. They created an America of perfect unity: all classes as one, the rural–urban divide breached, love and decency and neighborliness ascendant.'' And the primary agency of unity, on Bergman's reading, was a quality of ''whackiness'' deriving from the ''screwball'' idiosyncrasy of the primary characters.[35] An exemplary instance for Bergman is the rope-and-blanket routine Gable cooks up in the first auto-camp scene:

> When their night bus is halted by a torrential rain, Warne [Gable] unhesitatingly takes a single room for himself and the skittish millionairess [Ellen Andrews/Claudette Colbert] – and then proceeds to hang a blanket between their beds, calling it the 'wall of Jericho.' The blanket separates, but the offbeat act of putting it up brings them closer together. . . . The fact that Ellen is short of funds and dependent on Warne's lower middle-class street wit just to survive foreshadows the ultimate melting of class barriers between them.[36]

Bergman's generic understanding of *It Happened One Night* can be seen to follow Durgnat's description of genre logic; a particular part or property, the screwball whackiness of central characters, both categorizes and stands for the whole. (Later writers will narrow the generic reference even further, taking the aggressively screwball female lead as the genre's defining feature.)[37] Stanley Cavell, by contrast, expands the field of generic reference by choosing to consider *It Happened One Night* under the rubric of "remarriage comedy."

Cavell's understanding of the film, we should note, does not straightforwardly refute Bergman's. Indeed, Cavell incorporates Bergman after a displaced fashion by referring to a discussion by the anthropologist Claude Lévi-Strauss (in *The Elementary Structures of Kinship*) of the origins of the "marriage of chance, merit, or choice," as opposed (Cavell's words now) to that of "gift by kindred." Marriage by choice or merit only has social meaning, for Lévi-Strauss, "if it gives a girl from a superior class to a man from an inferior class, guaranteeing at least symbolically that the distance between the statuses has not irremediably compromised the solidarity of the group."[38] But Cavell does not, like Bergman, take the promise of class reconciliation through marriage as the primary or even the deepest of the film's implications. Rather, Cavell takes a basic task of the genre initiated in and by *It Happened One Night* to be an investigation of what marriage *is,* of what validates it, lends it social and personal legitimacy. Such questions, once raised, necessarily postpone or complicate assertions to the effect that marriage across classes is a social cure-all, especially if the society depicted (like the appealingly tolerant old auto-camp couple at film's end) is skeptical about the fact or the forms of the union in question.

In Cavell's usage, then, the part or property referred to by the appellation remarriage comedy involves the genre's (and the films') revisionary relationship to the history of comedy generally, especially to Shakespearean comedy. "A central claim of mine about the genre," Cavell writes, "is that it shifts emphasis away from the normal question of comedy, whether a young pair will get married, onto the question whether the pair will get and stay divorced, thus prompting philosophical discussions of the nature of marriage."[39] As Cavell elaborates in "A Capra Moment":

> The central idea is that the validity or bond of marriage is no longer assured or legitimized by church or state or sexual compatibility or children but by something I call the willingness for remarriage, a way of continuing to affirm the happiness of one's initial leap, as if the chance of happiness exists only when it seconds itself. In classical comedy people made for one another find one another; in remarriage comedy people who *have* found one another find that they *are* made for each other.

The greatest of the structures of remarriage is *The Winter's Tale,* which is, together with *The Tempest,* the greatest of the Shakespearean romances.[40]

Assumed here – and clearly evident in other films Cavell includes in the genre (*His Girl Friday, Adam's Rib, The Lady Eve, The Awful Truth*) – is that the central characters already *are* or *have been* married, hence a happy answer to the question of divorce will necessarily take the form of remarriage. The complication comes in the fact that remarriage to the same person calls into question the (as it were) "premarriage"; in what ways was it insufficient if its threads can be picked up yet again? This is complicated even further in two films of the genre – *It Happened One Night* and *Bringing Up Baby* – where no first marriage exists, or where the anticipated marriage involves a partner other than the one to which the central male (in *Baby*) or female (in *One Night*) is initially betrothed or wedded.

Cavell is alert to these questions, and the answer he gives, in the case of *It Happened One Night,* involves two features of the film (and the genre):

1. Legal marriage in these films does not by itself effect a "real" marriage, a realm of difference the genre undertakes to map out.
2. The marriage of Peter and Ellie at film's end feels as if "they are marrying again, and not merely because of the plain fact" that "the wedding night is shown to be set in yet another auto camp" but "specifically because what we have been shown in the previous auto camps is something like their marriage."[41]

The part-for-whole logic of generic description amounts to a species of metaphor; describing a film generically is a basic tactic of criticism, amounting to a claim that certain parts or patterns deserve special attention or invoke otherwise overlooked yet vital associations. Genres are also metaphoric in another sense, however, involving not the genre *term* but (rather) the object that it (re)describes, the text or the film that can also serve a metaphoric purpose, as a figure through which we rethink the world. In many respects the key difference between Bergman and Cavell is exactly the degree to which Cavell is more alert to this latter aspect of (opportunity for) metaphoric attribution.

Consider on this account the implications each derives from the first "wall of Jericho" scene in *It Happened One Night.* We have already summarized Bergman's view of the scene; putting up the rope allows Peter to be endearingly "whacky" and (I presume) sexually considerate. Cavell, by contrast, begins his reading of the film by construing the blanket/barrier as a virtual figure for the issues "of metaphysical isolation and of the possibility of community" as those questions have been elaborated by Lévi-Strauss and Kant.[42] Cavell will eventually go on to construe the blanket – especially as it functions in the penultimate auto-camp scene – as helping frame "a solution to the so-called problem of the existence of other minds."[43] (We need not run the whole exhilarating philosophical course of Cavell's interpretation to catch the sense in which the Jericho reference, say, connects the blanket and its fate to the founding or destruction of a culture.)

The key link here, for Cavell, involves two ways of taking the blanket:

1. as a figure of relayed or displaced perception (the blanket both conceals and reveals the realm of eros, of nature, reveals it by concealing it, as when Ellie undresses while Peter watches the blanket take on her shape); and
2. as standing (à la Bergman) for the conditions of human community, the realm of culture.

Our perception of the world is necessarily, on Kant's understanding of understanding, a matter of confinement, confinement (roughly) to the categories of language; in that sense there is always a barrier between ourselves and "the world in itself," the world apart from our presence to it, though that barrier *may* (like Peter's wall) reveal the world's presence to *us*. In the social realm, however, the barrier between the world as it stands and the world of our desires is less a logical than an ethical one; we may exempt ourselves from the human condition (this is roughly Peter's complaint against Ellie early in *It Happened One Night,* though his complaint is also a claim for exemption), but doing so is something *we* do, and can choose not to do. The only necessary (logical or grammatical) barrier between myself and the social realm is, says Cavell, that "I cannot reach this realm *alone*."[44]

Taking the wall of Jericho as concealing the self – wanting to conceal the self, to hide behind a blanket, or a story, as Peter does in running away from the second auto camp – is a way of refusing community, union, something we might call marriage. Taking the wall of Jericho, or the whole of *It Happened One Night,* as reflecting upon exactly that dilemma, by contrast, is Cavell's way of asserting community, the film's community with a particular dramatic tradition, Cavell's with the values he takes *It Happened One Night* and the other films of the genre to advance. To *describe* a film like *It Happened One Night* as a remarriage comedy is thus to emphasize certain textual features; to *interpret* it as a remarriage comedy is to take those features as bearing generally on our understanding of the world at large.

Two lingering but related problems with genre criticism are worth addressing briefly before we turn to the issue of film style. The problem in each case involves a question of values, of locating them, of contesting or revising them. The double difficulty at work here can be seen in the distinction Rick Altman makes in *The American Film Musical* between genre-as-ritual and genre-as-ideology, a distinction he rewrites as between "semantic" and "syntactic" approaches to genre study. Where the former is concerned chiefly with "common traits, attitudes, characters, shots, locations, sets, and the like," the latter is chiefly a matter of "constitutive relationships" among these semantic variables.[45] By defining a given genre as involving both of these conceptual sets, Altman is able to account for generic borrowing (the way a semantic element from one genre can be employed in another – film noir lighting, for example, in *It's a Wonderful Life*) and for generic consistency or durability (seen as involving stability at the level of a genre's underlying syntactical relationships, its "meaning-bearing structures").[46] This doubled definition of genre also allows Altman to account for what he calls the "cumulative" aspect of genre, which allows (in turn) for what he calls "symbolic spectatorship."[47] In viewing a film, Altman contends,

> the spectator must necessarily participate in two nearly identical but separable processes: (1) become engaged with a particular set of characters having their own specific problems calling for resolution within the limited context provided by the film at hand; (2) resolve a more general cultural problem which exists for the spectator thanks to tacit common-denominator processing involving numerous texts sharing properties with the one at hand.[48]

One catch in this anthropological picture of genre is that its "lowest-common-denominator" logic renders value judgments of particular films redundant if not impossible. Hence Sam Rohdie is compelled to admit, in concluding his "Totems and Movies" myth analysis of *Mr. Deeds Goes to Town,* that he finally cannot answer the question "why is *Mr. Deeds Goes to Town* a good movie?"[49] Not surprisingly, since "no single [genre] film can present the entire myth,'' as Altman notes by reference to Lévi-Strauss; it is rather ''the system of generic variations'' that generates ''a single coherent narrative mediating cultural contradictions'' thereby permitting ''symbolic spectatorship'' wherein ''particular objects and actions take on the new meaning provided by a broader cultural context.''[50] What lends cultural value to *Mr. Deeds,* under such a reading, can never be derived from the film itself. What matters in a given interpretive instance is not even those particular features or traits a given text shares with others of its kind but the fact that a minimal if crucial number of such traits is enough to call forth an effectively unconscious cultural prototype. The text at hand is merely a trigger; the prototype does the real mythological work of providing ''imaginary'' resolutions of ''real'' contradictions. (How a proposed solution to any problem, real or not, can be *other* than imaginary, in the sense of being imagined, is hard to picture.) However, the prototype is never really or fully ''there''; no wonder Rohdie missed it.

A related difficulty of structuralist theories of film genre is that efforts to ''read'' the prototype from the text in light of an anthropological collation of similar texts can never really rise to the status of critique, can never turn on the prototype in ways that will effect or change its implicitly conservative status. As Lévi-Strauss himself avers in ''The Structural Study of Myth,'' interpreting a myth is effectively to repeat (implicitly to reinforce) the myth: ''If a myth is made up of all its variants,'' then ''not only Sophocles, but Freud himself, should be included among the recorded versions of the Oedipus myth on a par with earlier or seemingly more 'authentic' versions.''[51] The logic of the common denominator apparently assures, then, that the critical element of even the most demystifying analysis will be mythologically factored out, so that neither artist nor critic can be understood as in a position to engage with culture at a conscious or effective oppositional level.

Like genre and ideology, the cognate concept of ''myth'' is a commonplace among Capra scholars, is therefore unavoidable in the present context, though it threatens to render criticism redundant or, worse, regressive. Nevertheless, it seems counterintuitive as well as counterproductive to accept the proposition that human beings are incapable of ''turning'' on their intellectual and cultural schemata; certainly people *claim* to be doing it all the time, nowhere more frequently or vehemently than in contemporary film scholarship. Perhaps we need a better, at least a different, concept of myth to work with. Again I turn to Stanley Cavell.

I do so by collecting thoughts from *Pursuits of Happiness* and Cavell's subsequent essay on "The Fact of Television." At issue in both are the problems that follow from thinking of "a genre as a form characterized by features, as an object by its properties."[52] And Cavell elucidates these problems by means of a distinction between "genre-as-cycle" and "genre-as-medium," a pairing that in many respects (e.g., its relation to Frye and Todorov) anticipates Altman's distinction between semantic and syntactic approaches to genre.[53] In Cavell and Altman both the idea of genre as a list of semantic features or properties only covers half the necessary conceptual ground. (That is the problem.) The other half of the territory of genre, however, is mapped quite differently in Altman and Cavell. In Altman's case the syntax of genre is mythic and largely unconscious, if only in the sense that the myth is only triggered by a film, is never fully present in it (to it). Cavell's notion of genre-as-medium, however, understands certain (Altman would say "exclusive") genres and genre films as not only incorporating a mythic intertext but as consciously interpreting, as revising, the myth in question, as remarriage comedy revises Shakespearean comedy by interpreting marriage as (by) divorce.

Underlying this view is the thought that "only the art can define its media, only painting and composing and movie making can reveal what is required, or possible (what means, what exploits of material), for something to be a painting, a piece of music, a movie."[54] A medium, a genre, is thus *not* something simply given, not a mere accumulation of semantic features or traits. Rather, "members of a genre share the inheritance of certain conditions, procedures and subjects and goals of composition," Cavell writes, and "in primary art each member of such a genre represents a study of these conditions, something I think of as bearing the responsibility of the inheritance."[55] Later Cavell will redescribe "the common inheritance of the members of a genre as a story, call it a myth. The members of a genre will be interpretations of it, or to use Thoreau's word for it, revisions of it, which will also make them interpretations of one another."[56] Later yet Cavell will take this mythic self-consciousness as an allegory of the relationships of the central characters in remarriage comedy: "Belonging," whether to a genre or to another, to a couple, "has to be won, earned, as by an argument of the members with one another."[57]

Cavell's understanding here of "interpretation" as crossing distinctions among the actions of characters and the symbolic "actions" of genre members can be extended by noting a second sense in which Cavell uses the concept of interpretation, as a matter of performing (thus interpreting) a text, as a musician performs (hence interprets) a score. "A performance of a piece of music is an interpretation of it, the manifestation of one way of hearing it, and it arises (if it is serious) from a process of analysis."[58] Here Cavell and Lévi-Strauss meet, not only in their shared reliance on music as a figure for analysis, but in agreeing that the analysis of a myth, the interpretation of an interpretation, yields yet another interpretation, another myth. As character to character, as lover to beloved, as genre member to genre, so finally film critic to film; each case is an instance of interpretation.

However, Cavell can be seen to turn on the assumption that often accompanies the Lévi-Strauss version of this story, the assumption that all versions of a myth function always at the same, effectively unconscious and culturally conservative, level. Yes, myths are in some sense all alike in being interpretations, as Capra interprets Shakespeare, Cavell interprets Capra, I interpret Cavell interpreting Capra, and so on. Therefore I can hardly deny to any other version of a myth whatever degree of self-consciousness I claim for my own. (I seem to be claiming considerable.) Myths may well be figures of and for interpretation, opportunities for our metaphoric attributions and deliberations; they may be good to think with, *bonnes à penser,* as Lévi-Strauss would have it.[59] So too, we have reason to hope, are we. Apart from that hope, there is no point in writing. I am obviously hopeful. Besides which, if Cavell is right in claiming that "a measure of the quality of a new text is the quality of the texts it arouses," then the evaluation problem also allows of (an ever tentative) solution; no film is ever any less valuable than the best available reading of it.[60] Put another way, the aesthetic or cultural value of a particular film is determined by, is argued by reference to, the quality of the aesthetic experience to which it gives rise, of which interpretation is both an essential and culturally negotiable component.

The Classical Narrative Cinema

Given the radical shift in the last several decades in the dominant genres of film criticism – from journalistic reviewing to academic close analysis – it is a major anomaly that discussions of film style in Capra have become (with few exceptions) less frequent and insightful rather than more so. In the thirties Capra was known chiefly as a stylist. In the words of Charles Wolfe, "The story material behind *It Happened One Night* and *Broadway*

Bill, many reviewers observed at the time, was not unique; what seemed to distinguish the films was Capra's treatment of this material: the behavioral charm of his actors, deft pacing, and a tone that was at once casual and vibrant.''[61] Yet the textbook Capra reproduced in primary anthologies is typically the Richards Capra, the populist Capra of genre and myth; in the words of Robert Sklar, ''Capra became known as a director with a subject rather than a style.''[62]

The idea that Hollywood's studio style was (as if generically) ''invisible'' we have already encountered. One of the earliest and clearest expositions of the logic of this claim is André Bazin's. Crucial here is Bazin's essay on ''The Evolution of the Language of Cinema,'' which effectively introduced the habit of describing Hollywood films of the 1930s as a ''classical art'' in which technique (chiefly film editing) is made subservient to dramatic enactment. Bazin describes a typical (if hypothetical) 1938 Hollywood shot sequence (establishing long-shot, cut-in close-ups, character-centered medium-shot) as exhibiting particular properties from which he derives his characterization of invisible or analytic editing. One is ''spatial verisimilitude, whereby the position of the character is always determined, even when a close-up cuts out the décor.'' And the other is an ''exclusively dramatic or psychological'' editing logic that ''does not add anything'' to the scene, that ''simply presents reality in the most effective manner. First of all by allowing one to see it better, and then by emphasising what needs emphasising.''[63] And *because* the ''only purpose of breaking down the shots is to analyse an event according to the physical and dramatic logic of a scene,'' the ''analysis is rendered imperceptible by its very logicality.''[64]

It is by now fairly clear that ''invisible,'' in such formulations, is to be taken metaphorically, as is the alleged viewer ''passivity'' that is typically taken to derive from it. Indeed, the two-stage model that allowed the imputation of spectatorial passivity – in which a generic dramatic scene is, as it were, ''preread'' and subsequently ''reread'' with little interpretive leeway or leakage – has been replaced by a much more complex model of ''classical narration,'' a primary feature of which is the intensely active (if often unconscious) role the viewer plays in comprehending even the most zero-degree Hollywood movie.

If (like Bazin) we equate narration chiefly with the camera, and subsequently declare the camera to be an invisible spectator whose traces are effectively masked or effaced by the logic of narrative, then the only fully visible aspect of the typical Hollywood film is the "narrative" itself. However, David Bordwell has demonstrated beyond all doubting that cinematic narrative is no simple or single thing; indeed, that something we might think of as a film's "story" is, in fact, never fully present, nor does it ever fully exist (except in rare cases) as a "profilmic" reality that the camera can be thought of as having subsequently "recorded." Accordingly, we would do better, on Bordwell's understanding, to give up the static two-term (narration/narrative) model by taking narration to be a dynamic process involving three conceptually separate though often phenomenally simultaneous systems from among the interplay of which the spectator constructs (is cued to construct) the mental object we normally refer to as a movie. We can define the three systems in question by means of two terminological distinctions, between Story and Plot, and between Plot and style.

"Story," in Bordwell's usage, refers to "action as a chronological cause-and-effect chain of events occurring within a given duration and a spatial field."[65] Key to the distinction between Story and Plot here is the matter of chronology; *flashbacks,* for instance, rearrange Story time by presenting an earlier event *after* later ones, though similar chronological shifts are familiar to us in the form of verbal reports, one character telling another of an action that happened at some earlier point in fictional or diegetic time. Because most films begin, as it were, in the middle of an action, *in medias res,* much of the Story is only reported, never presented. In that sense, the total Story is "never materially present on the screen or soundtrack."[66] By contrast, Plot time, or Plot order, is a matter of screen events, the order of "the actual arrangement and presentation of the [Story] in the film."[67] "The plot is, in effect, the film before us. The story is thus our mental construct, a structure of inferences we make on the basis of selected aspects of the plot."[68] Different Plots may thus yield (via selection) the same Story; different Stories may yield (from a filmmaker's perspective) quite similar Plots (e.g., genres).

The distinction between Plot and style involves similar complications. Though Plot refers to "the architectonics of the film's presentation of the [Story]," its "patterning is independent of the medium" in the sense that the same Plot "could be embodied in a novel, a play, or a film." What embodies the Plot in film, from which we will subsequently infer Story, is film style, "the film's systematic use of cinematic devices" – and style, like Plot, allows another range of variables.[69] Say that a given Plot requires two events to occur (be presented as occurring) simultaneously. "The simultaneity may be denoted by crosscutting from one event to the other, by staging the two actions in depth, by use of split-screen techniques, or by the inclusion of particular objects in the setting (such as a television set broadcasting a 'live' event)."[70] These "stylistic" options are not merely optional or neutral; it may well matter to the viewer or the maker which pattern is chosen in a given context. Moreover, the last of these options makes clear that the conventional distinction between the "telling" and the "told," between narration and narrative, is problematic; what is represented as part of the "narrated" world (a television) may well turn out to be a device for "narrating" that world. Bordwell's model of filmic narration is far more elegant and involved than this summary can possibly indicate. However, distinguishing among style, Plot, and Story allows us to characterize the classical narrative cinema as involving a particular range of relations among the three.

Story in the classical mode, for example, typically involves (is inferred from) a psychological or character-based model of cause and effect, often defining character action "as the attempt to achieve a goal," though the goal is usually reached only after considerable struggle and delay, often complicated by multiple cause–effect action lines. Plot, by contrast, typically involves a more abstract or dramatic pattern in which "an initial state of affairs" gets "violated" and then "set right": "The plot consists of an undisturbed stage, the disturbance, the struggle, and the elimination of the disturbance."[71] Plot requirements thus effectively eliminate Stories where goals are too readily achieved, where disturbance or struggle is lacking.

Furthermore style, in classical narration, "typically encourages the spectator to construct a coherent, consistent time and space for the [Story] action."[72] That is, consistency and coherency are assured by the continuity system of editing, which matches action, setting, gesture, dialogue, and so forth, across successive shots in such a way that cutting logic is subservient to Plot (hence to Story) logic, is in that sense "invisible." Key devices here include the "180-degree rule," which keeps the camera always on one side of a central (if easily shifted) axis of action so as to ensure consistency of background and decor, of screen position, of eye-line matches or glances, and of screen direction (direction of movement). The most common instance of this is the shot/reverse-shot figure in which conversations of facing characters are typically photographed, the two framed alternately over one character's shoulder, then the other's (Fig. 7).

Figure 7. Shot/reverse-shot in *Meet John Doe*.

We might describe classical narration, then, as a matter of "matching" – of matching style to Plot, thus providing a coherent dramatic space in which screen events can be enacted; of matching Plot to Story, in the sense that Plot is understood as providing all the knowledge we need to construct a consistent and coherent Story. "In all," writes Bordwell, "classical narration manages the controlled pace of film viewing by asking the spectator to construe the [Plot] and the stylistic system in a single way: construct a denotative, univocal, integral [Story]."[73] Such narration is hardly, *in toto,* invisible; at various points (e.g., the credits, montage sequences) the process of narration, of providing necessary information, is foregrounded. However, it is typically the case that the match of style and Plot to Story is so strong that the Story seems to tell itself. The motives of psychologically realistic characters drive the action; and aspects of the Story world are typically invoked to account for Plot resolution, the celebrated example being the deadline often seen in newspaper films like *His Girl Friday,* which provides an internal necessity for concluding the action of the film. We see an oddly literal instance of this in *Meet John Doe* in the promise Ann makes as John Doe to jump off the City Hall roof on Christmas Eve, a promise Long John Willoughby intends (for a while) to keep.

Our discussion of *Meet John Doe* – of its montage sequences, of its deeply problematic ending – indicates something of the difficulty that follows when Capra is read against these classical narrative norms. The match between Plot and Story is often rendered uncertain or ambivalent by virtue of the fact that Capra's characters – like Ann Mitchell and Long John Willoughby – are often profoundly unfocused, weakly motivated, decentered, following scripts laid out by others more than any goal-directed script arising from realistic plans of their own. From Harry Langdon to Peter Warne to George Bailey, Capra's protagonists are typically dreamers or visionaries whose goals are so diffuse or so improbable that they can barely serve by themselves to anchor narrative cause and effect. Thus it is typically the more antagonistic characters who have the plans or goals in Capra, and those goals or plans are often wildly sidetracked by circumstances – often a sudden death, as in *Mr. Deeds* and *Mr. Smith* – the effect of which is to delay goal-directed behavior in favor of moment-by-moment improvisations. The classic instance here might be *Lady for a Day* (or its remake, *Pocketful of Miracles*) in which Dave the Dude's gambling or racketeering plans are kept constantly on hold by the increasingly frantic "fairy-tale" scheme to pass Apple Annie off to her convent-educated daughter and prospective Spanish in-laws as Mrs. E. Worthington Manville.

Such a view of Story in Capra allows us to account for two commonly acknowledged aspects of his style. One is Capra's oft-noted willingness to let Story grind to a halt for the sake of more immediate visual and sonic pleasures or contemplations. The "Man on the Flying Trapeze" song sequence in *It Happened One Night* comes immediately to mind here; its Plot duration is wildly in excess of any Story-driven cause–effect necessity. Similar musical interludes are found throughout the Capra canon, from (at least) *The Miracle Woman* through *A Hole in the Head* and *Pocketful of Miracles*. Such moments are hardly matters of complete "free play" on Capra's part or ours. However, such moments typically are indicative of some "other" logic than that which seems to be driving events, a logic more of theme (in both the musical and cognitive senses) than of Story.

A second quality of Capra's style highlighted by the relative weakness of the Plot–Story match in Capra is the importance to his films of casting, of "stars," especially as casting introduces elements of generic "impurity," in Robin Wood's sense of the term. Though Capra's films are typically thought of as comedies of one stripe or another, they often draw upon the iconography of film melodrama, both for particular stars in lead roles (Barbara Stanwyck especially) and for a particular conception of character. Compare what I have already said about the "weakness" of psychological motivation in, say, *Meet John Doe* with the following passages from Peter Brooks's *The Melodramatic Imagination:*

> It is important that, in talking of affective structure . . . we not be deluded into thinking we are referring to the psychological structures of melodrama's characters. There is no "psychology" in melodrama in this sense; the characters have no interior depth, there is no psychological conflict . . . because melodrama exteriorizes conflict and psychic structure . . . . What we have is a drama of pure psychic signs – called Father, Daughter, Protector, Persecutor, Judge, Duty, Obedience, Justice – that interest us through their clash, by the dramatic space created through their interplay, providing the means for their resolution.[74]

A similar "exteriority" of significance is, of course, a staple of comic technique, on stage and screen both. It is part of Capra's cinematic genius that he can mix melodrama and comedy so effectively in the same film; and part of what makes that genius profoundly cinematic is its inspired reliance on casting, if not to fill "in," at least to fill "out," his characters, using actors *as signs* who exteriorize, make visible, the clash of values and styles. Something like this is surely what Stephen Handzo had in mind when declaring that "the face of Gary Cooper and *voice* of Jean Arthur," not the politics of populism, are the "real 'content' " of *Mr. Deeds Goes to Town*.[75] It is also akin to what David Bordwell had in mind when describing Long John Willoughby as "a character who *grows into* the star's persona." Thus Willoughby becomes "the rustic idealist John Doe because Willoughby was, in latent form, Gary Cooper to begin with."[76] In retrospect, I would add, we might well decide to attribute various depth-psychological states to Capra's characters; they certainly attribute such states to each other all the time, as does Capra via subjective sequences and/or point-of-view shots, techniques to which the melodramatic stage described by Brooks had no recourse. Our doing so, however, clearly requires a willingness to read their surfaces as deeply as possible, as signifying imaginative depths that neither they nor Capra are always capable of articulating in the normal language of social behavior. Thus to read Capra's style as invisible is a grievous perceptual and interpretive error.

We see a similar narrational complexity or disturbance when we turn from the Story–Plot relation to the Plot–style match in Capra. Though Capra's visual and sonic pallet is generally taken from the same technical store drawn upon by his Hollywood studio peers, Capra paid far less homage than many of his contemporaries to the editing conventions that rendered style subservient to narrative via match-on-action continuity. A corollary to the 180-degree rule, for example, is the 30-degree rule. Where the 180-degree rule works to ensure graphic continuity across shots by ensuring common backgrounds and positions, the 30-degree rule, which dictates that a change in camera position *must* vary by at least 30-degrees along the 180-degree arc established by the axis of action, guarantees that graphic change between shots will be great enough to mask over or distract from any minor changes in posture or positioning; shots too closely matched, especially those taken at the same angle from the action, are too easily read as mismatched if the match is anything but perfect. We typically call such mismatches "jump cuts."[77] Capra is famous for disregarding this convention.

The instance I have in mind – briefly discussed by David Bordwell and Kristin Thompson in *Film Art* – is from an early scene of *Mr. Smith Goes to Washington* in which Jim Taylor (Edward Arnold) and Senator Paine (Claude Rains) discuss whom the governor will appoint to replace the recently departed Senator Foley.[78] Taylor and Paine are in a conference room off of the governor's office, and Capra films their deliberation in a series of medium two-shots, all taken from the same angle, with the effect that cuts from one shot to the next change shot scale only minimally, and in such a way as to make the cuts instantly noticeable. A very similar sequence is that between Mr. Potter (Lionel Barrymore) and Uncle Billy (Thomas Mitchell) in *It's a Wonderful Life* in which Uncle Billy boasts to Potter of Harry Bailey's Congressional Medal of Honor and in the process slips the Savings and Loan's $8,000 between the folds of the newspaper he takes from and then returns to Potter (Fig. 8). Again, Capra sustains the same angle relative to the action, and cuts from medium-shot to tighter medium-shot and back again with only the slightest shift of scale. It is probable that cutting in both cases (and in the many similar instances elsewhere in the canon) follows from Capra's interest in acquiring certain readings or line inflections from his actors. However, his decision to ignore the 30-degree rule in the process does not of itself follow from nor is it fully explained by this essentially "theatrical" consideration.

Another rule Capra more spectacularly ignores is the 180-degree rule itself, sometimes to crucial stylistic and thematic effect across an entire film. A key scene of *Ladies of Leisure,* for example, finds Kay Arnold (Barbara Stanwyck) and Jerry Strong (Ralph Graves) in the latter's Manhattan penthouse studio. As the night grows longer Kay eventually faints – whether from the fatigue of posing while Jerry paints or as an act soliciting Jerry's sympathy is unclear, even to her – and Jerry offers her the couch immediately beneath the skylight as a place to sleep through the night. As they prepare for bed – putting bedding on the couch, changing into nightclothes, and so forth, a scene that in its back-lit erotic charge anticipates the walls of Jericho routine in *It Happened One Night* – Capra repeatedly cuts across the 180-degree line, framing Stanwyck either through or against the skylight while both she and Jerry (he in the adjacent bedroom) keep looking at the bedroom door between them.

An even more extreme example of line jumping occurs the next morning, when Jerry's railroad tycoon father appears during breakfast. By now Kay's hesitancy of motive has clearly given way to an almost hysterical affection for Jerry, prompted in large part by his considerateness of the night before, especially his touchingly parental gesture of covering her with an extra blanket while she feigned sleep. Once Mr. Strong enters, Kay retreats to the kitchen while Jerry listens to his father propose a double honeymoon trip to Paris, he and Mrs. Strong accompanying Jerry and his fiancée. Much of the scene is photographed in standard shot/reverse-shot with the two men anchoring the axis of action via eyeline matches. Repeatedly, however, we cut to a framing from the kitchen that places Kay in the shot, screen right, while the two men are visible in the background screen left, their screen positions reversed by virtue of Capra's having cut across the 180-degree line (Fig. 9). Moreover, once Kay is drawn into the conversation – by Mr. Strong's offer to buy her off at liberal rates – Capra continues to jump the line with nearly every cut of an extended passage of conversation.

It is not the case that any of these cuts, in either of the two scenes, is especially disorienting – despite the predictions of editing manuals. (Which is to say that the cuts, in fact, match.) Nevertheless, they *do* correlate with an aspect of uncertainty, ambiguity, reversibility. In the former scene Kay seems alternately pleased and disgusted with Jerry's proposal that she spend the night; in the latter she simultaneously asserts a kind of idealized domesticity (preparing breakfast, cutting flowers for the breakfast table) and a cynical party-girl acceptance of Mr. Strong's declaration that she is not, in fact, a model. Moreover, in both cases the editing pattern emphasizes the "fact" of lines; the "axis of action" itself, often embodied by a window or table edge, the door between Kay and Jerry, an architectural column that splits the screen between Jerry and his father at one point, the doorframe of the kitchen that splits the screen between Kay and the two men, and so forth. It is not hard to see such lines as tokens of the basic class and value conflicts that the film's larger action calls into question.

Two other connotation sets are also at play here, at least retroactively. The film's first pronounced across-the-line cut takes place during a dinner scene that features Jerry seated on the far side of a long table positioned perpendicular to the camera, his father screen left at one end, his mother screen right at the other. Again we get standard shot/reverse-shot editing on conversation, so that the table amounts to the axis of action. Twice, however, the camera jumps the line and frames the table from behind and to the right of Jerry's mother. At first glance it seems a matter of mere option. At the end of the sequence, however, Jerry's mother gets up from the table and glances over Jerry's shoulder, from a position "over the line," down to the table cloth, where he has written the word "Hope" twice, which we see from (roughly) her vantage point. Likewise, toward film's end we see a desperate Kay on a Havana-bound steamer, as the party-girl guest of Jerry's friend Bill Standish. (Kay is leaving Jerry at the request of

Figure 8. Jump-cut editing in *It's a Wonderful Life*.

his mother.) Kay leans on the rail as she waits for the boat to clear the twelve-mile limit so the bar can open and she can get "cockeyed." The cutting is complicated here by the fact that Capra intercuts action on the boat with action back at Jerry's apartment house. However, the shots of Kay alternate among extreme up-angle close-ups of Kay at the rail with stars behind her and down-angle shots over Kay at the rail to the water below; the rail itself amounts to a 180-degree line across which the camera repeatedly jumps.

I read all this as a meditation on hopefulness and hopelessness and especially on the gender politics involved. Hope, we might say, is the province of artists and women, people in some sense shut out of the workaday promises of the financial world represented by Jerry's father, who does *not* glance down to see Jerry's tablecloth jottings as he leaves the dinner table. Indeed, Jerry takes it for granted that Hope will have a woman's form; he hires Kay as his model because she seems, at some level, hopeful, or at least self-contained and self-directed. After all, he first sees her leaving a yacht under her own power, as disgusted as Jerry himself is with the pointless sexual raillery of the upper classes. (In fact, the first across-the-line cut occurs here, though the distance between Jerry and Kay makes it easy to miss.) Still, Kay's hope carries hopelessness along with it, especially when she comes up against the kind of class prejudice that even the sympathetic Mrs. Strong seems incapable of foreswearing. So crossing the line – like Mrs. Strong, like Kay Arnold – does not by itself guarantee success in life. It can just as readily find you hovering over the void and ready to plunge – as it does here when Kay jumps off the steamer, as it nearly does in *The Miracle Woman* when John Carson almost leaps from his apartment building or in *Meet John Doe* when John Willoughby comes close to jumping off the City Hall roof, as it does in *It's a Wonderful Life* when George Bailey hangs over another rail above another body of roiling water. Capra's legendary populist optimism hardly goes unchallenged in these instances.

Among textbook Capra essays only one attends very perceptively to the question of Capra's style, William Pechter's (aptly titled) "American Madness." Pechter begins by echoing Bazin's comments on invisible editing. Capra's style, Pechter writes, is one of "almost classic purity," a "style, one is tempted to say, based solely on editing, since it depends for its effects on a sustained sequence of rhythmic motion." Despite its purity, however, there is still something forced about it, especially so because (by contrast with Eisenstein's) Capra's style "has the effect of imposing order on im-

Figure 9. Crossing the "axis of action" in *Ladies of Leisure*. (*Ladies of Leisure* copyright © 1930, renewed 1957 Columbia Pictures Industries, Inc. All rights reserved. Courtesy of Columbia Pictures.)

ages constantly in motion.'' As a result, Capra's ''films move at a breathtaking clip: dynamic, driving, taut, at their extreme even hysterical. . . . The sheer speed and energy,'' Pechter goes on to remark, ''seem, finally, less calculated than desperate''; and it is in this quality of desperation that ''one sees again the fundamental nature of style as moral action: Capra's desperation is his final honesty. It ruthlessly exposes his own affirmation as pretense, and reveals, recklessly and without defense, dilemma.''[79]

We might paraphrase Pechter as alerting us to an element of ''mismatch'' in Capra, to a difference that troubles our conceptions of sameness, to a sameness that troubles our notions of difference. Much that we have already remarked upon in describing Capra's narrational strategies is obviously relevant here for allowing us to specify far more precisely *how* Capra manages to evoke such qualities as Pechter attributes to his films. On Pechter's description Capra pushes the classical narrative cinema to (at least some of) its limits. His accomplishment is unthinkable apart from the Hollywood tradition, amounts to one of its primary glories; but his accomplishment is exactly that he discovers or reveals the limits of that tradition by repeatedly, as it were, ''crossing the line,'' or walking it.

Capra *risks* difference, we might say, in the sense that risk in his films is both something imposed and something suffered. Capra imposes the risk of difference on himself, for example, in his habit of weaving divergent if familiar generic and intertextual threads together into strikingly singular and idiosyncratic patterns, as in the mixture of Thoreauvean transcendentalism, Shakespearean romanticism, and silent-comedy sight gags that Stanley Cavell elaborates in discussing *It Happened One Night;* or the mixture of film noir and small-town comedy motifs that Robin Wood discusses in his analysis of *It's a Wonderful Life*. A more literal task of melding opposites together is evident in Capra's stylistic habit of crossing the 180-degree line; a greater than normal measure of filmmaking skill is required to assure a fluid match of posture and action despite a complete change of background and the reversal of screen direction and position. It seems fairly clear as well that such passages should also be read as (at least potentially) motivated by aesthetic or artistic concerns beyond the compositional necessity of constructing a coherent and consistent temporal and spatial setting for the actions of goal-directed characters. Again, implications of *theme* are involved that suggest some *other* logic than that which seems most obviously present.

Such risk taking bespeaks a self-conscious virtuosity, as if Capra were trying to see how far he could go in elaborating upon the possibilities of the medium. This is the one-man, one-film Capra who "shoots as he pleases."[80] However, even here one senses a desire for recognition – an echo of Capra's almost frantic early 1930s campaign for an Academy Award, which he recounts in *The Name above the Title* – as if Capra were seeking to close the gap between himself and his public by opening and closing generic and visual gaps on screen. Indeed, in his later years this desire to match even took the form of reediting his films to account for audience reactions as tape-recorded at preview showings in order to make sure, for example, that the laughter elicited by one joke did not drown out or step on the next one.[81]

There is also a sense, however, in which Capra's desire for closeness can be understood as a matter of risks suffered rather than risks willingly self-imposed. A version of this is evident in Capra's penchant for jump-cut matches of nearly identical shots; similarity here has the effect of magnifying narrational difference beyond anything required by the logic of line readings, for example. A similar amplification of narration follows, I would suggest, from Capra's characteristic penchant for weakly motivated Story lines and protagonists. Instead of a clear cause–effect Story line that Plot can be readily understood as "following," Capra typically provides us with an improvisatory Plot that matches so closely with the improvisations of his characters as to amplify Capra's status as a guiding authorial presence. Again, near identity yields an obvious difference from the narrational modesty or homogeneity of the base-line Hollywood film, though a difference for which Capra is often chided.

Indeed, this different relation of Story and Plot, the collapse of Story *into* Plot, helps us account for Capra's notoriously problematic conclusions, of which the closing scene of *Meet John Doe* is only one spectacular instance among many. Such conclusions often seem arbitrary relative to the social logic of a film's depicted world. Clearly Ann Mitchell's hysterical claim that the John Doe movement will "grow" and "grow big" seems completely unconnected to the facts of the world she inhabits. However, the difference Capra suffers in such moments, asks us to suffer with him, is only arbitrary or narrationally forced on the assumption that the social logic of the depicted film world is the logic that matters most. Even in its failures and hesitancies, the conclusion of *Meet John Doe* is more usefully understood – *not* as Capra's quick and easy cure to social dysfunction or disaster – but as "figuring" (as standing for, as working out) the problem of authorship or language, a question that is logically prior to any prescriptions of the social engineering sort.

The difference connoted by this emphasis on language, to be sure, has its obvious dangers in the world of *Meet John Doe;* it is only by writing *two* letters, for example, one addressed "To All John Does Everywhere" and the other to Mr. Connell, that Long John can even begin to imagine that his suicide will stand to matter, despite his knowledge of Norton's power and resourcefulness. (Norton tells John that men are posted with instructions to hush up his suicide, in the event that John should jump, by destroying all evidence of John's identity. So identity is made *more* certain by duplication, even though duplication allows for its destruction, its deferral and dissemination?) However, authorship can also be a matter of more "positive" differences, as I have already suggested. This note is sounded in a quietly comic mode in *Meet John Doe* when the love-struck Long John elicits Mrs. Mitchell's offer to deliver John's marriage proposal to Ann on his behalf. More significantly, the film's closing sequence effectively urges (on this reading) that some acknowledgment of difference is necessary to the expression of community, in that sense to the expression of sameness, even to the expression of identity. Thus Long John Willoughby finally needs others to represent him, others who will speak the self that he is on the verge of destroying, even if the words they speak are echoes of his own, or of Ann's, or of her father's, or of our Father's; we might call this a matter of neighborliness, of nearness, of sustaining a language by speaking it together, by *meaning* it together.

Language, as Cavell and Kant and Lévi-Strauss alike remind us, may be a barrier. There is no world *beyond* it to which we have unmediated access. It may also be a screen whereby we reveal ourselves to others, hence a possible grounding for community, a world to which we do have access if we are willing, like Capra, to run the many risks of matching; the closer we get, the more difficult the match may become. Nothing guarantees the health or success of the human community; yet community is literally unthinkable apart from the willingness of its members to keep talking. On that account *Meet John Doe* may well be one of Capra's most abidingly successful and successfully communal films: in the spectacular sense (on Capra's recounting) that the ending Capra finally settled on was suggested after the film's initial release by a fan who signed his letter "John Doe," in the less spectacular sense that we are still talking about it, figuring it, are still figured by it. "Style as moral action" is a deeply apt description of the process.

You Can't Take It with You

I have described criticism as a mode of cultural conversation, of critics with each other and with the films they study. In the case of an open-ended film like *Meet John Doe* this process is readily evident, for example, in the ongoing debate about the aesthetic and ideological efficacy of the film's conclusion. Interpretations of the film are various; their variability has a history one can chart and to which one can contribute. The same cannot readily be said about *You Can't Take It with You,* where the range of interpretations has remained profoundly narrow and little changed over time.

Despite the fact that the stage and film versions of *You Can't Take It with You* were playing simultaneously in New York City and were thus available for comparison by the national press, *most* reviewers at the time of the film's initial release followed the lead of *Life* magazine in seeing Capra's version as a happy amplification of the Broadway original, the same in its general Romeo-and-Juliet outlines, yet made *more* of the same by the addition of scenes only hinted at by Kaufman and Hart (e.g., the night-court scene). Most critics welcomed Capra and Riskin's supplementary contributions as confirming the appeal of the eccentric Sycamore/Vanderhof clan while "widen[ing] the play's scope, reworking a wispy plot into a full-bodied narrative."[82] *Life* had predicted that "Capra's picture will bring a happy reacquaintance with America's best-loved stage family."[83] *Variety*'s reviewer confirmed this estimate in declaring Capra's *You Can't Take It with You* "wholly American, wholesome, homespun, human, appealing, and touching in turn."[84]

It is this very Americanness, however, that a minority of reviewers then and the vast majority of critics since have found distressingly characteristic of the Capra-Riskin elaboration of the play. Many latter-day Capra scholars avoid the issue by ignoring the movie; many of the essays on Capra's reputed populism, for example, rather inexplicably neglect *You Can't Take It with You* in their enthusiasm for treating the "Mr." films as a closed set – *despite* the politically significant fact that Edward Arnold, media mogul and villain extraordinaire in both *Mr. Smith* (as Jim Taylor) and *Meet John Doe* (as D. B. Norton), makes his Capra debut as an icon of capitalist excessiveness as *You Can't Take It with You*'s Anthony P. Kirby.[85] Charles Maland is almost alone among contemporary Capra critics in attending to *You Can't Take It with You* at any length, and even he finds moments in the movie – especially Grandpa Vandherhof's praise of Americanism – which nearly ''justify the critical claim that Capra is a blindly optimistic Pollyanna.''[86]

An early and especially interesting instance of this ideological discomfiture is James Dugan's *New Masses* review of *You Can't Take It with You.* Though Dugan and the audience with which he viewed the film responded differently, both he and the audience took Grandpa's tutelary remarks on Americanism straight and in so doing figure almost the entire range of responses to the film to date, either effusive praise or downright disgust:

> What the upper middle-class audience at Radio City cheered in the picture causes my alarm. In a speech inserted in the mouth of Grandpa Vanderhof (Lionel Barrymore) which was not in the play and has no organic place in the picture, the genial old zany remarks to his novelist daughter that she should put some ''ismology'' into her book. He goes on to explain that no contemporary novel should ignore Communism, fascism, and Nazism. Everybody who is disgruntled today, says Grandpa, goes out and gets themself an ''ism.'' This means that if you don't agree with what they think they'll bomb you. What Grandpa wants to boost is ''Americanism,'' and the old gentleman names a dozen American heroes to illustrate his point. The house came down.
>
> Now then, Riskin is no ignoramus. He is a grown man with a kindly feeling for the underdog – remember the exciting invasion of the farmers in *Mr. Deeds* and the whole bus sequence of *It Happened One Night.* When he begins to talk like Grandpa Vanderhof, naming the Communists along with Hitler and Mussolini as bombers, he is doing something that he very well knows is a lie. This disingenuous bid for reactionary applause, this seconding of the confusion hatched in the fink press is a burden no man of talent and decency can afford to carry.[87]

There are some obvious inaccuracies in Dugan's account of Grandpa's Americanism speech: Penny is a playwright, not a novelist; Grandpa urges a study of ''ismania,'' not ''ismology''; he mentions communism, fascism, voodooism, but not Nazism, and so forth. Even on Dugan's account, however, there is sufficient reason for doubting the wisdom of taking Grandpa's speech at face value, and in this regard Dugan is accurate enough; if resorting to an ''ism'' is a sign of disgruntlement that can lead in extreme cases to political violence, then Grandpa's speech (on Dugan's report) cannot be said to distinguish Americanism from any of the other isms under study, though Capra's legendary patriotism might make the distinction seem implicit. In fact, Grandpa *does* appear to make a distinction between the American ism and the others; after defining ismania in the inclusive and potentially self-contradictory terms suggested by Dugan, Grandpa goes on to list a number of figures from American history – John Paul Jones, Patrick Henry, Samuel Adams, Washington, Jefferson, Monroe, Lincoln, Grant, Lee, Edison, Mark Twain – none of whom, on Grandpa's account, resorted to isms when "things got tough." As if to confirm this latter claim, Grandpa invokes the following contrast: "Lincoln said, 'With malice toward none, with charity to all.' Nowadays they say, 'Think the way I do, or I'll bomb the daylights out of you.' "

Even on Dugan's abbreviated account, Grandpa's speech verges on incoherence or self-contradiction, which Grandpa apparently attempts to deny by reference to American history. What Dugan fails to observe is how the second part of Grandpa's speech continues the process of erasure or qualification. Almost all of the figures Grandpa cites – excepting Edison and Twain – are figures from the American Revolution or the American Civil War, in each of which people on both sides were "bombing the daylights" out of each other. Moreover, the speech Grandpa cites is Lincoln's Second Inaugural Address, the first in American history to be delivered during wartime; even while Lincoln was giving the address he commanded troops literally engaged in the final bloody stages of a long and brutal civil war. Given the fact that bombs figure so prominently in the movie version of *You Can't Take It with You* – the fireworks of Paul Sycamore and Mr. DePinna set against Kirby's munitions combine – it is hard to agree with Dugan in declaring Grandpa's speech completely out of place in the film. It must be granted, however, especially in view of the contradictions it generates, that "placing" Grandpa Vanderhof's speech is no easy matter.

My own view of the speech follows from a shift of perspective, taking it less as a piece of ready-made political wisdom than as an instance of artistic instruction, a view that depends on taking Grandpa as a profoundly self-conscious dramatist. Three scenes are crucial to such a perspective on the film:

3. the concluding sequence, especially Grandpa's advice to Tony and his harmonica duet with Kirby Senior;
2. the night-court scene, and especially Grandpa's fiction that the Kirbys had come

by the Sycamore house to purchase it, not for the purpose of meeting prospective in-laws; and

1. the scene with the Internal Revenue agent in which Grandpa refuses to pay more than $75 in back taxes.

I list the scenes in reverse Story order to mark the fact that this perspective works (at least for me) retrospectively; I take this retrospective shift to be roughly for viewers what Kirby Senior's ''conversion'' experience is for him, a matter of seeing old pictures differently. (Now I run ahead.)

I also list these scenes in reverse order to locate the moment in my own experience when I knew I had more to say about Frank Capra. It happened when I connected the concluding and the night-court scenes along ''dramatistic'' lines. Grandpa's status as a kind of improvisational dramatist is quite explicit in the film's concluding scene, most obviously when Grandpa responds to Kirby's despondent request for advice on parenting (saying he would ''give a fortune'' to make things good with Tony) by suggesting that Kirby should just play harmonica and let the crisis pass. He assures Kirby that the latter will be ''surprised what might happen,'' and he tells Kirby to ''swing it'' as they launch in to a rousing harmonica duet on ''Polly Wolly Doodle,'' which Grandpa knows full well (as indicated by close-ups of Grandpa looking up the stairway) will bring Tony and Alice down from the second floor hallway where Tony pleads with Alice to forgive him, thus reuniting father and son, Tony and Alice, Kirbys and Sycamores, all in one fantastic and self-consciously theatrical *kômos,* a grand finale that is equally as much Grandpa's as Capra's. Indeed, I think it is also fairly clear – especially when the film is considered in light of the Kaufman and Hart original – that Grandpa's artistry in bringing the whole cast together in celebration extends well beyond his use of music to call Tony and Alice down from upstairs.

Much is made, early in the film, of Grandpa's abiding affection for the brownstone family house the clan inhabits. (Grandma's fragrance has never left her bedroom; moving out of the house would be like moving out on Grandma.) Nevertheless, toward film's end Grandpa apparently thinks nothing about selling the house to Kirby's real estate agent, thus completing the land scam designed to force a competitor out of business. One might read this gesture on Grandpa's part as betokening despair at Alice's departure for Connecticut after her night-court renunciation of Tony and his family as snobs. Also, of course, Grandpa *is* playing for keeps in offering the home for sale; Rheba informs us (out of Alice's earshot) that she had seen a tearful Grandpa gazing at Grandma's picture.

However, only moments earlier Grandpa had told Alice he had sold the house because he "got tired of it, that's all." Furthermore, the fact that he *could* prod Alice with such a blatant fiction (especially given that *she* was the one who solicited Grandpa's reminiscences about Grandma) is also evidence of Grandpa's profoundly theatrical turn of mind. In Kaufman and Hart Alice retreats upstairs and *threatens* to leave the house, if she can ever get someone to call her a cab, a threat that causes some sadness but bears not at all on the prospect of the clan's continued residence, sans Alice, in their Manhattan home. In Capra and Riskin, by contrast, Alice is already long gone; Grandpa's sell-the-house scheme and the telegram announcing it amount to a calculated if desperate gambit to get her back, if only to pack up her things. The gambit works.

All of which urges the wisdom of attending as much to Grandpa's actions and their consequences as to his words per se. Applying this maxim to the night-court scene amply confirms the view that Grandpa's homespun "lilies of the field" zaniness is no less pragmatic than soaringly idealistic. The fact that needs explaining here is Grandpa's night-court defense of the Kirbys, a defense that *seems* designed to get them off the misdemeanor hook for the illegal manufacture of fireworks (of more than passing relevance given the film's munitions theme). It is easy to take this as just one more example of Grandpa's folksy kindheartedness. However, taking it that way requires one to ignore its consequences (and Capra's presentation of it, which focuses on Alice's response via reaction-shot close-ups of Jean Arthur).

Grandpa has set a test, we might say, that Tony fails by his silent if only momentary acquiescence to Grandpa's partial fiction (that the Kirbys were there to see Grandpa about buying the house). Moreover, when Tony finally does acknowledge the class prejudice that inclines his parents to accept Grandpa's fiction in lieu of the romantic truth of the matter, it is in the face of Alice's indignant test-passing wrath ("About time you spoke up"; "It's your family that isn't good enough. . . "). Indeed, in the commotion caused by Alice's angry outburst members of the press, previously denied entry, charge into the courtroom with flash-lamps blazing to document the moment when "Cinderella just told Prince Charming to go take a flying leap."

All of which ironically and very pointedly echoes Kirby's accusation, leveled at Grandpa in the drunk tank only moments earlier, that Vanderhof was using Alice's relationship with Tony to get a better deal on his house. Grandpa finds it rather funny that Kirby has been caught in his own trap (it was Kirby's real estate agent who tipped off the cops about the fireworks); Grandpa is a cagey comic dramatist indeed when he borrows Kirby's construal of events (that the love affair was really about real estate) and uses it measure for measure against him in court. (Despite the fact that both families are facing the same charges, when the judge calls the court to order the Kirbys and their brace of lawyers face the bench like defendants, while the Sycamores line up to the side of the bench, in the position typically reserved for jury members – one more reason for seeing Grandpa's gambit as putting Tony on trial.)

Grandpa Vanderhof, we might say, is a dramatist of the everyday who works by constructing situations that encourage people to think and act. He is also a student of rhetoric, as his habit of attending commencement addresses makes plain. The same can be said, quite obviously, of Frank Capra, especially so in the Internal Revenue and Americanism scenes of *You Can't Take It with You.* Indeed, as Dugan and many others have intuited, there is a powerful sense in which these two scenes especially can be taken as appeals applying *beyond* their immediate dramatic context. Just how their appeal *works,* however, can best be understood by taking that context into account.

The taxman scene is an interesting example because it comes closer than all the other scenes I have discussed (or will) to coming straight out of the Broadway original. To be specific, the argument between the Internal Revenue agent and Grandpa Vanderhof is almost word for word Kaufman and Hart.[88] Grandpa (in both) asks rhetorically, supposing for argument's sake that he *will* pay back taxes, ''What's the government going to do with it?'' In answer to which the agent supplies a long list of government officers and obligations, to which Grandpa replies (among other things) ''Not with my money.''

In the play, of course, Grandpa really does owe tax and really is playing for time. He eventually remembers that they had used his own name to get a burial certificate for Charlie the milkman who had lived with them for five years without ever revealing his last name. So Grandpa tells Internal Revenue (or so we learn in the last act) that his real name is Martin Vanderhof, ''Jr.''; it is the senior Martin Vanderhof who owes the taxes and he has been dead for eight years. In Capra and Riskin, by contrast, the scene concludes, after the frantic taxman departs in a crescendo of fireworks and xylophone music, with Grandpa saying "I was only having fun with him; I don't owe the government a cent." Of course, we have to take Grandpa's word on this latter account (and why not?), but doing so is interesting for changing our reading of the scene considerably compared to the Kaufman and Hart version of it. At the very least, we can say that the film Grandpa takes great pleasure in prodding others to examine their most deeply held convictions or assumptions. It is also worth noting that, in the film though not in the play, this entire exchange takes place in the presence of Tony Kirby, as if his convictions also are being prodded by Grandpa's tax-protest minidrama. (Indeed, Grandpa makes an explicit point of engaging Tony in a discussion of the matter after the taxman beats his hasty retreat.) Moreover, that prodding is clearly as much Capra's of the film audience as it is Grandpa's of Tony. It is less the conclusion of the argument that matters (Grandpa knows what he owes and has already paid up) than the fact that concepts are kept open for discussion.

That Grandpa's Americanism speech *can* be taken as banal political sloganeering is a fact well worth remembering. That it can (also) be taken differently – both more deeply *and* more literally – is equally true and noteworthy. *How* to take it differently, I am suggesting, is more than hinted at by later scenes in the movie; think of Grandpa as a self-conscious dramatist who fictionalizes his own in-the-world behavior so as to set the world to thinking. Part of the thought process initiated by Grandpa's speech I have already described in noting the various logical and historical inconsistencies or incoherences that mark his impromptu declaration. However, crucial to our grasp of what Grandpa's speech means in the larger context of the film follows from the fact – contra Dugan – that Grandpa does not offer this advice unbidden, out of thin ideological air. Rather, Grandpa's advice follows close upon, as if in answer to, Penny's repeated question, asked not only of Grandpa but of Donald, Mr. Poppins, even (over the phone) of Tony Kirby, "Have you ever been in a monastery?" It seems in Penny's current play she has written a female character in to a monastery, but draws blanks when it comes to writing her out.

Grandpa's first piece of advice to his daughter involves memory; he tells her to recall how she got out of jail once, advice Grandpa means figuratively, as applying to getting a character out of jail in some other play, but that Mr. Poppins takes (for the moment) literally, as applying to Penny herself. Her memory, it turns out, is somewhat faulty (though Alice has worked as a stenographer at Kirby and Company for months, Penny still thinks of her as working in a millinery shop) so Grandpa switches tactics. As if prompted by an exchange between Mr. DePinna and Mr. Poppins ("Oh, you're the iceman"), which obviously alludes to Eugene O'Neill's *The Iceman Cometh,* Grandpa suggests that Penny write a play about ismania, which Penny promptly construes as a theatrical device she can use to liberate Cynthia from the monastery. At which point Grandpa suggests that Cynthia be given Americanism.

Even at a fairly literal level, then, Grandpa's speech evinces a high degree of theatrical self-consciousness, complicated by the fact that Penny seems especially forgetful, as if she needs to be reminded periodically of the culture to which and for which she ostensibly writes. Also worth noting, however, is the physical "business" that goes along with Grandpa's recitation. During the first part of the discussion he is reading the newspaper, catching up with the world outside (e.g., he makes specific note of a large loan made by Kirby and Company); he folds up the paper and puts it aside just as he begins the ismania portion of the dialogue. As he continues talking he takes up a book and a magnifying glass and begins looking through the glass at stamps he has taken out of his coat pocket. To his immediate left (screen right) is a table; on the table are an archaic cigar lighter (familiar to most of us as a key fixture in Gower's Drug Store in *It's a Wonderful Life*), a framed photograph of Alice, and a pipe rack.

Given the fact that Grandpa makes a living appraising the relative value of stamps, or so one presumes from Alice's report that he gets well paid for his appraisals, and given the repeated associations in the 1938 discourse on "Frank Capra" of photographs and fires and the cinematic apparatus, I find the conclusion inescapable that Grandpa is a kind of stand-in for Capra, a figure for Capra's authorship. Indeed, it is hard to avoid connecting Penny's artistic problem, getting someone out of a monastery, with the narrative dilemma of Capra's immediately preceding film, *Lost Horizon;* and Grandpa's skill at appraising stamps – a kind of "moving picture," mechanically reproduced, often encountered in strip form – is another wildly apt analogy for Capra's skill as a judger and compiler of image strips, eventually destined for national (and international) distribution. James Dugan accuses Riskin (and, implicitly, Capra) of "doing something that he very well knows is a lie" in the ismania speech, but he misses altogether the reflexive quality of the lie in question, the sense that Grandpa and Riskin and Capra alike are equally aware of the fictions they generate and seek in various ways to bring their various (and respective) audiences to a similar state of self-conscious awareness.

Despite *You Can't Take It with You*'s theatrical origins, moreover, Capra underscores the film's reflexive dimension by means of specifically visual figures that help to embody and interpret the conflict of values and styles between Kirby and Grandpa Vanderhof. In Kirby's case the visual figure is the ornately framed formal oil portrait that comes to stand (almost literally) for the unbroken line of Kirby bankers stretching back (in Tony's exasperated estimate) some 9,000 years. The earliest indication of this correlation comes at the end of the first scene in Kirby's office. After a rush of expository dialogue setting out Kirby's real-estate/munitions-monopoly scheme and the federal government's complicitous acquiescence in it, Kirby gets up (a glass of bicarbonate of soda in his hand) and walks around his desk toward Tony, who has spent the last several minutes distractedly tending his nails. Kirby sits on the edge of his desk (screen right) to ask his son's opinion of the deal in progress; the pose he strikes in so doing duplicates that of the figure in an immense framed portrait, in the background of the shot, that dominates his equally oversized office.

Crucial here is the silent precision of Capra's *mise-en-abîme* framing of the shot, a framing that both confirms and undercuts Kirby's as-if-unconscious alignment of his own actions with those of his ancestors. Kirby seems almost childishly enthused by his own schemes, hardly pausing to register the thought that munitions are tools of destruction, anymore than Tony who subsequently jokes about his father's failure (as yet) to corner the slingshot trade. It is thus altogether appropriate that Kirby's deepest crisis of conscience should come in a conference room lined with similar ancestral portraits, one of which Capra cuts to, as it were, behind Kirby's back, as another instance of quiet narrational commentary. This man is driven by a history he barely seems to grasp; Capra's placement of him visually is a way of gaining perspective on Kirby's actions and values – negative values to the degree that their motives remain unacknowledged, positive values in the sense that they derive from a tradition of family loyalty, though a tradition become self-destructive given Tony's decision to quit the firm rather than accept the presidency of Kirby's new company. Indeed, after Tony shakes his father's hand in departing Kirby Senior sits as if frozen, his hand still extended, as if he too had finally been reduced to a motionless two-dimensional figure.

The other visual figure in question is the photograph, which can be understood as a matter of publicity and also as a token of cinematic self-consciousness. The former trope belongs quite clearly to the depicted world of the film. When we first see Kirby he is hounded by reporters and news photographers whom a Kirby and Company flunkey wards off ("No pictures!"). Furthermore, during the night-court scene, after the press barges in, Kirby covers his face with his arms while his wife faints dead away, as if publicity were (like ismania) a contagion to be avoided.

The equation of photographs with the apparatus of cinema is slightly more complicated for depending (in part) on more subtle cues. I have already mentioned the table next to Grandpa's favorite chair where he keeps his pipes and lighter and a framed photograph of Alice. Directly across the room from Grandpa's table is Penny's desk and behind it is the air shaft wherein Paul Sycamore and Mr. DePinna test out their fireworks. On the wall beside the air shaft window, and behind Penny's desk, are framed photographs of Alice and Essie. I take it that (at least) *some* relationship between women and photography and "light" is being quietly suggested here. I take the suggestion to be confirmed by verbal and visual details of the scene that immediately follows, between Alice and Tony in his Kirby and Company office.

Apart from the film's opening Wall Street sequence, in which Kirby's limousine pulls up in front of Kirby and Company, most of the early passages in the film retain a certain quality of staginess or theatricality; hence perhaps the common (though wildly inaccurate) impression that Capra and Riskin remained largely loyal to Kaufman and Hart's original script. When Alice answers the phone to field Rheba's inquiry about her dinner plans, however, the style of the film shifts from long-shots and booming voices to the intimacy of gauzy close-ups and whispered love lines. Indeed, Capra exaggerates the point by requiring Jean Arthur to answer the phone with her teeth (given that Tony has firm grasp of her hands), an action that would hardly work (or work nearly so well) on stage. Moreover, once it is subsequently settled that Tony is taking Alice out to dinner, he stops in midsentence to stare at Jean Arthur and declare that her beauty is otherworldly: "Maybe you're not real. Maybe you're a phantom or something. I keep expecting you to vanish." By itself, this attribution of ephemerality evokes the fact that film characters *are* phantoms of a sort, who *do* vanish when the lights go up. That this view stands opposed to some other is confirmed when Tony continues by telling Alice to sit ("Phantoms don't vanish very often from a sitting position'') and poses her with a flower beneath one of those Kirby family portraits (''That's a very lovely picture'').

The complexity of Alice's position in the film is well figured by this twin equation, of Alice with cinema and with formal portrait painting. She is the most Kirbyesque member of the Vanderhof/Sycamore clan, the only one who regularly works outside the home, for example, the one most set on soliciting the Kirbys' approval of her engagement to Tony. The equation comes to a climax of sorts in the courtroom scene after Alice has told Tony and family (in the reporter's words) to take a flying leap; she more or less does just that, jumping onto a table and ordering Mrs. Kirby to stay away from the Sycamore neighborhood the next time she wants to go slumming. While uttering the line Alice is framed with Gilbert Stuart's famous unfinished portrait of George Washington in the background (over the judge's bench), and when she has had her say she leaps off the table and out of the frame, like a vanishing phantom. Indeed, two brief shots of Alice racing from the courtroom are all we see of her until she returns from Connecticut in the film's finale. We might say she is declaring her independence of the Kirby side of her makeup. Or that she is pledging allegiance to the medium of motion pictures, by *moving*.

I have argued that Grandpa's Americanism speech is a kind of catalytic and self-conscious fiction. I have also noted the sense in which it allows for a simplistic construal. In concluding I want to put these two observations together by asking about the *general* relevancy of the film's patriotic dimension; granted that Grandpa's speech can be taken other than literally, we must still wonder about the fact that Grandpa does not invoke some *other* fiction, some other story. I find that my answer to this question keys primarily on scenes that seem little related to explicitly political issues, the Central Park ''Big Apple'' sequence, the subsequent restaurant scene, and the jail sequence.

At the heart of the matter is a contrast between Old World and, as it were, New World cultures or art forms – hence the general aptness of the Americana theme. For example, the Central Park scene, Alice notes as she and Tony approach a park bench, substitutes for attendance at the Monte Carlo ballet; Tony humorously acknowledges the shift by treating the park bench like a row of theater seats – hers is ''the second seat over.'' Tony and Alice converse a while about the courage it takes for people to follow their inspirations, about the excuses people offer for playing it safe – though extended long takes invite one's attentions to dwell as much on the shimmer of light off the lake in the background as on Tony's vaguely Emersonian dissertation on the energy in grass. However, it turns out that Tony and Alice have attended the dance after all, not the formally choreographed Monte Carlo ballet, certainly, but the more improvised and (in that sense) more democratic dance called "The Big Apple," which can be taught for a dime and learned of an instant, a fact that Tony connects to the institution of cinema by asking "Whatever happened to Astaire and Rogers?" – as if Tony and Alice were fully their equals, if not exactly in skill, at least in their capacity for vigorous and seemingly spontaneous fun.

The restaurant and drunk-tank scenes pick up on the contrast between Old World formality and position (on the one hand) and democratic spontaneity (on the other). In the former scene special emphasis attaches to the presence of several "four star blue bloods," among them British Lord Melville, who is pictured as drawing his family tree on a napkin or tablecloth. Tony asks if Melville is playing some "new game," and responds to his lordship's genealogical answer by observing that "family tree stuff went out with the buffalo," adding that Alice does not need a family tree because a Sycamore *is* a tree, unto itself. Tony then proceeds to disrupt Alice's discussion of her plans for introducing her parents to Tony's by an impromptu mime of a good-luck "scream"; when Alice screams to stop him, Tony tells the maître d' she has seen a mouse, which throws the whole blue-blooded crowd into a tizzy. In the latter scene the contrast involves Kirby's hierarchical sense of society as a jungle with himself the lion "on top" while his cellmates are the "scum" in "the gutter" – this set against the aesthetic and social unity imaged in Grandpa's harmonica rendition of "Polly Wolly Doodle" accompanied by the dancing of Mr. Poppins and Donald and the enthusiastic clapping and singing of nearly all their drunk-tank compatriots.

To be sure, Grandpa *does* blast Kirby's devotion to profits over people, in language taken largely from Kaufman and Hart's last act; the populist ideological charge here is palpable, if not very politically specific. However, the most telling gesture in the scene is Grandpa's subsequent apology and his gift to Kirby of his "birthday" harmonica, which Grandpa slips into Kirby's coat pocket behind his back. That Kirby's back is turned is significant; he has been stung by Grandpa's passionate sermon on the relative value of friendship, which you can take with you, and money, which you cannot. Furthermore, as Grandpa completes the gift-giving, Capra cuts to a group shot of Grandpa's down-and-out cellmates whose boozy WPA smiles express their approval of Grandpa's action, an acceptance of Grandpa's acceptance of Kirby's common humanity, for which the harmonica has come to stand as token. This is true in the obvious sense (available to Kirby's cellmates) that a harmonica is portable and can be competently played by almost anyone. It is also true in the sense that, in giving the harmonica to Grandpa originally, Alice (as it were) rewrites history by declaring that any day she gives a gift is a birthday, a ''new birth'' day. By giving the harmonica to Kirby Grandpa offers him the same chance, for a new birthright apart from the oppressive legacy of the Kirby clan.

I want to call what happens in the shot of Kirby's cellmates an interpretation, and to say further that the necessity of this interpretation follows from the fact that Grandpa's words are self-contradictory; he says what he means, and then apologizes, saying he did not mean it after all. In other words, Capra sets up this drunk-tank crowd as a surrogate audience, charging them with the responsibility of reading Grandpa's actions and bestowing or withholding their consent. The moment is one of many in *You Can't Take It with You* where the distinction between Story and Plot comes near to vanishing; characters within the film world (Grandpa, his cellmates) are depicted as acting in ways deeply analogous to human actions taking place beyond or behind that world – acts of creation (Capra's) and perception (ours). Moreover, it is exactly over the question of ''consent'' that Capra's interpreters, Dugan among them, typically balk. ''Because,'' as James Harvey puts it in discussing *Meet John Doe,* ''if that on-screen audience is always a lot nicer than the one we are sitting in, it is also, we recognize, a lot dumber – laughing at jokes that aren't funny and clapping for platitudes and speakers who call them 'little punks.' We can watch that audience on the screen, possibly even admire it, but we could never *be* it, any more than we can laugh at those jokes.''[89]

This latter claim, we should note, especially as Harvey applies it to *You Can't Take It with You,* depends on the view that Capra ''didn't like irony.'' Instead, ''He liked conversions,'' of the sort undergone by A. P. Kirby.[90] The irony Harvey and Dugan and others would prefer to see, of course, would involve some acknowledgment on Capra's part that the America he depicted is not the one in which he lived. According to Harvey, Capra's habit of thinking ''about all those masses of people out there as 'little' enough – cute and scruffy and starry-eyed enough'' is a way of avoiding having ''to think of them the *other* way these films show them: as ravening and demented, a mob clamoring for the hero's destruction. Capra's condescension is like Mr. Deeds's common sense – a protection from the world outside.''[91] But Harvey's unhappiness with Capra's lack of ironic self-consciousness evinces a blindness of its own, ironically enough; Capra's films *do* show us, on Harvey's own testimony, the *other* side of the mob, and they evidently do allow us to distinguish between audiences as depicted within the films and the audiences that (in turn) *view* those audiences, though doing so, of course, also requires *some* sense of their relationship. I want to say that the relationship is one of interpretation, a conversion of thinking in which we consent to the fiction of the world we are viewing for the sake of rethinking the world we inhabit.

Most criticism of *You Can't Take It with You,* by contrast, effectively eschews interpretation by assuming that the primary action and meaning of the film are a straightforward matter of Story, of Kirby Senior's conversion from tycoon to human being, as if that conversion should be understood as expressing Capra's unqualified endorsement of everything Grandpa Vanderhof says. However, even in Kirby's case, Plot and style provide narrational perspective that exceeds any explicit understanding available either to Grandpa or Kirby; strikingly, Kirby never actually *looks* at the Kirby family portraits in the conference room, seems positively to avoid looking at them, even if, in so doing, he looks *like* them. In saying that Kirby sees old pictures in a new light, then, I am speaking metaphorically. When attention is shifted to more overt matters of Plot and style, however, to the action of film and viewer, this description becomes far more literally accurate. Capra's narrational strategy in *You Can't Take It with You* is one that invites viewers to pay careful attention not only to words but to actions, and not only to the actions of his characters but (implicitly and explicitly) to the actions of his camera.

The primary outcome of paying careful attention to *You Can't Take It with You* is the repeated ''revision'' of understanding, taking Grandpa's Americanism speech, for exemplary instance, *not* as an unqualified assertion of political principle but as food for revisionary cultural thought. That it *can* be taken simplistically is necessary if revision is to take place. Furthermore, what is being revised, in Grandpa's speech and the film generally, is not only a political history but an aesthetic one, as the inclusion in Grandpa's list of national ancestors of Mark Twain and Edison (the latter one of cinema's founding fathers, a figure of ''light'') amply demonstrates. Indeed, in listing political and aesthetic figures together Capra offers a thumbnail theory of the role of art in the political process; art can help you rewrite the past by recollecting it, by reviewing it. I find it more than a little interesting that the figures who stand for this capacity, apart from Grandpa, are largely female – Penny, the playwright; Cynthia, her monastery-bound character; and Alice, initially trapped in the Kirby and Company "monastery" yet empowered by Grandpa's fiction (as he by hers) to declare her independence. Grandpa expresses his own authority, we might say, via the feminine principle, inspired by the memory of Grandma, inspiring in turn the expressiveness of Penny and Alice.

In the larger context of the film (and of American culture) it seems incredible that Grandpa's advice to Penny was ever taken straight; the ancestral past, whether the ancestors in question are founding bankers or founding fathers, is typically something to be self-consciously cut loose from or rewritten in that place we call America – especially these days, especially by women. (The degree to which Capra's own expressiveness takes feminine form will be a guiding question of the chapters that follow.) What is peculiarly American about *You Can't Take It with You* is less its overt attack on Old World money than its implicit acknowledgment that everyone can and must participate, like Kirby's cellmates, in those acts of understanding that make revision possible. Capra and Riskin's fairly radical rewrite of the Kaufman and Hart stage play is a way of aligning this democracy of interpretation with the democratic potential of the cinema, which has far greater power than theater to prod a whole nation into rethinking its cultural heritage. In that sense, *You Can't Take It with You,* like Stuart's portrait of George Washington, like Penny Sycamore's depiction of Mr. DePinna as a discus thrower, is profoundly unfinished, and always will be. To write the film off as too finished, as too polished, as if Capra had employed all his legendary filmmaking skill merely (in Otis Ferguson's words) to "make platitude boom like truth," even if Capra is pictured as self-deludingly wanting to believe the culturally unbelievable, is to miss altogether the picture Capra offers of himself in the figure of Grandpa Vanderhof, an almost Brechtian cultural iconoclast, someone who turns the culture's language back upon itself in ways that evince and encourage interpretive self-consciousness.[92] It is just *this* picture of Frank Capra and his motion pictures that subsequent chapters will seek to elaborate.

CHAPTER II

Melodrama and the Unknown Woman

Forbidden

A guiding thought behind much contemporary film criticism involves the intricate relationship of women, psychoanalysis, and cinema. "The 'stories' psychoanalysis tells, its fictions of subjectivity, are fully compatible with those proffered by the cinema," Mary Anne Doane writes in *The Desire to Desire*. "Reading Freud is often as strangely compelling as watching a woman's film," she goes on to say, in that each models "a more generalizable cultural repression of the feminine."[1] We might consider, on these accounts, the following exemplary "scenes," or "stories."

(1) A bookish woman known for her frumpiness and her reading glasses decides in a moment of crisis to take a sea voyage. On shipboard she meets a lonely husband of an invalid wife. Without revealing her real name or circumstances she welcomes his courtly advances. Once their ship has docked in a Latin-American port, they leave the boat together and consummate their relationship in a burst of light, though it turns out that the gentleman's guilt-tempered responsibility to his wife precludes the divorce that would allow the newborn romance to take the form of lawful marriage. At a later date, in a fit of weariness and self-pity, the gentleman threatens to foreswear the relationship as it currently (if imperfectly) stands, even if their "daughter" is bound to suffer in the bargain.

(2) A romantically inclined young woman devotes herself to the career of her socially prominent beloved. Unbeknownst to him, she bears his child; when asked, she refuses to reveal the father's name to the uniformed representative of the religiously affiliated institution where she has gone to give birth. She eventually marries, and her socially powerful husband threatens her lover's career if not his life. Her lover eventually dies, in part because of a letter received, as it were, too late, a letter revealing the identity of a hitherto unknown woman.

(3) A young woman enamored of romantic "pictures" falls in love with

the man of her dreams and bears his child, a daughter. She is courted by a working-class suitor. She eventually finds it necessary to visit the mansion where her daughter's father lives, to speak with the father's wife (an elegantly upper-class woman named Helen) to whom she delivers her daughter, though not without emotional strain, after which she is eventually discovered walking down a rain-slick city street.

Readers familiar with contemporary feminist scholarship on "the woman's film," or "melodrama," will certainly recognize these three stories as summarizing, respectively, *Now, Voyager* (1942), *Letter from an Unknown Woman* (1948), and *Stella Dallas* (1937). Reordered and reworded to account for differing emphases or inflections, every phrase in each of these stories is equally descriptive of Frank Capra's *Forbidden,* the only film in the Capra canon for which Capra claimed screen credit as writer of the original story (Jo Swerling is credited for adaptation and dialogue). Especially given *Forbidden*'s 1932 release date and its relative brevity (85 minutes), its status as a compendium of melodramatic motifs and situations is astonishing and deeply indicative of Capra's abiding connection to what Peter Brooks has described as "the melodramatic imagination." For clarity's sake, and in view of the film's lamentable obscurity, we had better sort *Forbidden*'s scenario out from the others, before attempting to assess the character of Capra's intervention into the development of melodrama as a cinematic genre. Hence:

(4) Pressured by time and a thoughtless colleague, town librarian Lulu Smith (Barbara Stanwyck) withdraws her life's savings and books passage for a Caribbean vacation. On shipboard she meets lawyer Robert Grover (Adolph Menjou) who reveals his sexual longings and (eventually, in Havana) his political ambitions. The voyage over, Lulu finds a job in the reference department of a newspaper in the (unnamed) city where Grover works. Grover visits her apartment on Halloween, but an ill-timed phone call and marriage proposal from Lulu's *Daily Record* colleague Al Holland (Ralph Bellamy) prompts Grover to reveal his identity and his marital status. In desperation, Lulu orders Grover out before she can reveal the fact of her pregnancy.

The child is born, a daughter Lulu names Roberta. Backed by the newspaper, which Al Holland now edits, Grover wins election as district attorney, though Holland fairly quickly grows dissatisfied with Grover's performance in office. Just as Grover's wife plans another trip to Vienna for therapy, one of Grover's investigators discovers Lulu's whereabouts and

Grover is united with his "family." No sooner united, however, than separated: A still amorous Al Holland chances upon Lulu, Roberta, and Grover in a city park. To avoid scandal, Lulu poses as governess to Roberta, whom Grover in turn describes as his adopted daughter. After delivering Roberta to the Grover mansion, Lulu attempts to break off her relationship with Grover, though on second thought she agrees to continue as his back-street lover, at which point she returns to the newspaper and is given a job as Mary Sunshine, the advice-to-the-lovelorn columnist.

Roughly eighteen years pass. Grover is running for governor; Holland is still bent on bringing him down. After receiving the nomination, Grover visits Lulu's apartment and confides his decision to go public with their relationship. Lulu advises against it, but appears to consent when he proves determined. The next day she accepts Holland's long-standing proposal, which prevents Grover's resignation from the governor's race. On the night of the election Holland reveals to Lulu over dinner that he knows the identity of the mother of Grover's daughter. Lulu and Holland quarrel over his plans to publish the story; she shoots him to death. Grover pardons Lulu after she serves a year of her murder sentence, and on his deathbed gives her a note acknowledging their relationship and bequeathing her half his estate. After Grover dies, Lulu walks distractedly through city streets, eventually discarding Grover's letter.

In applying to these four scenarios Doane's description of the woman's film – as evoking the cultural construction and repression of the feminine – we again encounter the paradox of genre in which *ex*pression and *re*pression go hand in hand. Doane and other feminist critics are especially interested in such stories for the contrast they apparently offer to the classical Hollywood narrative, which is taken to be male typical in its "address," featuring male protagonists whose goal-directed behavior anchors narrative cause and effect and whose gaze is typically "quoted" (via point-of-view shots) so as to give (male) viewers safe visual access to the erotic image of woman.

At a certain level, then, the woman's film seems to evoke an analogous yet feminine form of spectatorship, or "subject position"; women are central protagonists; theirs is the point of view represented. Furthermore, enactment of that story and vantage point requires the representation of female power, agency, and desire; requires, on film, the active cooperation of such world-historical agents as Bette Davis and Barbara Stanwyck. Yet the scenarios typically enacted limit the depiction of female agency to the domestic or erotic sphere, and even here female accomplishment or power is denied when the woman either fails to marry or loses her child (or both). Thus is repression expressed.

In addition, as Doane argues at considerable length, the ideological disturbance that follows from granting the power of the narratively active "gaze" to the woman is typically contained by depicting that gaze as "sick" or "paranoid" and then entrusting the eye-sick patient to the (implicitly repressive) care of male physicians or psychiatrists (e.g., Dr. Jaquith in *Now, Voyager*). The equation of woman and film here even allows an extension of the doctor–patient relationship to account for the excessive style of melodrama in general. The critic is the interpretive therapist; the film itself is a hysterical patient. As Geoffrey Nowell-Smith observes in "Minnelli and Melodrama,"

> Music and *mise en scène* do not just heighten the emotionality of an element of the action: to some extent they substitute for it. The mechanism here is strikingly similar to that of the psychopathology of hysteria. . . . The "return of the repressed" takes place, not in conscious discourse, but displaced onto the body of the patient. In the melodrama, where there is always material which cannot be expressed in discourse or in the actions of the characters furthering the designs of the plot, a conversion can take place into the body of the text.[2]

The confluence here of melodramatic and psychoanalytic categories suggests the inevitability that "meaning will out," that the very business of melodrama (and psychoanalysis) is, as Peter Brooks describes it, the "refusal of censorship and repression": "The melodramatic utterance breaks through everything that constitutes the 'reality principle,' all its censorships, accommodations, tonings-down. Desire cries aloud its language in identification with full states of being."[3] This utterance, moreover, "is motivated by a totally coherent ambition to stage a drama of articulation, a drama that has as its true stakes the recognition and triumph of the sign of virtue." Furthermore, the dramatists in question are equally those on stage, "within the conflictual system of the play," and the dramatist offstage, "within the medium of communication encompassing play and spectator, since the play strives toward making evident the very problematic that it takes as its subject."[4]

This intersection of melodrama and psychoanalysis is explicitly marked in *Forbidden* when Lulu Smith quite self-consciously likens herself to Cinderella. The fairy tale itself is a prototypical parable of female relationships and sexuality under patriarchy. And the psychoanalytic subtext here is made explicit when Lulu (now as "Cindy") describes herself as suffering a "complex," a fear that the clock will strike midnight. In view of the fact that (as we will soon learn) Grover's invalid wife is being treated, in the first decade of the twentieth century, by a Viennese physician and that her illness is such that she is incapable of childbearing and that she openly urges Grover to "have a good time," no questions asked, in her absence, it is hard to avoid the thought that Capra is literally suggesting a (Freudian) reading strategy here. Though what becomes of melodrama on film (as opposed to on stage) should not be presumed in advance, I assume that Capra's characters and Capra himself are equally (if also problematically, even tragically) devoted to a victory of expression over repression; such victories as they manage all require the hyperbolic rhetoric and expressive gestures typical of melodrama. We can begin closer analysis than plot outline allows by attending to how each of *Forbidden*'s three principle characters helps to enact the drama of signification and desire described by Peter Brooks.

Our first glimpse of Robert Grover, for example, follows quick upon his alcohol-induced misreading of the door of Lulu's cruise-ship cabin; what he assumed was cabin 99 turned out to be cabin 66. Rising from Lulu's bed as if still intoxicated, he wittily offers "33 apologies" – representing one possible construal of the difference between the action he attempted and that which he accomplished – before moving to the doorway and departing. No sooner does an inebriated Grover make his exit, however, than Grover reenters, now totally sober, to beg forgiveness and to chat about his being on holiday after a long stretch of nose-to-the-grindstone labor.

A drama is enacted here, a drama literally of recognition and misrecognition. Grover misrecognizes the room number of the cabin; for the purpose (we imagine) of confirming the innocent basis for his error he initially plays the drunk role in his actions and line deliveries, thus inducing a certain form of misrecognition in Lulu, though the drunk role he enacts (we have every reason to believe) is (was) in fact the truth of his circumstances. Moreover, the pattern of his actions here – his *acting* himself while not fully *being* himself, being, as it were, *beside* himself – is typical of the "role" he plays in the overall trajectory of the film. Though he *has* a political career – moving from district attorney to mayor to Congress to governor – that career is only represented in its private consequences; indeed, his rise to power is only made evident in the scrapbook ("Roberta

Her Book'') that is Lulu's only token of her maternity after she gives up her daughter to Grover and his wife. It is thus profoundly ironic that his chief qualification for his last public office – as detailed by the orator who introduces Grover to the only political rally we actually see – is his sterling record as ''husband and father,'' though neither of those words applies exactly as the speaker intends it.

We might well presume that, as a lawyer and legislator, Grover has an active relationship to political or social language – a relationship to which we are pointedly denied narrational access by a series of silences or hesitations. Grover fails to inform Lulu of his full name and marital status until considerably after their return from Havana, for example. When the phone rings in Lulu's apartment, he urges her not to answer it. When Al Holland comes to Grover's district attorney's office to ask why Grover can no longer ''behave'' as apparently Holland and the *Daily Record* expect him to, Grover complains about Holland's last editorial (which had claimed that Grover bought his last election with his wife's money) and promises to banish all of Holland's reporters from the building; when an investigator informs Grover only moments later of Lulu's whereabouts, he orders that no report be written. Indeed, after Holland encounters Lulu, Grover, and Roberta in the park, the subsequent decision to have Grover and his wife ''adopt'' Roberta is taken to solicit Holland's silence on the matter.

Grover's silence is perhaps best evidenced in his most public moments. What we know of Grover's nomination convention speech is acquired in silence (in a point-of-view shot of a corner of the speech's first page, a corner annotated in Lulu's hand); and when Grover gets up to deliver the speech Capra brings the scene to a quick close by fading out before Grover can get started. The closest we ever get to hearing Grover's public voice comes in the murder scene; while Lulu burns the evidence of her relationship with Grover his voice comes over the radio, though again the import is of hesitancy or reticence: ''I'm too excited to say very much but I want to thank all the good people who made my election possible.'' Notwithstanding, we must also allow that, at least in private, Grover can be profoundly, heartbreakingly, eloquent.

The scene I have in mind is that leading up to, falling away from, Lulu's Cinderella parable. On the way to Lulu's apartment Grover buys two *commedia dell'arte*–style Halloween masks and a bunch of long-stemmed flowers. He rings the doorbell; Lulu puts on a Latin-style phonograph record (in homage to their time together in Havana), and answers the door by opening a tiny porthole door at eye level. Through the porthole Grover inserts the wildly extended nose of his mask, and declares himself in quick succession a wolf in sheep's clothing and a census taker (Lulu replies that she lost her "senses" long ago). Once through the door Grover continues the census bit – asking for the names and ages of parents and children (all those social connections from which Lulu has cut herself loose) – while Lulu grabs the other mask Grover carries and begins to play along in what Grover announces as a "strange interlude," lines from an overtly and parodistically romantic play, spoken with masks down (Grover declares Lulu "the most beautiful flower in this lovely garden"; Lulu declares Grover her prince, her hero) alternating with more ordinary mock-marital discourse ("What have you got to eat?"), spoken with masks up ("Kippers, you pig"). (See Fig. 10.)

The playacting continues – masks alternately up and down – as Lulu and Grover go out to the kitchen and then return to the front parlor where Lulu promises to serve dinner (and to tell Grover her secret, of her pregnancy) as soon as Bob tells her whether he followed her instructions and (consequently) won his most recent court case. Grover asks Lulu if she is happy; she likens herself to Cinderella. Their conversation is interrupted by Holland's phone call and proposal. What had been playful and deeply erotic acting and mime becomes ominous silence; Grover lowers his mask over his face and tells Lulu, as her lawyer, that he "can't advise" her about marriage.

It is one of the most delightful and affecting scenes in all of Capra, recalling the first auto-camp scene in *It Happened One Night* when Peter and Ellie pretend to be married in order to throw her father's detectives off track (and where Ellie explicitly likens *herself* to Cinderella), or, in a different way, the scene in *It's a Wonderful Life* when George visits Mary at the Hatch house after his brother's impromptu wedding reception; in all three instances various sorts and tenors of "acting" serve finally (if for some only briefly) to open characters and circumstances to deeper levels of vulnerability and honesty than normal social discourse makes possible. There is an honesty in Grover's pretending to a mock rapacious sexuality, and his alignment of it with social bureaucracy, and yet a delicacy in the pretense that qualifies that picture without disallowing Lulu the chance to accept his self-characterization; like Pinocchio, he is a long-nosed liar. In admitting it, he might be, after all, a prince among men.

Within the context of Capra generally, Grover's public silence is itself

Figure 10. Impromptu gallantries in *Forbidden* and *It's a Wonderful Life*. (*Forbidden* copyright © 1932, renewed 1959 Columbia Pictures Industries, Inc. All rights reserved. Courtesy of Columbia Pictures.)

a sign of textual stress, a matter of excess; he is *too* silent. It is clear, for example, that Grover's silence is a primary factor in his apparently premature death. Yet I will eventually want to argue that Grover is also a token of expressiveness, even if the authorship of the story he acts out is a matter of some dispute. Indeed, that Grover "acts" out a story indicates that the conflict between his public persona and his private person is not absolute. It is clear that Grover literally rehearses his political speeches with Lulu, for instance; Grover is always acting, we might say. The difference between his public and private enactments seems to be that Grover's exchanges with Lulu take place on several levels, in several registers, mixing music, mime, fairy tale, and melodrama, a multiplicity splendidly visualized in the multiple "faces" on view during the Halloween sequence. This too is a form of excess, of supplementarity, though one that both Grover and Lulu apparently agree cannot be enacted in public, except perhaps in Havana.

A similarly convoluted (if finally less complex) relationship to language marks the Al Holland/Ralph Bellamy character in *Forbidden.* In Holland's case it is almost literally a matter of speaking two different languages – the first a poetic, explicitly pastoral language of ardor and affection, the second a ruthless dialect of journalistic hucksterism and sensationalism. One of the reasons that Holland is finally a less interesting character than Grover – to us, to Lulu – is his inability to grasp the creative possibilities implicit in this contrast of dialects.

Holland has a total of eight conversations (in seven brief scenes) with Lulu, most of them ostensibly focused on their personal relationship. Their second conversation – the stroke-of-midnight phone call Grover urges Lulu not to answer – is the occasion for his first explicit proposal of marriage. Their third conversation, after Holland discovers Lulu and Roberta in the park, finds Holland describing himself explicitly as an "ardent swain," though he quickly shifts gears and roles to that of muckraking journalist when Grover appears and claims Roberta (at Lulu's silent prompting) as his adopted daughter. Moreover, even when Lulu returns to the paper to ask Holland for a job – which he provides in the form of the Mary Sunshine column – the personal element of the relationship is never far in the background.

Indeed, in the second "movement" of the Mary Sunshine scene, Holland comes over to Lulu's desk to see what dirt she can deliver on Grover. Holland idealistically assures her that there "aren't any strings attached" to their personal relationship, though he notes she now works ''for the paper'' and expresses his (subsequent) displeasure when she refuses to provide any details about Roberta's birth, telling Lulu she will ''never make a newspaper woman.'' She asks if that means she is fired. He replies, jokingly, enigmatically, that she will (yet)''make a newspaper man''; in light of his many predictions that Lulu will wind up married to him,''make'' takes on a decidedly sexual import here, a prophetically unfriendly one given the mock ''punch'' that immediately precedes the line and that anticipates the right cross with which Holland eventually decks Lulu in the murder scene.

Holland's ''anything for a story'' hucksterism is more openly evident in those few moments when he is apart from Lulu – in the scene between himself and Grover in the latter's district attorney's office, for example. A more overtly telling instance of this stands as prologue to the Mary Sunshine sequence. Holland is barking orders *Front Page* fashion into various upright telephones between bites of coffee-dunked doughnut. Two stories are in the works. The first is about the death of some apparently wealthy antagonist who died at an hour inconvenient to a morning newspaper. Holland orders the reporter to ''work in a love nest angle,'' complete with a diagram of the apartment with a ''great big cross to mark the spot,'' a ''double cross'' Holland quickly adds in view of the fact that the deceased had never advertised in the paper. Almost as an afterthought Holland asks about a diary; ''that's alright, we'll write one here'' he responds in Charles Foster Kane fashion to the apparently negative answer his question elicits. Furthermore, when he hears (on another line) that a park commissioner has refused to talk with his reporter, he orders that a story be run on the commissioner every day, with the man's name misspelled every time it comes up.

The question of names, of how spelled, say, or how written, will return to haunt the relation of Holland and Lulu. However, as token of the de(con)structive conflict between Holland's two ''vocabularies'' we might cite the scene (just before the nomination convention) in which Holland proposes marriage to Lulu yet again. After a brief discussion of Holland's more-or-less dissolute love life, he idealistically assures Lulu he would ''do anything in the world'' for her. She promptly asks for two days off (to attend the convention), which Holland promptly (if half-jokingly) refuses. The subject switches to marriage; Lulu declares she is ''not the marrying sort'' and observes that Holland is already ''married'' to the paper; ''that comes first, always has, always will.'' The point is promptly exemplified when word arrives that bootleggers are shooting it out on the South Side: Holland immediately jumps up and barges to the nearest phone, where he begins barking orders, all hints of self-mockery gone from his voice, Lulu so deeply forgotten that the contradiction of his just-spoken words and his just-taken actions goes completely unnoticed. In this light it seems clear that Holland's pastoral idiolect is itself excessive, dissociated from the life he really leads, however ironically it echoes the erotic dimension of the Lulu–Grover relationship.

Assessing Lulu Smith's relationship to the language of desire is a matter of abiding complexity. According to Charles Maland, for example,''instead of empathizing with Lulu when she tells [Grover, after his nomination,] 'Your honors have been my honors, your success, my success,' . . . one feels more anger and pity toward a woman who seems never to have confronted her own human needs and desires.''[5] On Raymond Carney's understanding, by contrast, Capra ''seems to suggest, especially in the case of Lulu, in the Jamesian sense, that to have gotten nothing at all may actually be to have gained everything.'' Citing Grover's remarks (in Havana) about the ''worm'' of ambition, Carney suggests that *Forbidden* is better understood less as a parable of self-sacrifice than as a fable of desires explored and partly realized: ''*Forbidden,* in effect, takes as its subject the worm, the hunger, the desires that both [Grover] and Lulu feel within themselves. That defines a reality for them greater than any aggregation of nominally realistic facts or events.''[6]

The interpretive and moral question at issue here involves the extent to which the imaginative reality created by Grover and Lulu can stand as sufficient compensation for the various griefs they suffer. That issue cannot be addressed, however, without detailed consideration of the particular grievances in question. To paraphrase Freud, what does Lulu want? Put another way, to what extent are Lulu's desires genuinely ''hers''?

The answer to the latter question must be tentative, as it would be for any character, fictional or otherwise. (A desire is mine if I act upon it, accept responsibility for it, etc.) However, a case can certainly be made in Lulu's instance that her desire exists within obvious limits. The most obvious of these limits is that which decrees political success to be a male prerogative. Indeed, in the majority of the years covered by the film (some twenty-two years during the first three decades of the twentieth century) women did not enjoy the franchise. (Hence, perhaps, the odd force behind

Holland's query, in his last scene, as to whether Lulu has cast her vote for governor, a matter of signifying her desire, of balloting her secret.) Then again, Lulu's "worm," as she tells Grover in Havana, is Grover: His are the political ambitions. At least initially, then, politics are *not* Lulu's primary concern, though they become her concern as her relationship with Grover develops.

The clearest picture we get of Lulu's "ambition" is provided, quite literally, by her actions, only secondarily by her words. In the film's first sequence Lulu is late for work, for the first time in eight years, a lateness attributed by a library patron to spring fever. We are told by a second patron that Lulu has not missed a wedding in years. Once Lulu enters the library (after reading a valentine missive chalked on the library steps) her first gesture is to put a new rose in a vase on her desk and to stare at a framed print (seen in a zooming point-of-view shot) of a gallant soldier embracing a woman. When her library colleague asks her the time and checks her pulse, however, Lulu stands up self-assertively and declares that, if she owned the library, she would get an axe and smash it into a million pieces and then set fire to the whole town and play a ukulele while it burned. She sits down and checks the balance in her savings passbook, at which point Capra dissolves to a scene in the bank, during which Lulu espies (in another zooming point-of-view shot) another picture, a travel brochure featuring a Havana-bound cruise ship (Havana: The Land of Romance), at which point a match-cut dissolve transports us to what seems the very same cruise ship and thence (via a dissolve montage of music and dancing) to the ship's dining room where the question of sexual desire is openly posed, by the maître d' and headwaiter ("Two days out and still 'one' ") and by a resplendent Lulu herself.

Several elements of this series of actions stand out. One is the obvious and energetic *force* of her desire, imaged in the repetition of the zoom point-of-view figure and the dissolve; her desire is a desire *in motion,* a desire that threatens to obliterate limits of time and space. Another is the precise source and character of Lulu's object of desire. In one respect her desire is a matter of external views internalized, made real by the very force of absence: Lulu (as even the twin syllables of her first name would seem to indicate) longs to couple, to meet her match. That much we can readily infer from her glance at the print on the library wall. Then again, the entire Havana sequence also has the quality of interior desire expressionistically projected to encompass the entire known world. Lulu glances quickly at the menu and orders "everything," for example, before turning her attention to the couples around her. Her desire, we might say, is *for* desire, to be desired.

What she never expresses a desire for – until very late in the movie, when she finally accepts Holland's proposal – is legal matrimony. Indeed, during the Havana sequence she tells Grover they should become beachcombers for the rest of the century, living, she says, on worms, as if desire were its own sustenance. That people around and about Lulu – the library patron, Al Holland, even Grover himself in those self-pitying moments when he longs "to do the right thing" – should understand Lulu's desires as reducible to marriage is no reason for assuming that she shares their viewpoint, or for sharing it with them. Marriage is thus *not* something Lulu is called upon to give up, to sacrifice, *not* something she particularly or expressly *wants*. Arguably her deepest sacrifice is exactly a matter of accepting a proposal, not of foreswearing the very prospect.

Similar care needs to be taken in assessing the force of Lulu's abandonment of Roberta. After Grover reveals the fact of his marriage – and what seems to be his genuinely and exclusively personal reason at this point for not leaving his wife (involving his responsibility for her injuries) – Lulu at first expresses the desperate (yet characteristically *visual*) hope that, if she never sees Helen, she and Grover might go on as if Helen had never existed. In response, Grover remorsefully and conventionally asserts that he cannot offer Lulu marriage, nor can he offer her anything less, the implication being that he is calling their relationship off in a fit of noble feeling. At this point Lulu answers cliché with cliché ("You've had your fun and now you're fed up") and with all the profound sarcasm and desperation at Stanwyck's disposal, though her character clearly knows the charge is false in its specifics. Grover stands appropriately rebuked and leaves.

All of which is necessary background to assessing the logic behind Lulu's decision to give up Roberta. That Lulu understands the child as a substitute for Robert is indicated well enough by the name Lulu gives her, and by the curious fact that she does not want to see Roberta after the delivery, as if she were still angry with Grover. When we finally do see mother and child together, it is a bathing scene, and as Lulu dries Roberta off she promises to sing a song of moon and stars – at which point one recalls (Lulu recalls?) the equestrian ride along the moon-drenched beach that concluded the Havana sequence. When Grover shows up at her door,

Lulu reacts as if she had seen a (Halloween) ghost, and she retreats to her bedroom as Grover (in voice-over) begs her to let him in. As soon as Grover's voice fades, however, Lulu rushes to the hallway and calls down the stairwell after him. They are reunited. The child on the landing above them calls out angelically. Lulu looks at Grover and says, as if time had hardly passed at all: ''I forgot. Your daughter's name is Roberta.''

After this reunion events follow quickly that lead to the decision to turn Roberta over to Grover and his wife. Some readings of the film assume that the primary motive for the arrangement is to protect Grover's political career at Lulu's expense – which in some sense, I think, is true enough. However, that career has value in the film only and exclusively as it embodies the joint expression of Robert and Lulu's shared ambition. Lulu is thus in the position of needing to choose between, as it were, two children, two extensions of herself, Robert and Roberta. Giving Roberta to Robert is a way of keeping them both. Though agonizing, it is hardly a simple either/or choice, a thought that goes some distance in the direction of accounting for the odd tranquility with which, after her initial burst of anger at Grover and her circumstances on the night she leaves Roberta, Lulu returns to her life at the newspaper.

Indeed, the fact that Lulu is consistently represented as a working woman is a fact of the film too little noticed.[7] She begins the film as a librarian. Her first newspaper job involves the reference department, the clipping file, of *The Daily Record.* After Roberta's birth she works (so report has it) in some unspecified capacity at Brock's. After giving up Roberta she returns to the paper and inquires about the reference department again, but Holland assigns her to the Mary Sunshine column, replacing the kindly gentleman who had previously advised the lovelorn under that byline.

Lulu Smith thus joins a long line of Capra reporters, Peter Warne in *It Happened One Night,* for instance, or Babe Bennett in *Mr. Deeds Goes to Town* for another. Two of her journalistic Capra peers are especially important for assessing the value we might assign to Lulu's job status. The first is nearly her namesake, Stew Smith, the ''Cinderella Man'' reporter who marries into the upper crust in *Platinum Blonde* and who recovers his class senses by becoming a playwright, though the play he writes is uncannily like the life he leads. The other reporter, also played by Barbara Stanwyck, who signs a crucial document ''John Doe'' just as Lulu Smith signs one ''Jane Doe,'' who finds her difficult way in the world by helping to create a semifictional public figure whose crucial moment of self-revelation comes as he stands before the assembled multitude at a political convention, is *Meet John Doe*'s Ann Mitchell.

Perhaps the deepest implication of this intertextual connection is the reminder it offers of the generally "unformed" quality of Capra's major characters, a quality most noticeable in the habit they have of trying to create (or recreate) each other, and of recreating themselves in the process – a habit that allows action within the film world to stand as an allegory of the filmmaking process itself; characters direct and create each other and themselves as Capra directs and creates them. That it takes at least two to (re)make one is indicated clearly enough in *Platinum Blonde:* Stew Smith finally needs Gallagher's sexual and journalistic encouragement to become the playwright of his own life. In *Meet John Doe* this theatrical circumstance generates a virtual flood tide of authorships as Ann and then Norton and then Long John himself all strive to flesh out the "Be a Better Neighbor" philosophy Ann derives from her father's diary in ways that allow the realization of their deepest selves even as those selves are in the process of definition.

Forbidden provides a remarkably clear example of this enactment of the unformed or in-forming self. The most obvious fact to account for here is the odd "emptiness" of the political dimension of the movie. We have no idea as to the substance of Grover's political program apart from his antipathy to Al Holland. Among the critics who have written on the film there seems to be a vague consensus – derived perhaps from the track record of later Capra politicians, and from Grover's willingness to silence Holland by adopting Roberta – that Grover puts his political career before all personal or human concerns.[8] Indeed, this seems to be the genesis of Al Holland's enmity as well in his accusation that Grover financed his election to district attorney with his wife's money, as if he had married her for that very purpose. Grover denies the charge – a denial confirmed in every aspect of his remarkably open relationship to his wife – and it seems clear enough, given Holland's general lack of concern for journalistic veracity, that what galls him about Grover is some change of attitude, specifically some lack of gratitude or deference to Holland and *The Daily Record.* It is as if Holland wants to see himself reflected in Grover and becomes embittered when Grover declines the mirror role, a bitterness only exacerbated when it turns out that Grover is (was) Lulu's "boss." It is a matter of no little irony that Holland, by film's end, understands himself as a rival with Grover for Lulu when, in more literal fact, he is Lulu's rival for Grover. We might describe this as a contest of authorships. Holland's claim to authorship is obviously asserted when he confronts Grover in the latter's office. Lulu's claim to authorship is less explicit but no less significant, especially in light of her roughly twenty-year career as a journalist.

Certain local features line up here: Lulu's query in the first apartment scene as to whether Grover followed her advice in court, her silent nod to Grover in the park scene directing him to play the role of employer and adoptive father, her bitter remark on the night she leaves Roberta to the effect that Grover can just as well read his speeches to his wife, her handwritten comments on the speech Grover is set to deliver to the convention. However, the key event on these accounts comes the night of Grover's nomination when he informs Lulu that he is heartsick from all the years of deception and wants to go public with their relationship. Lulu at first objects, but Grover's determination and sincerity leave her only a single option if, as she had told Grover earlier, his success is her success. Like many a good director, she misleads her principle player, by agreeing to return with him to Havana – but her very next move is to accept Holland's marriage proposal, thus preventing Grover's withdrawal from the governor's race. The decision here is altogether Lulu's, not something asked of her by Grover.

Whether self-realization should *require* such a sacrifice is a good feminist question that the film does not so much answer as ponder. However, it is worth remarking that the question as Capra poses it has a decidedly subversive aspect, subversive in the sense that it calls into significant doubt strict gender-role assumptions, such as would take for granted, say, that Lulu really wants marriage (instead of authorship), really wants motherhood (instead of a career). Furthermore, when even these "substitute" desires are threatened – by Grover, by Holland – Lulu returns "the repressed" with a vengeance in that she is forced, if her visionary dream of authorship is to be realized at all, to enact a negative scenario of masculine self-assertiveness sadly typical of the culture she inhabits.

Crucial here is the framed print of the woman and the soldier at which Lulu gazes in the library before her coworker asks her what time it is ("Springtime," she responds). Among critics who mention the print it seems commonly assumed that Lulu imagines herself in the female position. However, the postures in the print – the female figure below the other, pressed down, as it were, by the man on top – are repeatedly enacted in the film, almost always with Lulu in the superior (top) position. As the dying Grover reminds Lulu, he was lying down when they first met, and during each of the two apartment sequences Lulu always takes the upper position whenever they sit together on a couch or in a chair. Moreover, the soldier is depicted as a Hussar, that is, as a cavalry soldier; it matters more than a little that Lulu is the one who suggests and thereafter leads the equestrian interlude on the moonlit beach. This identification of Lulu as a soldier engaged in a battle of authorships is confirmed by one of the film's most striking sequences, the murder of Al Holland.

Election night. Lulu and Al dine in their apartment, though in formal dress, which seems especially out of place (Lulu even asks Al why he is not down at the newspaper office) except as a narrational evocation of the formal dining we see during the shipboard and Havana sequences. In response to her question, Al tells Lulu he has almost solved the mystery of Grover's daughter; he asks her if she really loves him; Lulu replies that she married him and asks about Holland's new information. Lulu's response is transparent; an embittered Holland produces various documents – the hospital admissions card signed "Jane Doe," Lulu's last signed pay receipt from the paper, a photograph of Lulu and Grover pilfered from her trunk, a letter from Grover to Lulu that Holland had intercepted – that will enable him to kick Grover out of the governor's chair.

Lulu begs Holland not to publish the story; when he refuses she grabs for the letter. They struggle. Holland cracks her across the jaw. Lulu smashes a chair against the wall on the way down. Cut to a close-up of Lulu, standard key-and-fill lighting now replaced by extreme sidelight from screen left, the image now "thickened" by gauze or filters. Her lip bleeding (shades of George Bailey!), she retreats to the bedroom; just as Holland reaches the front door to leave, she appears in the bedroom doorway with a gun and tells Holland not to move. He comes toward her, swings the bedroom door shut in her face. Cut to a tighter shot of the door from Holland's side as bullets splinter wood; and then to a full-shot of Holland as he staggers around the room pulling down drapery and curtain rods before crashing to the floor. Cut, then, to a zooming close-up of Lulu (as if, in light of earlier zoom shots, Lulu were now seeing herself) after which she fires the remaining slugs into Holland's body, with more than a little righteous melodramatic gusto. A maid phones the police. Cut to a medium-shot of the fireplace as Lulu (from off-frame) consigns Holland's "proof" to the flames. Holland had rebuffed Lulu's entreaties by saying he would "commit murder for a story like that." She does; it is hers.

The emphatic narrational force of these various theatrical and cinematic gestures derives in large (if retrospective) measure from Lulu's initial interpretation of the library print. After gazing at the embracing soldier and his woman, after suffering the taunt of her colleague, Lulu jumps up and expresses the desire to smash the library to bits and to burn the whole town down with it to the accompaniment of her ukulele. This is pretty much what she does in murdering Al Holland; while the radio plays on, wood is smashed and splintered, a room is torn to pieces, worlds are consumed by fire, and three lives are effectively lost in the process.

Holland dies outright. Grover, by now portrayed as a hysteric whose mental distress is written large across his tortured body (the radio announcer has Grover rising from his sickbed to address well-wishers upon his gubernatorial election victory), will soon go into the final decline leading to his death a year or so later, and Lulu resigns herself to a lifetime without Grover (a decision already taken, however, in marrying Holland). Especially given Holland's behavior as a kind of self-appointed social superego, noted comically in his repeated complaint about a light left burning in the newsroom, it is not hard to think of Lulu's usurpation of male-typical prerogatives and weaponry as patriarchy's well-deserved comeuppance, as expressing and returning the force of repression that had consigned her desire and creativity to the cultural margins – or at least to the "woman's pages."[9] This Mary Sunshine burns like fire. (So too does Capra's image of her.)

It is easy, in light of *Forbidden*'s final scenes, to take it as one of Capra's most pessimistic exercises in cultural mythmaking or interpretation, especially when the dying Grover commends Lulu for being a "good loser," especially when Lulu disappears at last into the crosswalk crowds of the film's closing street scene. Nevertheless, such a reading must overlook the fact that Lulu and Capra both succeed after a fashion, succeed together, as it were. What each succeeds *at* is the creation of a series of images that opens up the question of theatrical and sexual collaboration.

Key here are two primarily visual motifs by means of which Capra can suggest the more positive exchange of traits and roles that characterizes the relationship of Grover and Lulu. One of these is the stairway, taken as an emblem of transit, as a stage for the movements of desire. This connection of stair steps and desire is first suggested in the library scene; Lulu pauses on her way into the library to read a valentine message chalked onto the first of the steps leading up to the library entrance. The equation is repeated and sustained when Lulu makes her two grand entrances into the ship's dining room, and later when Lulu and Grover are reunited on the interior stairway of her second apartment building. That desires are not all painlessly realized is indicated by Capra's framing of Lulu at the foot of the large stairway in Grover's mansion while Helen thanks Grover for finding Roberta, and where Helen subsequently questions Lulu about her "references" as a governess – at which point Lulu bolts from the premises in a fit of maternal desperation.

A second "narrational" figure – one that Capra had developed with considerable sophistication as early as *That Certain Thing* and that plays an especially resonant role in *The Bitter Tea of General Yen* – is the doorway. Doors, like stairways, are entrances and exits simultaneously. In addition to being passageways, doors also are a matter of frames and of framings. In *Forbidden,* Capra evokes these implications to emphasize the fluidity of human identity, as if the doorways were proscenium stages for theatrical enactments, places where characters can "play" themselves, or play another; as if the door frames also served as mirror frames, inscribing a space, a glass, within which characters can see themselves reflected as (in) each other.

This is almost literally the case in the first doorway scene, involving Grover's reverse-image misreading of Lulu's cabin door (66) for his own (99). It is also an apt description of the opening movement of the Halloween sequence discussed earlier where Grover and Lulu alternate masks and lines. Keeping in mind that Grover brought flowers for Lulu on the latter occasion (eventually revealed in the kitchen when Grover "magically" opens the dumbwaiter door), we can see the last Grover–Lulu apartment scene as mirroring the first, though now it is Lulu who provides the explicitly theatrical surprise – the red carpet, the "Grover for Governor" pennant/sash – and Lulu who provides the flowers that she strews along Grover's path, literally leading him into the flat.

The deepest implication of this mirror figure involves the androgynous interchange of roles and responsibilities that it suggests. Lulu is always a slight and feminine Barbara Stanwyck; Grover is always the mustachioed and masculine Adolph Menjou. Nevertheless, within the context of their relationship, she is the director, the leader, he the one who takes direction, even if the scenario enacted began with him; by film's conclusion it is her story, the product of her authorship, while he is the hysteric who begs his beloved to run away from it all. To be sure, Lulu's "masculinity" has its murderous aspect. Grover's projecting of himself (his nose) through a door is done in (serious) jest; Lulu's similar projections, the bullets that pierce the bedroom door in the Holland apartment, are in deadly earnest. However, the interchange of roles and positions, which is the distinguishing characteristic of the relationship of Lulu and Grover at its best, is clearly the film's image of the good, against which we read the mental and social rigidity that characterizes Holland's behavior both personally and socially.

This exchange of dreams and vantage points between Grover and Lulu can equally be taken to figure the relationship of analogy or mutuality that binds Lulu as "auteur" to Capra. We have characterized action within the film world as a matter of enacting desire, finding a way to speak it or represent it, which can mean finding the right actor, or the right director, or the right combination. In the world of *Forbidden* such matches are hard to come by, hence the melodramatic extremity of its situations and scenarios. That such matches are potentially comic (in the deepest sense, as enlivening, as re-creating) is evidenced during the Havana/vacation sequence and the first apartment scene. We might cite here as token the delightful exchange between Grover and Lulu in the Havana nightclub when he describes her as the dream girl (were he an architect, not a lawyer) he would design; as he talks, Lulu mimes his every gesture, right down to the twirling of "her" mustachios just as he twirls his.

The match of camera and character, of Capra and Lulu, is implicit, I have suggested, in the overall trajectory of the film. It is rather emphatically underscored on three particular occasions, all of them involving an almost literal matching of frames. The first such match of Lulu's "frame" and Capra's comes in the first dining sequence, aboard the Havana-bound cruise ship.

Even before the explicit frame match Capra suggests a kinship of camera and character in the sequence of cinematic events that literally introduce Lulu to the dining salon. After the zooming point-of-view shot of the travel brochure, we dissolve – via graphic match on the brochure ship image – to a ship on the high seas and thence to a montage sequence (also involving superimposed images) of dining and dancing that begins on a long-shot, taken from behind the band, of the sweeping salon stairway in the background. Dissolve to a slightly closer shot of the band, from a different angle, the stairs now out of the picture, over which is superimposed (in successive dissolves) close-ups of singers and string players, after which we dissolve (again) to a position looking down on the dance floor from the stairway, at which point the camera pans emphatically right to frame Lulu in her new-bought finery. The narrational emphasis here needs emphasizing. The camera is equally "with" Lulu, on the stairs, and "ahead" of her, anticipating her, as if representing her anticipated view of herself, though from a position that is obviously *not* exactly hers.

Once Lulu is seated at her table we get an almost textbook study of the point-of-view editing figure: shots of Lulu glancing off-frame followed by shots (presumably) depicting the objects of her gaze, hence her gaze itself. That these "views" are not exactly objective is emphasized at the end of the sequence, when a man who is the object of Lulu's explicitly erotic gaze gestures as if in response, as if inviting himself to her table (Fig. 11). Stanwyck's Lulu – in one of the most delicate and shattering passages of acting in all of Capra – responds in turn with profoundly ambiguous gestures of eyes and mouth and shoulders, as if saying and not saying yes, finally raising her glass as if in greeting and (yet also) in defense. Capra then cuts to a full-shot, Lulu at her table screen left, as the man enters from screen right and proceeds past Lulu to a table behind her – a sight gag lifted whole cloth, both in its framings and its poignancy, from Chaplin's *The Gold Rush;* yet also a sight gag, of mistaken identity, which (in retrospect) looks hopefully forward to (in that sense *stands for,* almost literally occurring, one imagines, at the same time as) Grover's mistaken identification of Lulu's cabin door as his own.

This sense of an action taking place off-frame that somehow matches up with an action taking place on-frame characterizes the moment when Capra underscores his kinship with Lulu by matching his frame up with hers. Lulu has four "glances" in the point-of-view sequence, the first and third point-of-view shots being single takes, the camera panning to represent Lulu's searching gaze, a search she hopes is over when (in the fourth glance) she finally sees an unattached (at least unaccompanied) young man. In the second point-of-view shot, however, Lulu's gaze lingers on the space of the dance floor, on dancing couples. Instead of maintaining the single take by which the character's gaze is effectively "quoted," Capra claims authorship of the shot, without denying Lulu's copossession of it, by *cutting* from couple to couple, rather than panning. Either device would have done the job of depicting Lulu's interest in "coupling"; only cutting effectively "couples" the camera's gaze with Lulu's, no longer merely quoting but inhabiting the view, literally sharing its subjectivity, its power of selection.

A similar sharing of the frame, of the power of selection, of subjectivity, is evident in the "Roberta Her Book" montage sequence (recounting Rob-

Figure 11. The erotic gaze in *Forbidden*. (*Forbidden* copyright © 1932, renewed 1959 Columbia Pictures Industries, Inc. All rights reserved. Courtesy of Columbia Pictures.)

erta's childhood and Robert's rise to power) wherein Capra quite emphatically attends very specifically to the *process* by which the book is constructed. At the end of the Mary Sunshine sequence we get a point-of-view shot of Lulu's typewriter as she composes her first piece of advice to the lovelorn ("Dear Perplexed: If you love him, stick to him") from which Capra dissolves to the cover of "Roberta Her Book." The camera tracks back to a slightly longer shot as a newspaper is opened up and laid down over the book from screen left; a woman's hands scissor a picture of Helen Grover and Roberta out of the paper. We then dissolve to a shot from the same angle as glue is applied to the back of the clipping and the clipping put in place, at which point the camera tracks in to a slightly closer shot followed by a dissolve to what seems (by virtue of a tilt from headline to caption) a point-of-view shot of someone "reading" the book.

The sequence goes on, and concludes (roughly eighteen years later) with another shot of a letter being written. However, even this abbreviated description makes evident how thoroughly this passage mirrors the point-of-view match effected in the dining salon sequence. Again a kinship of view is suggested by spatial contiguity of camera and character – on the stairs, in Lulu's flat – which is confirmed by an explicit gesture of matching, in this case the track-in and the dissolve effectively closing the angle that initially distinguishes the camera's vantage point (roughly over Lulu's right shoulder) from Lulu's own.

Beyond that, it is worth noting the way in which Lulu's cut-and-paste artistry and its product, a series of images arranged so as to tell a story in which male and female (Robert and Roberta) are equally, almost indistinguishably represented, is an obvious echo and representation of Capra's artistry and product, which also amounts to a series of images cut and pasted in sequence so as to enact and depict a collaboration that strives to express the inexpressible, the *Forbidden*. To love someone, as Lulu apparently understands it, is to "stick to" the beloved; for Lulu and Capra both "sticking" is a matter of editing, of representing, of authorship, though an authorship in both cases that is split or shared, Lulu with Grover, Capra with Lulu.

The last frame match I want to consider involves the film's last sequence, Lulu weaving her disconsolate way through sidewalk crowds after leaving the governor's mansion. She pauses in her journey to read Grover's last testament before discarding it. During this passage Capra frames Lulu against a shop window. On the window glass are the words "Art Shop";

in the window, *mise-en-abîme* behind Lulu, is a portrait, of a seventeenth-century Dutchman to judge by the posture and the clothing of the subject. Though I have been unable to identify this as representing a particular painting, it certainly brings quickly to mind the central figure of Rembrandt's *Night Watch* (as it is popularly known) and also, perhaps, Rembrandt's *Portrait of Burgomaster Jan Six*. What are we to make of the implicit equation of foreground and background "pictures" here?

I answer by noting that Rembrandt, alone among Dutch artists of his generation, is widely known for his astonishing number and variety of self-portraits, many of which feature Rembrandt in explicitly theatrical costumes, as acting a role. In this light I am led to say that Stanwyck wears the costume and acts the role here and that the role she acts, stands in for, is Capra's authorship. Indeed, her last gesture before walking away is to scrap Grover's proposed ending in favor (as it were) of Lulu's. Capra's audacious yet oddly muted allusion to Rembrandt is, I would urge, a similar sort of "throwaway," an acknowledgment that authorship is at issue, an assertion as well that the figure on view is authored differently, is a moving picture that stops and then starts up again, not caught forever in a singular posture.

The other factor worth accounting for here is Capra's use of the Art Shop picture to suggest a certain commonality of technique shared by the media of painting and film, having to do with "illumination." I have already discussed the scene of Al Holland's murder, the sudden shift that takes place from standard Hollywood lighting to extreme side lighting, eventually specified as deriving from the fire in which Lulu burns the evidence and beside which she finally stands as she listens, her body shaking uncontrollably, to Grover's brief radio speech. In view of the implicit equation of Lulu and the Dutch-style portrait, hence of Capra and Rembrandt, I cannot resist the thought that Capra here aligns his visual style with Rembrandt's; each uses extreme contrasts of light and dark, typically attributed to (but wildly exceeding the power of) off-frame or side-of-the-frame lighting sources, a fireplace, a lamp, a window, to suggest a fullness and depth to the image, ambiguity too, which more realistic lighting schemes could not possibly approach. We might call this a matter of "visual melodrama," painting with fire and shadow things that cannot be represented by (as) simple daylight alone.[10]

These last few comments return us to the question of genre, itself a kind of shadow hanging over this discussion, though a shadow expressly forecast in my compound chapter title: "Melodrama and the Unknown Woman." In posing (then postponing) the question of what becomes of melodrama on film I wanted to mark for future reference an aspect of incoherence arising from the "doubling" of expression attributed (variously) to melodrama by such critics as Peter Brooks and Geoffrey Nowell-Smith. Both agree that melodrama is characterized by an excess or fullness of expression, but it is not always clear who is speaking and under what pressures, or what they are speaking, or to whom it is spoken. Put another way, who is conscious of what?

In Chapter 1 I quoted Peter Brooks to the effect that "there is no 'psychology' in melodrama" because characters "have no interior depth." Melodrama, he goes on to say, "exteriorizes conflict and psychic structure" into "a drama of pure psychic signs."[11] In that same chapter I briefly allude to Stanley Cavell's discussion of the second wall of Jericho scene in *It Happened One Night* as reflecting upon the philosophical problem of "metaphysical isolation," which sometimes takes the skeptical form of doubting or denying "the existence of other minds" – as Peter doubts and denies Ellie in sending her back around the blanket after evoking the image of a Pacific island where "you and the moon and the water all become one." In which light we might say, as Brooks eventually does say, that melodrama aspires to a state where nothing is unknown or denied, where there is no psychology, in the sense of an "unconscious," because everything already *is* conscious; making everything perfectly expressive – as in the gestures of "self-nomination" by means of which melodramatic stage characters explicitly declare their moral natures – is thus an ambition shared alike by melodrama and psychoanalysis. It is also closely akin to philosophical skepticism as Cavell describes it in *The Claim of Reason* where it amounts to a wish that "the connection between my claims of knowledge and the objects upon which the claims are to fall" will "occur without my intervention, apart from my agreements."[12] Melodrama and skepticism are (at least potentially) alike, then, in expressing a desire to avoid the human, the world of psychology, of desire, of language, a world of impure signs and endless necessities for agreement. Both the skeptic and the melodramatic character seek a world of certain knowledge, what Brooks calls the "moral occult." Hence perhaps the odd sense (alluded to alike by Brooks and Nowell-Smith) in which the "dream" of melodrama always seems on the verge of nightmare or hysteria, as if the figures projected by the play or film in question were (in turn) projections or symptoms of some off-frame (unconscious) agency; a world of perfect signs is a world of horror and inhumanity, however human the desire for it.

I describe this crowded intersection of generic and philosophical issues here primarily as background for noting the ambiguous generic status of *Forbidden,* as being midway between what Cavell has called remarriage comedy and what he subsequently describes (derives) as "the melodrama of the unknown woman." The difference between the two genres might be described as a matter of knowledge, of who has it and who gets it and how.

Classical comedy (New Comedy) knows what marriage and desire both amount to; marriage is society's mode of consenting to or sponsoring desire. In remarriage comedy, however, and in the Shakespearean precedents from which it derives, this sponsorship is insufficient. The moral of *Antony and Cleopatra,* on Cavell's understanding, is that "no one any longer knows what marriage is, what constitutes this central, specific bond of union, as if it is up to each individual pair to invent this for themselves."[13] It marks the kinship of remarriage comedy and melodrama that in both genres erotic desire is *already* fully incorporated, if not exactly or even nearly fulfilled (the characters have often already been married, or have borne children), and that in remarriage comedy it is typically the male of the pair who is most explicitly cast in the teacher or "professor" role (Peter Warne's lectures on doughnut dunking and piggybacking and hitchhiking in *It Happened One Night* are classic examples), which often results in a betrayal of his capacity for villainy or brutality, a capacity often depicted, as Cavell elaborates by reference to the home movie sequence in *Adam's Rib,* in terms derived from melodrama.[14]

That the man has something, some knowledge, that the woman needs is a way these films have of marking the larger sphere of inequality within which and from which equality is to be won. Cavell calls this winning a matter of creation or recreation: "The demand for education in the comedies presents itself as a matter of becoming created, as if the women's lives heretofore have been nonexistent, as if they have haunted the world, as if their materialization will constitute a creation of the new woman and hence a creation, or a further step in the creation, of the human."[15] The form that this education typically and world-famously takes is what Cavell, following John Milton, has called "meet and cheerful conversation." These characters may not exactly know what marriage is, having already discovered that something they once (upon a time) took as marriage did not quite take;

what they do know, beyond the shadow of all reasonable doubts, is how to go on talking about it.

Accordingly, what distinguishes remarriage comedy from the melodrama of the unknown woman, especially in view of their shared concern for the recreation of the female human, is that in melodrama "this change must take place outside the process of a mode of conversation with a man (of course; since such a conversation would constitute marriage)." Bravely, in light of the latter comment, Cavell elaborates by going on to speak from the vantage point, in the voice, of a melodramatic heroine addressing her comic sisters on the topic of their differences: "You may call yourselves lucky to have found a man with whom you can overcome the humiliation of marriage by marriage itself. For us, with our talents and tastes, there is no further or happy education to be found there; our integrity and metamorphosis happens elsewhere, in the abandoning of that *shared* wit and intelligence and exclusive appreciation."[16] Indeed, when women in these melodramas do talk to men, the result is typically *not* a matter of conversation, of interchange between intellectual equals; rather, it results in what Cavell, speaking of Bette Davis in *Now, Voyager,* describes as a genre-defining "irony [that] serves to isolate the woman of this melodrama from everyone around her, or almost everyone. It is a question whether it also isolates her from us. Hence I speak of the genre, adapting its title from one of its members, as the study of the unknownness of the woman."[17]

I collect these formulations here partly for future reference but chiefly because they provide terms for describing the generic complexity of *Forbidden,* especially as that description poses the question of whose desire is spoken or denied in the film. That *Forbidden* is *some* kind of woman's film is beyond denying, as is the fact that it takes speaking and writing as life-or-death issues. That it is also an important precursor of *It Happened One Night,* and hence of the entire remarriage comedy genre, is also clear. However, Capra works a strange reversal of emphasis in the relation we might expect between the film's two couples – Lulu–Grover, Lulu–Holland – and its two primary genre threads.

Thus it is the more positive relationship of the two that depends most deeply on the conventions of melodrama. Though Lulu and Grover sustain what amounts to a lifetime relationship, it is a relationship repeatedly marked, as if punctuated, by ironic "arias of divorce" of the sort Cavell takes to define the melodrama of the unknown woman. After Grover tells

Lulu about his invalid wife, which he takes to mark the end of his relationship with Lulu, she tells him sarcastically to "go ahead, be noble," after which she hands him his hat and slams the door in his face. After Lulu leaves Roberta with Helen, she and Grover finally wind up on a park bench, in the rain, where she tells him that she is not old and he is not the only man in the world – "I don't have to stop living, not for you, not for anybody" – after which she strides off into the rain-drenched distance, leaving Grover alone on a park bench. (She eventually returns.)

Indeed, despite the marvellous reciprocity of the Lulu–Grover relationship, there is next to nothing to suggest that, like the educating husband of remarriage comedy, Grover "teaches" or gives Lulu anything beyond the simple fact that his ambition, his worm, provides the raw material for the story that Lulu eventually stages and records for her picture book. Even this aspect of their relationship seems beyond him at crucial moments, as he demonstrates when he proposes to go public with his love for her, regardless of the consequences. It is a scene strikingly like the last scene between Charlotte Vale and Jerry in *Now, Voyager,* in which Jerry threatens to remove his daughter from Charlotte's care by saying that "No self-respecting man would allow such self-sacrifice as yours to go on indefinitely," to which she replies, with withering Bette Davis irony, "That's the most conventional, pretentious, pious speech I ever heard in my life. I simply don't know you." What Cavell says of Jerry in *Now, Voyager* can equally well be said of Grover, that in speaking on behalf of social convention, by invoking a conventional picture of sexual honesty and responsibilities, each man proves (the conditions of) the woman's existence by proving how little he knows her, how "unknown" she finally is to everyone but herself.

A similar reversal of expectation marks the Lulu–Holland relationship. I have already remarked upon Holland's oddly pastoral courtship vocabulary. Precisely because he is always overstating the romantic case, and because Lulu always responds in similarly ironic kind, their conversations take on something of the wit that characterizes the verbal exchanges of partners in remarriage comedy; they are always talking about marriage. That the wit here masks a quality of violence is evidenced in Holland's habit of punctuating their conversations by assaulting someone, usually with a piece of food – an apple core, a doughnut – tossed at someone's head. (The echo here of the food motif in *It Happened One Night* is hard to miss, especially when Lulu answers Holland's query about what happens when the unstoppable force meets the immovable body by concluding that "they start a restaurant.")

Indeed, if anyone can be said to teach Lulu it is Al Holland, and the lesson he teaches involves the potential murderousness of art, at least as art is conceived in the male-typical society he inhabits. (When Lulu levels a gun at Holland he offers to get a photographer, as if shooting with a camera were as deadly as with a revolver.) Holland would "commit murder" to get the dirty goods on Grover, to write the story his way. Lulu does. Indeed, for the sake of getting her writerly way Lulu destroys two (or three) alternative endings (shades of *Meet John Doe!*): the story Holland would have written for the front page; Grover's "do the right thing" letter wishing her well after her marriage to Holland, the letter Holland intercepts and that Lulu burns to ashes; Grover's last will and testament.

The price Lulu pays for claiming authorship is one of almost total isolation, at least from the world she inhabits; the only men with any claim to know her are dead. In the world of theatrical melodrama described by Peter Brooks, such isolation is the antithesis of "the melodramatic imagination" wherein "the sign of virtue eventually confronts all witnesses, on stage and in the audience, with its liberation from oppression and misprision."[18] In *Forbidden,* by contrast, the sign of virtue does not so much confront the world as haunt it in the figure of Lulu Smith, a figure whose self-creation remains unfinished because unacknowledged by any possible audience.

Of course, I have spoken of Capra and Lulu as collaborators, so we might say that Capra is also a spirit (say a Halloween ghost) haunting the world of *Forbidden,* like Lulu an absent presence, and therefore a being fit to acknowledge her authorship by asserting his own, as I argue he does by framing Lulu against the Art Shop window display in the film's last sequence. Of course, such a claim is second cousin to Al Holland's threat to go public with the details of Roberta's birth, to use Lulu's story against Grover; one could argue that Lulu's failure to sustain an acknowledged existence is a function of the fact that she had nothing but male-typical "pictures" of authorship to work with, or male bosses, however subversively she worked with them. In that sense Capra's appropriation of Lulu's story might well be taken as yet one more chapter in the sadly melodramatic history of male villainy; in "speaking" Lulu Capra destroys her, uses her for his own ends, makes her story his, as some accuse Freud of using his female patients' stories more to further his own purposes than to assist in the realization of theirs.

An alternative picture, which does not so much deny as further interpret this sad history, is to say that what is forbidden in *Forbidden* is the female voice. What is not altogether forbidden, in our world at least, is Capra's attempt to speak the female in himself by assigning authorship to Lulu, trying to see the world, almost literally at times, through her eyes. At the very least, we can say that the Capra of *Forbidden,* like Lulu in the film, like the film itself, remains largely unknown, unacknowledged. Indeed, in *The Name above the Title* Capra goes out of his way to dismiss the film as uninteresting, describing it as "two hours of soggy, 99.44% pure soap opera."[19] I find this denial deeply haunting, as if Capra were deeply haunted by a better self than the Capra-corn optimist associated with his more overtly political parables. In its incipient and awkward feminism, however, *Forbidden* is arguably one of Capra's most deeply political movies, despite its avoidance of the nuts and bolts reality of representative democracy. Much of the interest of his subsequent "Mr." films, I will argue, derives exactly from the way in which their political overtones work in counterpoint with the feminine voice elaborated in *Forbidden.* To avoid hearing that voice, I contend, is to deny Capra altogether.

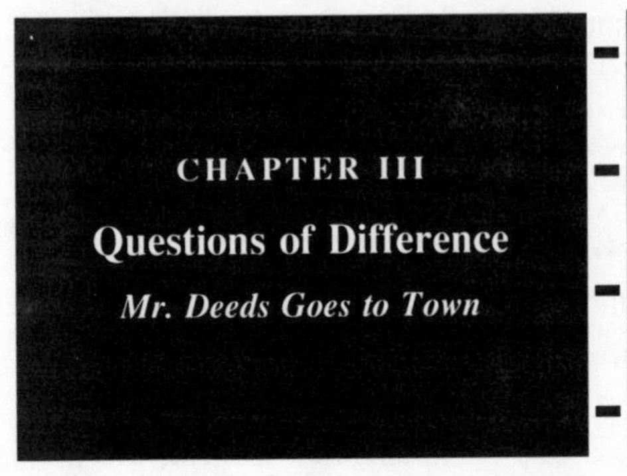

CHAPTER III

Questions of Difference

Mr. Deeds Goes to Town

In the Preface and Chapter 1, I not only sketch out an "institutional" picture of Capra's place in film history but do my best by reference and example to demonstrate some of the interpretive limitations that both empower and undermine that picture. Capra criticism is hardly a closed shop. However, on at least one account there is an extraordinary measure of unanimity: Just about everyone agrees that *Mr. Deeds Goes to Town* marks a crucial turning point in Capra's relationship to his craft and his public. In the words of Morris Dickstein, it was "not until the story of that 'simple honest man' Longfellow Deeds, as played by Gary Cooper," that Capra found "the perfect vehicle for his new gospel, from which he claims never to have strayed." Though Deeds inherits $20 million at the film's beginning, it is "a matter of remarkably little interest to him, until, two-thirds of the way through the film, he (and Capra) happen to notice the Depression, which had scarcely intruded into *It Happened One Night* (1934). This sets Deeds off doing good deeds, pursuing a New Dealish but paternalistic scheme to give away parcels of farmland. Deeds, like Capra, has at last found a purpose serious enough to justify his good fortune."[1]

Many elements of this passage are worth dwelling on. Dickstein (more or less) echoes James Dugan's *New Masses* discussion of *You Can't Take It with You* in locating the Capra "shift" by reference to the moment in *Mr. Deeds* when the distraught farmer breaks into Longfellow's mansion.[2] Equally typical is Dickstein's reference to *It Happened One Night* as providing the most immediately telling measure of Capra's progress in the direction of "social responsibility." Most significantly, the passage is typical for being a decidedly retrospective assessment of *Mr. Deeds,* in noting, for instance, Capra's messianic claim about the whole of his subsequent career.

As Gerald Weales points out, assessments of *Mr. Deeds* as displaced autobiography or personal testimony were far from the rule at the time of the film's initial release; its "very favorable first reviews tended to welcome the movie as another Capra comedy."[3] However, since the 1971 publication of *The Name above the Title,* it has been all but impossible to avoid the Capra–Deeds equation. Capra explicitly repeats his oft-made claim that with *Mr. Deeds* he shifted his goals and his methods: "Beginning with *Mr. Deeds Goes to Town,* my films had to *say* something." "And regardless of the origin of a film idea – I made it mine."[4] However, the crucial factor that makes the temptation to equate Mr. Deeds and Mr. Capra well nigh irresistible is less Capra's explicit statements to that effect than the extent to which Frank Capra's life story as recounted in *The Name above the Title* parallels crucial elements of the *Mr. Deeds* film story.

The central character in each, for starters, is top honcho in a backwater light factory – Deeds as coowner of a tallow works in Mandrake Falls, Capra as the ace director and primary meal ticket of Columbia Pictures. Each is a popular poet on a contract whose sentimental fables circulate via mechanically reproduced images – Deeds's occasional-verse postcards, Capra's academy-ratio film frames. Each then experiences an unexpected turn of fortune that suddenly renders him a public figure of almost national proportions – Deeds as the inheritor of $20 million upon the sudden death of his globe-trotting, bank-owning uncle, Capra as the director of *It Happened One Night,* which unexpectedly swept the major Oscars in February of 1935. Each thereafter confronts a series of stories leading to disillusionment if not downright panic – for Deeds it is the series of "Cinderella Man" newspaper stories penned by Babe Bennett (Jean Arthur); in Capra's case it was the "trivial" story material he encountered after all the *Happened One Night* Oscar hoopla. Each responds to disillusionment by attempting to retreat from responsibility, Deeds by returning to Mandrake Falls, Capra by feigning or giving in to illness. In each case retreat is cut short, or so the story goes, by a total stranger who invades the poet's inner sanctum and confronts the malingering do-gooder with the selfish error of his way.[5] After which, as Capra and nearly everyone else tells the tale, he resolved "to *say* something" with his films, beginning with *Mr. Deeds Goes to Town,* which also concludes when a folk poet finally decides to break his silence and "say something."

A common reading of the difference this say-something difference makes comes from the region of genre studies, involving the distinction frequently drawn between "screwball comedy" and "populist comedy." In the work of Wes Gehring (particularly) the distinction hinges on questions of gender and class, with screwball comedy understood as representing a (not so temporary) swerve from the main tradition of American humor as personified by the rural "crackerbarrel philosopher" – best exemplified on film by Will Rogers. Whereas populist comedy retains the rural and paternalistic emphasis of crackerbarrel humor, screwball comedy shifts focus from country to city, from middle to upper class, from male-dominant action lines to female-dominant story matter (e.g., the flight of "madcap heiress" Ellie Andrews in *It Happened One Night*). The moral of the story, as Gehring and others typically construe matters, is that Capra no sooner helped to inaugurate the screwball genre than he abandoned it. "After *It Happened One Night,*" writes Gehring, Capra's "career took a fascinating but decidedly nonscrewball turn. The Capra heroes who follow, like the classic trio of Mr. Deeds, Mr. Smith, and John Doe, are from the American humor tradition of the political crackerbarrel, hardly that of screwball comedy."[6]

A far more interesting version of this genealogical thesis is James Harvey's. In *Romantic Comedy in Hollywood, from Lubitsch to Sturges,* Harvey is very explicit in defining the difference that sets screwball comedy apart from its immediate dramatic and cinematic predecessors. Screwball comedy is thus similar to the (often musical) comedy of Ernst Lubitsch in its emphasis on wit and eroticism, but differs to the degree that screwball wit (both verbal and visual) does not ironically undercut or isolate its characters, an isolation Harvey takes as typifying an essentially European form of social skepticism. Screwball is also similar to sophisticated stage comedy of the Noel Coward sort in its focus on a "knockout couple," but screwball managed to avoid the empty and self-congratulatory acceptance of class privilege that typified Hollywood's appropriation of "the continental, neo-Molnár style."[7] Finally, screwball is similar in its energies and urban iconography and its verbal sound to the "wiseacre" world of Hecht and MacArthur's *The Front Page* – its Chicago a fully American equal to the mythical Paris of Ernst Lubitsch – yet its idealistic vulgarity tends *not* to be personified in the solitary and essentially antiromantic (however deeply erotic) figure of a James Cagney or a Jean Harlow.

Key words in Harvey's elaboration of his case and his subsequent application of it to Capra are "condescension" and "surprise." Each of the predecessor genres Harvey discusses is characterized by some form of condescension, of director to his characters or his audience, of upper-class characters to their lower-class counterparts, of one member of the tough ''mug'' couple to the other. What seems most surprising and exhilarating about screwball comedy on Harvey's understanding is exactly the absence of this aspect of superiority or inequality, in every dimension. Indeed, Harvey takes the first auto-camp scene in *It Happened One Night* as epitomizing the genre and Capra's connection to it in the way that each character's words and actions (the camera's actions too) repeatedly take the other and the viewer by happy and thought-provoking surprise – so much so that the whole world of *It Happened One Night* comes to seem suffused (as by Joseph Walker's deeply expressive black-and-white photography) with an aspect of expectation or yearning: ''The world the movie shows us is a world waiting to be transformed.''[8]

Like Gehring, however, Harvey sees *Mr. Deeds* as a betrayal of the screwball promise of *It Happened One Night.* Partly, this involves a shift in gender politics. Jean Arthur is both the screwball heroine *and* the humorless heavy, constantly calling into doubt the capacity for equitable laughter that *It Happened One Night* had so strikingly promoted. Gender notwithstanding, Harvey's deepest complaint about the post–''conversion experience'' Capra involves the ''self-consciousness'' of his condescension. Cooper's Mr. Deeds, writes Harvey, ''is self-conscious about being *un*self-conscious. And in this respect above all he represents Capra's dilemma, too.'' Typical of Capra's self-conscious ''naturalness'' for Harvey is the final harmonica duet in *You Can't Take It with You,* which Harvey describes as being at the same time ''one of the great exhilarating events of thirties comedy'' and a ''skillful counterfeit, a hyped-up, efficiency expert's version of something Capra had done with more conviction earlier on.'' As a general Capra result, ''the flow of rhetoric about goodness and kindness and caring about your neighbor seems so utterly remote from any real experience of doing good or attempting it that it becomes finally offensive. Even a little crazy. But that, I think, is finally its appeal.''[9]

In dwelling on the retrospective unanimity of opinion in regards to *Mr. Deeds* I am *not* maneuvering to denounce retrospection in the name of some less mediated relationship to the film. Indeed, my references to genre history lay groundwork for eventually recontextualizing *Mr. Deeds Goes to Town* along considerably different lines. Before doing so, however, I want to ponder further the claims made by Gehring and Harvey to the effect that *Mr. Deeds* differs from its Capra predecessors in its political focus and in the greater degree of its authorial or aesthetic self-consciousness.

Of course, it is no simple matter to describe a film or a scene as political

– even as that term has typically been employed in populist discussions of Capra where its meaning is inevitably and easily measured against the explicit representations of electoral politics in films like *Mr. Smith Goes to Washington, Meet John Doe,* and *State of the Union.* Certain scenes in *Mr. Deeds* seem clearly enough to fit under this populist rubric. Deeds's visionary response to Grant's Tomb – invoking both the bitter legacy of the Civil War and the more hopeful farmstead-to-White House trajectory of Grant's life story (''Things like that can only happen in a country like America'') – is an obvious case in point, though its ideological implications are sketchy at best, especially in view of the scene's dramatistic status as a parable of interpretive variability.[10] Also of obvious political import are any number of self-controverting courtroom remarks by lawyer for the plaintiffs John Cedar to the effect that Longfellow's scheme to dispose of his fortune by bankrolling farmsteads, apart from proving Deeds mentally incompetent, risks ''fomenting a disturbance from which the country may not soon recover'' despite the fact that the ''government is fully aware of its difficulties and can pull itself out its economic ruts without the assistance of Mr. Deeds or any other crackpot.'' (If help is not needed, how is the offer of it socially debilitating?)

The ambivalence or contradiction that marks each of these latter two moments effectively requires some placement or translation if they are to gain narrative force. Thus Raymond Durgnat, to take a significant example, discusses the political rhetoric of *Mr. Deeds* as a matter of strategic ''paraphrase'' that allows Capra to address the issue of the Depression without the kind of ''too accurate a description'' that would ''run the film head on into all sorts of depressing controversial reflections.''[11] A similar interpretive strategy allows Glenn Alan Phelps to claim – contra Durgnat's subsequent description of *Mr. Deeds* as ''propaganda for a moderate, concerned, Republican point of view'' – that Longfellow's plan to share his wealth, far from supporting private volunteerism, undercuts it by showing how the distinction between private and public is far from secure.[12] ''If Deeds's private scheme can do so much to help society,'' writes Phelps, ''might it not be easily deduced that private actions have been preventing needed improvements in the public realm?''[13] The point to make, if we assume only as much interpretive leeway as is evident in the examples of Durgnat and Phelps, is that Capra's films before *Mr. Deeds* are shot through with political implications.

As my references to Dickstein and Dugan and Durgnat indicate quite clearly, politics in *Mr. Deeds* and its predecessors boils down quickly to the Depression. For some (at least) the Depression is effectively personified by the gun-toting farmer who bursts into Longfellow's mansion and berates him for feeding doughnuts to horses while displaced people starve. However, by that standard – and keeping in mind the striking emphasis on food that characterizes any number of Capra films from *That Certain Thing* (1928) onward – the scene in *It Happened One Night* (right after the "Flying Trapeze" songfest) when a starving mother faints on the north-bound bus is just as deeply political, as much a token of social deprivation and displacement, as the *Mr. Deeds* scene. (Mother and son have spent all of their money on tickets for New York City, where the man of the family has lately found work.) Indeed, one of those haunting, thought-inducing details that Harvey praises in his discussion of *It Happened One Night* is relevant here. When Ellie rises from sleep on the morning of the first auto-camp scene, Peter directs her to the communal "showers and things." Clad in Peter's pajamas and bathrobe, Ellie walks between the cabins (the camera tracking with her in long take). What we see, even if she does not, is kids playing and various residents raking the cabin yards. The latter is rather anomalous behavior for transients. As Harvey makes the point, "We don't get the feeling that people like this have left their homes so much as that they make them, as they find them, on the road," a Depression-era "rootlessness" that Capra pointedly takes for granted.[14]

Or consider, if explicit depictions of poverty accompanied by explicit discussions of politics are what matters in determining the difference of *Mr. Deeds Goes to Town,* the opening few moments of *Lady for a Day* (1933). The film's first several shots are of beggars, one a blind accordionist, another a legless pencil peddler, yet another selling flowers, Apple Annie herself moving against the flow of the Manhattan crowd selling apples. Two of the beggars check in with Annie, who asks each how they are doing ("How's business?"). The legless one answers "Terrible. Looks like everybody's broke. Must be tough on them," indicating by a nod of the head that "them" are the better-dressed sidewalk passersby. To which Annie replies,"Stop yapping, didn't you hear the president over the radio?"[15] (In a subsequent exchange between Annie and the Hotel Marberry doorman, we discover that the latter has upped the price on hotel stationery because the guests are no longer leaving things in their rooms. "It's conditions," he says sadly if matter of factly.)

Two elements of this latter scene deserve comment for elucidating Capra's general approach to economic issues. One is his willingness to bring poverty and comedy together, something he had been doing well before the Depression set in. Indeed, there is something almost surreal (and Chaplinesque) about Capra's representations of lower- or working-class life that connotes both intimacy and anxiety. Witness here the sequence in *That Certain Thing* when Molly Kelly returns in the rain from her fairy-tale wedding night to face the angry residents of her working-class tenement: The point-of-view montage of distorted faces is fully the nightmare equal in its force and bitterness to the last montage sequence in *Meet John Doe* where Gary Cooper is haunted by similarly accusatory faces. Many of Capra's earlier Columbia pictures are equally matter of fact about the brutalities of economic hardship; that few people seemed to notice this aspect of his filmmaking until *Mr. Deeds* says more about Capra's audiences and critics than it does about Capra. Like the legless beggar said, when "they" are broke, it is a national issue. Also worth noting in this regard is how often in Capra's pre–*Mr. Deeds* films the primary victims of economic and social hardship are female, like Apple Annie, like Molly Kelly in *That Certain Thing,* like Kay Arnold in *Ladies of Leisure,* like Florence Fallon in *The Miracle Woman*. Perhaps the real differences to be pondered here are these:

1. Capra did not achieve public acclaim until *It Happened One Night,* where the primary victim is less a victim of hardship than of wealth – despite Capra's quiet efforts to place that victimization (as when Ellie lines up for the showers and things at the first auto camp) within a larger economic context.
2. Capra was not credited with a significantly political vantage point until the victim of wealth was (like Longfellow Deeds) an heir rather than an heiress.

Though Gehring's screwball versus populist comedy rubric finally does not very aptly describe the relation of *Mr. Deeds* to Capra generally, for implying that Capra had ignored economic issues prior to making *Mr. Deeds,* there is a kind of truth to it that we would do well to remember: Audiences have sometimes found it difficult to take women seriously as agents of (figures for) political insight or action. Indeed, I will eventually want to argue that the most interesting implications of *Mr. Deeds Goes to Town* involve exactly the difficulty of accepting a feminine vantage point. However, conviction on *that* account requires some response to James Harvey's claim regarding Capra's narrational self-consciousness in *Mr. Deeds*. If Capra's self-consciousness is to be equated directly with that attributed to Longfellow on Harvey's understanding of the film, it is hard to imagine how Longfellow's (or Capra's) attitude might include a positively feminist component, especially given his treatment of Babe Bennett.

The question of self-consciousness and the difference it makes as regards *Mr. Deeds Goes to Town* can be very tricky. For Harvey, self-consciousness is nearly synonymous with condescension. And by "condescension" Harvey has in mind an almost defiantly self-congratulatory if not self-pitying attitude that Capra's characters seem to adopt toward those less fortunate or less generous. The degree of Harvey's exasperation (shared by many) is evident in his description of the *Mr. Deeds* courtroom sequence, in which Longfellow's response to the charge of incompetence

> is to stop talking. To anyone. When all the while it is perfectly clear that the absurd suspicion could be disposed of in an instant, and he could be saved from the loony bin if only he *did* talk, even just a little – no, never mind. Let his friends and supporters sweat and plead – they do, they do. He just sits there in the courtroom – *don't mind me,* he seems to be saying, as he turns his suffering beautiful face, mute and reproachful, to the heroine and the farmers, to the crowd, to the judge, to the camera, to us.[16]

Nothing funny or screwball or very endearing in all that.

Part of the "trickiness" of this passage and of Harvey's often astute chapter on Capra generally is that Harvey attributes self-consciousness to Capra almost entirely in terms of actors and acting style – precisely those features the antagonists of the classical Hollywood film take as "naturalizing" bourgeois ideology by distracting viewer attention from the "constructedness" of film space and film time, thereby rendering film style (and its manipulations) "invisible." What I find most anomalous about all this – despite my predictable disagreement with Harvey's understanding of the film – is the basic accuracy of Harvey's stylistic description of *Mr. Deeds*. Though the idea that Capra's pre-*Deeds* films *ever* lacked for self-consciousness or reflexivity is deeply false – as *Forbidden* alone would indicate – the fact remains that the self-consciousness of *Mr. Deeds* is unusual in that the film rather strikingly eschews or downplays many of the stylistic devices by means of which Capra more typically suggests a narrational presence.

Montage sequences, we have repeatedly seen, contravene the standard time–space coordinates of classical narrative and allow authorial intervention into or commentary upon the film's depicted world, in part by connecting the world narrated to the world of the depicting narrational instance itself; such sequences are *only* visible to a world beyond the film world. Capra's skill with and reliance upon such sequences is legendary. Still, by contrast with montage sequences elsewhere in Capra, those in *Mr. Deeds Goes to Town* are at most functional, employing the compression of montage for exposition's or iconography's sake and for little else. Compared to the run-on-the-bank montage sequence at the center of *American Madness,* for example, even the most elaborate montage sequence in *Mr. Deeds* must be described as an instance of classical narration at its concisely efficient best.

Or consider Capra's use of special lighting effects in *Mr. Deeds.* Though various silhouette lighting schemes in *Mr. Deeds* are striking – especially the famous shot of a silent Deeds framed against the cagelike window of his hospital room prior to the trial – there is nothing in *Mr. Deeds* to rival the glittery black-and-white expressionism of the Havana sequences in *Forbidden* or the crossing-of-the-stream sequence in *It Happened One Night.* A number of scenes in *Mr. Deeds* come close enough to ponder on this account – the scene in the rain outside the Semple mansion when "Mary" faints on the sidewalk, the Central Park conversation-become-duet of Arthur and Gary Cooper, the proposal scene that takes place on a brownstone stoop in a nighttime fog – but each scene on its own seems to lack the excessiveness with which Capra typically correlates extreme visual with extreme emotional and sexual states of being, as if he had gone out of his way to isolate visual and emotional elements that he normally brings together.

Or consider how in *Mr. Deeds* Capra downplays the acting theme that allows many of his pre-*Deeds* films to acquire a reflexive narrational dimension quite apart from manipulations of editing or lighting. *The Miracle Woman,* for instance, anticipates *Meet John Doe* in having a central character of a messianic bent who turns out to be the creature of show-biz calculation; Florence Fallon, like Long John Willoughby, is literally acting a role, and she finally encourages others to "act" for the sake of her deception (as John Carson pretends, toward film's end, to have regained his sight through Florence's "miraculous" intervention). Even a film like *American Madness,* ostensibly focused via its bank-run story on economic questions, acquires much of its interest via a theatrical subtext. In an early scene various tellers agree to keep straight faces when Matt Brown (Pat O'Brien) delivers his customary morning joke; Mrs. Dickson uses an evening at the theater as a cover for a surprise anniversary party; the police detective who suspects bank cashier Cyril Cluett of complicity in the murder and robbery that initiates the bank run solicits his confession by pretending (via a staged phone call) to have a talkative Dude Finley in custody; and so on, and so forth.

It is hardly true that acting is absent from *Mr. Deeds Goes to Town.* Much of it, however, tends to be subsumed by other forms of social exchange. Lawyers, for instance, tend to act on behalf of their clients – like the lawyer representing the common law wife of Longfellow's uncle, like John Cedar himself, especially in the courtroom sequence – a fact that tends to minimize the exclusively theatrical elements of their performances. Likewise, the *literati* who razz Deeds about his postcard poems are acting when they seem to welcome him (and Babe) to their restaurant table – but the point here is how quickly Deeds sees through the act. Even Babe Bennett – to whose "Mary Dawson" act Deeds remains almost inexplicably blind until Cobb forces the issue (who else *but* Mary is witness to all the actions reported in the papers?) – seems quickly "untheatricalized" by the personal sincerity of her questions and of Longfellow's answers, to the point where Babe Bennett seems more the fiction than Mary Dawson. Put another way, the relation of Babe to Deeds is in its genesis profoundly unlike that in *Meet John Doe* between Ann Mitchell and Long John Willoughby; Ann *creates* John Doe by scripting him, while Babe's reports are, in fact, pretty accurate as far as we have access to them.

An alternative reading of the *Mr. Deeds* difference – one that will eventually help us to puzzle through the question of how a film can be self-conscious while seeming to erase the marks of self-consciousness – is Raymond Carney's. Among the many changes in Capra's style that Carney observes in his discussion of the period between *Lady for a Day* and *Lost Horizon* three are especially noteworthy:

1. Capra's "camera moves back from the frequent gauzed close-ups of *Ladies of Leisure, Forbidden,* and *Bitter Tea* to take in social surroundings relentlessly impinging on the central characters."
2. "With *Deeds* Capra's work shifts from privileging predominantly visual structurings of experience to contrasting visual and verbal structurings," a contrast literally figured in the film's second half by the character of Babe Bennett who

does her melodramatic best to speak on Longfellow's behalf during the trial scene.

3. Capra's work shifts "from predominantly female protagonists to predominantly male," a "shift from more or less passive, visionary central characters to more or less active, practical, worldly ones" reflecting "Capra's increasing willingness to explore biographical similarities between himself and his central figures."[17]

This collection of features *can* be accommodated to a Harveyesque reading that takes *Mr. Deeds* as Capra's attempt to say something about American society circa 1936 by placing Deeds in a dramatic social circumstance that requires him to speak. However, differences in what Carney and Harvey mean by "social" argue against doing so.

The desire to link Capra's increased attention to the social and verbal placement of his characters to a particular political movement or agenda has a long and unproductive history; the rush to affix a political label has far too often served as a way of denying (rather than elucidating) the complexities of the films. We would do far better, on my view, to follow Carney's lead in taking Capra's meditations on social relations both more literally and more figuratively. Put another way, we can say that *Mr. Deeds Goes to Town* is concerned with the social *as such,* with its underlying conditions and possibilities, possibilities against which any particular set of social arrangements can (must) be adjudged. Carney's "social" is considerably more expansive and self-conscious than Harvey's.

The primary evidence in support of the claim that *Deeds* is concerned with the social *as such* is the film's sustained interest in the raw *fact* of language. This concern is most obviously evident in the courtroom sequence. Indeed, Raymond Carney has described Longfellow's courtroom performance – against the view that Deeds is a sort of inspired simpleton – as instancing a perspicaciously linguistic grasp of the essential "structurality of structure." No more the simpleton than Rousseau or Derrida, Longfellow

> systematically takes up each of the major pieces of testimony that have been used against him by the witnesses and lawyers in the hearing and (most brilliantly and exuberantly in the case of the testimony of the Faulkner sisters) reveals the essential textuality of the discourse, tracing and explaining to the court the particular set of arbitrary codes, assumptions, and consistencies that generate the text and attempt to control and limit its interpretation.[18]

The "textuality" of the courtroom scene can also be understood more literally. The trial itself has a proscribed procedure, rules of order and evidence and authority that can be bent but not broken. Indeed, the existence of rules and precedents is made most explicit when Babe Bennett, in her passion, seeks to bend them in the service of language: Deeds must be made *to talk*. Twice, moreover, explicit definitions are called for, once for "pixilated," once for "doodling." (In each case a local or archaic usage – both are associated with Vermont – is given new currency, for a larger community, in the very *act* of defining it.) Beyond all that, there is a marvellous chorus of accents foreign and domestic to account for in the string of witnesses John Cedar calls upon to prove Deeds insane – the Irish brogue of the cop, the operatic Italianate trills of Madame Pomponi, the cockney lilt of the hansom cabby, the Brooklynese chin music of Deeds's half-baked bodyguard, the Viennese schmaltz of Dr. Van Haller. The case Cedar presents is as much a study in phonology as in sanity, a study (in both the linguistic and psychological realms) of similarity and its differences.

Many other moments and features of *Mr. Deeds Goes to Town* could be adduced to confirm the view that language is an abiding concern throughout. Always alert to the odd word and ready to seek its rhyme, Longfellow is (and is named after) a widely popular American poet, for example, and is in the habit of quoting another, Henry David Thoreau. The plot to railroad Deeds to the nuthouse derives from his desire to see and Cedar's to hide "the books." However, the most significantly linguistic aspects of *Mr. Deeds* are (1) its sustained concern with the reach and meanings of specific words or concepts and (2) its repeated examinations of the underlying social protocols of speech acts.

Instances of the former are the courtroom discussions of "pixilated" and "doodling." (Note how the psychological and the textual are paired here.) "Pixilated," for example, is synonymous with "balmy" (or so a doctor tells the presiding judge) and is clearly intended by the interrogating Cedar as another word for "crazy." "Crazy" itself threads through the film from early to late. Babe's editor gloats that the other papers will go "crazy" with envy and frustration after the publication of Babe's first "Cinderella Man" story; Deeds himself, the morning after his "bender," describes his poetic drinking companion as "crazy," and he subsequently reports to Mary that his opera-board colleagues think *him* "crazy" for wanting to "run the opera like a grocery." (Food again!) Moreover, Babe's editor declares *her* "crazy" when she eventually proposes to tell Deeds the truth over lunch. Add to "crazy" itself a whole warp's-worth of synonyms – "nitwit," "nuts," "mad," "idiot," "funny," "silly," "haywire" – and you have a very complex conceptual fabric indeed. Among other words or concepts that are similarly elaborated – by repeated use in different contexts, or by the use of different synonyms in similar contexts – are "natural," "laughter," "show," "real," and "see." As token of the general linguistic wit on display in *Mr. Deeds,* equally humorous and apt though readily enough overlooked as generic bric-a-brac, I cite the moment when Deeds seeks to leave his mansion only to be confronted by his bodyguards, one of whom summarizes their duties as follows: "No matter what we see, we don't see nothing, see?"

Carney's claim that *Mr. Deeds* marks a Capra shift (with considerable help from Robert Riskin, no doubt) in the direction of the social and the verbal is more than confirmed by this emphasis on "vocabulary." His subsequent claim that Deeds's courtroom theatrics reveal the "arbitrariness" of all discursive systems prompts a moment's pause, especially when "arbitrary" is taken in its Saussurean sense as *merely* arbitrary or conventional, as if (to simplify only a little) knowing a language were basically a matter of knowing the meanings of words.

My hesitancy is prompted by Stanley Cavell's work in "ordinary language philosophy," especially his study of what we might term the language of skepticism. Cavell finds the skeptic's case deeply human, as we have noted in our discussion of melodrama, in its desire for a certain (specific, absolute) connection to the world of objects and beings. Cavell also finds that case and the language presenting it oddly empty in that the desired certainty is defined (in advance) by an absence, by the skeptical knower's lack of intervention or implication in those human agreements that make up our world, a lack motivated by the fear that such agreements are *merely* arbitrary or conventional, a matter of mere words. Cavell's reply is that our knowledge of the human world is always already so certain that we are often forced into actively denying it in pretending to the passivity of the skeptical proof. Underlying that reply is a chain of revelations about the nature of language, that, for example,

> the extent of agreement is so intimate and pervasive; that we communicate in language as rapidly and completely as we do; and that since we cannot assume that the words we are given have their meaning by nature, we are led to assume they take it from convention; and yet no current idea of "convention" could seem to do the work that words do – there would have to be, we could say, too many

conventions in play, one for each shade of each word in each context. We *cannot* have agreed beforehand to all that would be necessary.[19]

Cavell is not exactly denying here the social nature of language; far from it. Rather, he is pointing to its *depth* and to our rootedness in it, "For nothing is deeper than the fact, or the extent, of agreement itself." Indeed, Cavell elaborates the concept of agreement by means of a musical analogy that seems deeply appropriate when applied to such a jolly good tuba player as Longfellow Deeds: "The idea of agreement here is not that of coming to or arriving at an agreement on a given occasion, but of being in agreement throughout, being in harmony, like pitches, or tones"; people are thus "mutually voiced with respect to [language], mutually *attuned* top to bottom."[20]

This depth of attunement is quietly attested to at various points in *Mr. Deeds Goes to Town* when characters ask questions in ways that presume underlying agreements, as when Cedar (in court) asks Babe whether she works for the newspaper, assuming the present tense still applies. She shows it does not (and gets Cedar's goat) by saying "No." (She quit.) A far more spectacular instance of this is the scene at the Mandrake Falls train depot when Cedar and Cobb question the stationmaster about Longfellow Deeds. They want to know how to find him so they can break the news about the Semple fortune, yet they do not ask where to find him, asking instead if the stationmaster knows Deeds, if he knows where Deeds lives, and so forth. As if sensing that Cedar and company are withholding something, the stationmaster continues about his business (until Cobb grabs him) and answers their questions as literally as possible. The scene is typically taken as an affectionate portrait of rural naïveté; just how naive is opened to doubt when the stationmaster delivers the crew to Longfellow's house and replies to the housekeeper's observation that Deeds is elsewhere by saying that he "knew it all the time," but the men said they wanted to see the house: "Can't read their minds if they don't say what they want." Of course, he *has* read their minds, infers (I take it) that their words are insufficiently forthcoming (is more right, in this, than he knows), and serves them tit for tat by giving them exactly that for which they asked.

This brief aside on language theory is hardly out of place in discussing a film so obviously concerned with language. Indeed, part of what distinguishes Carney's reading of *Mr. Deeds* from Harvey's is his attribution to Deeds, hence implicitly to Capra, of an abiding interest in the social dynamics of rhetoric or style. By contrast, Harvey's understanding of ''rhetoric'' in *Mr. Deeds* equates it fairly restrictedly with questions of ''goodness and kindness and caring about your neighbor,'' a rhetoric Harvey finds deeply objectionable because its self-congratulatory self-consciousness is too easy, too dependent on a condescending picture of the poor that, far from sympathizing with their plight, falsifies it, as if fearing the truth. Listen on these accounts to Harvey's description of the farmer's confrontation with Deeds:

> The poor man who comes on with a gun finally says ''Excuse me'' for pointing it and ends up just the way these movies like their poor people: weak and lovable and grateful. But the real focus of this sequence is Deeds himself, sitting across the table while the farmer eats – watching him in silence, chin in hand, making welling-eyed little grimaces and blinking his encouragement whenever the man looks up. Cooper's self-consciousness is so pronounced that Deeds seems moved by his own emotion as much as by anything else.[21]

''Silence,'' for present purposes, is the key word here, for allowing us to construe the notion of cinematic self-consciousness negatively. I have already discussed some of the stylistic devices Capra does *not* resort to in *Mr. Deeds* to the extent that he does elsewhere. For someone familiar with Capra, the silence on these accounts is deafening, as of things not so much lacking as repressed. I have also alluded to the theatricality trope by which Capra often invokes a reflexive analogy of character and director. Indeed, another trait that Carney takes as distinguishing early Capra from later is the frequency with which later Capra characters – Long John Willoughby in *Meet John Doe,* for example – are depicted as supporting players in some larger social drama, as opposed to the free-lance on-the-margin writers and painters and impromptu self-dramatizers of Capra's early Columbia pictures. I have already observed that this aspect of *Mr. Deeds* is relatively weak, as weak as Cedar's court case. I have also noted the sense in which the Longfellow Deeds story and the Frank Capra story are cognates; each is an author who represses his own voice and eventually finds that voice when confronted by the impassioned voice of another (or several others). In which case we might aptly say that the dominant narrational trope of *Mr. Deeds Goes to Town* is less theatrical than sonic – a matter of ''echoes.''

An interesting number of film-textual features line up here: the stationmaster's repeated ''Good morning, neighbor'' as he tries (or doesn't much) to talk to Cedar and Cobb; Deeds's habit of rhyming (and the fact that his chief "puzzle" on this account, "Budington," is the middle name of the author of the original "Opera Hat" short story upon which *Mr. Deeds* is based); the moment when Deeds confronts two mugs in the mansion foyer and hears them say, in chorus, "we're your bodyguards"; the passage of the courtroom scene in which the two Faulkner sisters take turns repeating each other ("Must we have the echo?" is the judge's comment). Most spectacularly, there is the scene in Longfellow's mansion when Deeds, on the second-floor landing, calls after one of the staff, only to hear his voice echo from the distance. Deeds tells Walter to shout, eventually enlists another servant or two in the chorus, and finally makes his exit by saying, enigmatically, "Let that be a lesson to you."

I take both the lesson and the scene of instruction here as offering the same advice: "Listen for echoes." Among those echoes is a scene from Capra's *Platinum Blonde* in which Stew Smith, likewise a "Cinderella Man" uncomfortably ensconced within a palatial old-money estate, discovers the echo-chamber properties of the mansion's main entryway and bids his butler, as Deeds bids his, to join in and pipe up. The analogy is not exact. Stew Smith's situation is depicted as that of "a bird in a gilded cage," a cage from which, at best, Stew can hope to fly; Deeds, by virtue of his fortune, is free to give away the cage, and to invite the whole world in to watch him do it.

This lack of exactitude is crucial to the way the echo trope functions in *Mr. Deeds,* especially as that trope invokes an element of cinematic self-consciousness. In short, an echo is a "return" of sound, a sound sent out, projected, that then comes back after an interval, sometimes in ways that the sender can hope to harmonize with by (as it were) re-sounding. Something else that threatens to come back differently, after an interval, is "the repressed." In which case I am led to say that the self-consciousness of *Mr. Deeds Goes to Town* is evidenced by a species of "muteness" that finally must be seen as a cover story, a means of denying some *other* story, but another story so central to the mind of its creator that it cannot help but return, like an echo. I want to postpone, for the moment, the question of Longfellow's "other story." But Capra's crucial other story in *Mr. Deeds* is clearly *American Madness*.

Any number of local details could be cited to establish the aptness of the *Madness–Deeds* analogy, from the way the architectural motifs of the *Deeds* courtroom, for example, rather strikingly replicate the "X" motif of the doors to Tom Dickson's Union National Bank in *American Madness,* to the way certain casting decisions help to replicate the power relations between antagonists and the hero in each film; the chair of Dickson's board of directors is played by the same actor who depicts the acting-chair of the opera board in *Deeds,* while another member of Dickson's board is the "Budington" of the "3 Cs and the little B" law firm aligned against Longfellow Deeds in the later movie. Moreover, at the macro or thematic level, there is the whole issue of sanity – with its various *American Madness* cognates: crazy, mad, silly, "I lost my head" – that is explored at considerable depth in both films. As the chair of Dickson's board puts it, upon deciding to help stop the bank run by depositing his own funds, "If everybody's going crazy I'll go crazy too."

What echoes most profoundly from the earlier film to the later, however, is a kind of subtextual logic linking a number of key scenes: of a man refusing to answer questions under interrogation despite the testimony of a dotty old lady, of a man telephoning a woman to ask for some truth of her identity, of a man with a hidden gun, of a man posed mutely against a window while someone pleads with him to shrug off despair and take on his accusers and responsibilities. Of course, there are (at least) two "mutes," if you will, in *American Madness,* and the relation of one silence to the next is nearly that of cause to effect; Matt Brown refuses to tell the police where he was at the time of the robbery and murder to avoid revealing that he had seen Mrs. Dickson with Cyril Cluett at the latter's apartment, while Dickson's suicidal silence upon learning something like the truth from Cluett confirms Brown's (and Dickson's) painfully conventional assumption about the nature and dynamics of (in)fidelity: It is the woman's fault and the man who suffers. Most Capra critics, rather tellingly, avoid discussing the sexual subplots of *American Madness* in their rush to connect Dickson's banking philosophy – a liberal one of keeping money in circulation by making loans on the basis of character rather than hard collateral – to Capra's reputedly populist ideology. What such a view of *American Madness* studiously ignores is a deep link between the bank run and the film's female characters, a link quite exceeding in interest the fairly explicit thematic link between having "faith" in one's friends and depositors as well as a "faithful" wife.

Two aspects of *American Madness* point to a larger view of the "economy" of human relationships than is typically attributed under the populism rubric. One involves the weak "security" of the line between sane and crazy as epitomized in an implicit comparison (almost to the point of equation) between the board of directors and Dude Finley's gangsters. The analogy is first suggested by the way each group of characters is introduced; in each case female secretaries on an upper level comment upon their entrance, and each sequence features a conspicuously mobile down-angle shot that "leads" the men deeper into the space of the bank. Moreover, the analogy is confirmed by cross-cutting: While Dickson and the board debate the value of liquidity and collateral – Dickson boasts that he has never lost money, has always been 100 percent right – Finley pushes Cluett to pay up *his* losses while Cluett asserts he was crazy to gamble, a remark that comes back to haunt the film when, toward the end, Dickson describes his last-second depositors as bucking ten to one odds as a way of encouraging his board members to get similarly crazy. All of which I read as quietly linking male-typical brutality (gangsters, the robbery-and-murder sequence) to the "normal" conditions of the economy.

The other strain of *American Madness* that argues against a simplistically populist reading of its economic aspect is the role that women play in the bank-run plot. Most obvious here is the female aspect of the rumor mill. Though men figure prominently in the spread-the-word montage sequence, it *begins* with the bank's ditzy-blonde telephone operator who seems to lack meaningful work of any sort; about all we see her do is gossip with sister operators. However, in some ways the real beginning of the bank run is the robbery, an oddly essential part of which involves Cluett's efforts to establish an alibi with Mrs. Dickson, who winds up going out with Cluett when her forgetful husband stands her up. (The "oddity" here involves the way the alibi scenes effectively replace the event of the robbery itself, of which we only see the concluding moments.) Indeed, the only time a version of the word "American" is heard in the film is when Phyllis Dickson jokingly asserts that Cluett deserves a medal as "America's comfort to misunderstood wives."

The misunderstanding in question is Dickson's. In Dickson's first scene he promises Phyllis (over the phone) that he has not forgotten the plans she has made for that evening, plans that she later tells Cluett she has been making for months, as if that were all she had to do. Dickson promptly forgets, and in his wife's presence. When she reminds him, he apologizes and urges her to go out with the girls for the night, promising to take her out the following evening for dinner and dancing. No sooner is the promise made than Dickson sits down at his desk, Samson walks in with some papers, and Dickson begins a rat-a-tat tirade about people who "can't make up their minds," telling Samson to set up a contract signing for the following evening, the evening he has just promised to Phyllis. Capra cuts to a close-up of a thunderstruck Phyllis as her husband's voice continues over, at which point the image fades to black, as it will some moments later over the long-shot of the fallen bank guard at the end of the holdup sequence, as if Phyllis and the watchman were equally ghosts fated to haunt the world of the film.

What is mad about this America is the way it literally forgets its women, leaving them, as Phyllis Dickson remarks, without "any part" in life's drama. The marginality of women is repeatedly and pointedly observed during the film's climactic bank-run sequence, in the figure of the woman who is last seen sinking to the floor under the rush of customers, for example, or in the old lady who keeps repeating that her husband's life insurance money is at risk, all that stands between her and the "old ladies home." Indeed, *American Madness* almost forgets itself on this account when Phyllis pleads with Dickson to go back out and fight for the bank and the depositors. Instead of holding on the conversation of husband and wife Capra cuts away to the hubbub on the bank floor, thus cutting out whatever logic Phyllis uses to get from the claim that Dickson had made her feel like "an outsider" to her subsequent urging that there is something "more important" than their marriage. As most critics understand *American Madness,* Tom Dickson is Capra's resident surrogate in the film, the master of ceremonies whose institutional ease and skill are the echo of Capra's. On my reading, Capra's deeper affinity is with Phyllis Dickson, as someone who throws parties nobody attends, as someone who senses that her efforts at establishing a community of appreciation are of secondary value by contrast with a primary (primarily male) world of power and privilege, as someone who haunts the world, as if barely present in it or to it.

Questions of gender and repression, we can at long last see, are thus common to discussions of *Mr. Deeds* and its intertexts whether those discussions begin from the provenance of genre theory or focus more explicitly on questions of film style. Gehring effectively represses the feminine by declaring *Deeds* a populist comedy, which comes near to equating political wisdom and masculinity. Harvey condemns the politics of *Mr. Deeds* (and Mr. Deeds) as presupposing the superiority of the self-consciously sentimental Capra hero over the sophisticated screwball heroine played by Jean

Arthur, as if Capra's task in *Mr. Deeds* were exactly a "repression" of the screwball feminine that Capra had given surprising expression to in *It Happened One Night.* Even at the stylistic level, the narrational self-consciousness of *Mr. Deeds Goes to Town* is evidenced primarily by practices or tokens of repression, by the repression of the stylistic excessiveness that marks so many of Capra's pre- and post-*Deeds* films, by taking as the film's primary intertext a film that few viewers could be expected to have seen or well remembered and a film (moreover) that takes as *its* subtext the question of the marginality of women. James Harvey's claim that *Mr. Deeds Goes to Town* is the first of Capra's self-conscious films and is typical (in this) of those that follow is thus deeply flawed. The theatrical trope that typifies films both before and after *Deeds* (e.g., *The Miracle Woman, State of the Union*) gives the lie to the general applicability of Harvey's understanding. His chapter on Capra is nevertheless useful for alerting us to the peculiar "partiality" of the reflexive dimension of *Mr. Deeds,* the sense in which its mode of self-consciousness is primarily a matter of "un-consciousness."

I spoke earlier of echo and the way echo requires an interval, a difference, a distance. I also spoke of *American Madness* as being the "other" story that *Mr. Deeds Goes to Town* metaphorically represses and (in repressing) expresses, and of Mr. Deeds as being, in a way, an echo of Frank Capra. At least one difference between Capra and Deeds is that Deeds is far less conscious of his other than Capra. Capra's other story is quite aptly and strategically remembered. The flurry of scenes derived from *American Madness* comes in a sudden burst in *Mr. Deeds* beginning with Longfellow's phone call to Mary/Babe asking her to tell the truth, just as Dickson had asked his wife her whereabouts of the night before; in both cases the form of the question is such that truth is as much repressed as requested. We then get the scene of the almost suicidal gun-toting farmer invading the mansion, followed quickly by the run on Longfellow's fortune and then his subsequent arrest culminating in his Dickson-like silence at the window of his guarded hospital room.

In evoking various *American Madness* scenes as the "unconscious" of *Mr. Deeds* I mean to capture the sense in which they lie behind or beneath the surface events of the later film, *not* that Capra was unaware of his actions in replicating shots and situations from one film to the next. In the case of Longfellow Deeds, however, the unconscious is both something remembered, as from the past, and newly acknowledged, within the present.

What Deeds is explicitly unconscious of is Babe Bennett, an unconsciousness effected in part by his own skeptical gesture of denial. What I take Deeds to be implicitly unconscious of – what Babe Bennett becomes a figure for – is the feminine side of himself, his own "repressed femininity." On such a reading the genre distinction between populist and screwball quickly collapses for depending on overly strict gender distinctions, and the question of the condescending falsity of Longfellow's self-consciousness will have a new answer, especially so as Longfellow's courtroom victory will be seen as the triumph of his feminine side, not a triumph *over* the feminine as figured by Babe Bennett.

The path to this view of Mr. Deeds begins (began for me) in Stanley Cavell's more recent work on film genre where *Mr. Deeds* is taken as exemplifying certain aspects of "What Photography Calls Thinking" and the kind of "Romance" (and marriage) for which Cavell is willing publicly to offer "Two Cheers" (rather than three).[22] What Cavell says specifically about *Deeds* is fairly abbreviated, and is concerned almost exclusively with the courtroom sequence. At issue (for Cavell) is *why* Deeds finally decides to speak up, what role the camera plays in that decision and his subsequent demonstration of sanity, and how we are to understand Deeds's prior muteness, especially as it aligns him with the suffering heroines of melodrama and therefore (romantically) with Babe Bennett. What Cavell says on these accounts is said against a far larger background, however, portions of which I have already sketched out, a story of skeptical doubt about the world's very existence, as of a dream one might hope or fear to awaken from, of which Descartes's famous "I think, I am" proof of existence (the *cogito*) took itself to be the antidote, and of which cinema, on Cavell's reading of it as "a moving image of skepticism" by which our senses "are satisfied of reality while reality does not exist," is taken as the perversely perfect embodiment, a world present to me while I am not present to it, a world existing apart, therefore, from my agreements or attunements and thus (consolingly) beyond the reach of my responsibility.[23]

Three clauses of that story are especially resonant when considered in relation to *Mr. Deeds Goes to Town*. The first of these involves Cavell's picture of the skeptic as "madman," as someone literally angry with the world, whose "self-consuming disappointment" with language's inability to certify the connection of self to world seeks "world-consuming revenge."[24] Given Cavell's claim that cinema is "the moving image of skepticism," and his frequent description of skepticism as the wish to exist ''outside language games'' and hence outside ''the social as such,'' I find myself thinking of Longfellow Deeds as allegorizing cinema's skeptical provenance; he literally steps outside language games by refusing to defend himself and therefore helps sustain the picture of himself as a madman.[25] This connection between Longfellow's anger at the world and his denial of language is periodically (parodistically) made manifest by his habit of punching his interlocutors in the kisser, as if to knock the very words from their mouths. I also take another of Cavell's descriptions of the skeptic, as someone fated to ''haunt the world'' he has withdrawn from, as marking a route to therapy, at least to the extent that the description aligns Deeds with the (as yet) uncreated women of remarriage comedy and also with the voiceless women of melodrama, all of whom, in some sense, haunt the world (of men).[26]

A second clause in Cavell's recounting of the skeptical problematic involves his concept of ''inheritance'' as a mode of interpretation or conversation. Cavell elaborates a version of this concept as it pertains to film genre in *Pursuits of Happiness.* ''The idea is that the members of a genre share the inheritance of certain conditions, procedures and subjects and goals of composition, and that in primary art each member of such a genre represents a study of these conditions, something I think of as bearing the responsibility of the inheritance.''[27] Part of the inheritance remarriage comedy is heir to and interprets is Shakespeare's *The Winter's Tale,* which Cavell has repeatedly declared ''the greatest of the structures of remarriage'' and has repeatedly construed as enacting the skeptical problematic under the sign of jealousy and in the form of a world-consuming doubt on the part of Leontes as to whether a nearly born child is his.[28] Listen now to some passages from Cavell's discussion of Emerson's ''Self-Reliance'': ''First, language is an inheritance. Words are before I am; they are common.'' ''Writing . . . is an expression of the proof of saying 'I,' hence the claim that writing is a matter, say the decision, of life and death, and that what this comes to is the inheriting of language, an owning of words, which does not remove them from circulation but rather returns them, as to life.''[29] (The echoes of *The Winter's Tale* here – of entities owned or disowned, rejected or acknowledged; of beings returned to life, as if from death – indicate something of the continuity in Cavell's range of interests and examples.)

If skepticism, on Cavell's accounting, amounts to a refusal of language, a refusal of human connection and attunement, it makes considerable Cavellian sense that remarriage comedy would virtually "demand" portrayals of "philosophical conversation" in which "questions of human creation . . . and the battle between men and women for recognition of one another . . . are given expression."[30] Later in *Pursuits of Happiness* Cavell will use similar terms to describe the as-if marriage of Peter and Ellie in *It Happened One Night:* "In those films talking together is fully and plainly being together, a mode of association, a form of life, and I would like to say that in these films the central pair are learning to speak the same language."[31] A related point is that the dialogue that results, for all its depth and poetry, tends to pass "without notice, as unnoticeably trivial." "These film words thus declare their mimesis of ordinary words, words in daily conversation."[32] We have already noted how the dialogue of *Mr. Deeds Goes to Town* entails a systematic examination of its central terms, an examination barely remarked upon in the extensive critical literature. That this examination amounts to an instance of "ordinary language philosophy" is a claim fully warranted by this neglect. Further confirmation (if needed) comes from the fact that "bearing the responsibility of an inheritance" is exactly what Mr. Deeds *does* when he goes to town. Moreover, he finally "bears" that responsibility by "owning words" and "returning" them to "circulation." When he finally decides to speak (in concluding another fable of jealousy and disputed patrimony) he speaks his "two-cents worth," as if words were common and commonly affordable coin, and the effect of his rhetoric is exactly to assert a commonality of human behavior, something everybody does, Deeds calls it "thinking," though the signs of thought vary in particular cases: O-filling, doodling, ear pulling, nail biting, eye twitching, tuba playing, and so forth.

Indeed, as Deeds words the thought world, naming its signs, Capra (as Cavell elaborates) *shows* the world, and shows it explicitly *to us* in a series of close-ups obviously unavailable to (not needed by) Longfellow's on-screen audience. Indeed, this "alignment" of Deeds and Capra's camera in the courtroom sequence, apart from confirming their status as echoes of each other, puts in some perspective Capra's decision to avoid stylistic excess in *Mr. Deeds,* as if he too wanted to speak (at least this time) in cinematic "common coin." (No wonder that a critical tradition that takes *Deeds* as its thematic and stylistic benchmark has proven so inadequate to Capra's accomplishment!)

A third significant clause of the skeptical problematic I want to mark in passing involves Cavell's various inflections of the concept of "romance."

In "Two Cheers for Romance" Cavell juxtaposes his way of taking and using romance with that often employed in feminist critiques of the institution of "romantic marriage," where romance refers to a kind of passional excitement and plenitude for which legal matrimony (and the woman's, though not the man's, subsequent "confinement to domesticity") is the asking price.[33] We might call this a sociological understanding of romance. Cavell's understanding of romance is simultaneously philosophical and literary. Philosophically, "the romantic" refers on Emersonian grounds to "the continued search for a new intimacy in the self's relation to its world" – a relation skepticism effectively denies in its disappointed desiring, and which Descartes's speaking of the phrase "I think, I am" undertakes to restore by asserting his own existence to the world, hence the world's (God's) to him.[34] Literarily, romance refers to a specific generic tradition wherein marriage stands as an image of personal and social renewal. Cavell offers only "Two Cheers for Romance" because the genre of remarriage comedy effectively acknowledges the shortcomings of legal marriage – by showing, among other things, that sexuality and desire are *not* identical (or else the first marriage would be marriage enough), and that the societies in which such remarriages take place are largely incapable of understanding or sponsoring the desires – for reciprocity, for mutual autonomy, for conversation – that motivate them. That "Two Cheers" are well deserved, however, follows from the fact that remarriage on Cavell's understanding provides a modern trope or version of Descartes's *cogito,* one that proves simultaneously the existence of each partner to the other and hence the (potential) existence of "the social as such," a place where one cannot go *alone.*

In Chapter 2, on *Forbidden,* I alluded to Cavell's interpretation of Shakespeare's *Antony and Cleopatra* as a precursor of remarriage comedy, its moral being "that no one any longer knows what marriage is, what constitutes this central, specific bond of union, as if it is up to each individual pair to invent this for themselves."[35] The philosophical element of the story is evident in Cavell's claim that "the invention of marriage *is* [Cleopatra's] response to Antony's abandonment [of the world]; it is a return of the world through the gift of herself, by becoming, presenting herself as, whatever constitutes the world."[36] The general relevance of all this to Capra is evident in the way that this description applies equally well to the second auto-camp scene in *It Happened One Night,* where a confessedly skeptical and disappointed Peter offers up an almost literally fantastic picture of a world where "you and the moon and the water all become one" as a way of denying the reality of love, and of a woman "that's real, somebody that's alive." To which picture Ellie responds by offering herself as token of that world and its reality (her offer silently underscored by Capra's marked shift to soft focus, which shows Ellie literally *as one* with, by evoking, the dreamily fantastic presentation of the preceding crossing-of-the-stream sequence, where Peter and Ellie and the moon and the water *are* shown *as one*).

The specific relevance of these chained asides on philosophy and genre to *Mr. Deeds* involves an element of role reversal or bisexuality that can be traced from *Antony and Cleopatra* through *It Happened One Night* to *Mr. Deeds*. Various characters in Shakespeare's play comment on the exchanges of identity between Antony and Cleopatra, the way Antony "is not more manlike/ Than Cleopatra," nor she "More womanly than he."[37] Similarly, though Ellie's transgression of the wall of Jericho in the second auto-camp scene of *It Happened One Night* announces her status as the woman of Peter's dream, she does so dressed in his pajamas, implicitly the attacking trumpet-blowing Israelite, while he reclines on his bed, hands behind his head, elbows out, like an actress in a glamour pose; it is Peter, moreover, who is assigned to play the Cinderella role, fleeing the ball in the dead of night, and it is Peter, in the second scene, who uses the leftmost bed, which Ellie had claimed in the first auto-camp scene.

Mr. Deeds, in a way, doubles or echoes this reversal; in the later film it is the man who is the heir(ess), the woman who is the reporter on the story. Beyond that, on Cavell's reading, an important consequence of Longfellow's courtroom dissertation on thinking is to show that the "I think, I am" proof of existence has a passive or silently feminine side: Thought (hence existence) reveals itself to sight, to the camera, whether the thinker wills it or no, voices it or no. Additional consequences follow:

1. Even in his silence Deeds effectively speaks (so the *real* question is why he agrees to attend the hearing *at all,* if the point is simply a matter of not cooperating).
2. *When* he speaks his two-cents worth aloud, Longfellow is effectively acknowledging his kinship with Babe Bennett, who has, as it were, lent him her voice at the hearing by speaking on his behalf.

Cavell says that Deeds has stopped running from his desire, as Babe (in admitting her love for Deeds) has stopped running from hers. For each, the shoe or slipper fits. More philosophically, also more literally, we can say that Deeds's recovery of voice reverses (as from passive to active) the proof of existence. His running away from Babe – most spectacularly after *she* reads *his* poem aloud – denies her full existence by denying her a visible "other," hence denying her the world, someone to whom she is visible. Yet Longfellow's poem, wherein Deeds portrays himself as "handcuffed and speechless" in Babe's "presence divine," anticipates the courtroom scene by declaring *his* silence to be the source of *her* otherworldliness. Indeed, his implicit refusal to hear her out over the phone, or over lunch, expresses not only his anger and disappointment but a desire that she had not told him the truth, had not spoken at all, had remained an imaginary being, a "damsel in distress." (Here is where Longfellow's blindness to Babe's real identity despite the evidence of her stories finds its placement.) By speaking up in court Longfellow thus breaks the skeptical spell, accepting her as (in the words of Peter Warne) somebody "that's real, somebody that's alive."

I suppose no more than Cavell that a reading of *Mr. Deeds Goes to Town* as exemplifying or inheriting the goals and procedures of ordinary language philosophy is anything but controversial. That the film *is* deeply and abidingly concerned with language is beyond doubting; nor is much imagination required to see its concern with sanity, with strangeness, with abnormality, as synonymous with a concern for what is "ordinary" to human beings and behaviors. In the present context I want to rephrase the latter concern as applying to questions of gender, on the understanding that it is an essential feature of remarriage comedy "to leave ambiguous the question whether the man or the woman is the active or passive partner, whether indeed active and passive are apt characterizations of the difference between male and female, or whether indeed we know satisfactorily how to think about the difference between male and female."[38] One reason that "there can in general be no new social reconciliation" in remarriage comedy (by contrast with classical comedy) is that the society depicted typically "does not regard the difference between men and women as the topic of metaphysical argument [call this philosophy]; it takes itself to know what the difference means."[39] Whether or not *Mr. Deeds* can be read as philosophically engaged will depend on the reader's willingness to engage the question of gender or difference philosophically.

What I have said on these accounts thus far is pretty sketchy beyond saying that Cavell's work on film genre got me started. Any number of local moments in *Mr. Deeds* can be cited to advance the claim that Longfellow Deeds has a feminine aspect. Cavell cites Cooper's legendary "beauty" as a property explored in Capra's oddly posed shot of Deeds lolling on his bed while talking to Babe; we see a similar shot of Loretta Young (as Gallagher, "one of the boys") in *Platinum Blonde*. Here I would enlist the movie's several Christ references (Deeds is the son of Joseph and Mary Deeds), on the premise that (to quote Luce Irigaray again) Christ is the "most feminine of all men."[40] Equally relevant here is the fact that Deeds inherits his uncle's fortune via the maternal line of descent; Semple was his mother's maiden name. Longfellow is wont (on Babe's report) to speak of carrying his someday bride over a honeymoon threshold; the only person carried across a threshold in the course of the film is Longfellow. There is also the imaginary girlfriend of Longfellow's Mandrake Falls boyhood, with whom he would take long walks in the woods. In discussing her with Babe, Longfellow describes his motive as a matter of having "always wanted someone to talk to"; one of the charges leveled against him by the Faulkner sisters is that he always talked to himself. I take the self to whom he was always talking to be this feminine self, the feminine side of his being. Perhaps Babe's description of Longfellow as a "Cinderella Man" is better understood as an intuitive insight on her part than as a smart-alecky put-down.

To say that Deeds has a feminine self is one thing; to say that Babe Bennett *is* that self is another, though substantiating that claim would further confirm the initial premise. Here is the place to note the degree to which – and in ways perhaps *never* fully known to Deeds – Babe and Longfellow echo each other. Each, on our first view, is seen playing with an object identifiable as a children's toy; the tuba mouthpiece Deeds has been awaiting for weeks because local kids keep swiping them for bean shooters, the piece of rope with which Babe plays while her editor berates his staff for fumbling the Deeds story. Each is a writer, and each traffics on demand in the common sentimental coin of the community in which he or she lives. Indeed, Babe's "Cinderella Man" headline, apart from raising the role-reversal issue, locates her tale or fantasy in a realm not far removed from that of Longfellow's imaginary girl. Each experiences a sudden piece of good fortune – Longfellow's inheritance, Babe's Pulitzer Prize – and for each good fortune leads to a species of muteness or silence. In Longfellow's case the muteness comes on gradually, a matter of fending off "moochers" until the greatest moocher of all, John Cedar, decides to strike and shut Longfellow up for good. In Babe's case there is her silence at the staff meeting to account for, along with the fact that she had not *already* gotten the goods on Deeds; in fact, it takes the promise of a vacation, a break from writing, to get her moving at all. Longfellow and Babe are both forced to change residences – Deeds from Mandrake Falls to the Semple mansion, Babe from her own flat (which we never see; her newspaper office seems as much of a home as she has) to Mabel Dawson's. Moreover, each at a crucial juncture seeks to flee the city: Babe to avoid hurting Deeds any further, Deeds to avoid further hurt after Cobb breaks the news that Mary Dawson is in fact Babe Bennett. Both of these latter moments are marked, we should note, by similar shots, of Deeds or Babe looking disconsolately out a window.

The thought of Babe as Longfellow's other dawned on me past doubting when I connected two scenes repeatedly cited in discussions of *Mr. Deeds,* the courtroom scene and the farmer scene. At issue here is a certain asymmetry of cause and effect. It is commonly agreed that the turning point in the trial is Babe's confession of love for Deeds – despite the fact that Deeds refrains from speaking his two-cents worth until after several other parties (Cobb, MacWade, various farmers) join in the chorus. The impression is strong, on the basis of Cooper's expression in response to Babe's admission, that Longfellow's mind is made up as soon as Babe speaks the truth, and that his subsequent delay is a matter of wonder and curiosity. However, it was *not* Babe's truth speaking earlier that had caused him to lose hope and voice; he was already planning to return to Mandrake Falls, had long ago determined to give away his fortune, *before* Cobb spilled the Babe Bennett beans and the farmer invaded the mansion. Indeed, the straw that breaks his back is not Babe's betrayal but Cedar's legal action alleging insanity. So why does Babe's confession of love turn Deeds around?

Before answering that question let me note two elements of the farmer scene that typically go unremarked. One of these is the farmer's characterization – offered as if in explanation of his own crazy actions – of his wife, as someone who says "everything is going to be all right." I take it that Deeds is more or less saying this, on a grand scale, in his homesteading scheme, an interpretation confirmed during the subsequent run-on-the-mansion sequence when Deeds asks an applicant if he is a farmer, to which the man replies "Yes, mam." The other overlooked element of the farmer scene involves its echo of an earlier scene. Before Cobb tells Longfellow who Mary is, Deeds hustles about the mansion checking on preparations for lunch. At one point he sits down at the table to check the sight lines and asks one of his staff to sit in the place set for Babe. The man does so, and Deeds instructs him to lean forward while leaning forward himself; the two men wind up as mirror images of each other, Deeds with his right elbow on the table, the butler with his left elbow similarly anchored. I take the whole episode in its silent elusiveness to be a parable of similarity and difference, and implicitly of sexual difference. (The point is reinforced by one of Capra's most outrageous mismatches. In the establishing shot, after Deeds first sits down, he has his pipe in his right hand. In the subsequent medium-shot he has his pipe in his left hand. As if there were really two ''sides'' to Longfellow Deeds?) When Longfellow subsequently sits down to watch the farmer eat, the farmer sits in Mary's place – but Deeds adopts the same elbow-on-the-table pose as in the earlier scene, as if he too were in the wife position.

What triggers Longfellow's silence, I now want to say, is the complete and legally sanctioned denial of his ''feminine'' capacity for nurturance, in which light Cavell's various hints to the effect that Deeds in his silence is related to the unknown women of melodrama acquire considerable explanatory force. Indeed, the ''isolated heroine'' of melodrama in this case is Longfellow Deeds, and the isolation is less a function of ignorance on the part of some representative male (Grover in Capra's *Forbidden,* for instance, or Jerry in Irving Rapper's *Now, Voyager*) than of an institutionalized ''maleness'' that locks Longfellow away and puts him on trial. Moreover, what saves the *Mr. Deeds* day is *not* the kind of ''meet and cheerful'' conversation that marks remarriage comedy; nearly every exchange of words between Deeds and Babe is colored by hurt or nostalgia or longing. Rather, what returns Longfellow to life is the fact that Babe acknowledges her love in public, a gesture that Cedar ironically characterizes as *her* acknowledgment of Longfellow's weakness (''Why shouldn't she defend him? It's a tribute to American womanhood, an instinct to defend the weak''). Babe plays the educator role typically played by the male in remarriage comedy, and the instruction she provides is an object lesson in unknownness. What she proves beyond the shadow of all doubt is that she was unknown to Deeds. In saying that her example helps return Longfellow to life, to words, I further interpret her instruction as a lesson in admitting to one's vulnerability, one's ''womanhood.'' She says that Longfellow's silence follows from the fact that he had been hurt. What she demonstrates in her passion is that one can hurt and speak at the same time.

By speaking in response, Deeds acknowledges *her* reality and his own as well. Together they speak "the social as such," the dream of a common language in which one's otherness and vulnerability are publicly recognized as a fully sufficient proof of human existence.

Among the many promissory notes I have written there are two I feel compelled to expand upon by way (in lieu) of conclusion, one involving the question of Longfellow's presence in the courtroom *at all,* the second having to do with the film's political dimension. I take the former question as relating to James Harvey's charge that Cooper (and Capra) are insufferably and condescendingly self-conscious in their display of kindness and generosity, as if Cooper's silence in the courtroom were a show of kindness somehow gone crazy in its excess, as if Capra and Cooper were really (unconsciously) out to punish the (on- and off-screen) audience for lacking a like measure of generosity. On my view there is nothing unconscious about it – beyond the (obviously significant) fact that nothing is said. Rather, I take Longfellow's silent presence as an overt challenge to the "linguistic sanity" of the culture he inhabits. Babe tells the court that Longfellow's words had been "twisted." I understand his silence accordingly to be claiming that the culture has twisted its words to death, past recovery. I take his presence thus to be a form of revenge and rebuke. What he seeks is the skeptic's reassurance that language really *is* untrustworthy; that he needs reassurance indicates that he does not really believe it.

We can say that the self of which Longfellow Deeds is self-conscious is that of a ghost haunting the world, a skeptic, a film viewer, a woman. We can describe the action of the film as an allegory of public acknowledgment that renders that ghost temporarily real. Most of Capra's pre-*Deeds* films, as we have seen, are deeply political in their implications. Indeed, *American Madness* provided lengthy and specific discussions of economic theory to an audience obviously alive to the issues. However, those discussions go on, literally, behind the closed doors of the bank's boardroom. What is lacking in *American Madness,* though not in *Mr. Deeds,* is the depiction of an overtly *public* discussion of those issues. Of course, *as depicted* the issues in *Mr. Deeds* are somewhat less public; Deeds never claims that his giveaway scheme has implications for public policy. However, by the kind of metaphoric logic invoked by such as Durgnat and Phelps, it is clear that the sanity on trial in the case of Longfellow Deeds is less Longfellow's than that of the culture at large, hence the enthusiastic reception of the film by left-wing journalists. Indeed, what seemed most astonishing to those initial reviewers was less the overt outcome of the film or the hearing than the mere fact that the farmer (and his cohorts) appeared *at all,* were given a voice, "speaking the language of workers, saying the things workers all over the country say."[41] What renders this culture crazy, what twists its words, we might say, is a species of deafness. Capra is accordingly to be praised as much for listening as for saying something.

A voice to which that culture continues for the most part to be deaf is the feminine voice that echoes across the movie. This is true in the obvious sense that it has taken over fifty years for Capra critics to hear the film differently, to see that Babe Bennett, for example, is as central to the film as Longfellow Deeds, is as clearly Capra's surrogate (contra Carney) as Deeds himself. As token of that deafness I cite the film's true conclusion, which critics hardly ever touch upon, and which is itself a parable of female silence and isolation. After Deeds is declared the sanest man ever to enter the courtroom, he is carried in triumph out of the room, though Capra's camera dwells chiefly on his discomfort and on Babe's displacement, her exclusion from the celebration.[42] After a wipe cut we return to a long-shot of the courtroom, empty except for three women, Babe Bennett and the two (whispering) Faulkner sisters. A hubbub is heard in the hallway outside, and Deeds, his clothes ripped, dashes into the courtroom, closing the doors behind him as if to keep his pursuers at bay. He picks up Babe, as if preparing to carry her over some threshold. In so doing he repeats and revises his first moment with her, when he helped her up off the sidewalk after she "fainted" outside the Semple mansion. Cavell understands this moment as evidence of the film's relationship to remarriage comedy. He also notes how the honeymoon posture of Babe and Deeds depicts them as in search of a suitable threshold, "of some inner place they have to discover together."[43] The point I would make is that the only visible threshold – standing between Babe and Deeds and the world at large – is blocked by a mass of men. I think of them as Capra critics, so intent on praising Longfellow's immediate victory that they overlook its deeper significance. I take it that Capra's deeper loyalties are fully exhibited by the fact that his camera dwells, as if forever, on the female side of the line. "Still pixilated."

CHAPTER IV
Glimpsing the Eternal
Lost Horizon

Of the many incidents recounted in *The Name above the Title* perhaps none is more prophetic of the current state of Capra studies than the story Capra tells of the production of *Lost Horizon,* which culminates in a scene where Capra, distraught after a disastrous preview showing of a three-hour version of the film, rushes into the Columbia cutting rooms and orders Gene Havlick "to take the main title from the beginning of the *first* reel of the picture and splice it onto the beginning of the *third* reel."[1] At issue, finally, is the essentially antagonistic relationship between Capra and (most of) his critics, by contrast with the far happier relationship he has enjoyed with audiences over the years. On Capra's understanding, ironically, it was the hostile preview audience that effectively saved the film: "One small, seemingly insignificant change had turned an unreleasable, unshowable picture into the *Lost Horizon* that was welcomed by the world; a picture about which thousands of fans were to later say in their letters: 'I have seen it as many as twenty times.' "[2]

The idea of "salvation" can be taken quite literally here, not only by reference to the film's initial commercial fortunes, but also in the sense that the 1971 publication of Capra's autobiography prompted a campaign, begun in 1974 under the auspices of the American Film Institute, to restore *Lost Horizon* to its original (road-show) running time.[3] It is ironic that a film *about* preservation and restoration – it is Father Perrault's avowed intent that Shangri-La will serve as an archive to which the world can turn to recover the beauty of its culture after indulging in an "orgy of greed and brutality" – should thus become such a famous example *of* preservation and restoration. It is more ironic yet that the result is a film decisively "unlike" any version that audiences were likely to have seen from the time of *Lost Horizon*'s original road-show release in 1937 through each of the various "edited" versions that Columbia Pictures (and numerous television stations) successively exhibited over the years.

Most Americans in 1937 saw a version that ran nearly 117 minutes, cut down from the 132-minute version shown on the film's initial release in New York and Los Angeles. The restored version approximates the latter, but only by recourse to a mix of footage from various 35mm and 16mm prints and footage "made up" via freeze frames and production stills to fill out the seven-minute difference between an original sound track and the best available combination of image tracks. The result is a kind of palimpsest that tempts us to imagine some earlier, some more perfect version that, like a "lost horizon," we can never quite glimpse, or glimpse beyond. By the same token, the marks of "erasure" are repeatedly foregrounded and in such a way as to make the historical "process" that yielded the present version of the film a constant presence and issue. In part because I am interested in the process by which Capra has made himself known, partly also because the AFI-restoration print is likely (and deserves) to become the standard version of the film for the foreseeable future, the present discussion takes the restored print as its text.

The oddly uncalled-for moral Capra draws from his account of the production of *Lost Horizon* has to do with the validity of film criticism, though no working film critic was involved in the decision to "Burn the First Two Reels" (as Capra entitles his chapter on the film). Capra nevertheless draws the conclusion that "big-time film critics are wrong in insisting they view a film alone in private projection rooms" because "the audience is always right."[4] All of which is an instance (in Kenneth Burke's happy phrase) of "prophecy after the event"; though Capra appears to limit his frame of reference to the period before the release of *Lost Horizon,* it is clear that his bitterness over the film's critical reception lingered well into his retirement. Indeed, even among Capra's most eloquent latter-day advocates there are those – Charles Maland and Raymond Carney, for example – who are still unhappy with the film, an unhappiness Maland tries to explain and that Carney avoids acknowledging by repeatedly adducing the film in related contexts while never seriously discussing *Lost Horizon* for itself.

Is *Lost Horizon* merely a bad Capra film or is it a bad film altogether? For most the case against *Lost Horizon* involves a general sense that the film is altogether too atypical, too un-Capra. Unlike the films of Capra's populist trilogy, *Lost Horizon* is not set in America; its hero is not a visionary Jeffersonian simpleton whose naive idealism is tested by powers of greed and corruption but finally vindicated with the democratic assistance of the "little people"; its production is not characterized by an economy of means calling forth Capra's legendary flair for inspired improvisation and the down-home symbolism of doughnut dunking and tuba playing but is, rather, an upscale affair involving elaborate sets and a mellifluous orchestral score. Most of all, especially by contrast with *Deeds* and *Smith* whose eponymous heroes endure elaborate pedagogical rituals of doubt and humiliation, *Lost Horizon* seems "dramatically flat." In the words of Charles Maland: "From the start, Conway is presented as a confident, serene man. When placed into Shangri-La, he has no reason to leave. Though absence of conflict may create a wonderful society, it's no way to construct a film."[5]

It is equally common, however, to find *Lost Horizon* an embarrassment for exactly the opposite reason – because it is in certain crucial respects *too* typical, the most openly fantastic instance of Capra's "fantasy of goodwill" formula. Like Capra's other films, writes Ellen Draper, *Lost Horizon* "celebrates an ideal of social purity; but it displaces that ideal into the remote mountains of Tibet, and offers us a chance to examine the assumptions on which Capra's democratic ideal is based." And once displaced, "Capra's vision of American independence and assertiveness . . . becomes a libertarian nightmare."[6] In the pungent language of Elliott Stein, Capra's Shangri-La

> is run as a benign dictatorship where Tibetans toil to permit lamas and guests the leisure to contemplate their own white navels. When the High Lama (Belgian) finally gets around to wheezing out his wisdom to his chosen (English) successor, it boils down to this: there would be no bread lines or labour trouble if the planet were one big John Doe Club ruled by a lamaocracy.[7]

As these various estimates of *Lost Horizon* well attest, the "typicality" question admits of no simple answer; Maland and Draper clearly share a (roughly populist) view of what "Capra" amounts to, yet its applicability to *Lost Horizon* is evidently troubled and troubling. If we ask how *Lost Horizon* fits into the Capra canon as it existed in 1937, a number of features (of the canon, of the film) stand out. Most contemporary commentators saw the film as a generic and stylistic experiment, obviously unlike *Mr. Deeds,* and unlike Columbia product generally in the generous budget Capra got Harry Cohn to devote to it.[8] However, to this point in his career Capra had undertaken little else *but* a series of generic and stylistic experiments

– among which we can include his male-buddy/special-effects action pictures (*Flight, Dirigible*), gangster films (*The Power of the Press, The Way of the Strong*), melodramas of various sorts (*The Younger Generation, The Miracle Woman*), protomodernist meditations on the status of art and artists (*Ladies of Leisure, Platinum Blonde*), romantic fairy-tale comedies (*Lady for a Day, It Happened One Night*), not to mention Capra's extraordinary habit of bringing various generic strains together in particular films, often in odd and productive ways (*Forbidden*).

Indeed, *Lost Horizon* is remarkably similar (as we will see) to *The Bitter Tea of General Yen,* and it shares a number of important features with *Mr. Deeds*. Moreover, *Deeds* and *Lost Horizon* were in various stages of production simultaneously; on some accounts (see Behlmer) it was the necessity of delaying photography on *Lost Horizon* to accommodate Ronald Colman's schedule that dictated the order of production and release, *not* some semiteleological sense that *Deeds* should have priority for being more truly ''Capra.'' Certainly *Deeds* would not have seemed paradigmatic until *Mr. Smith* was released in 1939.

The juxtaposition of *Bitter Tea, Mr. Deeds,* and *Lost Horizon* provides occasion for proposing a different prototype of the ''Capra story'' than that typically encountered under the populist fantasy of goodwill rubric. Considering Capra as a political populist almost inevitably places the emphasis on the (notoriously problematic) outcomes of his films, as if they were all best understood as realistic recipes for practical political action. In earlier chapters I have focused especially on Capra's abiding interest in language as a precondition for political thought, hence for political activity. Another way of characterizing this interest is by noting an almost ''anthropological'' strain in Capra, which has the effect of throwing emphasis onto the beginnings of his films.

The Capra story, we might say, often begins with some form of social rupture – a death, a revolution of some kind – that has the effect of transporting the Capra hero from a familiar role or position into a foreign environment, often epitomized by a palatial house of some sort, usually empty and cavernous except for ''native'' servants who do their best to indoctrinate the main character into his or her new (social) role. Often, however, the role is not altogether new; it represents an expansion or distortion of some social ideal the character already holds, and in ways that put that ideal to the test, a test the character or the ideal often fails, or comes near to, as the evangelical missionary enthusiasm of Megan Davis (her naive desire to "tame" bandit generals) gives way before the genuine charm and thoughtfulness and emotional courage of the general she finally encounters in *The Bitter Tea of General Yen.*[9]

Bitter Tea, Mr. Deeds, and *Lost Horizon* are thus all alike in beginning with some turmoil that results in something like a kidnapping; literally, in *Lost Horizon,* where transport is by airplane, almost literally in *Bitter Tea* and *Deeds* where Megan Davis and Longfellow Deeds each winds up on a train in the custody of people native to the eventual destination (Yen's summer palace, New York City). Indeed, in two of these three cases the journey is undertaken at night, while characters sleep; the world they wake up to seems never quite to lose its aura of dream work or fantasy, and the act of awakening, by the same token, is always potentially threatening, as of a forced return to some lesser reality. Furthermore, what is typically at stake is very rarely the social status quo; only in *Bitter Tea,* among the three films currently at hand, is there a genuine shift of political power, if only from one warlord to another. Rather, the emphasis tends to fall upon the *process* by which ideals and communities (if only a community of two) are formed, a process foregrounded precisely in the differences made evident in the clash between one culture, one dream, and another.

I have alluded to Capra's lingering unhappiness with the critical reception of *Lost Horizon.* Part of this unhappiness surely followed from the film's middling box-office fortunes relative to its extraordinary (for Columbia) production costs; it was not the spectacular bottom-line success Capra enjoyed with *Deeds* or, for that matter, with his succeeding film, *You Can't Take It with You,* both of which also earned Capra Academy Awards as best director. It is my considered (if admittedly speculative) opinion that Capra's deepest regrets followed from the failure of most critics – even those who had seen the full road-show print – to acknowledge the astonishing degree to which Capra and Riskin had reconfigured, to the point of reconceptualizing, James Hilton's immensely popular and (therefore) well-known novel. (The *Time* magazine critic was only a little more emphatic than most of his peers in declaring that Capra had "had the good judgment to leave the story almost exactly as it was written.")[10] Put another way, *Lost Horizon* represents one of Capra's most spectacular assertions of his one-man, one-film brand of film authorship; that it remains to this day so deeply misappreciated almost justifies Capra's legendary crankiness with his critics.

It is beyond the scope of this chapter to detail all the many changes Capra and Riskin introduced into Hilton's story; likewise beyond its scope is any attempt to annotate the many differences between the film's road-show print and its various cut-down versions (again, see Behlmer and Frank). Suffice it to say that it is the general (and deeply ironic) trend of the process of condensing the film to make it seem more and more like the Hilton original, less and less like the film Frank Capra directed. One change (or set of them) in particular is worth noting, however, for showing the extent of the Capra–Riskin "revision" of Hilton's tale, and also for the light it casts on the charges of racism entered by Elliott Stein. At issue is the basic motive and mechanism by which it is decided to kidnap Conway and his companions.

In Hilton's novel, as Father Perrault explains matters to Hugh Conway, the motive behind the kidnap plot is openly racial and, more significantly, *not* particularly focused on Conway himself. In response to Conway's question ("Why we four, out of all the rest of the world's inhabitants?") the High Lama explains his (as it were, archival) recruitment policy, based on the desire "to have with us people of various ages and representative of different periods." Unfortunately, the locals (Tibetans, Chinese) are "much less sensitive" to the restorative powers and (literally narcotic) processes of Shangri-La, few of them lasting much beyond 100 years of age. By contrast, the "best subjects, undoubtedly, are the Nordic and Latin races of Europe," though there is also the (racially based) hope that "Americans would be equally adaptable." Given a twenty-year hiatus in recruiting resulting from World War I and the Russian Revolution, which effectively halted all travel in the region of Shangri-La, and the recent deaths of several members of the lamasery, a crisis point was reached, to which one of the local fellows responded with "a novel idea" involving the new technology of air travel (in short: if Europeans will not come to you, go to them and fly them back).[11] Father Perrault's eventual decision to entrust the future of Shangri-La to Conway is only arrived at, then, long after the fact of abduction and as the result of innumerable lengthy interviews in which a crucial feature is Conway's "passionlessness" (as Father Perrault puts it), the aftermath (Conway explains) of his experiences during "1914–1918," a state of mind that allows him to accept his kidnapping with equanimity and makes him a perfectly suitable (and European) candidate to succeed Perrault as the High Lama; it is as much Shangri-La's isolation as its ostensible mission that Hilton's Conway finds attractive.[12]

In the Capra–Riskin *Lost Horizon,* by contrast, the impetus to shanghai Robert (versus Hugh) Conway to Shangri-La comes from two effectively different characters. One of these, most crucially, is Conway himself, no longer Hilton's passionless low-level functionary of the British Consular Service with "few close friends and no ambitions" but (as his brother George endlessly reminds people, Robert Conway among them) the inevitable choice as the next Foreign Secretary of England.[13] Conway is also, it turns out, a world-famous author of philosophical musings, as Father Perrault informs us in his first words to Conway (all Capra–Riskin, having no equivalent in Hilton). Perrault expresses his long-standing admiration for Conway, and not for Conway "the empire builder and public hero" but for the Conway who wrote that there "are moments in every man's life when he glimpses the eternal." That Conway is evidently a visionary of sorts matters more than a little here, as qualifying him to assume the leadership of Shangri-La. Equally crucial, however, is his "doubled" public profile, as diplomat and as author – which provides fictional allowance for the proposition that he is singled out not by virtue of his race but for his particular abilities and talents, which are well enough known to make such a choice possible, even from a great distance.

The second character who plays a crucial role in the plot to kidnap Conway, for whom there is barely precedent in Hilton, is a female inhabitant of the lamasery, Sondra Bizet (Jane Wyatt), whose duties include music instruction of the valley schoolchildren, and whose pastimes include pigeon keeping (shades of Jeff Smith!). On Perrault's report, she has read Conway's books, and has arrived at a "profound admiration" for him, an admiration in her case clearly involving sexual as well as philosophical motives. It is at her suggestion that Conway is brought to Shangri-La, though Perrault's report of this fact and a subsequent discussion of it between Sondra and Conway in her pigeon house (Fig. 12) – during which she elaborates on the emptiness she saw in his writings ("All I saw was a little boy whistling in the dark") – were both missing from the 117-minute general-release version of *Lost Horizon*.

An important consequence of the reader–writer relationship of Sondra and Conway is effectively to relocate the race issue. That Conway is required to act in racist ways is made evident during the Baskul sequence when he tells George not to let any natives aboard the rescue planes; that he personally regrets these actions is made clear (in another piece of the film missing from at least some of its versions) when Conway, slightly drunk and sleepy, asks George in midflight whether he has filled out a report on the evacuation and whether, in so doing, he mentioned, in addition to the ninety white people rescued, that they had "left 10,000 natives down there to be annihilated." One can thus readily assert that Capra and Riskin were well aware of the racist potential of Hilton's novel pointed to by Elliott Stein. Moreover, Capra had been equally as explicit about questions of racial and cultural prejudice in *The Bitter Tea of General Yen;* blindness about such matters is not the issue. Nevertheless, a version of the charge can still be urged, as the contrast with *Bitter Tea* makes evident.

In the earlier film we do get an explicit and explicitly sympathetic treatment of interracial sexual attraction and relationships. On the one hand this could be taken as evidence that the Anglo–French relationship of Conway and Sondra ought not to be understood chiefly in racial terms, though it seems unlikely Sondra would fall in love in absentia with, say, a Hindu mystic, given the generally western bias of Father Perrault's archival imagination, especially as realized in Capra's Frank Lloyd Wright version of Shangri-La. Still, it must also be noted that the cross-racial romance of Megan and Yen in *Bitter Tea* is, after all, enacted by two Caucasians, Barbara Stanwyck and Nils Asther. A worst-case interpretation of each film might take the obvious moments of racial broad-mindedness as a kind of cover story that only serves to hide a deeper sort of racial antagonism. Yen winds up dead, after all, as does Maria in *Lost Horizon;* the latter is depicted as Russian, but is portrayed in her last moments by an elderly Oriental woman. Is the only good Chinese a dead Chinese? Is the attraction of Shangri-La, in other words, its unacknowledged status as a bastion of white rule (even Chang, clearly Chinese in the novel, is played by H. B. Warner in the film) in the midst of an indigenously nonwhite population (portrayed, no less, by a cast drawn from various Native American tribes)?

The worst-case answer to this question is an ambivalent "yes," most regrettably so toward the end of the film in view of the stereotypical portrayal of the porters who know so little about mountaineering that they take thoughtless potshots at their lag-behind charges and precipitate an avalanche in the bargain. However, even in the worst case we can say more positively that at least Capra addresses the issue with unusual candor for his era. Moreover, the worst case is largely predicated on the view that Conway is to be understood as essentially satisfied with and by Shangri-La; hence the charges of "dramatic flatness" and the general puzzlement at his willingness to leave it all behind for George's sake. This latter view is understandable though not finally sustainable when judged against the AFI-restoration print.

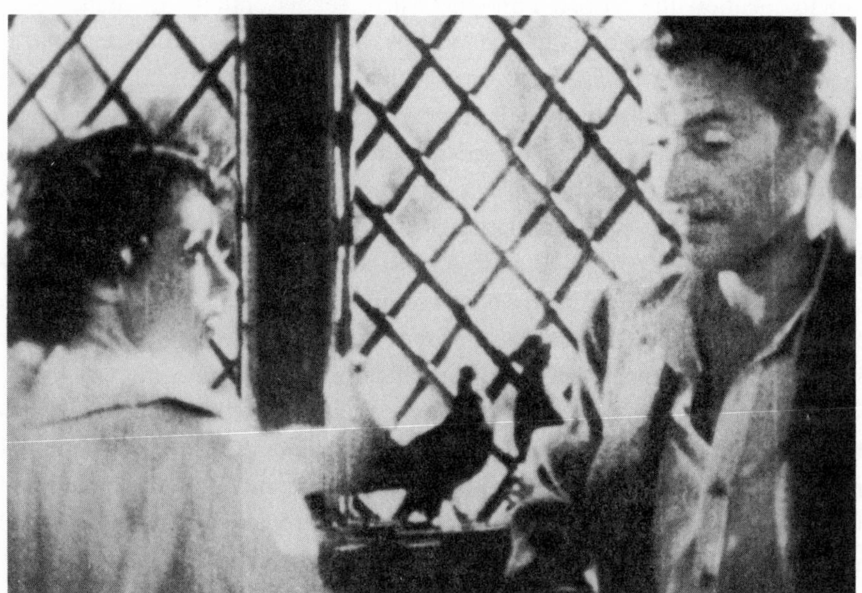

Figure 12. The aviary scene in *Lost Horizon.* (*Lost Horizon* copyright © 1937, renewed 1965 Columbia Pictures Industries, Inc. All rights reserved. Courtesy of Columbia Pictures.)

I have already alluded to a segment of the film, missing from most prerestoration prints, in which a weary and somewhat inebriated Conway queries his brother about the report on the Baskul evacuation. In response to Robert's evident skepticism George urges his brother to rest; Robert takes the urging as occasion to renew his attack on the ethics of the foreign service ("Can't you just see me, Freshy, with all those other shrewd little foreign secretaries . . .") and he rambles on to express a pacifistic vision ("I'm not going to have an army. I'm going to disband mine. . . ") that he knows full well will get him "slapped straight into the nearest insane asylum." George takes the whole monologue as nonsense, a sign that Robert had better stop drinking, as if it were only the liquor talking; Robert (in response) offers sarcastic reassurance that he will "be the good little boy that everybody wants me to be" but only "because I haven't the nerve to be anything else."

Two elements of this exchange are worth dwelling on. One is the evidence it gives of Conway's visionary predilections, predilections of which most of his lamasery interlocutors are well aware (and of which George, not to mention the British Foreign Office, seems entirely ignorant, as if George had never read his brother's books). Thus Chang expresses amazement at Conway's amazed response to his lecture on the philosophy and history of Shangri-La by wondering how Conway could fail to recognize one of his own dreams when he sees it. Thus Father Perrault literally quotes Conway to Conway on their first meeting. Thus Sondra answers Conway's query about the strange familiarity of Shangri-La by saying that Conway has ''always been part of Shangri-La without knowing it,'' as if the very emptiness she had seen in his books were a space, a ''valley,'' of which Shangri-La's Valley of the Blue Moon were the embodiment. A clearer instance of a dreamer confronting his dream is hard to imagine.

A second crucial aspect of Conway's pacifistic vision is the deep ambivalence with which he expresses and eventually confronts it. In the initial revelation of Conway's ideals he is defensively ironic in his recitation and fully aware of the doubled life he leads as diplomatic troubleshooter and visionary philosopher; he has nerve enough to make the Baskul evacuation seem like an only slightly frenzied package tour rushing to make connections (hence the frequent comments about Conway's serenity) yet he lacks the nerve to put his philosophy into practice beyond expressing aspects of it in his writing.

Indeed, Conway continues to be skeptical and dissatisfied in various ways throughout his stay in Shangri-La. Much of this is evident in the film's dialogue, some of it cited earlier, much of it progressively cut out of various prints of the movie. Conway is fascinated by Shangri-La, alright, but that fascination takes the form of continuous questioning and repeated expressions of puzzlement and doubt, interspersed with knowing (occasionally nostalgic) references to the world outside. At one point, for instance, he tells Sondra that he is waiting for ''the bump,'' for the rough landing that will wake him up, as if he were still sleeping, the rescue plane still heading to Shanghai. Nevertheless, he quickly avers that the world outside seems like a dream to him now, and asks Sondra whether she has ever wanted to go there (''It's not so bad, really'').

The anthropological or epistemic ''relativity'' implied by Conway's almost Descartian declaration that each world he lives in is a dream of (and to) the other is marvelously captured in one of the film's loveliest passages, which follows quickly upon the dialogue cited earlier. Sondra and Conway recline together in the shadows of a classically tended garden, his back against a column, she against him, in his arms. He, it turns out, is her dream; she asks if she is forgiven for summoning him to Shangri-La. He repeats her word, in an interrogative tone (''forgiven?''), and then answers with a kind of parable:

> You know, when we were on that plane I was fascinated by the way its shadow followed it, that silly shadow racing along over mountains and valleys, covering ten times the distance of the plane and yet always there to greet us with outstretched arms when we landed, and I've been thinking that somehow you're that plane and I'm that silly shadow and that all my life I've been rushing up and down hills, leaping rivers, crashing over obstacles, never dreaming that one day that beautiful thing in flight would land on this earth and into my arms.

Much of the quality of this passage is in the playing, in the look on Jane Wyatt's face, in the tone of Ronald Colman's voice. Furthermore, in light of the film's conclusion, to which we will return, the last several phrases have a prophetic ring as predicting exactly what Conway will do in his superhuman efforts to return to Shangri-La. Here I want simply to notice an aspect of ambivalence, verging on incoherence, in what is unquestionably Conway's moment of deepest contentment. How an object's shadow can travel ten times the distance of the object is hard to picture, for example, though how it can *seem* to is vaguely comprehensible from the viewpoint of the passenger seat of an airplane, the passenger seeming static relative to the seat while the shadow races relative to the ground, especially so when the earth's surface is wildly variable in its topography. Beyond that, it is worth noting a certain reversal of positions. In fact, the kidnapped Conway was the airborne passenger, Sondra was the one awaiting on the ground; yet in Conway's parable she is the (male) plane, he the (female) shadow with outstretched, winglike or birdlike arms.

There is an intricacy and complexity to the dialogue of *Lost Horizon,* only hinted at in my last few paragraphs, that is both admirable and risky and owes hardly anything to James Hilton, despite the widely shared conviction that Capra's general problem with the film was a talkiness resulting from too slavish a mimicry of the novel. The theme of Conway's general ambivalence about Shangri-La does not depend, however, on language alone. Indeed, the ludic ''doubleness'' implicit in the film's dialogue is also elaborated in explicitly visual terms.

Partly what I have in mind here is a series of classical Capra sight gags, some more obviously comic than others. The most overt of these involves the Edward Everett Horton character, Alexander P. Lovett, on his first morning in Shangri-La. The scene begins with a medium-shot of an ornate curtain from behind which a sword of some oriental stripe extends, its wielder apparently practicing thrusts of some sort. Then Lovett pokes his head out from behind the curtain, looks round suspiciously, as if afraid of being spied upon, and then returns to his swordplay, sharpening a pencil with the weapon in his hand. We might think this a throwaway moment, a typical Capra grace note, yet the hint of self-conscious theatricality, on Lovett's part, on Capra's, urges us to keep it in mind, to seek for less obvious analogues.

At least two come to mind. One involves the scene that immediately follows, in which Sondra leads Conway on horseback through the woods. Despite the fact that she repeatedly stops and waits for Conway to catch up, and despite the undercranking of the camera, which makes Conway's horse seem to run at an excessive speed, he can never close the distance between them. At one point, indeed, she walks her horse behind a rock at the foot of a waterfall. Only seconds later Conway (finally) arrives in the same spot, looks around as if Sondra and her mount had disappeared into thin air, only to discover that Sondra has somehow managed to get herself and her horse to the top of the waterfall, as if by (cine)magic. A similar (if less emphatic) moment comes quickly after the crash of the airplane that delivers Conway and company. In long-shot we see George leave a door on the right side of the plane while Robert leaves moments later from the left side. We then follow Robert, who stumbles and falls as he climbs over the wing, into the cockpit, where he finds the pilot dead, after which George, head start or no, finally makes his entrance from the other side of the cockpit.

I take all three moments as microparables of vision and its contingency, the way it depends on expectation, the way expectations can be manipulated or confounded or fulfilled. Doubts are raised, we might say, and raised visually. A far more crucial species of visual doubting is evident in a series of "looks" enacted by Robert Conway. Two such are justly famous, in part because they deeply echo one another:

1. Conway's first sight of Shangri-La, which Capra stretches out with a complex series of glances and point-of-view shots as Conway looks back through the stone archway to the wind-swept pass and then turns to gaze (again) at Shangri-La and the valley before and below him; and
2. Conway's last look at Shangri-La, where a very similar series of shots depicts

Conway's parting gaze before he turns his back and joins George and Maria in their perilous journey.

It is fairly clear that these latter two sequences have something like doubt at their center, though a paucity of dialogue leaves characterization of it to the viewer. Three other looks – only one of them having any real equivalent in Hilton – are equally crucial to the claim that Conway never stops doubting Shangri-La, if only for showing how sustained this pattern is across the whole film.

Arguably the most crucial of these looks comes at the end of Conway's first audience with Father Perrault, which *begins* with Conway's astonished recognition – via Conway's (panning point-of-view) glance at Perrault's crutch and his single foot – that the High Lama in fact *is* the same Father Perrault who (on Chang's report) founded the monastery in 1713. The question of sight (or insight) is sustained in the scene, not only by Perrault's citation of Conway's glimpse-the-eternal conceit, but also by Perrault's explanation of the "reason" for Shangri-La and the subsequent abduction of Conway, the "meaning and purpose" of which derives from "a vision" that came to him long ago – a vision (taken fairly literally from Hilton) of nations "strengthening not in wisdom but in the vulgar passions" that would doom every book and treasure to destruction unless they are preserved, to which task Perrault dedicated himself and his lamasery.

As Perrault finishes his recitation he rises to prophesy the immanent fulfillment of the Christian ethic wherein "the meek shall inherit the earth." Conway seems deeply moved, and he impulsively kisses Perrault's hand. This latter action is filmed in close-up, the camera staying on Conway as he says "I understand you, Father"; and then the camera holds on Conway as the latter stands fully upright and looks off-frame at Perrault, saying nothing, simply looking, his torso half-turned, as if to leave, though with a look on his face that indicates, at the very least, puzzlement if not downright doubt, doubt for which there is no real equivalent in Hilton, however faithful to the novel much of the scene's dialogue remains.

This visual trope of "holding" a look beyond the temporal requirements of the dialogue, as if both character and camera doubted dialogue's capacity for closure or intuited meanings beyond or beneath the reach of language, recurs on at least two other occasions. The first comes late in the film, though before Conway's last visit to Father Perrault. Just as Conway finishes a courtyard conversation with Barnard (Thomas Mitchell) on the topic of providing indoor plumbing to the villagers, George walks by and Conway accosts him, saying that he has, in his silence, been behaving ''like a child.'' George avers there is nothing to discuss and leaves the frame. Again, the camera holds on Conway, as he watches George depart, and again what seems at stake is some manner of anxiety, an anxiety or doubt I take to be as much self-directed as George directed, in view of the several references (Conway's among them) to his own status as a little boy, a ''shrewd little foreign secretary,'' ''a little boy whistling in the dark.''

The last of these three looks comes in the climactic sequence in Conway's apartment in which George and Maria convince Conway to accompany them. The scene is more complex in Capra than in Hilton, in part because it condenses two different scenes from the novel, and partly because, unlike the novel, it includes (crucially, as we will see) the woman who has arranged for the porters.

Once Maria has proven her determination to leave Shangri-La – despite Conway's inquiry about her age (according to Chang she is an old woman, who will revert to her normal appearance upon departing from the valley) and despite his accusation that she is lying – Conway moves across the room, away from George and Maria, and stops, his head nearly framed by a mirror in the background as he gazes off-frame. The change-of-heart moment in Hilton comes when Hugh Conway stands on a balcony and gazes ''at the dazzling plume of Karakal,'' the mountain that dominates the valley; the change of heart itself is reported by an omniscient narrator who describes Conway's descent into madness (''For even as he nerved himself, he saw the corridors of his imagination twist and strain under impact; the pavilions were toppling; all was about to be in ruins'').[14] In Capra, by contrast, Conway's doubt is evidenced chiefly by his distanced yet deeply interior glance, understood as culminating a series of such glances, and by a self-deprecating laugh that Conway chokes out before asking if the porters are all ready to go – a laugh echoing that with which Conway (early in the flight from Baskul) deflates George's impassioned recitation of the factors making Conway's appointment as foreign secretary an absolute necessity (George: ''You can laugh if you want to but who else can they get?''). None of which amounts (yet) to an explanation of Conway's decision to leave Shangri-La. Still, it seems perfectly clear that Conway's departure, whatever the reason, is not represented as a renunciation of certainly held convictions, no matter what Conway may explicitly say to George in defense of his desire to stay.

I began by reference to Capra's account, in *The Name above the Title,* of the circumstances leading up to his decision to "Burn the First Two Reels" of *Lost Horizon,* taking the fable as emblematic of Capra's stormy relationship with his critics. The parable is also emblematic in another aspect. I have in mind the episode, reportedly after the film's successful second preview showing, when Capra ducked out of the studio victory party and headed for the Columbia cutting rooms: "I ran up to the cutting rooms, took those blasted first two reels in my hot little hands, ran to the ever-burning big black incinerator – and threw them into the fire. Being nitrate film, they flamed up with a whoosh that lit up the night sky."[15] At issue here is the remarkably *visual* quality of *Lost Horizon* and of Capra generally, an aspect of his filmmaking that is almost universally ignored under the classical narrative cinema rubric, which tends to emphasize the "transparency" of the image, the represented signified at the expense of the representing signifier. Nevertheless, an enduring aspect of the Capra legacy is Capra's repeated experiments with the expressionistic potentials of the cinema, especially of black-and-white photography, for which Capra's parable about "lighting up the night sky" with a "whoosh" of burning nitrate – regardless of the literal veracity of Capra's recollections on these accounts – can stand here as token and as pointer.

Of course, an ironic effect of the AFI restoration of *Lost Horizon* is to shift viewer focus repeatedly from the world depicted to the medium in which that depiction takes place – to the process, that is, of narration, as that process has waxed and waned in emphasis over the course of the film's history. Evidence of *re*construction – images that suddenly freeze while the matching voices continue to deliver dialogue, say, or that suddenly go grainy in midsequence – is equally evidence of the film's "constructedness" in general. But there is ample reason for suggesting that the original road-show version of *Lost Horizon* was equally as concerned with questions of viewing and of (film) authorship, as much of the foregoing discussion has indicated.

Perhaps the most (literally) spectacular evidence of this concern on Capra's part with the materiality of the film image – a concern sparked perhaps by the film's unusually generous production budget – involves Capra's devotion to exploring the dynamics of light and lighting effects. Here too, we should observe, Capra drew inspiration from the Hilton novel, which is itself punctuated by emphatically visionary moments, though typically the vision is such as to reassure the Hugh Conway character in the midst of his various trials. Consider the following passage, from the novel's second chapter, marking the sunrise following the dead-of-night crash-landing of the hijacked aircraft:

> Framed in the pale triangle ahead, the mountain showed again, gray at first, then silver, then pink as the earliest sun rays caught the summit. . . .It was not a friendly picture, but to Conway, as he surveyed, there came a queer perception of fineness in it, of something that had no romantic appeal at all, but a steely, almost an intellectual quality. The white pyramid in the distance compelled the mind's assent as passionlessly as a Euclidian theorem.[16]

Such emphatically visual moments as these seem, if only in retrospect, at least as crucial a factor in prompting Capra's desire to acquire film rights to the novel as its openly fabulous story, yet here too Capra revises (literally: reenvisions) Hilton's conceit in such a way as to significantly modify the implications that follow from this shared emphasis on seeing or on "sights."

A good example here is the visual treatment Capra affords the scene of Father Perrault's death. Most elements of the scene – the chiaroscuro illumination that outlines figures in the frame, the curtained window, the idea of flickering lights – are found somewhere in Hilton's descriptions of Perrault's quarters. However, Capra's recombination of them does not suggest, as in Hilton, the certainty and continuity of knowledge (Hilton's Perrault counters Conway's reference to the Dark Ages, for instance, by discussing the "flickering lanterns" of knowledge that illuminated the medieval gloom).[17] The emphasis in Capra falls rather on the ephemeral quality of human life, even among the most long-lived. Capra frames Conway and Perrault with a large candle and candle stand between them as the ostensible light source; the effect is to render the top half of the frame a blank wall, a glowing screen, the light from which is reflected back upon the characters, rendering them mere outlines in the darkness of the lower portions of the frame. Moreover, just as Perrault dies, Capra cuts to the window, to show a breeze moving the curtain, and then back to Conway and Perrault as the breeze blows out the candle, casting the room ever deeper into darkness, the only illumination the moonlight caught in Father Perrault's wispy white hair. The candle-flame/breath-of-life analogy verges, of course, on the banal; but there is a wild, nearly uncanny precision in the shift from dark to darker, or from light to lighter, that emphatically underscores the risky and ephemeral nature of human effort, of human life itself.

A second example of Capra's play with, interest in, the expressive effects of lighting comes in the film's spectacular first sequence, which can be understood quite literally as a study in techniques of illumination. Conway's basic task is to shepherd a number of Europeans aboard rescue aircraft, which we see departing and arriving through the course of the scene. Just as the last planes are set to land the power goes out, cut off by attacking rebels, casting the landing strip into darkness. Without missing a beat, Conway grabs a kerosene lamp and starts off toward the hangar, his lantern a bobbing light in a roiling sea of darkness as Conway retreats from the camera. Once he gets to the hangar he clears out its inhabitants, opens the spigots on a brace of petrol drums, and then tosses the lantern onto the gas-soaked floor, at which point a ball of fire explodes up toward the camera. Even the film's first shot – masses of people running toward the camera from a burning city in the far background – is notable for its *noir*ish side-lighting, the work of Capra's long-time director of photography, Joseph Walker. However, with Conway's burning of the hangar the deep contrast of light and darkness becomes a matter of explicit representation, especially so as Conway (in the foreground) waves a signal lantern toward an airplane in the background that is itself little more than a silhouette against the burning hangar in the far distance.

In this latter gesture Conway can clearly be seen as a kind of stand-in for Capra, directing lighting and action in a manner closely akin to that of a film director. That Conway ought to be taken as a figure of and for cinema is indicated by our very first view of him, very precisely framed as a silhouette shadow against and within the rectangular glass panel of the door leading to the airport waiting room. The frame motif will be picked up in various ways throughout the film; some characters will be literally framed *within* the image, by the windows of the aircraft (the natives who refuel the plane), by mirrors (Lovett), by the frame of a loom (Maria and George), whereas in other instances the film frame itself will be foregrounded by its explicit power of exclusion (as when Sondra "disappears" during the waterfall sequence). The equation of shadows with projected images will also be frequently repeated, most spectacularly during the funeral procession in which torchlight (echoing the lantern light of the first scene) will cast massive shadows, against the blank white lamasery walls, of mourners passing through the precincts of Shangri-La.

Such general references to (analogues of) the materiality of cinema gain added force and point when aligned with more specific allusions by which

Capra asserts a number of important intertextual relations between *Lost Horizon* and his earlier work. I have already commented on the general similarity of *Lost Horizon* and *The Bitter Tea of General Yen,* though at this general level we would do well to recall the implicit role-reversal equation of Megan Davis (in *Bitter Tea*) and Robert Conway (in *Lost Horizon*); each is effectively kidnapped, and for each the hideaway subsequently arrived at embodies some aspect of the central character's imagination, through which the character confronts, as it were, his or her deeper self. That this similarity matters more than a little is indicated by the way specific shots in each film's opening sequence (mostly involving fleeing refugees and truck-borne soldiers) almost duplicate each other from the earlier film to the later, and the significance of the connection is further confirmed, late in *Lost Horizon,* by a verbal echo of a crucial and deeply self-conscious scene from *The Bitter Tea of General Yen.*

The *Bitter Tea* moment follows an expressionistic dream sequence wherein Megan Davis/Barbara Stanwyck experiences the stirrings of desire, though in oddly stereotypical and explicitly cinematic (montage) form, as if her desires drew their inspiration from a history of moviegoing. She awakes from her trance to find Yen standing behind her, in full oriental regalia, and as he joins her on the balcony overlooking the ornate garden of his summer palace he observes that it is the season of the "cherry blossom moon" wherein homage is paid to "the god of love." Megan expresses doubts about Yen's sincerity; Yen wonders if Megan thinks the Chinese incapable of love and asks (as if in reply) if she has ever read Chinese poetry or heard Chinese music: "Have you ever seen our paintings," he goes on, "of women walking among fruit trees, where the fruit trees look like women, and the women look like fruit trees?"

The analogous moment in *Lost Horizon* literally enacts aspects of Yen's description of the potential unity of art and nature. After their conversation in the aviary, Conway and Sondra walk through a cherry orchard, though the walk is accomplished via fairly obvious back projection that renders the orchard expressly "cinematic." They stop at a fence, framed by branches and blossoms (as the balcony rail in *Bitter Tea* is framed by the garden beyond), at which point Conway expresses (yet again) his sympathetically bemused skepticism, declaring Shangri-La "inconceivable" and Sondra herself a source of further confusion exactly in her familiarity, her ordinariness. However, that quality is explicitly related, in Conway's mind, to aesthetic properties: "All the beautiful things I see," Conway observes, echoing Yen, "these cherry blossoms, you, [are] all somehow familiar." The importance of aesthetics is subsequently confirmed, moreover, when Conway defends his desire to stay in Shangri-La by telling George that the secret of Shangri-La is "fantastic and sometimes unbelievable but so beautiful."

The general self-consciousness and Capra typicality of *Lost Horizon* is further confirmed by (at least) one other set of significant intertextual relations, these between *Lost Horizon* and *Forbidden*. There are some obvious similarities of situation between the two films; in each an isolated yet visionary young woman known for her reading habits manipulates the career of an up-and-coming political figure depicted as witty and sophisticated (and mustachioed), a connection confirmed by the change of Conway's first name from Hugh (as in Hilton) to Robert. When Sondra chases after the departing Conway shouting "Bob, Bob!" one can hardly help hearing it as an echo (having seen *Forbidden*) of Barbara Stanwyck shouting the same words as she chases after a departing Robert Grover (Adolph Menjou) midway through the earlier film.

Three specific connections between *Forbidden* and *Lost Horizon* are worth observing here. One involves a remarkable escalation of extreme lighting effects toward the conclusion of each film, a consideration I wish to postpone for the moment. Another connection involves the drunk scene in each movie, a link complicated by the fact that the drunk in *Forbidden* seems not so drunk after all. In the earlier film the drunk is Menjou; his mistaking Lulu's shipboard cabin for his own seems simultaneously innocent (in the sense that we do not doubt his having *been* drunk) and expressive of his deeper (erotic) desire, understood in part as a matter of dissatisfaction with his work life. When Lulu discovers him, he *acts* drunk in a gracefully apologetic manner, though it seems *only* an act, moments later, when he suddenly acts perfectly sober. Robert Conway's drunk act, also born of work and world weariness, seems less an act (in the theatrical sense) but is no less indicative of his deeper desires and selfhood; the analogy with Grover's "as-if" inebriation in *Forbidden* gives reason for wondering how much a role the drink *really* played in Conway's decision to speak his heart. (A moment's scan of the Capra canon raises any number of similar questions of similar scenes – Connell's drunken denunciation of Norton in *Meet John Doe*, for instance.)

A last link between *Forbidden* and *Lost Horizon*, already alluded to, relating as well to the illumination issue, involves the horse-riding sequence of *Lost Horizon,* for which there is no precedent at all in Hilton, but which is clearly and deeply related to the equestrian sequence that concludes the Havana episode of *Forbidden.* The riding sequence in the earlier film only requires five shots, of an ecstatic Lulu Smith galloping her horse along the spectacularly moonlit beach in advance of Grover and his mount; as in the riding scene of *Lost Horizon,* obvious cinematic wizardry is used, a back-projection close-up (in this case) of Lulu turning to look back at Grover (as Sondra repeatedly looks back at Conway) while her hair flies wildly about her, followed immediately by a long-shot of Grover and his horse with the camera looking directly into the light-drenched surf in the background.

It is as visually striking a sequence as any in Capra, and has an obvious kinship to the scene in *It Happened One Night* when Peter carries Ellie across a moon-drenched stream. However, the transcendental force of this visual crescendo also depends on, gains emphasis from, the immediately preceding scene, in which Lulu, despondent at the prospect of returning to the mainland on the morrow, asks Grover if they can stay. ''For another week?'' he asks; ''another century,'' she replies, adding that they can live on ''worms'' – *Forbidden*'s shorthand (Grover tells us earlier) for dreams and ambitions – as they lead the life of beachcombers. Whether we should take the reference to beachcombing as a prototype of Shangri-La's archival motif is a question I will only raise, though in each case the basic idea is to wait for the world's ruination while living on its margins and gathering its lost treasures. Clearly the idea of desire expanding weeks into centuries – while lovers, associated in each case with animal energy, with the play of light on water, of water on skin or hair, continue to exist at an ever closing but never quite closed distance – cannot help but evoke its later elaboration in the equestrian interlude between Sondra and Conway in *Lost Horizon.*

This intertextual kinship of *Forbidden* and *Lost Horizon* prompts consideration of the latter's capacity to sustain a feminist reading, the possibility that *Lost Horizon,* like *Forbidden,* might instance a (somewhat) feminine voice or vision. A certain flexibility of gender roles is clearly evident in the Conway–Sondra relationship, as we have seen. Two other thematic threads of *Lost Horizon* are worth following out briefly in this regard, the first having to do with the explicitly feminist perspective of the Isabel Jewell character (Miss Stone), a perspective increasingly cut from the film as it suffered repeated reediting, and the second having to do with the Thomas Mitchell–Edward Everett Horton duo.

At least as they stand in the AFI-restoration print, Miss Stone's more overtly feminist comments can and should be allowed to speak for themselves, though we should not forget the commercial censorship that denied them a voice over the course of the film's history. In *Lost Horizon*'s initial sequence, for example, she volunteers to suspend the "women and children first" rule, urging Conway to "take some of those squealing men with you first" because "they might faint." Later, after the crash landing and George Conway's near hysterical outburst at the thought of slow starvation, Miss Stone delivers the following bitterly and openly feminist diatribe, for which there is no precedent whatsoever in Hilton: "A year ago a doctor gave me six months to live. That was a year ago. I'm already six months to the good. I'm living on velvet; I haven't got anything to lose. But you, you the noble animals of the human race, what a kick I'm going to get out of watching you squirm for a change. What a kick!"

The implication here that women are always living under conditions of slow starvation is hard to miss. Somewhat easier to miss – especially in the film's shorter versions – is an implicit equation of Miss Stone and George Conway. Early on, before the crash landing and George's subsequent despondency, Miss Stone suffers a similar fit of hysterics, clearly (in her case) brought on by illness, altitude, and lack of oxygen; before Barnard and Conway can calm her down she tries to jump from the airplane and needs to be held down on a couch to the rear of the aircraft cabin (where George had slept the night before). Later, in a scene now pieced together from production stills and freeze frames (depicting Miss Stone as lying on her bed while Chang stands in the doorway), she tells Chang, in another burst of male-directed bitterness, that the only help she wants from him is help in leaping off the lamasery cliff to the valley below (for which task, as she tells him echoing Conway, she has not "got the nerve"). The obvious point to make here is that she and George are the most openly hysterical of the film's characters – she clearly more from the ill effects of tuberculosis and maltreatment at the hands of men than from lack of fortitude – and that George is the one who in fact carries out her threat to jump, leaping to his death in a fit of "squealing" male madness when he discovers near film's end that Maria has reverted to her natural age and appearance. I take the George–Miss Stone equation and the gender reversibility it implies to be quietly confirmed, midway through the movie, when George (like the distraught farmer in *Mr. Deeds*) runs amok with a loaded gun in the hope of forcing the truth from Chang. Like Miss Stone earlier, he has to be forcibly subdued and is subsequently restrained on a bed. Equally telling here is the fact that of the five European characters in the scene, only Miss Stone and George are dressed in slacks; Lovett, Barnard, and Conway are all attired in skirtlike oriental garb.

The Barnard–Lovett duo is generally discussed, when discussed at all, in terms of Edward Everett Horton's status as a light comedian; hence his frequent exchanges with Thomas Mitchell's Barnard come under the heading of comic relief. However, these exchanges also raise large-scale issues of status and position, chief among which are questions of gender role. The status question is seen, for example, in the fact that Conway initially boots Lovett off the last rescue plane, on the rushed assumption that Lovett's oriental garb indicates a native rather than a British subject in local mufti; when Lovett explains his paleontological discovery to Barnard, it is chiefly in terms of the knighthood that awaits him in England for discovering that particular bone *in Asia,* thus linking physical and social position. When they awake the next morning, it is Barnard's observation of the position of the sun relative to the aircraft that informs Conway and company they are off course – which prompts a grumpy and incredulous Lovett to observe that any child knows, when facing the sun in the morning, that north is always to one's right (he says, getting things backward), to which Barnard replies that he gets confused, being left handed. The position question is also raised during the second dinner sequence, when Barnard reveals his true identity as Chalmers Bryant, wanted far and wide for stock fraud; he delivers a few almost philosophical remarks on the humor in his rise from "slew-footed plumber" to "great civic leader" and his subsequent fall to the status of criminal fugitive.

The "fluidity" of social and physical positions marked out by Barnard and Lovett is also specifically elaborated in gender terms, chiefly by costume and dialogue. The former we have already noted, though we should remember here Lovett's extreme discomfiture, his first night in Shangri-La, with the vaguely feminine (by western standards) ankle-length oriental robe he is given to wear. The dialogue in question punctuates three separate scenes, the first two casting Lovett in the female role, the last assigning that status quietly to Barnard.

Both of the former instances are in scenes that begin with Lovett complaining about his "ridiculous clothes." Once the plane has taken off from Baskul and Lovett has explained his unregistered self to the Conways, Barnard asks him about his line of work and expresses skepticism about Lovett's self-predicted knighthood. Lovett takes offense, Barnard replies "okay, brother," to which Lovett takes additional offense, to which Barnard replies "okay, sister." The next morning, after Barnard bids him "good morning, Lovey," Lovett insists upon his full name, saying "I didn't care for sister last night and I don't care for Lovey this morning." Furthermore, after the completion of their first meal in Shangri-La Barnard suggests that he and Lovett play honeymoon bridge, though he happily agrees to double solitaire when Lovett demurs, telling the latter: "I'm your man, come on, Toots!"

In Barnard's case the gender-role shape shifting comes in the second dinner scene, the only one attended by Miss Stone. Barnard comments that she looks beautiful without her makeup, without her mask. Lovett asks Barnard to drop his own mask. Conway seconds the motion by urging Barnard to "unbosom" himself, to which Barnard agrees, saying that he is perfectly willing to "let [his] hair down," whereupon he reveals himself as Chalmers Bryant, ex-plumber and fugitive from international justice, yet the implication remains that, in revealing his "true self," Barnard/Bryant is revealing his own femininity, his own vulnerability. Taken singly, of course, most of these lines come off as snappy and slightly risqué Hollywood patter; taken together, in the context of the film as a whole, they considerably advance *Lost Horizon*'s status as an almost anthropological meditation on the sociology of human desire.

The importance of this last claim to an understanding of *Lost Horizon* is confirmed, in my mind, by the scene immediately preceding Conway's parable of the shadow and the plane, though that recitation itself raises important issues of role relativity and gender exchange. Conway queries Sondra about her desire to see the outside world, and tries to tell her of its attraction for him, having to do with the fullness of the struggle with which people naturally seek to make a place for themselves (a speech that echoes Robert Grover's discussion in *Forbidden* of the worm of desire that drives people to be sharp and creative).

Sondra repeatedly interrupts Conway's discourse by asking "why?" Conway responds by playing both roles in a drama designed to prove that "why" is the most annoying word in the English language, the first role that of an exasperated mother, the second role that of mother's little darling who insists upon sticking her fingers in the salad bowl rather than use a fork. To the daughter's "why" Conway retorts (among other things) "because mother read it in a book somewhere." When Sondra-as-daughter asks (again) "why?," Conway-as-mother responds with a threat; because "if mother's little darling doesn't take her fingers from the salad bowl this instant mother is going to wring her little neck.'' Sondra asks Conway playfully if he would like to wring her little neck as she runs away into the garden; when Conway catches up to her in the colonnade she asks again, and he responds by grabbing her neck with both hands, a grip halfway between a choke hold and a caress. They kiss, and Capra dissolves to the scene of the reclining lovers that culminates in Conway's shadow-and-plane parable.

Several features of this scene bear emphasizing. Most obvious is the exchange of gender roles, Conway playing both mother and daughter until Sondra (in yet another exchange) takes over the latter part; again Shangri-La is depicted as (in some ways) confounding strict gender expectations. Another crucial element, cutting somewhat *against* the latter's implication of flexibility, involves the ''textual'' basis for the crisis of authority that Conway's little drama enacts; its ''point'' is a linguistic one, and its (ostensible) source is a book dictating the behavior appropriate for children. Despite the implication that the dictate is *only* a dictate, moreover, Conway (ambivalently) ups the dramatic ante by threatening force, though whether as proof of the rulebook's destructive arbitrariness or as an expression of his own frustration remains unclear. Clear enough, however, especially in light of Conway's subsequent parable of plane and shadow, is the implied equation of sheltering, welcoming wings or arms and the hands that can mime strangulation, as if death, darkness, and desire were all of a piece.

I remarked earlier that Conway's ambivalence toward Shangri-La in some way prepares for but does not by itself explain his decision to leave the Valley of the Blue Moon, a decision that most critics find deeply puzzling. Their puzzlement of itself argues *against* trying to explain Conway's decision in realistic or political terms; in many ways the political element of *Lost Horizon* is equally and as symptomatically ''empty'' as its counterpart in *Forbidden.* There is even less sense in Capra than in Hilton that Shangri-La's social mission as a cultural repository is in any way threatened by Conway's decision, whichever way it goes. Indeed, as was often his practice, Capra literally shot several endings for *Lost Horizon* (again, see Behlmer), which I take as a marker of the essential open-endedness of the Capra story in general, where endings are less important than beginnings. Three aspects of *Lost Horizon*'s concluding sequences are especially interesting once focus is shifted away from the political specifics of Shangri-La taken as a model society.

The first of these involves the introduction of Maria (Margo) into the scene where George (Mallinson in Hilton) convinces Conway to leave with him. Her (rough) equivalent in Hilton, Lo-Tsen, plays no direct role in the scene except as a subject of conversation; the last straw for Hugh Conway, which weighs him down unto literal madness, is Mallinson's declaration that he and Lo-Tsen had slept together. (Whether Hugh Conway's disappointment is focused more on his loss of Lo-Tsen to Mallinson or Mallinson to Lo-Tsen is decidedly undecidable.) In Capra, by contrast, Maria is brought in by George as proof of the latter's assertion that Chang and Perrault and company are a bunch of "loose brained fanatics" who have "hypnotized" Conway. Curiously, in both novel and film, the argument between Mallinson/George and Conway quickly boils down to the question of age, and most specifically the question of whether the apparently youthful Lo-Tsen/Maria is an old woman who will revert to her natural age upon leaving the valley. (The "curiosity" here, of course, is the irrelevance of Maria's age to the larger political function of Shangri-La, though this is far less curious, I would argue, in Capra than in Hilton.) However, in Capra the woman is allowed to voice her own desire and she does so in terms that Conway evidently takes as voicing *his* desire as well.

I draw the latter conclusion partly from the fact that Maria's appeal works where George's does not. Several elements of her appeal, in addition, echo earlier moments in the film and in ways that effectively assert Maria's kinship with Conway. In explaining her desperation to leave, for example, she testifies that Chang has repeatedly prevented her escaping and punished her various attempts, even to the extent of locking her "in a dark room," a phrase that I hear as echoing Sondra's description of Conway as "a little boy whistling in the dark" and alluding as well to Conway's status as a figure of darkness, shadow, and light that is developed in the film's opening scene. After Maria pleads her case, furthermore, George urges (in voice-over) that Maria was "kidnapped two years ago just as we were"; here we might well recall Conway's comment to Sondra that his kidnapping was "a crime, a great crime," his acceptance of which he finds extremely troubling, as if he has not fully accepted it at all (any more than Maria).

Equally significant to the claim that Maria "speaks" for Conway is the gesture by which the latter responds to George's description of Maria as a kidnap victim; he grabs her by the shoulders and backs her against the door, declaring her "every word" a lie. Conway's movements here – by contrast with his (Colman's) graceful deportment everywhere else in the film – are profoundly awkward, as if he can barely bring himself to press the accusation. Moreover, the pose in which he and Maria wind up, his arms extended, his hands near her neck, her back against the door – emphatically recalls the moment when Conway playfully threatens to wring Sondra's neck. To the extent that Conway and Sondra, as object and shadow, are mirror images, so too (in a way, to that extent) are Conway and Maria. Indeed, Conway's vulnerability to Maria's appeal depends greatly on her willing acceptance of the vulnerability to aging and death that (on Chang's account) she expresses in acting upon her desire to escape. Even if her kidnap story is a fiction, she takes complete responsibility for whatever fate awaits her. Capra and Riskin make no particular attempt to *explain* her desire, apart from assigning it to a woman, a victim, like Miss Stone, of slow starvation, of desire's lack. In acceding to her desire Conway effectively acknowledges his own.

Another curious feature of the film's concluding scenes is the fact that Conway – after Maria ages and dies and George leaps to his death – does *not* return *immediately* to Shangri-La, if returning to Shangri-La is the point once Chang's veracity is confirmed. Matters of memory and narration intersect here. Hilton's Conway *must* return to civilization so that his story can be told and recorded; the middle chapters of the novel are presented as a third-person transcription (by Rutherford; Gainsford in the film) of Conway's first-person narration that the novel's first-person narrator and Rutherford discuss in the book's epilogue, in ways which (as it were) confirm the truth of Conway's story. Moreover, Hilton's Conway is clearly on the verge of madness when he departs Shangri-La (the last we see of him in the novel); his amnesia is therefore perfectly credible, as is his determination (upon regaining his memory) to return to Shangri-La, though his return trek is not in the least detailed.

Capra's Conway, however, is *not* presented as deranged and his amnesia seems largely the result of exposure to the elements. Moreover, unlike Hilton's Conway, Capra's is a public figure whose disappearance, whose return to "civilization," and whose subsequent recovery of memory and escape from Gainsford's custody are the stuff of worldwide headlines, not to mention the tale Gainsford tells at his London club upon returning from his year-long trek after the elusive Conway. Especially in view of the toast that Lord Gainsford offers to Conway, expressing the hope that Conway and everybody ("we all") will find some Shangri-La, and in view of the extraordinary close-up in which Capra catches light in the circle of glasses raised skyward in salute, from which the image dissolves to a wind-swept Tibetan glacier, I am inclined to read Conway's decision to go on after his brother's death as a narrational metaphor by which Capra suggests that civilization in general suffers from amnesia, a loss of ideals, for which Conway's amnesia is a figure and his recovery an exemplary cure.

A last feature of *Lost Horizon* worth pondering involves the implications of the film's last few shots, especially as they raise issues of "readability." It is commonly assumed that Conway *reaches* Shangri-La in the film's last moments, or at least has reached a point where the entrance to the valley is in view – as indicated by an editing trope (Conway glancing off, followed by a shot of the railed archway seen earlier) commonly understood as representing a character's gaze and its object. However, when Conway experiences this vision, he is depicted as standing on a glacier, despite the earlier trek sequence in which the pathway to Shangri-La is represented as a series of ledges or bridges along high-mountain cliffs or ridges. (Even here there is an ambiguity. Capra *wipes* from the last ledge shot of Chang and party to the shot, taken from the valley side of the arch, of the exhausted travelers first entering through it. My willingness to take these actions as roughly continuous, despite the ellipsis implicit in the wipe figure, follows from continuity in the music and from the rail visible through the archway, implying a steep drop below.) Even if we assume that Conway knows where he is, is near in fact to Shangri-La, however, there is no way of taking the point-of-view shot here (as it were) literally given its represented dimensions, taken roughly from the position (in space, off the cliff?) from which Sondra was last photographed leaning on the rail and looking after Conway. Any nearby glacier would be far below the archway entrance; Conway's "view" of the archway must be taken (at best) as a *memory* sparked by proximity.

Crucial to my own understanding of this final moment is the fact that Conway is presented, in the glance shot, with the sun screen left over his right shoulder while he looks up and off frame right. I take this moment as culminating a series of shots from the second trek sequence, both before George's death and after, in which Capra escalates lighting and framing effects, most notably a number of shots where actors are off-frame while their larger-than-life shadows move across the screenlike whiteness of various snow formations. In the context of *Lost Horizon*'s general self-consciousness about the materiality of cinema, such images can be understood as emphatic parables of cinematic "projection." In which light

I want to say that the Shangri-La Conway ''sees'' in this last shot is, as if literally, his shadow, his projection, a memory that always walks on before him. Read vis à vis Conway, this ''vision'' differs in at least one crucial respect from the Shangri-La seen earlier in the film; this vision is *his* vision, the result of *his* efforts and struggle, of his desire. Given Conway's deep kinship to Maria, and in view of Gainsford's description of Conway's superhuman efforts to go beyond the limits of any humanly known world, there is also something self-deluding if not downright suicidal in Conway's Capra-like claim to authorship of his own story, a claim he asserts by kidnapping *himself* to Shangri-La despite the best efforts of Gainsford and the Foreign Office to restrain him. Nevertheless, acting that story out is also a way of taking responsibility for it – something Conway could not have done by merely sitting tight in Father Perrault's lamasery – and it provides occasion for uniting his activist and visionary selves.

What is ''right'' about Shangri-La is finally its vision of an ordinary life protected from the extraordinary pressures of a world gone communally mad. Barnard goes back to plumbing; Lovett returns to the classroom. This world is also ordinary in the sense that its (as it were) middle-class women (George and Robert Conway among them) seem confined by a class structure to lives comprised of hobbies and handicrafts, weaving, raising pigeons, and so forth. That, finally, is also what is wrong with Shangri-La, as Conway and any number of critics over the years have intuited; hence his (their) desire to escape. Even Sondra, though raised in Shangri-La since infancy, seems aware at some level that the world of Shangri-La is as much a trap as a haven; hence her reading habits and her request for Conway and her subsequent agony, despite Chang's reassurance that Conway will return, when Conway leaves Shangri-La. Her conviction that everyone should come to Shangri-La is equally a wish (as Conway points out) that Shangri-La should cease to exist as a society apart; Conway's escape, at some level, grants Sondra her wish, in that now she too is connected to the world beyond the pass, as that world itself is reminded of ideals it has forgotten, the ''ideal'' itself among them.

My reference to Sondra as a reader, and to reading as connecting her (eventually) to the world outside the one she now inhabits, allows me to reconfigure the ambiguity of the film's last point-of-view shot. In brief, I take the ambiguity as token of a potential collapse of narrative into narration via a match between Conway and Capra; each ''projects'' a vision, and their projections (taken together) put the viewer in the position of *willing* whatever conclusion is derived from the film. Thus one *can* understand the images comprising Conway's trek away from Shangri-La and back as somehow representing a real departure and a real arrival. To do so, however, requires overlooking the literal fact that the footage used derives (quite obviously) from a variety of sources; the trekking figure that binds the sequence together, when not literally a shadow, appears in a variety of costumes and variously embodied. Even the obvious Capra-directed studio footage emphasizes the "constructedness" of the image. When George and Conway try to help a fading Maria to her feet, Capra poses them on a ridge, their figures in silhouette against a roiling cloud of backlit snow; after George dies Conway treks onward and is suddenly caught in silhouette on what is obviously the same set, regardless of distance traveled. The last two Himalaya sequences thus continue the cine-"magic" of the film's many sight-gag moments, all of which invite the viewer to acknowledge complicity and assume at least some responsibility for the views shown and taken.

Such cinematic gestures are Capra's escape from the narrative structure of Hilton's fable, as they depict Conway's escape from the "siiken bonds" of Perrault's Shangri-La; in each case authorship is claimed, responsibility taken, though that responsibility is more to a process of realization than to any particular instance of it. Eternity, we might say, is not something glimpsed once and for all; it is rather, to paraphrase Conway, a matter of moments, of taking them, of projecting them. Among Capra's films none has been more variously projected than *Lost Horizon,* a variety that the AFI-restoration print emphatically preserves and proclaims. That its critics persist in taking it (*when* they take it) within the most narrow interpretive limits almost justifies Capra's legendary authorial moodiness. By the time he was writing his autobiography, it must have been depressingly clear that such interpretations were a precondition that made the progressive destruction of Capra's *Lost Horizon* possible. That Capra was himself a party to the process must have made for bitter gall indeed.

CHAPTER V
"This Is a Man's World"
Mr. Smith Goes to Washington

I have already noted the temptation to take Capra's "Mr." films as a closed populist set. A related tendency takes the entire Capra canon as inscribing a parabolic trajectory that tops out with the trilogy and *It's a Wonderful Life* and heads downhill from there as the social conditions that contributed to Capra's popularity changed beyond his recognition or adaptation. Implicit in this latter picture of Capra is a fairly stable set of generic and ideological imperatives, a populist mythology that Capra was destined (as it were) to discover and represent. In the words of Jeffrey Richards, "There is a clear development in the emergence of the classic Capra hero" that culminates in the Lincolnesque Longfellow Deeds: "He combined the innocence, determination and innate goodness of the Langdon character with the common sense of the earlier urban heroes" and in so doing "provided the pattern for the subsequent [Capra] heroes" played by Cooper and Stewart, both of whom "are popular archetypes of the good American," in that sense "perfect Lincoln–Christ figures."[1]

Charles Maland and Raymond Carney both give reasons for doubting the general accuracy of this picture. Maland observes how Capra's life story hardly conforms to this simple rise-and-fall logic, describing it instead as a "wavy and at times jagged" pattern of "striking successes . . . quickly undercut by personal disappointment or disaster."[2] Indeed, it is an uncanny fact of his career that Capra repeatedly rejected his Hollywood persona and position, creating disasters when disaster did not befall him of its own accord, becoming hysterically ill after the success of *It Happened One Night,* for example, or rejecting a big-bucks contract with Fox after making *Arsenic and Old Lace* in favor of joining the U.S. Army Signal Corps. Of more interpretive moment is Raymond Carney's assertion that "Capra's so-called development" proceeds "less along a straight line of artistic 'progress' than as a series of continuous self-corrections or repeated adjustments of course along previously taken paths.''[3] An important duty of the present chapter is to specify how or in what respects *Mr. Smith* differs from *Mr. Deeds,* a difference more than simply hinted at, if my feminist reading of *Mr. Deeds* is still convincing, in the tag line I have taken for this chapter's title.

My reason for breaking the chronology of the trilogy set by discussing *Meet John Doe* in Chapter 1 was to counter the teleological compulsion to reduce *Deeds, Smith,* and *Doe* to a common ideological denominator, by equating the central character of each, for example, with the others or with the mythological gods of the populist American pantheon, Washington, Jefferson, Lincoln, and Grant. We have already seen how tempting literal-mindedness can be on these accounts: Capra's primary characters are populist simpletons, therefore Capra is a populist simpleton. I will eventually want to agree that *Mr. Smith Goes to Washington* strives at several levels for a melodramatic kind of moral clarity. However, the rich tradition of commentary on the film provides evidence aplenty that such clarity does not come simply or easily, at least not in this middle installment of Capra's Cooper–Stewart trilogy.

The conventional way of observing the complexity of the film's ideological project is by emphasizing the film's ''ethos of vocality'' elaborated in Jefferson Smith's virtual ''apprenticeship in public speaking.''[4] Features activated in such readings typically include Jeff's ''immaturity,'' simultaneously political and sexual; and the fact that his position as a U.S. senator, credentialled *to speak,* on *behalf* of constituents, literally and figuratively positions him as a token of ''representation.'' Jeff's task, through the course of the film, is thus to find ''a mature voice – a voice that can confirm and assert his true identity'' while ''simultaneously discovering a voice which permits him to articulate the significant thoughts and feelings of the masses.''[5] Jeff barely *has* a voice at the film's beginning – we do not even *see* him until some fifteen minutes or so into the movie – and the voice he has at film's end is exhausted to the point of silence under the strain of his filibuster. Whatever ''voice'' Jeff has at film's conclusion is clearly a matter for interpretive conjecture, *not* of an unequivocal *presence.*

Behind this obviously problematic equation of ''identity'' and ''voice'' is a composite picture of the social force and fact of language drawn (loosely) from Lacanian psychoanalysis and from speech-act theory. Each is vaguely (partially) allegorized in the narrative trajectory of *Mr. Smith Goes to Washington.*[6] The crucial event in the Lacanian scenario of language acquisition and subject construction, for example, is the moment when the father intervenes between mother and child, demonstrating her lack (of power, of ''the phallus'') and thereby breaking the illusory ''mirror-stage'' bond between mother and child, replacing it (and the Imaginary ''identification'' which it allowed) with language, which is itself nothing but a series of sonic and graphic differences ''sutured'' together, under the threat of castration, into a seemingly coherent and transparent discourse that the child-as-subject ''identifies'' with by speaking it, though such (ostensibly ''free'') speech really only amounts to accepting one's subjugation to the Symbolic ''Law of the Father.''[7] Something very much like this happens to Jefferson Smith. A patriarchal representative of the Law (Governor Hopper) comes in the night to the home Jeff shares with his mother to inform Smith of his (providential) appointment to the United States Senate. Our first glimpse of Jeff comes as the bombastically rhetorical governor introduces him to the farewell banquet celebrating Jeff's appointment, before which gathering a visibly discomfited Jeff Smith is obliged *to speak*. Moreover, the speech he gives effectively subordinates his own voice to that of his senatorial colleague, Joseph Harrison Paine, to judge by Jeff's comment that Paine has served so ably that a second senator is hardly necessary. Indeed, Jeff's promise to do nothing that would ''disgrace the office of United States Senator'' places his voice and service explicitly under the sign of negativity, under threat, a threat (like castration) disavowed or repressed via identification with the Father.

Speech-act theory, unlike Lacanian psychoanalysis, is less concerned with how language is acquired than with how it is used.[8] Two aspects of speech-act theory have recently been taken up by Capra critics, its focus on ''rules,'' or ''conditions,'' and its concern with the ''performative,'' or ''dramatistic,'' aspect of language. What distinguishes speech-act theory from, say, a theory of syntax or grammar is that the latter is relatively unconcerned with the social contexts of language use. Speech-act theory, by contrast, extends the notion of rule to cover the pragmatic conditions within which a speech act takes place, conditions that help to *define* a given speech act *as* an act of a certain kind, a promise, say, or a wedding. A performative, in speech-act parlance, is a locutionary act in which saying *is* doing (the matrimonial ''I do'' is a classic example). The advantage of such a theory to critics of *Mr. Smith Goes to Washington* should be fairly obvious. As critics have repeatedly observed, Jeff Smith's education into language only *begins* with his banquet acceptance speech. Thereafter he undergoes an extended apprenticeship in the procedural rules and conditions that enable him, for example, to seek "recognition" from the president of the Senate, to introduce his bill establishing a National Boys' Camp, to yield or not to yield the floor, to compel the presence of a quorum in the absence of one, to "speak his piece" to the point of exhaustion in the film's climactic filibuster.

One of the many complexities such a picture of language introduces into considerations of *Mr. Smith* involves the extent to which the Law of the Lacanian Father is coextensive with the rules that govern who may speak and how within the theater of representative government embodied in the Senate chamber. That publisher-industrialist James Taylor (Edward Arnold) *functions* as a kind of linguistic lawgiver is evident not only or chiefly in his ability to promote political candidates in his newspapers but rather in the odd contrast of magnitude between the Willet Creek landscam that Jeff's Boys' Camp bill runs afoul of and the massive weight of influence Taylor exercises toward the film's conclusion when he seems to have near complete control of the national press and media corps: Why would someone with that much clout risk it all for the sake of some garden-variety graft? We are little tempted to answer that question in plausible psychological terms; James Taylor is hardly a realistic piece of portraiture. Rather, his excessiveness marks him as the very sign of social power, a power exercised chiefly as and through language, giving orders to some (to Governor Hopper, to Joe Paine) and silencing others (Jeff Smith). The uncanny sense in which Capra's *Mr. Smith Goes to Washington* seems to anticipate the linguistic theories of political modernism is confirmed by Raymond Carney's astute descriptions of Taylor's role in the film: "The Taylor syndicate has established as the lingua franca of political life a self-contained system of political rhetoric emptied of all personal values." "The film imagines a world in which, if not necessarily then at least conceivably, speakers are spoken by their texts, and not the other way around."[9]

A central Lacanian tenet might well be adduced here, to the effect that desire is coincident with language, in that both are a function of lack or absence. Reading Jefferson Smith according to "prototype" schemata of the Jeffrey Richards sort encourages the assumption that Jeff's political ideals are fully formed and in place from the film's beginning. However, such a view of Jeff ignores the way his "political or expressive agenda . . . keeps shifting from scene to scene."[10] The Boys' Camp notion, for instance, though dear to Jeff's heart, is less something he pushes than something he is pushed into – by the press, by Senator Paine, by Saunders. By film's end his only real goal is just to keep talking, as if the very possibility of free speech depended on his ability to hold the floor by continuing to voice the discourse of democracy. Like his fellow journalist and namesake Capra cousin, *Forbidden*'s Lulu Smith, Jefferson Smith is best thought of as "a fugitive figure of desire in quest of a destination or point, which recedes as fast as it is attained."[11] In more Lacanian terms, Jeff has no way of defining his desire until he learns how to speak, a task that takes nearly the entire Plot duration of the film; moreover, any desire that *can* be spoken, at least as Lacan tells the story, is less likely to be Jeff's than that of the Father for whom Jeff speaks.

That *Mr. Smith* is profoundly concerned with institutional or structural matters – as much with the who and how of speech as with the what and why – is confirmed by the film's intertextual relationship with *Forbidden*. Both films have successful politicians (Grover, Paine) as central characters, both of them "actors," each possessed by a politically debilitating secret and a longing to confess; but in neither film do we get any sense of the partisan "substance" of political dispute. The closest we get to conventional partisanship in either film is the distinction made early on in *Mr. Smith* between the majority and minority leaders of the Senate, a purely "relational" definition. This "blankness" is confirmed in *Mr. Smith* by the title of the only legislative bill, apart from Jeff's, that we hear anything about, the "Deficiency Bill," the virtues of which seem generally agreed upon, though upon which (obviously) decisive action is still pending, as if an inability to act were exactly the deficiency in question.

The question of what Jefferson Smith wants is less easily answered, I have suggested, than many critics seem ready to assume. Far clearer, in my current view of the movie, is what Jefferson Smith does *not* want – adult responsibility of the sort that got his editor-father murdered (silenced) for opposing mining interests in an earlier land-grab scheme. During his filibuster Jeff starts to read the Constitution of the United States, beginning with the Preamble. Had Capra not cut away to the battle between Taylor's syndicate and the *Boy Stuff* brigade we might well have heard Jeff recite the following language from Article I, Section 3, Part 3: "No person shall be a senator who shall not have attained to the age of thirty years." In light of which we might well begin to wonder at the more perversely adolescent aspects of Jeff's behavior, despite his apparent age. He is totally deaf to the sarcasm of Susan Paine's constant remarks about his "little feathered friends,'' for instance, as if he were so flummoxed by the thought of sex as to have lost his senses (not to mention his hat) altogether. (When Jeff first meets Susan and her three friends at the train depot, they demand $1 each for the milk fund; Jeff concludes he owes the four of them $5.) Or we might wish to ponder further Jeff's response to the largely humorous (rather than vicious) treatment he initially receives at the hands of the Washington press corps, walking off the Senate floor in a vengeful huff in the hope of punching out the offending scribes.

Underlying Jeff's strange behavior, I take it, are questions of memory and history. The issues are explicitly voiced in the scene alluded to in the title of this chapter, for example, where Joseph Paine distinguishes between two *kinds* of history before urging Jeff to ''forget'' Taylor and what Taylor said and to remain silent during the final debate on the Deficiency Bill. The first history Paine alludes to is that which can be ''absorbed'' by ''seeing sights,'' as Jeff sees them during the Vorkapich-depicted tour-bus montage immediately upon his arrival in Washington. The other history – of how states and empires were made ''since time began'' – is the history of ''compromise'' by means of which ideals are traded for power, the implication being that ideas are effectively *powerless*. It is Jeff's burden, and Capra's, to prove him wrong, by *refusing* the repression of history and voice upon which Taylor's success depends.

The repression issue is *not* confined, however, to the manifestly political plane of the film. Jeff Smith, for example, has a curious habit of making as-if universal pronouncements that he repeatedly fails to abide by or live up to, sometimes without any explicit or conscious regard for the discrepancy between his words and his deeds, as if he had totally forgotten his previous declarations. Early on Jeff avows a willingness to let Senator Paine cast the state's only vote in the Senate, yet after the Press Club crowd derides Jeff as a ''Christmas tiger,'' prepared to nod an automatic stooge-like ''yes'' in response to whatever his senior colleague might say, Jeff corners the latter in the ornate Paine flat and declares himself eager to study bills before voting on them, as if his own voice suddenly mattered. Paine promises advice to Jeff regarding upcoming votes, and Jeff responds, without any apparent reference to his earlier pronouncement: ''That's just the point – there's no reason for me to be here at all.'' (Here is where a somewhat desperate Paine picks up the Boys' Camp cue from Jeff's news conference and urges him to work it up as a bill.) Or consider a line from the filibuster sequence, after Jeff reads from the Declaration of Independence and then declares (like a good speech-act theorist enumerating felicity conditions) that "you're not gonna have a country that can make these kinds of rules *work* if you haven't got men that've learned to tell human rights from a punch in the nose." Thus far, at least, the only nose puncher in evidence is Jeff himself – a point his impassioned delivery of the remark overrides entirely.

One of the most important lines in the film is Jeff's declaration to Senator Paine, as they train their way to Washington after the farewell banquet, that "one man by himself can't get very far" when he "bucks up against a big organization." Coming on the heels of Paine's recitation of the facts surrounding the death of Jeff's father, among them that Joe Paine and Clayton Smith were "twin champions of lost causes," the line applies as much to Paine as to the elder (or the younger) Smith; with Clayton's death Joe Paine lost his twin, became "one man by himself." It is commonly assumed that Jeff's one-man filibuster represents the younger Smith's self-conscious repudiation of this defeatist conclusion, an assumption we will examine more fully in due course. I describe the scene at length, here, as marking the place where a certain set of facts suddenly lined up to raise the repression issue in ways that profoundly reordered my sense of the entire movie.

The tone of the brief train scene between Jeff and Paine is deeply nostalgic, sparked by Paine's observation, upon being handed a copy of *Boy Stuff,* that Jeff is just like his father, printer's ink in his veins, hat always on and ready for journalistic battle. Jeff recalls his father saying that "the only causes worth fighting for were the lost causes," to which Paine replies: "You don't have to tell me, Jeff. We were a team." Indeed, Paine remembers being there to see his martyred "twin" slumped over "that old roll top desk, still with his hat on" – a recollection that prompts Paine, like many a Capra dreamer, to gaze out the window of the train, as if the ideal were just off-frame and visible to those with eyes to see it. At which point one cannot help but wonder how it happened that Senator Paine was apparently taken completely by surprise at the bon-voyage banquet when Jeff *begins* his speech, after declaring his admiration for Paine, by noting that the senator and his late father were best friends and schoolmates. Paine's expression shifts markedly, he leans forward and gazes down the table to Jeff's mother, who nods in reverse-shot response – as if Paine had been completely unaware that Jeff was the son of his best friend and alter ego.

At the time it seems a grace-note moment, a matter of happy surprise. However, Paine's subsequent recitation on the train renders deeply problematic this apparent lapse of memory, as if something well beyond mere forgetting were at stake. It seems highly unlikely that Paine could simply have forgotten that his best friend had a son, especially not when the son's unusual first name is Jefferson, especially not when the child was old enough at the time of his father's death (which Paine personally witnessed) to have secure recall of conversations in which Clayton Smith described Joe Paine as "the finest man he ever knew."[12] By the time Jeff throws Paine's recollections back at him – in the closing moments of the filibuster – it seems beyond doubting that Jeff is less a figure of emotions "recollected in tranquility" than of the deeply repressed newly returned, and with fierce ideological vengeance. At which point we are free to ponder whether Paine had ever *really* forgotten at all, especially in light of his obvious discomfort about the whole Willet Creek affair and his subsequent support of Governor Hopper's decision to defy Taylor's expressed wishes by appointing Jefferson Smith to fill out the deceased Sam Foley's term. As Paine puts it to Taylor: "A young patriot – recites Lincoln and Jefferson – turned loose in our nation's capital. Ya. I think it's alright." Jeff's are not the only desires "turned loose" in the course of the movie.

I have described Jeff Smith as striving to find words for his desires. I also suggested that such striving has its negative aspect, in the sense that knowing one thing can be a way to avoid knowledge of another. We can rephrase this latter claim in light of Joseph Paine's forgetfulness by asking what Jeff Smith has forgotten. The most obvious candidate is "history," a consideration that first dawned on me in connection with the oft-discussed bill-writing scene in Jeff's office. Attention usually focuses on the latter half of the scene, in which Jeff struggles to find words for the spirit he wants the camp (and the bill) to embody. During the scene's first part, however, Jeff listens as Saunders explains the process by which bills are drafted, considered, and voted up or down. The bit is played for comedy, especially by a world-weary Saunders. Clarissa's sarcasm is more than matched, however, by Jeff's naïveté about procedures, some of which (the legislative calendar, say) do seem reasonably arcane from a layman's standpoint. However, Jefferson Smith is not exactly a layman. This is the young Boy Ranger patriot who knows what Washington and Lincoln and Jefferson said "by heart." So how is it that Jeff does not know what a congressional committee is or does – as if Lincoln, say, had never tangled with one? Indeed, Capra stages the scene as a remake of the scene between Sondra and Conway in *Lost Horizon* in which the former (a pigeon fancier too, like Jeff) plays the innocent "child" to Conway's "mother," pestering Conway by repeatedly asking, as Jeff asks the motherly Saunders, "why?" Sondra (Jane Wyatt) has the excuse of her isolation in Shangri-La to explain her ignorance of the outside world that the kidnapped Conway (Ronald Colman) inexplicably longs for; hence her curiosity, which Conway deflects by staging their little play. By contrast, Jeff's naïveté seems oddly willed, especially in view of Chick McGann's comment that Jeff had done nothing during the two-day train trip to Washington but recount the history of the United States. What *kind* of U.S. history is it that can escape all knowledge of how Congress operates?

The same kind of history or historical consciousness that allows Jeff to know absolutely nothing about the likes of James Taylor, one might respond. In the published script, it bears saying, Jeff *does* know at least something about Taylor.[13] In the movie, however, Jeff's ignorance of Taylor and the kind of political power he exercises is total, despite the fact that Jeff's own father was a victim of political assassination; Smith's response to the discovery of corruption, especially after he sees its power to rewrite the script of reality, literally "forging" his identity during the committee hearings called to investigate Paine's Taylor-made charges against Jeff, is a total loss of voice amounting to a skeptical renunciation of the world at large, as if the *difference* between constantive and performative, between signified and signifier, were beyond Jeff's comprehension, and this despite Jeff's journalistic (textual) heritage. By contrast, the world Jeff lives in is chock-full of ordinary people who know very well who Taylor is and what he represents, at least at the film's beginning: for example, the members of the Citizens' Committee who protest the proposed appointment of Horace Miller ("a party man," "Taylor's stooge"), not to mention the Hopper kids, most of them Boy Rangers, who hesitate not at all in razzing their father about his subservience to Taylor ("I wouldn't appoint an old twerp like Horace Miller, Taylor or no Taylor"). How the editor of a statewide weekly, himself the son of a crusading antimonopoly journalist, can avoid knowing the identity of the state's chief publishing magnate and political kingmaker, when everybody *else* seems to know, is hard to figure except as an instance of willed ignorance. That Saunders must eventually reassure Jeff that Lincoln too had his Taylors and his Paines – when the history of the Civil War is shot through with shady dealers and war profiteers – only confirms the wild excessiveness of Jeff's ignorance, an ignorance Jeff hides (from himself) by recourse to a form of textuality, speeches memorized by heart.

A primary instance of repression by textual substitution is Jeff's Boys' Camp bill. Strangely enough, Jeff's discussion of the spirit he longs to embody in his document acknowledges (as if unconsciously) the way documents can repress: "Boys forget what their country means – by just reading 'the land of the free' in history books." The implication is clear that reading history can deaden some prior state of knowledge. I want to say that the Boys' Camp bill itself fulfills a similar diacritical function for Jefferson Smith. That Senator Paine intends it to divert Jeff's attention away from the Deficiency Bill is clear enough. That Jeff welcomes the diversion should also be clear. When he approaches Paine after confronting the press corps it is with the apparent conviction that he ought to study legislation before voting on it, despite his earlier view to the contrary; by the time he leaves his desire is (instead) to "do just that one thing" while in Washington. That his Boys' Camp bill (that one thing) amounts to a sustained effort on Smith's part to avoid responsibility by continuing to live a Boy Ranger life is variously confirmed. Despite the substantial stack of mail we see on Jeff's desk upon his midafternoon arrival at his office, and the promise from Saunders that far larger stacks will "start pouring in from all over the country," Jeff anticipates a busy evening writing letters and explicitly rejects Clarissa's suggestion that he dictate them ("I couldn't talk letters. I just have to sit here and scratch them down"). In the script it is clear that Jeff intends to write chiefly to "the Rangers and Ma."[14] In the film what seems clear is that Jeff intends to do nothing *but* write letters for the rest of the day, as if he had no other duties to attend to, studying bills, perhaps, or attending committee meetings, for example? When Paine meets Jeff on the Senate floor for the first time he explains his tardiness by saying "I was in committee," making it clear, before Saunders makes it clearer, that senators do much more than give speeches. Nearly all of Jeff's energies, by contrast, are devoted to Boys' Camp matters, energies that are expressed almost exclusively by the production or reproduction of text.

It is striking how seldom Capra scholars have taken him to task for all this *Boy Stuff* stuff. Nick Browne is more emphatic than most in this regard. "It's far from clear," writes Browne, "that Capra understands that his audience – projected more or less as a boy scout troop – is also composed of women. Nor is it clear that Capra insofar as he inscribes an audience understands the distinction between a child and an adult.''[15] Much that I have already said about Jeff's excessive childishness refutes the latter claim while acknowledging its relevance. It is certainly true that Senator Paine takes himself to know the difference when he tells Jeff that ''This is a man's world'' by contrast with the Boy Ranger world Jeff ordinarily inhabits. Nevertheless, Browne is certainly right to suggest that the overt ''masculinity'' of *Mr. Smith Goes to Washington* is problematic – all the more so in view of my repeated claims to the effect that Capra is something like a feminist. Should we take Paine's assertion on this account as *mere* description, then, or should we hear ''man's world'' as a form of narrational accusation, at least as it applies to the film's depicted world where ''you've got to check your ideals outside the door, like you do your rubbers''?

Any answer we might provide to that question must eventually confront the fact of Clarissa Saunders. Plot outlines of *Mr. Smith* rarely go beyond noticing that Clarissa coaches Jeff when the time comes for him to filibuster, as if the film's real struggle were entirely one between Jeff and Taylor. That is certainly the way Taylor and Paine tend to see things. When further explanation for Clarissa's presence seems called for, critics typically appeal to the notion of genre, describing her as the love interest that enables Capra to ''bring together in a self-validating configuration, comic form, Christian mythology, and American ideology,'' as if the combination were designed to impose narrative closure and avoid a Story dilemma that Capra could not resolve in sufficiently ''realistic'' terms.[16] However, such descriptions tend to ignore the fact that *Mr. Smith* is one of Capra's *least* erotic movies, at least as measured by the standards of sensual longing on view in *Forbidden,* say, or *It Happened One Night* or *Lost Horizon.* To the extent that comedy (or Capra's cinematic inheritance of it) involves the visually erotic, there is more to be said on the matter of genre as it pertains to *Mr. Smith* – a topic to which we will return.

The most common explanation for the presence of Clarissa Saunders, however, involves her status as an ''identification,'' or ''conversion,'' figure, an audience surrogate. As Charles Affron puts it, Saunders is ''the representative of the most jaded among us.''[17] In her frustration she describes Jeff as ''an infant with little flags in his fists,'' for example, quick upon his arrival in Washington. Nevertheless, she is moved by Jeff's lyrical description of his Willet Creek Shangri-La, and ''if she can be moved to tears and to love, so can the whole democratic nation.''[18] Of course, there are several such viewer surrogates in the film, many auditors and many audiences (e.g., those who hear radio newsman H.V. Kaltenborn describe Jeff's filibuster as "democracy's finest show"), and the differences of knowledge among them can be taken to "inscribe," or "project," the ideological position(s) taken up by the film's off-screen viewers. In the words of Brian Gallagher, "Only we – and within the diegesis, our surrogate, Saunders – know who Smith really is, and to the extent we affirm the rightness of Smith's actions we are also meant to affirm the stated ideological underpinnings – idealism, democracy, individualism – of those actions."[19] In other words, Saunders and other narratively privileged auditors, the viewer included, know far in advance of the film's various on-screen audiences the truth of Jeff's claims regarding the Willet Creek affair. By associating this literal truth of its depicted world with a set of ideological truths obviously derivable from ours, the film effectively forces the viewer to take the latter "truths to be self-evident," or so it is claimed.

The idea of "force," or "inscription," in these latter formulations obviously carries a negative charge. In more Lacanian terms, Saunders "represents" the viewer, is the very sign of our freedom to reject Jeff's ideological naïveté; yet that sign eventually functions less to "free" our speech than to "speak us," by defining our relationship to "the Law" in ways we seem unlikely to interrogate, much less oppose. Put another way, what Saunders finally represents is (textual) repression. "By the end of the film," as Brian Gallagher notes, "she is reduced to virtual silence and denied a central place in the action – i.e., she watches and listens to Smith's filibuster from the Senate gallery."[20] Like the viewer – who also watches and listens – Saunders is eventually repressed by the very language she had hoped to hear spoken.

A number of film-textual details can be adduced to fill out this picture of the "muteness" of women in *Mr. Smith Goes to Washington.* A version of this mute woman motif is always on view whenever Saunders struggles to coach Jeff across the expanse of the Senate chamber. Of course, she is not *always* silent. When the vice-president hesitates to recognize Jeff prior to the vote on the motion to expel him from the Senate, Saunders calls out on Jeff's behalf ("Let him speak!"). Also, toward the end of the filibuster, upon learning that Taylor thugs are attacking Jeff's Boy Rangers, Clarissa calls upon Jeff to stop. Important as these exceptions may be, however, it remains true that Saunders's more normal forms of communicating with Jeff during the filibuster sequence are visual – hand gestures, facial expressions, brief written notes, words more mimed than spoken. Nor is Saunders the only mute female in the movie. I have already noted the moment when Jeff's mother leans forward, over the banquet table, and says a silent hello to Joe Paine. (It is worth noting that when women talk to *each other* in the film, Ma Smith and Clarissa, for instance, though also Clarissa and Susan Paine, it is over the phone, at a distance.) Another silent woman is the governor's wife. We first see her as she listens to her husband talking via telephone to Joe Paine and then Jim Taylor as the news of Sam Foley's death makes the circuit. As her husband says "Yes, Jim," his wife nods in sarcastic agreement, and then observes that Taylor would probably drop dead if her husband ever said "No." I might also cite the use of American folk tunes in the *Mr. Smith* sound track as extensions of this mute, or absent, woman theme. Precisely because of their familiarity, such melodies tend to go unnoticed; we get music only, no words. It is worth noting, however, that three of the primary themes of the movie are tunes – if music evokes lyrics – about missing or absent women, "Darling Clementine" for one, "Jeannie with the Light Brown Hair" for another, not to mention that "Red River Valley" from which they say some bright-eyed woman will soon be leaving.

We have already noted the paradox of film genre by which expression and repression go hand in hand. We have also alluded to the claim that the viewer of classical narrative films is typically conceived or inscribed, by point-of-view shots for example, as male. The fact that a mute woman like Clarissa Saunders is frequently taken as the primary viewer surrogate in *Mr. Smith Goes to Washington* is thus doubly expressive of repression, an implicit acknowledgment that women are more typically denied agency and the gaze. Indeed, one of the key differences between *Mr. Deeds* and *Mr. Smith* is that the acknowledgment of sexual difference, which the earlier film manages only at the deepest subtextual level, is so openly accomplished in the later movie. Put another way, the repression of women is openly expressed in *Mr. Smith Goes to Washington* in ways that far exceed the paradoxical repression of the feminine on view in *Mr. Deeds*. We have Joe Paine's testimony to the effect that the film world of *Mr. Smith* is a "man's world," for instance, a claim amply confirmed by the degree to which the Taylor machine is populated almost entirely by cigar-smoking "old boys." The issue of female ability and its second-rate recompense is openly addressed when Clarissa confronts Paine in his office with the declaration that she "wasn't given a brain just to tell a Boy Ranger what time it is," to which outburst Paine responds (surrounded the while by photographs of male politicians) by offering her "one of the biggest jobs in

Washington'' when Paine moves (or so he implies) into the White House. The clearest acknowledgment that women are at a disadvantage in the world of work and politics is offered by Jeff Smith, during the bill-writing scene, when he tells Clarissa that she has done awfully well ''for a woman,'' and this despite the fact that he has never met anyone ''more intelligent or capable.''

The family resemblance of Clarissa Saunders and *Forbidden*'s Lulu Smith ought to be more than apparent by now. Each is a token of repressed femininity; each is a gazer who, one way or another, drops out of sight. In the script version of *Mr. Smith* there is a scene in which Clarissa telephones Chick McGann to set up a bogus date, thus to free Jeff from his bodyguard and clear the way for Nosey and his fellow newshounds to grill Jeff on his first night in town. Her *nom de phone* is Lulu Love. In the film the Lulu–Clarissa connection is rather more subtly suggested, by mute gesture rather than dialogue. The first thing we see Lulu do upon arriving at the library in *Forbidden* is to replace the flower in her desktop vase with a fresh one. The first thing we see Saunders do in *Mr. Smith,* once she gets off the phone with a frantically Smith-less McGann, is to finish arranging flowers in a vase on *her* desk. Numerous other details reinforce the connection, but most notably the way Clarissa stands to Jeff Smith as Lulu stands to Bob Grover, as ''writer'' to ''reader.'' Each woman authors (or authorizes) the man's speeches, and in each case the relationship is emphatically marked by a point-of-view shot from the man's perspective in which he reads an intimate note, written in the woman's hand, before beginning to speak, the woman looking on from a distant balcony all the while.

I adduce the Lulu–Clarissa connection here as much for difference as similarity. Most crucially, the writer–reader relationship in *Forbidden* is erotic before it is political. Grover's is the worm of political ambition; his political career only provides Lulu (almost literally) with a figure for desire, a means for expressing her own. In *Mr. Smith,* by contrast, the desire expressed in Jeff's speeches is in significant ways Clarissa's before it is Jeff's, even if he too, like Grover, becomes a means of (as it were) delivery. Moreover, the desire in question here, to make a long story shorter, is Clarissa's desire not only to quit the political life she has been leading but to bring Taylor's political machine down in the bargain.

I imagine this claim will prove controversial, to judge by all the criticism that focuses on Jeff Smith as the film's prime populist mover. Any such controversy risks confirming the view that Saunders is the film's primary figure of repressed desire, by further repressing it. However, I would add that the expression of this desire, as in the case of Lulu Smith, involves, as it were, the "return" of the repressed, which Saunders accomplishes by repressing in her turn. What she represses – by denying it to Smith and Paine alike – is her knowledge of how each intends to use Willet Creek. Simply put, it is Clarissa Saunders who precipitates the Willet Creek affair, and in that sense authors the ideological combat of Jeff Smith and Jim Taylor.

It is Clarissa, for example, who sets up Jeff's first press conference – specifically, she says, to finance the new wardrobe she needs before quitting her job and skipping town (shades of Lulu Smith!) – the results of which include:

1. the surfacing of Jeff's Boys' Camp idea and the subsequent report of it;
2. Jeff's confrontation with the press upon reading those reports; and
3. Paine's suggestion that Jeff write up the bill in lieu of reading any others.

I grant that Clarissa could hardly have foreseen all these consequences. However, the scene in Jeff's office when she explains how legislation becomes law makes it profoundly clear that she has all the knowledge necessary to anticipate the consequences of her subsequent actions, all of which push consistently in the direction of confrontation. To continue the list:

4. She withholds from Jeff (if just barely) her knowledge that Paine already has plans for Willet Creek (had Jeff known, he would probably have approached Paine for advice, which Paine would have happily provided by urging Jeff to consider an alternate site, as he testifies he *did* during the hearings of the Committee on Privileges and Elections).
5. She withholds from Paine the fact that Jeff's bill specifies Willet Creek as the camp site, so that Paine does not hear of it until (at the very moment) it becomes a matter of public record, a publicness Clarissa seeks to confirm by getting Diz Moore out of bed to witness the show.
6. She does *not* tell Jeff about the plot to kidnap him to a diplomatic reception so as to keep him off the Senate floor when the relevant portion of the Deficiency Bill is due for its last reading, in which plot she actively collaborates by taking Jeff out shopping for the appropriate bib and tucker.
7. However, she *does* tell him about the Willet Creek crux once it is clear beyond doubting, via the kidnap scheme, that something crooked is in the works, despite

the fact that it is hardly likely (on her own account) that Jeff's bill will ever come up for a vote.

None of which, we should note, is truly necessary to set up the film's basic Story conflict. Jeff could have had his Boys' Camp idea in mind from the beginning, and could have taken seriously his senatorial duty to read upcoming bills before voting, which would have precipitated the same Willet Creek showdown between Smith and Taylor. By assigning this narrational task to Clarissa Saunders, however, Capra declares (yet again) his feminist loyalties. Indeed, this equation of Clarissa and Capra as coauthors (note the echo of the names, hers an expressly feminine name that she ordinarily represses) is confirmed in one of the film's most openly self-reflexive moments, of which there are many, when Clarissa details for Diz Moore the dramatis personae of the "little play" she has so deftly and openly constructed to (as it were) "catch the conscience of the King." Jeff is "Don Quixote Smith, man with bill"; McGann is "One of the supporting characters"; Paine is "The Silver Knight, Soul of Honor – on a tightrope." Moreover, while Saunders provides the voice-over, Capra provides the images, cutting from one player to another at her direction, the shots taken from camera positions only vaguely related to the spatial position occupied by Saunders and Diz in the Senate gallery. (Compare this to the more obviously conventional point-of-view cutting of the earlier sequence in which a page explains to Jeff the social geometry of the Senate chamber.) As in the very similar sequence in *Mr. Deeds,* in which Longfellow's comments on the testimony against him are accompanied by cutaway shots of the witnesses in question, shots that are both unnecessary and unavailable to the film's on-screen audience, so too in this sequence the intrusiveness of narration is emphasized by the film's direct address to its off-screen audience, in which Capra is to us as Saunders is to Diz Moore.

Saunders's status as Capra's primary on-screen surrogate is securely established by the time of Jeff's first speech and is confirmed on subsequent occasions. When she is absent – as when Smith rises to speak against the Deficiency Bill or is asked to testify before the Committee on Privileges and Elections – Jeff is quickly silenced. When she returns – at the Lincoln Memorial, looking down at Jeff, like a waiting Lincoln come to life – Jeff rediscovers his voice, finds a way to speak again the "fancy words" that the actions of Taylor and Paine had rendered apparently useless. (That this recovery of language amounts to Jeff's discovery of maturity is emphasized by the casual way he asks Clarissa where they can get a drink – implicitly something alcoholic – as they leave the Lincoln Memorial.) A consequence of taking Clarissa as Capra's authorial surrogate is to render the whole question of surrogacy or agency in *Mr. Smith* far more complex than it is typically pictured. Equally complex is the question of Clarissa's motive. That is, having established that Saunders effectively authors the film's primary actions, we still do not know *why* she does it. Or perhaps the problem is that her explicit statements of motive ring oddly false, as if here too a species of repression or substitution were at work.

The incoherence of Clarissa's actions first dawned on me when, just prior to digging the Deficiency Bill out of her office files, Clarissa turns to Jeff and announces that Diz Moore is the man she intends to marry. We cut away to a brief medium-shot of a drunken Diz confirming his status as Clarissa's fiancé, then to close-ups of Jeff and Clarissa. Before Jeff can say a word, Saunders blasts him for his silence: "Why don't you say something – don't just stand there?" Several intertextual threads come together here, as if something more were going on than seems readily apparent. What comes most immediately to mind is a deeply analogous moment during the night-court scene in *You Can't Take It with You* when Alice turns to Tony (or Arthur turns to Stewart) and blasts the younger Kirby for *his* silence ("About time you spoke up!"). The earlier scene, I have argued, is clearly a piece of improvised theater, staged by Grandpa Vanderhof to test Tony's commitment to Alice, a test he nearly fails. That the *Mr. Smith* version of the scene is equally theatrical is evident on several accounts. We know, on the basis of scenes Jeff does not witness, that the engagement of Saunders and Diz should not be taken seriously, at least as an erotic proposition. The probability that Jeff would in fact *be* in his office, writing more letters, is already clearly established; Saunders knows she will have a particular and particularly interested audience for her seemingly hysterical departure scene. Moreover, the immediately preceding restaurant scene, in which an ostensibly inebriated Clarissa proposes to Diz in language echoing that of the bill-drafting scene, is too self-conscious by half to be taken "straight." Indeed, like many another Capra drunk – Grover in *Forbidden,* Conway in *Lost Horizon* – Clarissa *uses* the excuse of drunkenness (like a good speech-act theorist) to get at the truth, though the truth most obviously in question has to do chiefly with the Willet Creek affair. So what seems less than readily explicable is why Clarissa uses the prospect of her marriage to Diz

Moore as prologue to her spilling of the Willet Creek beans. What's love got to do with it?

My answer to the latter question requires asking another that is equally as puzzling – What's Susan Paine got to do with it? When Clarissa is not evoking Jeff's idyllic description of the wonders of western nature – for Diz in the restaurant or (sarcastically) for Jeff in his office – she returns (as if) compulsively to the topic of Susan Paine. While Diz mixes before-dinner drinks in her apartment, for example, Saunders expresses her general disgust with the Taylor crowd in terms that are doubly canted. In the first place, she construes Jeff's situation as a "fight," though she knows full well Jeff's bill will probably bog down in committee, not to mention the likelihood, implicit in Paine's unhappy decision to have Susan snatch Jeff from the Senate floor on the afternoon of the Deficiency Bill's last reading, that the bill's passage will render moot any dispute over that particular camp site, leaving untouched the more general issue of the camp itself.[21] (There *is* no fight until Saunders makes it one!) Second, within this already canted context, Saunders characterizes the Taylor and company tactics by sexually loaded reference to Susan Paine: "It's clouts below the belt I can't take. Sicking that horrible dame on him – when he's goofy about her." She repeats herself in the restaurant scene, though upping the ethical and sexual ante by describing Susan in decidedly phallic terms: "Steering a poor dope up blind alleys for that grafting Taylor mob is low enough. But helping that dame cut him in little bits and pieces." All of which is rendered deeply problematic by the fact that Jeff's relation to either woman is all of four days old – and his relation to Susan, as far as Clarissa has evidence, amounts to little more than a once-confirmed newspaper report that Jeff finds Susan pretty and his comical loss of hand–eye coordination when he tries to take off his hat and talk to Susan on the phone simultaneously. Indeed, the only explicitly goofy person we see in the course of the film is, in fact, Clarissa Saunders, a goofiness she admits to Diz, as the filibuster gets started, and to Jeff, in a note quoting Diz, even later.

Clarissa's description of Jeff's situation as a fight is clearly a matter of self-projection, a (doubly) self-fulfilling prophecy. The same can be said of her description of Susan Paine as a femme fatale. At a fairly obvious level, Clarissa's excessive anxiety about Jeff's goofiness is a displaced version of her own; her fear that Jeff will be hurt expresses the fear that *she* will be: "I don't have to take it. I won't be party to no murder." However, the murderess in question is less Susan Paine than Clarissa Saunders, as her own remark about "helping that dame cut him in bits and pieces" half indicates. Clearly, Jeff is *not* in love with Susan Paine nor does he really stand to be hurt by her glamorous insincerity. Once Clarissa spills the Willet Creek beans, no mention is made of Susan Paine *at all;* telling Jeff the truth about Susan is less an emotional favor than a prod to action. What seems at issue in Clarissa's Susan Paine fixation is the latter's implicit status – confirmed early by her father's declaration to McGann that Susan "isn't here to carry out assignments like that for anybody" and late by the appearance of Jim Taylor waving a diamond bracelet before a bevy of Susan-like lovelies – as a political prostitute. Clarissa's identification with Susan is thus symptomatic of her own institutional circumstances under patriarchy; her condemnation of Susan is equally condemnation of herself. Indeed, the film represses the moment when Paine (evidently) reverses himself and asks Susan's help in keeping Jeff occupied; what we get instead is the subsequent moment when Susan asks for Clarissa's assistance in getting Jeff properly attired for the reception, as if the dirty task were being passed along to Saunders.

However, Saunders is obviously not content simply to quit and have done with it. Rather, like Lulu Smith, Saunders evidently has visions of bringing the whole show down with her. Her description of Jeff as someone who is vulnerable below the belt, and specifically to twisting or cutting knives, casts Jeff in the female role, as someone Clarissa is prepared to *use* for her own purposes. Moreover, the pain of it all for Clarissa seems to condense around the fact that Jeff's words are, somehow, her words, as his silence is eventually a version of her silence, the result of male-typical "Taylor-made" repression. Hence, perhaps, the ironic force with which "pain(e)" is made to rhyme with "dame" in the apartment scene. Mr. Smith is Clarissa's masculine self, we might say, empowered to speak on the Senate floor in her stead, as Babe Bennett is the feminine alter ego of Mr. Deeds whose voice he effectively "borrows" during the sanity hearing. Clarissa's identification with Jeff makes him her "twin," a sisterly champion of lost feminist causes, someone who can see the country through Lady Liberty's eyes, as Jeff urges his Senate colleagues to see it during the filibuster. Indeed, in so doing Jeff openly echoes Clarissa's own Lincoln Memorial conceit about the kind of faith that enables one "to lift his thought up off the ground." No longer alone, Clarissa can now "buck up against a big organization," though doing so, as Clarissa indicates when she describes the filibuster scheme to Jeff as a forty-foot dive into a tub of water, comes something near to being suicidal, a classic Capra leap into the void.

Two aspects of this leap require further comment. One of these involves the erotic component of the Saunders–Smith relationship. An obvious point of comparison here is the *It Happened One Night* auto-camp scene in which Peter Warne both arouses and denies the desire of Ellie Andrews via his Pacific island soliloquy. Jeff's tête-à-tête dissertation about Liberty and the Capitol dome and the wonders of nature occasions a similar arousal in Clarissa, an arousal marked in both cases by Capra's emphatic shift from key-and-fill medium-shots to gauzy soft-focus close-up, as if to mark the woman's desire to merge into the liquid space evoked by each man's fantasy of a singularly unified nature, a nature "full" of wonder, in which "you and the moon and the water all become one."

A way of marking the *difference* of the two scenes is to note the temporal placement of each. Peter's speech comes late in *It Happened One Night.* It culminates a whole series of scenes – the first wall of Jericho scene, the scene of Peter carrying Ellie across a moonlit stream, the subsequent haystack sequence – that are deeply erotic, not only in the actions and emotions depicted (Ellie flipping her lingerie over Jericho's wall), but in Capra's expressionist visual treatment as well, which tends to emphasize the almost symbiotic relationship of water and light – via rainwater on windows or by light reflected off the dancing surface of a country stream. By the time Ellie, dressed in Peter's pajama's, asks from her side of the rope-and-blanket screen whether Peter has ever contemplated marriage, the aura of frustrated sexual desire is palpable and deeply threatening, as Peter's subsequent speech makes clear, though his assertion that "somebody that's real, somebody that's alive . . . don't come that way any more" is contradicted by every word he speaks. The world he describes as distant beyond reaching is right there, is the life he has just lived and is living, in the sense that his words are equally as descriptive of scenes we have already witnessed as of some otherworldly paradise. The fact that Ellie fully shares his fantasy only makes it more threatening by making it that much more real, more present.

Jeff's speech, by contrast, comes relatively early in *Mr. Smith Goes to Washington.* It is arguably his first piece of extended discourse. What lies behind it, moreover, is not a series of bedroom scenes charged with physical longing but, chiefly, a pair of Slavko Vorkapich montage sequences, one moving us from the governor's mansion to the bon-voyage banquet, the other comprising Jeff's tour of Washington sites and monuments. The first montage introduces the star motif – referring as much to James Stewart, perhaps, as to the superimposed flaglike stars answering to Governor Hopper's half-cynical description of the banquet as ''star-spangled'' – and the motif of the Capitol dome; both motifs figure importantly in the second montage sequence and in Jeff's spirit speech itself. The tour montage is also deeply ambivalent, despite Jeff's wide-eyed presence. At a certain level it represents Jeff's passionate vision of American history – a passion subsequently qualified by Jeff's apparent ignorance of that history. A good many shots from the sequence, however, are shots *of* Jeff, so at least some external perspective is suggested. Indeed, the middle passage of the tour montage dispenses with the glance shot of Jeff altogether in its depiction of Civil War statuary and headstones, including a bas-relief battle sword and the tomb of the unknown soldier, tokens perhaps of the phallic violence of which Jeff strives to remain unconscious, though his absence from the image half implies that these images, more than the others, are truly Jeff's, however deeply repressed they may be, so that *our* view of them is also understandable as a matter of narrational direct address. Put another way, the sight-seeing montage is not unitary but deeply conflictual in its implications, a conflict underscored by superimposing a waving-flag star motif over the Civil War monuments and headstones, as if this star-spangled spectacle were equally as subject to ideological manipulations as the bon-voyage banquet.

When an impassioned Jeff Smith strides to the window of his office and points to the Capitol dome in the distance, then, as betokening the spirit he wants his Boys' Camp bill to embody, the passion in question is clearly something *other* than that which is on display in *It Happened One Night,* regardless of the more obvious similarities between these two scenes – and this despite the odd fact that Clarissa Saunders, for the only time in the film, appears in a costume that is openly sexual, a diaphanous white blouse over some kind of dark bustier! I take this latter feature and Jeff's apparent blindness to it as indicating that the eroticism of his relationship with Saunders is, as it were, pre-Oedipal, not a matter of confirmed (ego) ideals and (gender) roles but of unfocused sexual and political energy, a kind of ''transitional realm'' where choices and objects are fluid, like the water-filled landscape of the rural paradise Jeff evokes for Clarissa.[22]

That this energy is potentially dangerous is already evident from the montage sequence and is subsequently confirmed by Clarissa's remarks to

Jeff at the Lincoln Memorial. Liberty and death go hand in hand. However, all Jeff's talk about living as if you had just seen the light at the end of some "long dark tunnel," coupled with the breastlike fullness of the Capitol dome, also evokes a more positive fantasy, of birth-giving and maternal nurturance – at which point Jeff's rapt attention to Clarissa's account of how bills are considered can be understood as a version of Lacan's Imaginary mirror phase in which mother and child express mutual attunement by means of vocal tones and facial features quite apart from the semantic import of what is spoken. This aspect of the bill-writing scene *is* decidedly erotic, but an eroticism less evocative of adult sexuality than of the childhood play upon which adult sexuality eventually draws inspiration. Indeed, by casting Jeff as her extempore Don Quixote Saunders seizes the opportunity that play affords to identify herself with Jeff by enlisting him in her cause, as her representative. In that sense, Jeff "gives birth" to Saunders by allowing her, as it were, to give new birth to him, sending him out into the world – hence perhaps the "transitional object" rag doll Saunders takes out of her desk and waves around to punctuate her seemingly drunken disputation on political poltroonery. This almost childlike "more perfect union" of Jeff and Clarissa is subtly confirmed by a moment midway through the bill-writing scene when Capra uses a wipe–dissolve match-on-action to equate Clarissa's shadow, moving left to right as Clarissa goes to get paper and pencil, with Jeff Smith, who paces back and forth across the same space in search of words for his ideals. I want to say that Clarissa Saunders and Jefferson Smith, like Sondra and Conway in *Lost Horizon,* are each shadows or projections of the other. Their very mutuality betokens their vulnerability, their individual weakness in the face of worldly danger. That they face it together indicates that something like love has everything to do with it.

The other aspect of the Saunders–Smith leap into the void worth noting briefly is the way it echoes Capra's own immanent leap into the capitalist void as an independent producer-director – a subject of fan-mag speculation as early as August 1938 when Capra hit the cover of *Time.* For Capra and Clarissa alike, "Don Quixote Smith, Man With Bill" is a farewell production that bids adieu to a particular set of institutional circumstances, a production amounting almost literally to a declaration of independence after which easy reconciliation with the status quo ante will be extremely difficult. Each, literally, manufactures a crisis situation that requires the frantic and (variously) open manipulation of all available media resources, chief among them the voice and person of Jimmy Stewart, but including as well the press and the theatrical and sonic resonances of the Senate chamber itself. Clarissa could hardly be planning to take another government job in the near future, despite Joe Paine's last-minute confession. Capra's depiction of the relationship between big business and big government hardly seems designed to calm the waters set roiling by the ongoing dispute within Congress and the Justice Department over the studio practice of block booking, a practice that Capra would subsequently seek to ''buck up against'' in making and marketing *Meet John Doe* after his departure from Columbia Pictures.[23] Indeed, Jim Taylor's ''Buy it or wreck it'' philosophy of media acquisition and control cuts pretty close to the capitalist Hollywood bone – thanks perhaps to screenwriter Sidney Buchman's leftist leanings – and the accusations against Jeff Smith, both on the Senate floor and in committee, always hinge on his desire to ''profit'' from his position, to the point where ''profit,'' ''graft,'' and ''fraud'' become effectively synonymous, in the film world if not in ours. Small wonder that the film engendered such vehement opposition, for being anti-American, upon its premier and initial release.

In discussing *Mr. Deeds Goes to Town* I devoted concerted attention to its stylistic reticence, its self-consciousness evident chiefly as a function of an implicitly feminist un-consciousness. I have already noted the way in which the gender repression on view in *Mr. Smith* is far more openly expressed, a textual feature, in light of Clarissa's status as Capra's narrational surrogate, which also bears on the degree of artistic self-consciousness on view in *Mr. Smith Goes to Washington*. Nearly everything I have thus far written about the film stands behind the claim that *Mr. Smith* is one of Capra's (and Hollywood's) most decisively self-reflexive movies. Indeed, Raymond Carney describes the whole of the film as a contest of aesthetic styles in which the impersonal montage style of the Taylor machine stands opposed to the far more ''melodramatic'' and personal mode of expression practiced by Jeff and Clarissa, a contest that comes to crescendo during the filibuster sequence when close-ups of Jeff reading (as if to himself) from St. Paul's letter to the Corinthians are flooded out of the frame by the rushing montage of Boy Rangers and Taylor goons locked in near-mortal struggle over the issue of whether Jeff's truth will be heard back home.

As token that Capra's narrational self-consciousness extends *beyond* his use of surrogate authors – Taylor, Vorkapich, Clarissa Saunders – I want to pick up a stylistic thread left hanging in Chapter 1. In "Picturing Capra" I cited a scene early in *Mr. Smith* in which Taylor and Paine discuss the prospects for replacing Sam Foley, a scene filmed largely in a series of medium two-shots taken from the same angle, thus breaking the 30-degree rule. The result is a series of mismatches, most spectacularly when Capra cuts from one shot to another in such a way that Joe Paine's crossed hands suddenly criss cross, right hand over left hand instantly becoming left over right. Given the *substance* of the scene – involving Paine's expressed desire to drop the Willet Creek scam and Taylor's retort that it would be a "crime" to do so, especially in light of the danger delay would pose to Paine's national ticket aspirations – I find it tempting to think here in terms of a "double-cross," of Taylor, say, by Paine – which, after a fashion, is pretty much what happens. The issue of the Taylor–Paine match is also raised in more obvious terms, by dialogue, as noted, but also by the only significant break from the two-shot pattern, an over-the-shoulder insert of a newspaper page featuring a full-bleed picture of Joseph Harrison Paine ("Scion of Patriots"). Apart from the obvious fact that true patriots do not indulge in environmentally reprehensible real-estate scams at the expense of the public purse, the photo is also a mismatch or misrepresentation in strictly *visual* terms. The Paine we see in most shots wears glasses; Taylor's "patriot" does not.

A similar species of mismatch is evident when the scene is repeated on two later occasions. In all three scenes, the dialogue sounds basically the same themes – Paine's discomfort with the Willet Creek affair, Taylor's reply by reference to future political prospects – but Capra's visual treatment shifts markedly from scene to scene, a difference marked for future reference by the initial series of mismatched shots. The second scene, taking place in Taylor's Washington, D.C., hotel suite just before he attempts to buy Jeff off, again has Taylor and Paine tête-à-tête in an anteroom, but jump-cut two-shots are now replaced by extended long takes and a moving camera that tracks in and out as Paine and Taylor move together or apart, eventually reversing screen positions.[24] The third scene, taking place in the same room during Jeff's filibuster, goes for yet a third treatment, not jump cuts, or long takes, but classical shot/reverse-shot close-ups. In David Bordwell's lingo this amounts to "parametric narration," a mode in which film style functions independently of Story or Plot. Capra's narrational independence is, by the third instance, clear enough. However, style also serves a commentative function; the deeper Paine goes into the Willet Creek affair, the more pressingly conventional and restrictive become his visual and political relationships.

Capra's narrational "presence" is thus emphatically marked in *Mr. Smith Goes to Washington,* by visual strategies, by use of surrogate narrators. Another aspect of cinematic self-consciousness in *Mr. Smith* is a matter of intertextuality. I have already had occasion to note the film's indebtedness to *Forbidden, It Happened One Night,* and *You Can't Take It with You.* A more elusive but ultimately more crucial intertext of *Mr. Smith* is *Lost Horizon.* Any number of local moments (beyond several already mentioned) could be cited to affirm the connection: Jeff looking out his window at the Capitol dome, for example, echoes the moment when Conway gazes out a window at the snow-capped peak that dominates the Valley of the Blue Moon. Or the gender-fluid comradeship of the Thomas Mitchell and Isabel Jewell characters in *Lost Horizon* – especially in view of the latter's explicit feminism – could be seen to anticipate the similar pairing of Thomas Mitchell and Jean Arthur in *Mr. Smith.* However, what is most at stake in the *Lost Horizon–Mr. Smith* comparison is finally the question of film style. Briefly put, the stylistic "expansiveness" of *Mr. Smith* – the full-throated orchestral score, the virtuoso montage sequences and lighting effects, even the impassioned address to moral and political issues – is almost unthinkable apart from the chances Capra took and learned from in making so openly epic a film as *Lost Horizon,* however poorly the latter film has fared with critics.

The melodramatic "excessiveness" of both films – especially the way narration in each doubles the actions of characters or pressures the depicted world to yield up otherwise repressed or occulted meanings – marks both as instances of "the melodramatic imagination" described by Peter Brooks. That *Mr. Smith* is generally taken as the more successful movie might reflect a deeper kinship of subject and technique than is on view in *Lost Horizon,* to the extent that melodrama is a historically "democratic" genre, its events taking place in a topical world where the traditional "sacred" exists only as remnants or fragments (Saunders: "Pray, Diz, if you know how"), where "feudal" powers threaten virgin daughters of subordinate classes (Jeff: "For a woman you've done awfully well"), where virtue is expressed as and in the "individual act of self-understanding" or public "self-nomination" (Clerk: "Mr. Smith?" Jeff: "Here!"), and so forth.[25] Both for its characters and its creators, melodrama "strives to find, to articulate, to demonstrate, to 'prove' the existence of a moral universe which, though put into question, masked by villainy and perversions of judgment, does exist and can be made to assert its presence and its categorical force among men."[26]

In thus undertaking to enact the signs of virtue in the most explicit and public of manners, melodrama "represents a democratization of morality and its signs."[27] That the resulting representations are so excessive and hysterical is a sign that morality is indeed a "performative," a matter of (something like) *speech acts,* not the simple rehearsal of some mythological prototype, though "fragments" of myth may well abound. By the same token, melodrama also entails a conservative (or nonprogressive) element, an element Brooks elaborates by contrasting melodrama and comedy:

What is being blocked in melodrama is very seldom the drive toward erotic union. . . . What is blocked, submerged, endungeoned is much more virtue's claim to exist qua virtue. Thus with the triumph of virtue at the end, there is not, as in comedy, the emergence of a new society formed around the united young couple, ridded of the impediment represented by the blocking figure from the older generation, but rather a reforming of the old society of innocence, which has now driven out the threat to its existence and reaffirmed its values.[28]

The paradox of melodrama, as being both radical and regressive, echoes the paradox of film genre. An additional level of complexity is introduced into such determinations, however, when we recall how remarriage comedy differs from classical comedy at exactly the same point where melodrama differs: In melodrama and remarriage comedy alike, social progress is "blocked" by a kind of social ignorance, in each case an ignorance of something like the transcendental, something that could figure real social transformation. Cavell sketches a comic version of that figure as follows in *Pursuits of Happiness:*

Comedies of remarriage typically contain not merely philosophical discussions of marriage and of romance, but metaphysical discussions of the concept that underlines both the classical problem of comedy and that of marriage, namely, the problem and the concept of identity – either in the form of what becomes of an individual, or of what has become of two individuals. On film this metaphysical issue is more explicitly conducted through the concept of difference – either the difference between men and women, or between innocence and experience, or between one person and another, or between one circumstance and another – all emblematized by the difference, hence the sameness, between a marriage and a remarriage.[29]

The blockage in remarriage comedy comes about because the society typically depicted "does not regard the difference between men and women as the topic of metaphysical argument; it takes itself to know what the difference means," which means "there can in general be no new social reconciliation."[30] Indeed, what is most melodramatic about remarriage comedy is a potential for violence that is repeatedly associated with a "fixed" or "split" picture of sexual difference. We see this most clearly in Cukor's *Adam's Rib* where Adam's appearance as a melodramatic "despoiler of virtue" in a silent (home) movie links up with the way his "manly" behavior in the main plot is understood as "a melodramatic threat to the romance of his and Amanda's marriage."[31] We see a similar threat to romance, equally violent and monstrous, at work in *It Happened One Night,* where Cavell interprets Peter Warne's interpretation of the wall of Jericho as follows:

> What it censors is the man's knowledge of the existence of the human being "on the other side." The picture is that the existence of others is something of which we are unconscious, a piece of knowledge we repress, about which we draw a blank. This does violence to others, it separates their bodies from their souls, makes monsters of them; and presumably we do it because we feel that others are doing this violence to us. The release from this circle of vengeance is something I call acknowledgment.[32]

The connection between melodrama and masculine brutality, the latter understood as ignoring or denying some usually female (or feminine) other, is repeatedly enacted in Capra. Part of what makes *Forbidden* so deeply fascinating is the way Lulu and Grover repeatedly encounter and *survive* exactly this dilemma – not just once, as is typically the case in remarriage comedy, but time after time over a twenty-year span. The connection between acknowledgment and something like marriage is also a standard Capra motif – hence, perhaps, the credit usually accorded to *It Happened One Night* as the founding instance of screwball or remarriage comedy. Even here the connection is tenuous; Cavell discusses at length the fact that Peter and Ellie do not *begin* the film married to each other, which leads him to wonder what marriage amounts to and how Peter and Ellie's time together on the road provides sufficient basis for their eventual (re)union. The same questions far more obviously apply to the relation of Jeff and Clarissa in *Mr. Smith Goes to Washington,* which seems on the face of it decidedly less erotic or adult than the relationship of Peter and Ellie in *It*

Happened One Night. So what basis is there for hoping that Jeff and Clarissa will, in some meaningful sense, "remarry"? To answer we evidently need some way of connecting childhood and adulthood, of connecting male and female, a picture of sexual and social development that offers a plausible account of how inequality is both maintained and overcome.

The key here – suggested variously by Freud, Lacan, Cavell, and others – is the link between childhood experience and the structure of adult sexual and social relationships. Nearly all scenarios of human development focus on the difficult and paradoxical process of "differentiation": "the individual's development as a self that is aware of its distinctness from others."[33] We have already seen how *Mr. Smith* can be understood as enacting the Lacanian picture of these matters, though Lacan's picture is that the difference is never, finally, *real,* and (less certainly) that the process is fairly singular or punctual, a matter of identification shifted once and for all from mother to father, from the Imaginary to the Symbolic. Both Cavell and Jessica Benjamin, by contrast, see the process as a matter of never-ending and creative *tensions* in the relation of self to other, though in Benjamin's view *establishing* that tension is the most difficult problem with which parents and children are tasked, especially in contemporary western societies. "The need of the self for the other is paradoxical," Benjamin writes in words that echo Cavell's speech-act theory analyses of acknowledgment, "because the self is trying to establish himself as an absolute, an independent entity, yet he must recognize the other as like himself in order to *be* recognized by him"; "at the very moment of realizing our own independence, we are dependent upon another to recognize it"; "and this, in turn, means I must finally acknowledge the other as existing for *himself* and not just for me."[34] When acknowledgment is refused, especially in infancy or early childhood, the whole world of reciprocal differences and acknowledgments goes with it; what remains is Hegel's master–slave version of the paradox in which the world is either dominated or submitted to, the latter often by means of an idealized picture of the former. The slave identifies, that is, with the idealized master as a way of denying the powerlessness of the slave position, though only at the cost of continued subordination, continued inequality.

Benjamin makes this last point in terms that are especially resonant as they apply to *Mr. Smith Goes to Washington:* "Identification with the aggressor, embodying the wish to merge with and be like the all-powerful other, is an effort to escape the necessity of destroying the father." "That this acceptance of powerlessness in the guise of autonomy may deny our responsibility to care for others is rationalized by the notion that we can, after all, do nothing to help them.''[35] I take these two sentences as an apt description of Jefferson Smith's paradoxical circumstance. Though a walking repository of American ideals, Jeff has a curiously passive side that comes through most clearly in his supposition, expressed in discussing his father's death with Senator Paine, that ''when a fellow bucks up against a big organization like that, one man by himself can't get very far, can he?'' We might say that Taylor is the master here, and Jeff the slave who denies his own anger and autonomy and responsibility to others by idealizing the Law of the Father. That this idealizing on Jeff's part marks his kinship to Taylor, and serves to mask a capacity for violence, is fully on display when Jeff dashes around Washington, D.C., punching out reporters for the sin of misrepresentation. One of Capra's classical sight gags underscores the point. We have already noted the star motif that initiates the bon-voyage banquet; once the star-spangled montage resolves itself we get our first real glimpse of Jeff, and we eventually see another reproduction of Gilbert Stuart's portrait of George Washington. When Jeff subsequently accosts one reporter in a Capitol Hill hallway and knocks him for a loop, the camera shoots the punch almost from the reporter's perspective, a close-up of Jeff with a portrait of a young George Washington in the background. Once hit, the reporter ''sees stars,'' mostly close-ups of the starlike pattern of the marble floor; and when he comes to after Jeff's hasty departure he focuses on the portrait of Washington, as if it had been George himself who threw the punch. The implicit equation of Taylor and Jeff is not exactly or merely funny, especially not when their violence is (falsely) attributed to, is in that sense masked by, a national idol or ideal.

Central to Benjamin's elaboration of the psychology of development is the ''rapprochement'' phase in which the child's instinctive assertion of omnipotence is (ideally) matched by a caregiver's both asserting and *sharing* a recognition of human finitude or limits, the difference between wants and needs, say; narcissism or omnipotence on both sides of the parent–child dyad is given up in favor of the mutual attunement that *discovers,* as both revealing and creating, the real world, the ''intersubjective'' world, a world of *shared* tensions and responsibilities. Crucial to this phase is a process of ''destruction,'' as defined by D. W. Winnicott, in which the child's natural aggression toward the parent takes the form of ''a refusal, a negation, the mental experience of 'You do not exist for me,' whose favorable outcome is pleasure in the other's survival."[36] It is as if the desire for a world of shared experience is finally (contra Freud) more basic than the desire for control or for fantasy gratification; what destruction really destroys is boundless fantasy. Apart from the uncanny way in which Winnicott's summary of the destruction phase of rapprochement describes Peter Warne's actions and motives in the second auto-camp scene of *It Happened One Night* – his denial of Ellie's reality by sending her back to her side of the blanket – there is an obvious echo in Benjamin of Cavell's whole remarriage paradigm, in which a marriage is destroyed so that it may subsequently and pleasurably survive. That this destruction partakes of the childish, portrayed by forms of game playing and often infantile bickering, by characters learning to "speak the same language," is a point Cavell repeatedly makes, often by noting the odd *lack* of children in the films of the remarriage genre. "Almost without exception," Cavell remarks, "these films allow the principle pair to express the wish to be children again, or perhaps to be children together. In part this is a wish to make room for playfulness within the gravity of adulthood. . . . If it could be managed, it would turn the tables on time, making marriage the arena and the discovery of innocence."[37]

I have already noted the mutual attunement of Jeff and Clarissa on display in the crucial bill-writing scene of *Mr. Smith Goes to Washington,* which might aptly be described as enacting "the discovery of innocence." It is clearly the childhood feature of the remarriage genre that *Mr. Smith* inherits and interprets, as if elaborating the premarriage phase that other films of the genre only allude to, the rapprochement that prefigures remarriage. However, something beyond innocence is also in train here. Clarissa is far from innocent in plotting to destroy the Taylor political machine. The logic of events runs something like this. Clarissa recognizes Jeff's idealism as a disguised form of aggression, an aggression that has its basis in the failure of rapprochement brought about by the assassination of his father when Jeff was of a tender age; Jeff's father did *not* survive, so Jeff could not work through the Oedipal crisis, could not fully believe in his *own* survival, and therefore does not yet live in the real world. Clarissa also recognizes James Taylor as a figure of infantile omnipotence, writ large as Hegelian mastery, a mastery that she takes as figuring her own doctor-father whose great largesse, though a matter of kindness to unfortunate patients, left Clarissa and her mother in the financial lurch, where still she dwells. Her kinship with Jeff thus provides both the occasion and the means for a ''slave revolt'' (or children's crusade) that will destroy the patriarchal status quo that is itself symptomatic of arrested social development. Whether it can or should survive destruction is a good question – made all the better by the global political situation at the time of the film's release on the eve of World War II.

The better hope, for which Jeff's Boys' Camp stands as emblem, is for restoring to the world a sense of difference and of mutual attunement – of finitude mutually shared – that will stand in significant opposition to the destructively ''omnipotent'' childishness that characterizes the world as it stands. On this account we might well note how Jeff's filibuster both enacts and depends on a series of differences or distinctions. Jeff describes his Boys' Camp as providing an education in difference, an education the ''man's world'' of the film desperately needs: ''It seemed like a pretty good idea, getting boys from all over the country, boys of all nationalities and ways of living, getting them together; let them find out what makes different people tick the way they do.'' Jeff's subsequent reverie about seeing America through Lady Liberty's eyes includes a view of freedom that incorporates differences of ''race, color, or creed'' within a shared picture of human freedom and decency. A number of less obvious details also contribute to this elaboration of difference – Jeff's distinguishing among various ways of yielding the floor, for instance; or his observation that certain parts of the Declaration of Independence give him a greater ''kick'' than others; or his conviction that rules derived from ''the consent of the governed'' will not work ''if you haven't got men that've learned to tell human rights from a punch in the nose''; or his quoting St. Paul to the effect that, among faith, hope, and charity, charity is the greater virtue; or his invocation, by quoting that ''one simple rule: 'Love Thy Neighbor,' '' of Christ's parable of the good Samaritan in which neighborliness is explicitly defined as a matter of ''otherness.''

Of course, Jeff's picture of difference is still couched in distinctly masculine terms; we hear nothing about a girls' camp or a kids' camp. Indeed, the society on view in the film continues to see human endeavor in strictly masculine and *individual* terms, which the film curiously and repeatedly defines as a position of weakness, of isolation, for which Jeff's filibuster is taken to be the ultimate expression, ''one lone and simple American holding the greatest floor in the land.'' In the words of one senator: ''Most of us feel that no man who wasn't sincere could stage a fight like this.'' But, of course, ''no man'' stages it, certainly not a ''lone and simple'' one; Clarissa

Saunders is the dramaturge, Jeff Smith the actor who takes direction and "grows" in his role. Indeed, the last thing Jeff reads before Clarissa encounters him at the Lincoln Memorial are the closing lines of Lincoln's Gettysburg Address, including something about a "new birth of freedom," of "government of the people, by the people, for the people." Jeff thinks the words (by now) a bunch of "hooey." But Clarissa – who had early on aligned herself with Lincoln, as someone awaiting another – gives new birth to Jeff, as he had given new birth to her earlier. Moreover, what seems to turn Jeff around is less what Clarissa has particularly to say – indeed, her filibuster scheme is not revealed until it is subsequently enacted; all she asks from Jeff is the willingness to act – than it is her manner of saying it, the confidence of her claim that not everyone in Washington is a Taylor or a Paine, the passion of her praise of "common rightness." This too is an instance of "attunement," of "speaking the same language."

Capra's combination of comedy and melodrama in *Mr. Smith* thus requires a revision of the Brooks description of the latter as emphasizing self-understanding or self-nomination. It is easy enough to see how "the social as such" is a realm where one cannot go alone. Indeed, the speech acts by which melodramatic stage characters declare their moral natures are never completely solitary in that there is always (necessarily) an audience. What Capra emphasizes in *Mr. Smith* is the degree to which the self is always already social, a matter of collaboration, of mutuality, of acknowledgment. The American dream of starting over again from social scratch finds its most basic expression in Jeff's conviction, uttered on the verge of collapse, that "Somebody'll listen to me." Only by *sharing* ideals do ideals gain the power to sustain us, to sustain the world. Only by acknowledging "the other" is there a world to be sustained. The great anxiety in the latter moments of *Mr. Smith* is that Jeff will not be acknowledged. How far that anxiety is Jeff's is uncertain; he only reads a few of the Taylor-made telegrams that Paine delivers to the Senate chamber, and those he describes as lies. The greater anxiety by far is Clarissa's – who knows as Jeff does not the full and dreadful specifics of Taylor's media blitz against them – and if hers, then also Capra's. Both are mute artists who work behind the scenes, absent presences who depend on others to voice, hence to share, their ideals. For each the great nightmare is that no one is listening. Until Clarissa Saunders is fully acknowledged by critics and viewers as Capra's feminine other, she and Capra will both remain, in a fully modern and melodramatic sense, "unknown women." This is a man's world indeed.

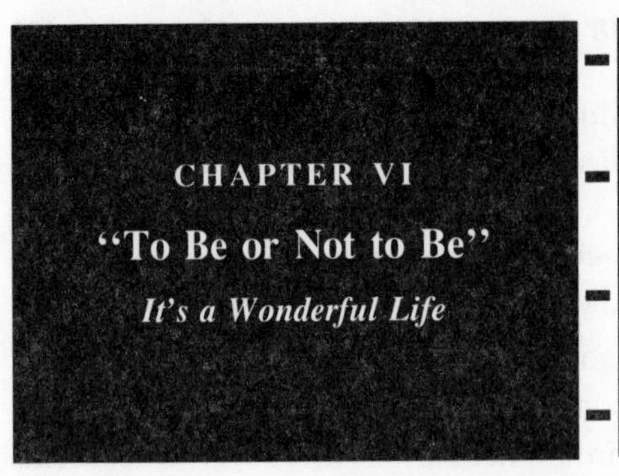

Let us begin somewhere near the beginning. Another snowy Christmas Eve. George Bailey, leaning on a bridge rail over a voidlike body of water, the snow-covered rail itself an image of the edgeless line between the nightmare "nontime" of George's hellish descent into "Pottersville" and the "real time" of his impending return to Bedford Falls, begs his guardian angel and finally the Lord himself for help: "Please, God, let me live again" (Fig. 13). In fact George repeats the wish, folklore fashion, three times; the last two "wishes" are uttered in close-up, George's elbows bearing his weight against the bridge rail while his fists press into his eyes. Most readings of the line take it as denoting George's desire to escape the film-noir horror of the Pottersville he has just experienced. I want to say that a deeper (if no less literal) understanding of the wish follows from George's recognition that he *had* been living, living *at all;* asking to "live again" acknowledges his life to date as his own, as a *life* – despite the view, held alike by George and many critics, that his life to date has been lived, as it were, in shadow, a shadow cast by Henry F. Potter, by Peter Bailey, by Mary Hatch, by Bedford Falls, by whatever it was that prevented George from realizing his dreams of travel and knowledge and accomplishment. Furthermore, I imagine this recognition to be accompanied by some kind of inner vision, figured by George's rubbing of his eyes with his fists, in which George *sees* his life as *his*. The life he sees, indeed, is "wonderful," full of strange and fantastic beings, himself among them. I take it he is seeing the same film we are seeing, have just seen, are reseeing in memory. Before going on to share or read this vision I want to reread some passages of my own life, to (re)trace the path that brought me here. We are near the end we began with; time for a flashback.

Here I invoke a claim first urged in the Preface, that *all* criticism is effectively a matter of retrospection, of revisioning. An important measure

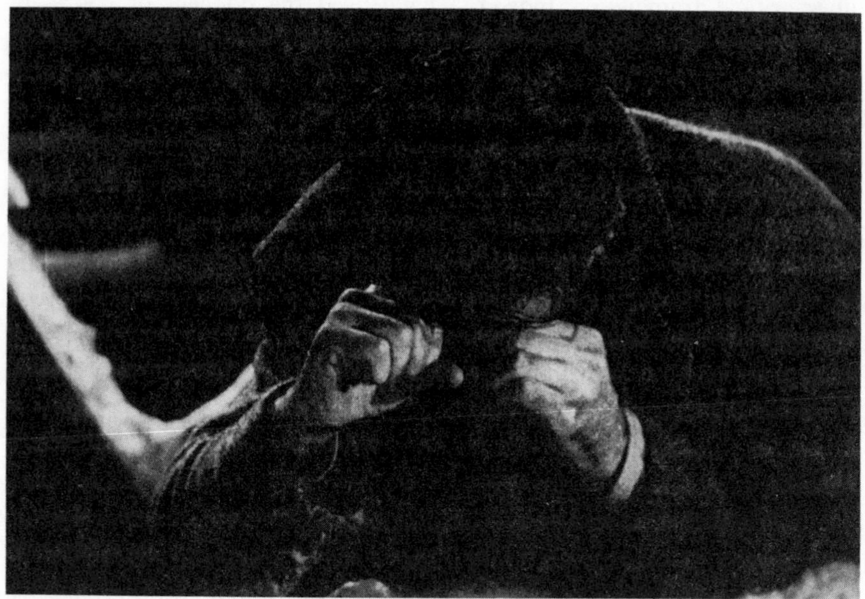

Figure 13. "Please, God, let me live again."

of Capra's ongoing stature in film study is the degree to which his films repeatedly "reread" themselves and each other in ways that encourage viewers to undertake a similar mode of interpretation.[1] Recall how the night-court scene of *You Can't Take It with You* prompted my rethinking of Grandpa Vanderhof's Americanism speech, for instance, or how the recollections shared by Jeff and Senator Paine during the brief train scene in *Mr. Smith* prompted my reconstruing of the latter's forgetfulness during the banquet scene as a species of repression. Even the standard interpretation of Capra acknowledges this "revisionary" tendency of his accomplishment in tracing the declining political efficacy of Capra's populist heroes against the allegedly stable background of their prototypical Lincolnesque ideals: Deeds wins handily, Smith just barely, Doe is lucky to survive at all.

In promising to defamiliarize Capra I assume a similar diacritical obligation; my task is inevitably a historical one, of displacement and replacement. Some initial "placement" was accordingly necessary, for which purpose I invoked two interpretive contexts or traditions, one deriving from the study of film genre, the other from the study of film style. In retrospect, both traditions can be seen to employ a similar part-for-whole categorical logic. I have hardly sought to provide a theoretically complete account of either critical framework. Indeed, I have used the concept of genre, by reference chiefly to Cavell on remarriage comedy and Brooks on melodrama, to raise questions pertaining mostly to matters of gender and desire. I have used the concept of the classical narrative cinema, as elaborated via distinctions among Story, Plot, and style, to ponder matters of narration. Against the view that Capra's films are best understood as male-centered parables of individualism triumphant rendered transparently available in the invisible language of Hollywood, I have urged that Capra's deepest affinities are with his female characters – even and especially in the ''Mr.'' films – whose task, like Capra's, is exactly a matter of making the invisible newly visible, expressing the socially repressed, if not to the world they inhabit, at least to the world(s) of their projection.

Plotting *It's a Wonderful Life* against this background proves (aptly enough) to be a frustratingly difficult task, in part because other critics have already made the case or cases I had originally expected to make, in part because I now find myself disagreeing with certain of the arguments involved. Capra critics are almost unanimous, for example, in observing that *It's a Wonderful Life* makes the process of cinematic narration unusually explicit. The ''apparatus'' of cinema, figured in the facts of projection and perception, is allegorized in the flashback that comprises the bulk of the film, accompanied by the voice-over commentary of Joseph (the celestial projectionist) and Clarence Oddbody (the celestial ''viewer in the text''). Two moments in this interpretive undertaking are frequently noted as ''baring'' the cinematic ''device'' (Fig. 14):

1. the initial ''frames'' of the interfilm, which a wingless second-class angel like Clarence cannot bring into focus without Joseph's assistance; and
2. the first time we see James Stewart as George Bailey, in the luggage shop, where the image of George freezes so Clarence can ''take a good look'' (shades of *Meet John Doe!*).

Also typically discussed under the ''narration'' rubric is the Pottersville sequence, also seen as a matter of divine authorial intervention, to the extent that Clarence, with Joseph's apparent approval, grants George's wish that he had never been born.

What to make of this narrational explicitness is subject to some dispute. Kaja Silverman invokes the Lacanian picture of subject positioning – in which Imaginary identification with the maternal is replaced by Symbolic

Figure 14. "Baring" the cinematic "device" in *It's a Wonderful Life.*

identification with "the Law of (God) the Father" – to suggest that the narrational component of *It's a Wonderful Life* is doubly coercive or repressive, allowing us to identify equally with George and with Clarence, each of whom stands at a masochistic distance "from the discursive apparatuses which define them" and that thereby, as it were, define *us*.[2] Indeed, the fact that George and Clarence "mediate" the ideological distance between heaven and earth, almost literally traversing it, allows us "to enter with pleasure into George's pain, to expose ourselves to lack and insufficiency with the confidence that these things will not only be condoned, but will provide the means whereby we too are integrated into a celestial plenitude and sufficiency." As a serious explanation of how minds acquire language or the cognitive capacity to apprehend and be moved by films, the Lacanian paradigm invoked by Silverman, especially as it applies at the narrational level, is no longer very credible, in part for being so obviously self-contradictory. The film's "dual interpellation prevents us from ever really calling into question the sacrifices required of George," we are told.[3] Yet Silverman encounters little difficulty exempting herself (and her reader?) from the prohibition. As a ''mythical'' figure for interpreting the social force and reach of language, however, the Lacanian picture is obviously productive; we will return to Silverman's reading of *It's a Wonderful Life* in short order.

The more usual understanding of the narrational explicitness of *It's a Wonderful Life* is elaborated by critics like Robert Ray and Robin Wood who construe the film's assertively overt narration as a matter of difference or ''impurity,'' as a symptom of underlying ideological contradictions that the film strains to ''contain.'' Both assume that (as Wood has it) ''a central ideological project'' of *It's a Wonderful Life* is ''the reaffirmation of family and small-town values that the action has called into question.''[4] Moreover, the film's success (in Ray's analysis) ''depended utterly on George's vision, provided him by Clarence: the chance to see what Bedford Falls would have been like if he had never been born. That vision was the movie's great trick.''[5] That it is *only* a trick, however, Hollywood sleight of hand, is attested to chiefly by style.

Partly this trickery involves the ''familiarity'' of George's nightmare, in which the ''iconography of small-town comedy is exchanged, unmistakably, for that of film noir.'' Though noir iconography differs from that of the film's daylight world – ''police sirens, shooting in the streets, darkness, vicious dives, alcoholism, burlesque shows, strip clubs, and the glitter and shadows of noir lighting'' – it is still (generically) familiar, a matter of common Hollywood knowledge.[6] Nevertheless, the resulting juxtaposition of genre worlds, on Ray's account, yields ''an unsettling sense of their proximity.'' ''In Capra's film, the natural evolution of the movie's early street scenes into the Pottersville vision retroactively [reveals] the barely controlled *noir* elements existing just beneath the surface,'' confirming ''the presence of the previously repressed *noir* world in the body of the Classic Hollywood mythology.''[7] Indeed, Ray goes Wood one better on these symptomatic accounts in claiming that Capra, in order to repress ''the utter emptiness of American Life'' as it is revealed through and to George Bailey, had little choice but to break the cardinal rule of classical narrative style by making ''the invisible style visible'' via the projection and freeze-frame devices of the noirish flashback sequence, despite the more normal practice of subordinating style to narrative in order ''to establish the cinema's illusion of reality and to encourage audience identification with the characters on the screen.''[8]

It is clear from the progress of Ray's larger argument that he takes the visibility of style in *It's a Wonderful Life* as an exception that proves the Hollywood rule. Rule or no rule, one can only agree that stylistic questions come bewilderingly to the forefront in the Dreamland sequence of *It's a Wonderful Life*. In the words of Raymond Carney, "the dreamland sequence is more than the demonstration of a psychological and social truth. It is, first and foremost, a bravura cinematic performance" in which Capra flaunts his "dazzling cinematic ability to *reimagine everything we have already seen in the film in a new way*. . . . We do not see just two styles; we see that everything we have seen or will see is style," we "see that there is only the seeing."[9] The problem *I* encounter in the face of this overwhelming (if somewhat contradictory) evidence of Capra's stylistic extravagance in *It's a Wonderful Life* is the implication that something genuinely new is at work here, as if *Wonderful Life* were Capra's most radical stylistic experiment, a claim I find almost empty in the present context. Extravagant and self-conscious the film may be, but how is it any more narrationally extravagant or self-conscious than *Forbidden* or *Lost Horizon* or *Mr. Smith Goes to Washington* or *Meet John Doe* or (for that matter) *Arsenic and Old Lace?* I have argued all along for the view that Capra is a deeply and overtly self-conscious artist. Repeating the claim here thus seems pointless, unless the claim can be urged in terms specific enough to account for the difference of this film from the others, something that none of the available accounts really manages.

A similar ambivalence shadows my understanding of the gender *politique* of *It's a Wonderful Life*. The most subversive, most progressive, and most consistently ignored component of Capra's filmmaking, I have claimed, is his repeated depiction of female desire as existing on or beyond the margins of the conventional system of sexual relations, often in ways that explicitly challenge the sexual/political status quo. Central to this claim is an understanding of "female" that allows its applicability to Capra's male characters, who often seek out the female in themselves, their own capacities for dreaming and gazing and mute contemplation, as a means of confirming their own existence and identity. The fact that this capacity for spiritual androgyny is typically expressed in the context of what might well seem a conventional heterosexual relationship allows the view that Capra's "Mr." films, for example, are "comedies" in the classical New Comedy sense of the term, boy-gets-girl despite the opposition of an Oedipal *senex* figure.

Conspicuously lacking in Capra, however, are those public ceremonies or sacraments that would bind the lovers to society in ways that would allow their wedding to symbolize social renewal or rejuvenation. Indeed, something we almost never see in Capra is a completed wedding ceremony, which, if it takes place *at all,* takes place off frame. More typical, especially in the trilogy films, is a marriage proposal, never explicitly responded to, based on false assumptions – Longfellow's poetic proposal to ''Mary Dawson'' in *Mr. Deeds,* for example, or Long John Willoughby's asking Mrs. Mitchell to propose to Ann on his behalf before Connell spills the political beans about Ann's collaboration with Norton. Neither woman gets (or takes) the chance to say the conventional ''Yes,'' even after the truth comes out. Babe admits her love for Deeds under oath, as Saunders confesses hers to Jeff during the *Mr. Smith* filibuster; Ann pleads with John ''to keep fighting'' (''We can start clean now! Just you and I!''). But a conventional marriage seems out of the question in all three cases, if only because the experience the characters have undergone renders them decidedly unconventional to begin with, even if we assume that something like a wedding will eventually take place. It is exactly this difference from classical comedy that Cavell's remarriage paradigm undertakes to account for, a difference that sets Capra's central couples at an unmistakable remove from the culture(s) they inhabit.

We see a similar ambivalence about marriage in *It's a Wonderful Life.* Despite the oft-repeated claim that *Wonderful Life* is something straight out of Andy Hardy or Norman Rockwell, awash in ''good neighborliness'' and family unity, Harry Bailey does *not* bring his fiancée home to meet the folks before tying the proverbial knot. The wedding takes place off frame, out of town; Ruth is simply a surprise Harry springs on George and Uncle Billy at the railroad depot (Harry: ''Meet the wife!'' George: ''Why don't ya tell somebody?''). For that matter, we do not actually see George and Mary exchanging vows. Rather, Capra wipes from a close-up two-shot of George and Mary embracing to an extreme close-up of cousin Tilly shouting ''Here they come!'' as George and Mary descend the stairs to begin their honeymoon trip. The closest we get to a ceremony here is the front-porch wedding photo that Cousin Eustace frames and shoots with his old-fashioned box camera and tripod.

Against this larger background, the relationship of George and Mary seems excessive in its conventionality, even though we do not get to see the preacher. This accommodation to convention is especially marked in Mary's case. She certainly *seems* content to enact the conventional female role, as Raymond Carney observes:

Whereas George continually moves, physically and imaginatively, outward, conquering external spaces, Mary placidly possesses and fills interior spaces, in her pregnancy, her sitting still at home, and her thriving in the bosom of the family as she fixes up the Granville place. Even her initial wish on the windows of the Granville Place in the "Buffalo Gals" scene was only that she and George might one day live together in that house.[10]

Furthermore, this degree of conventionality is repeatedly measured in the film against the sexual standards at play in Capra's *Forbidden,* which surfaces time and again as a crucial intertextual element of *It's a Wonderful Life*.

Among the many moments or scenes of *Forbidden* that are echoed in *It's a Wonderful Life* one in particular is crucial. I have in mind the first post-Havana meeting of Grover and Lulu. Lulu has a secret to tell, associated with a picture hanging on her kitchen wall. Grover arrives with Halloween masks, which subsequently allow the two of them to play games, among which is an exchange of as-if magical gallantries, Grover's provision of flowers, Lulu's offering her hand to be kissed, Grover bowing extravagantly to kiss it (see Fig. 10). As she moves to answer the door Lulu puts a record on; the tune she plays specifically evokes a memorable night of her past life together with Grover, a night of moonlight and water and explicit sexual desire. A phone call from a potential suitor interrupts their intimacy by raising the specter of marriage, a topic that Grover seeks desperately to avoid. Accusations follow, equally bitter and false.

The scene at Mary's house in *It's a Wonderful Life,* where a disaffected George winds up after leaving the impromptu reception for Harry and Ruth, is manifestly a remake of this scene from *Forbidden,* even if several of its elements – the Elizabethan exchange of gallantries, say, or the idea of "costumes" (the masks of the earlier movie replaced by athletic regalia in the later) – have already come into play in the "Buffalo Gals" scene. In the proposal scene there is, again, a secret to tell – Mary's love for George, George's for Mary – again associated with a picture, not the sketch of a sleeping child we see in *Forbidden* but Mary's cartoon of George lassoing a reluctant moon. Again a woman puts on a record for the purpose of recalling a memorable sexual encounter; "Buffalo Gals" is the tune this time. Again we get a phone call from a potential suitor (Sam Wainwright) that brings up the question of marriage (Fig. 15) – of George to "that broken down old Building and Loan," of George and Mary to each other – the result of which is bitterness and shouting and tears. Which makes it all the more striking that Mary – whose kinship to Lulu is eventually confirmed in the Dreamland sequence where she appears, like Lulu in *Forbidden*'s first scene, as a spinster librarian – should exist so totally *within* the bounds of sexual convention. Lulu's secret, after all, is her out-of-wedlock pregnancy, which seems far more a token of illicit satisfaction than of a yen for conventional domesticity of the sort that Mary gladly seeks.

It is the virtue of Kaja Silverman's reading of *It's a Wonderful Life* that it specifies at considerable depth the "domestic" matrix that characterizes life in Bedford Falls. Silverman takes for granted that "cultural subjectivity, in both its male and female versions, consists of a compulsion to repeat experiences which are instinctually unpleasurable, and involves an ever-increasing accommodation of passivity and masochistic pleasure." (Civilization is a source of pain, on this account, yet somehow we learn to love it.) In Capra's culture and our own, this masochistic accommodation "is usually associated at the manifest level only with the female"; male subjectivity ordinarily avoids or denies the inevitable sense of pain and loss by identification with "the law" and with the positive symbolic attributes that accrue to the "paternal" position: "knowledge, potency, legal authority, linguistic, monetary, visual and narrative control, etc." Moreover, what Capra brings to light, on Silverman's reading, largely by employing Christianity as the film's "structuring discourse," is the distance of the male subject from the ultimate source of paternal authority and reward (from "God"). Instead, Capra provides a series of mediating figures (Joseph, Clarence, Peter Bailey, George) that defer satisfaction and thus make "startlingly evident the necessary cultural subordination of the male subject, as well as his full participation in the passivity and masochism usually associated with the female subject." Put another way, "The film effects the forced identification of the male subject with a 'weak' or 'castrated' father" whose legacy is not power but pain and suffering, a legacy of "lack."[11] That cultural force is involved and necessary is measured, for Silverman, by the frequency with which George's expressed desire to escape is almost immediately matched or countered by a crisis that binds George ever the more securely into his Bedford Falls persona.

Though I have lately come to disagree with crucial elements of Silverman's interpretation of *It's a Wonderful Life,* my earlier chapters are obviously indebted to her founding claim that, in a way, George Bailey is the primary female character of the film, perhaps in all of Capra. Indeed, the connection of femininity and Christianity is one I explicitly make in my

Figure 15. "The chance of a lifetime."

discussion of *Meet John Doe,* especially as it figures (toward the film's conclusion) into the exchange of identities between Ann Mitchell and Long John Willoughby. We can see a similar crossing of identities between George and Mary without going much beyond the film's intertextual references to *Forbidden.*

Though Lulu is more obviously a prototype of Mary, there are any number of moments when a kinship of Lulu and George is as forcefully suggested. While George and Uncle Billy await the arrival of Harry (and Ruth) at the train station, George shows Billy a fistful of travel brochures ("Europe," "South America") that recall the travel brochure ("Havana – Land of Romance") that sparks Lulu's travel plans in *Forbidden.* When Violet Bick subsequently espies George hanging out near the Bijou cinema and asks "Georgie-Porgie" where he is going, George replies "I'll probably end up down at the library," to which Vi responds: "Don't you ever get tired of just reading about things?" The association of George with books, with language, with libraries, connects him not only with Lulu, also explicitly portrayed as a reader, but also with the Mary of the Dreamland sequence; I will eventually want to say that the explicitly masculine Mary (decked out in glasses, a mannish coat and hat) is the "other" self that

George both fears and desires. In which case I find it significant that the child George is most closely associated with, whose "petals" are the clearest tokens of his own identity, is Zuzu. The name is an obvious echo of Lulu, and both Lulu and Zuzu are associated with flowers and with dreaming and, after a fashion, with death: Lulu obviously, in shooting Al Holland to death in *Forbidden,* Zuzu in the gesture by which George places his hand on her forehead, as if shutting the eyes of a corpse, after telling her to go to sleep so she can dream about her flower (" . . .and it'll be a whole garden").

Silverman and I agree that there is *something* exceptional about *It's a Wonderful Life,* in both cases something having to do with the film's emphasis on the domestic or the everyday. Nevertheless, there are two reasons for pondering further her account of *It's a Wonderful Life* as a parable of desire denied and Christian accommodation to a life of lack:

1. The "Christian" logic of Clarence's demonstration to George has little if any bearing on the lesson he learns, despite the film's obvious reliance on a biblical intertext.
2. It is far from clear *what* George does or does not want.

I have already alluded to the former crux in suggesting that George's wish to "live again" amounts to an acknowledgment that his life was, indeed, his. This must be put together with the fact, first observed by Barbara Deming, that "we never see [George] accept the basic premise upon which [Clarence's] argument rests: that [Dreamland] *is* simply a demonstration of what the town might have been," which affords George a view of "what a difference his life has made to others."[12] Absent from both my own account and Deming's is *any* sense of the classic Marxist critique of religion, that it offers otherworldly glory in (bogus) recompense for earthly suffering, though Robert Ray's description of the vision as a "trick" comes pretty close. Certainly *George* receives no comfort from the knowledge that (in his world, if not ours) there is a God and hence a heaven, a life of the world to come. Nor is he chastened by the thought that his life was "wonderful" in terms of the difference he made in the lives of others. What George responds to most deeply is the repeated lack of recognition he encounters in what seem to him still familiar places and faces ("Mary, it's George! Don't you know me?"). The lesson he finally learns is less how much Bedford Falls needs him than how much he needs and wants

Bedford Falls ("I need you, Mary! Help me!"). So how does George's need for recognition trigger his subsequent acknowledgment that the life he lived, wonderful or not, was *his?*

That is a difficult question to answer, especially to the extent that George's failure to recognize his life *as his* follows from the uncertainty of his desires. Most readings of the film, Silverman's included, take for granted that George wants to leave Bedford Falls and see the *National Geographic* world, desires that Bedford Falls, in its various avatars, manages to frustrate; his father dies, his brother marries, his own mother matches him up matrimonially with Mary Hatch, his forgetful uncle loses $8,000 worth of Building and Loan funds, not to mention an avuncular guardian angel who prevents him from committing suicide. Some readings expand the range of George's desires to include more derivative "superego" motives, chiefly associated with George's father and the desire, shared by Peter and George Bailey alike, to stand up against Henry F. Potter, "the richest and meanest man in the county." However, any number of details can be cited that complicate the standard picture of George Bailey as a study in unalloyed frustration.

The most spectacularly overlooked of these details involves the film's most concerted examination of the act and fact of "wishing." After dancing the Charleston in the high-school swimming pool, George and Mary walk home, in clothes borrowed from the high-school athletic department (he in football togs, she in a male-sized bathrobe) to the tune of "Buffalo Gals." The uncertainty of George's desire comes out when George tries to pay Mary a compliment: "If it wasn't me talking, I'd say you were the prettiest girl in town." She asks why he does not just come out and say it, a question he dodges by asking how old she is, which leads to some confusion about what "older" and "younger" mean. George then steps on the dragging belt of Mary's borrowed bathrobe and mutters an archaic Elizabethan apology ("A pox upon me for a clumsy lout") as he hands it back to her, at which point she offers her hand to be kissed (Fig. 10). He apparently has more than hand-kissing in mind, she turns and walks away, and George stops her by offering to "throw a rock at the old Granville house."

Rock throwing, as local folklore has it, is synonymous with wishing; as George tells Mary, it amounts to a *test* of wishing, as if the purity or efficacy of the wish depends on the wisher's aim: "You make a wish and then try and break some glass. You got to be a pretty good shot now-a-days, too." George heaves away, breaks a window pane, and Mary asks him "What'd you wish?" to which George responds with his oft-cited litany of desires, "a whole hatful" of wishes, to "see the world," "go to college," "build things." George's list is apparently endless, so Mary stops the recitation by picking up and heaving her own rock. George asks her what she wished, to which she offers two responses:

1. She walks away, singing "Buffalo Gals" (as if the current moment, wherein she and George "dance by the light of the moon," *were* her wish, no more, no less).
2. When pressed, she refuses to reply on the grounds that, if she told, "it might not come true."

Most readings of these events take them not so much literally as "conventionally," as a matter of narrational "exposition." Thus the rock-throwing device is a "meet-cute" way of authorizing George to tell Mary (hence the viewer) what he wants and who he is. Except that Mary is hardly unfamiliar with George. She grew up with him, after all, not to mention the earlier scene, at the soda fountain, where he had made his desires, or so he had thought, emphatically clear ("I'm going out exploring some day, you watch. And I'm going to have a couple of harems, and maybe three or four wives"). So Mary's asking George what he wished for – especially in light of her subsequent remark to the effect that telling a wish cancels it – is really a *test* of George, of whether he still wishes his old wish, or wishes it enough to keep quiet about it. Moreover, George's willingness to tell can easily be read as expressing the desire to cancel the wish, assuming that George's command of local folklore is a match for Mary's (he does not dispute her claim on these accounts). It may even be that George has a better wish in mind, evidenced by the fact that his offer to throw the rock in the first place expresses a desire to stay close to Mary. Indeed, George's desire to exchange wishes here is quietly confirmed in the subsequent proposal scene. George *does* in fact leave Mary, as Grover leaves Lulu in *Forbidden,* but he returns, to get his hat, the same hat that he describes to Mary as the repository of his desires.

Further complicating our understanding of what George wants is the almost nightmarish frequency with which George's desires are in fact realized, either outright, or in some displaced fashion. Our earliest view of George, for example, has him sliding down a snowy embankment on a shovel. Once at the bottom, he puts his megaphone to his mouth and provides a voice-over commentary on the next contestant: "And here comes the scare-baby, my kid brother, Harry Bailey." Harry replies that he is "not scared" – which the subsequent course of events, especially Harry's war record, would seem to confirm – but George's description becomes a prophecy fulfilled when Harry hits thin ice at the far end of his slide and goes through. George – whose own slide had clearly been on the shorter, less risky side – suddenly has a reason to come to Harry's rescue, to be the brave hero for Harry's sake. A comparable sequence of events occurs in the subsequent drugstore scene. George sees Gower distressed over the death of his college-age son, asks if he can help, is told no, but soon finds occasion for rendering heroic assistance when he discovers the poisoned capsules a drink-befuddled Gower had mistakenly prepared. The implication that even the most casual of George's desires will be realized at the risk of death is horrifically confirmed on the night of Harry's graduation party. Despite George's belief that he'd be "bored to death" if he attended the party, attend the party he does as a means of cutting short his "last meal in the old Bailey boardinghouse" and thus avoiding his father's brooding ruminations to the effect that "This town is no place for any man unless he's willing to crawl to Potter." Any number of critics have noted the sense in which George's departure here is death dealing; it is Peter Bailey who eats his last meal, or "last supper," not George, as if that were George's desire all along.

A more "positive" species of displacement is in evidence when Harry Bailey returns from college with his new bride. One of the wishes in question here is that expressed by George and Mary together in their extempore harmonizing of "Buffalo Gals," the most emphatic line of which involves dancing by the light of the moon. The wish is literally fulfilled by Harry and Ruth. She is the daughter of a Buffalo glass manufacturer, hence a "Buffalo Gal," and the last we see of them in the sequence has them dancing together in the background of the shot, framed in the front doorway of the Bailey house, while George and his mother discuss Mary on the front sidewalk, by moonlight, I imagine.

His mother's mention of Mary Hatch prompts what seems a different wish in George, an alternative version of the moonlight scenario. After his mother hands him his hat, George proposes to "go out and find a girl" (implicitly *not* Mary) with whom to "do a little passionate necking," a task that takes him downtown, where he looks first at the Bijou Theatre, then at a passing woman, and then at Violet Bick. George proposes "to make a night of it'' with Vi, which for him means going up to the falls (''It's beautiful up there in the moonlight''), then up to the top of Mount Bedford (to ''smell the pines''), and so forth. Vi will have none of it. However, George's fantasy of a shoeless walk through the grass obviously recalls (for us, for him) his earlier postdance escapade with Mary; when we first see George and Mary in their athletic togs they are coming from a field of some sort, at the edge of town, it would seem. The sense that Violet is a figure here for Mary is confirmed when George finally winds up at the Hatch place. As he and Mary stand together, framed in *her* doorway, he comments on her dress, as he had on Vi's in the ''carriage trade'' scene; and in one of his few attempts at conversation he tells Mary that her house ''still smells like pine needles,'' which obviously connects Vi and Mary in his imagination. Indeed, by the logic of cancellation invoked in the ''Buffalo Gals'' scene, George's obsessive (and quite true) attestation that he ''didn't tell anybody I was coming over here'' renders his presence all the more an open secret, hence (in fact) his wish, as it had been all along. (No wonder he leaves his hat!)

George's problem, we can say, like Robert Conway's in *Lost Horizon,* is less a clear cut matter of getting what he wants than of knowing what he wants when he gets it. Putting it that way allows some truth to the view that George wants to get out of Bedford Falls, wants to see the world. However, it also allows the claim that his desire to leave is equally well understood as a cover story, a displacement or denial of other or deeper wishes. George's ''lasso the moon'' trope is deeply reminiscent on these accounts of Peter Warne's Pacific island soliloquy in *It Happened One Night*. Far from being a simple expression of Peter's desire, it clearly functions as a denial of Ellie's, of her reality as a desiring being, flesh and blood. In asking Ellie ''Where are you going to find her, somebody that's real, somebody that's alive?'' Peter commits an act of spiritual violence, denying Ellie's reality by soliciting her consent to the proposition that women ''don't come that way anymore.'' George is up to similar spiritual mischief in his own Pacific island soliloquy, at the soda fountain, when he tells Mary of Tahiti and the Fiji Islands and of the harems and wives he hopes for, implicitly excluding her from the list. George Bailey's deeply conflicted perspective on existence is epitomized in his reply to the wish Mary expresses in the ''Buffalo Gals'' scene to live in the old Granville place someday (''It's full of romance''). George retorts, ''I wouldn't live in it as a ghost.'' In other words, he would rather die first. That he eventually consents to living there, gladly enough it seems, can be taken to mean that he believes himself already dead, the ghost of his own existence, haunting himself.

Several systems of significance contribute to the view that George is devoted, after a fashion, to death or to something quite like it. Looming large among them is the film's basic narrative framework, flashing back in time from a point very near to George's impending suicide. Also in train here are any number of verbal references to death, uttered either by or in reference to George. In promising Mr. Gower never to disclose the mistaken prescription, for example, George affirms his sincerity by saying "Hope to die, I won't." Of course, in saying it he reveals it, to Mary, who is still sitting at the soda fountain, and who is explicitly depicted as well within earshot (she is shown to cringe when Gower slaps George). George repeats to Mary the proposition first directed to Harry that he (had) expected to be "bored to death" at the graduation party. The neighbor who watches George's courtship of Mary finally expresses his frustration by saying "Why don't you kiss her instead of talking her to death?" There is Potter's never-disputed characterization of George as someone "who's been dying to get out on his own ever since he was born." Then there is the wish that follows upon George's rescue of Clarence, the wish that he had never been born in the first place.

Related to the death issue is the film's treatment of time. Any number of Capra critics have noted how time seems somehow frozen in Bedford Falls, often for the purpose of claiming that Capra is unknowingly stuck in an idealized nineteenth-century view of America. Still, no less a light than Uncle Billy is well aware of the curious fact that "nobody ever changes" in Bedford Falls; Capra's assignment of the line to Uncle Billy, famous for his scatterbrained absentmindedness, portrayed as a reaction to the untimely death of his wife, ought to raise some doubts about Capra's supposed naïveté on these accounts. Indeed, time in Bedford Falls seems deeply and systematically "out of joint." Specifically, George seems simultaneously older and younger, concepts of which his conversation with Mary shows him to have a weak grasp. Thus George's father assures George that he was "born older" than Harry when they discuss whether or not Harry could handle the Building and Loan position George is about to hand down to him. Thus Harry refers to George as his "kid brother" at the graduation dance.

The sense that time in Bedford Falls is somehow out of sync is confirmed by a number of allusions to *Lost Horizon*. Both *Lost Horizon* and *It's a*

Wonderful Life are utopian fantasies. In each case the utopian is associated with an aspect of timelessness. Indeed, *Lost Horizon*'s Father Perrault anticipates both Clarence (in his benevolent ''longevity'') and Henry F. Potter, another apparently ageless, silver-haired patriarch. (Potter's appearance never really changes, despite the film's twenty-six-year time span.) Yet timelessness in both cases is cause for deep disquiet, especially on the part of someone named George who finds the prospect of extended residency unsettling to the point of madness. When George Bailey runs frantically down the main street of Pottersville, the first dive he sees is the Blue Moon Bar, as if to confirm the continuity of anxiety that unites George's ostensibly utopian day world and his explicitly distopian night world (Fig. 16). Like George Conway in *Lost Horizon,* who feels trapped in the Valley of the Blue Moon, George Bailey feels trapped in Bedford Falls, caught in a timeless nightmare. Part of what George assumes or wishes when he throws his rock at the Granville place is a knowledge of ''what I'm going to do tomorrow and the next day and next year and the year after that,'' as if time for him were always already frozen. Perhaps a clockmaker like Clarence Oddbody really is the kind of guardian angel George needs, someone who can tell time, or keep it, or start it.[13]

Another form of ''living death'' in the Bedford Falls that George projects is the fate of female existence, life as a woman. Silverman argues a general correlation of masochism and femininity in her reading of *It's a Wonderful Life*. However, a number of details specify femininity as something George explicitly fears, fears becoming, hence wishes. For example, when Marty Hatch asks George to dance with his little sister, George reluctantly agrees, and urges Marty to hurry the introduction, to get it over with, lest George get stuck ''being wet nurse for a lot of. . . .'' The sense that associating with girls or children makes George girlish is then picked up, years later, when Potter calls George in to offer him a job. Potter's sales pitch amounts largely to describing George's life in George's own terms: ''Yes sir, trapped into frittering his life away playing nursemaid to a lot of garlic-eaters. Do I paint a correct picture, or do I exaggerate?'' (Later, when George begs Potter for help, Potter opines that George ''used to be so cocky,'' the implication being that he is no longer cocky, i.e., masculine.) The sense that marriage is emasculating is confirmed in the proposal scene when George tells Mary in an angry voice that he does not want to get married. By the time his resistance collapses, marked by his repeating of Mary's name, getting ''married'' and getting ''Maryed'' sound strikingly alike.

Figure 16. The "Pottersville" montage.

One other aspect of femininity as George sees it is worth observing, one that links women and "ghosts" and film viewers. The concept of the "vanishing female," the female as "phantom," is one we have encountered before in Capra; in *Forbidden,* when Lulu vanishes at last into a crosswalk crowd; in *Lost Horizon,* when Sondra and her horse disappear from the mountain pool and appear, moments later, at the top of the falls (shades of George's speech to Violet Bick!); in *You Can't Take It with You,* when Tony describes Alice as a phantom, or later when she leaves the courtroom and flees to Connecticut. *It's a Wonderful Life* plays on this motif at least twice. The first is when George promises to show a frustrated (and by now absent) neighbor "some kissing that'll put hair back on your head." Mary bolts, right out of her bathrobe, the belt of which George has stepped on (yet) again, leaving an astonished George looking down at the empty garment, as if he really expected Mary to be somewhere still in it, lost among the folds. Likewise, when Ma Bailey urges George to pay a call on Mary, George assures his mother that he knows what she is up to: "I can see right through you."

The implication that women are transparent, or invisible, is playfully enough suggested, yet that playfulness becomes nightmarish in the Pottersville sequence, in which George himself is effectively invisible, there but not there, visibly present but socially, humanly absent. In being a ghost who haunts Pottersville, George becomes a figure of (for) the film viewer, seeing a world that is (in Cavell's lingo) present to him while he is not present to it. We might call him an unknown woman. That this is what George both fears and wishes is confirmed at the end of the fantasy sequence when George confronts the spinster version of Mary, who is also a version of himself, a "reader."

Pottersville, we can say, has always been a version of George Bailey's desire or anxiety, Bedford Falls without him. Until George presents himself to Bedford Falls, Bedford Falls will not be fully present to George. He remains, as ever, a ghost. Indeed, when George, during the Pottersville sequence, flees in desperation from the front porch of Ma Bailey's Boarding House, he runs into an excruciatingly tight and deeply enigmatic close-up, as if to press to the limit the convention of the "invisible camera" (Fig. 17). Either the camera is invisible or immaterial or somehow George is, despite the camera's presence, as if it could pass right through him. That we see a similar shot, as George tries to leave the Building and Loan office after the board of directors elects him executive secretary, is another indication of the continuity of anxiety that binds George's two worlds together.

Echoes of Jessica Benjamin's theory of intersubjectivity are sounded in several of my last few sentences, to the effect that human reality and identity are created and discovered *between* people, by acts of mutual recognition or acknowledgment. Such echoes will doubtless have a place in any full description of the logic by which George Bailey's recognition of his *need* for recognition, his realization of his own status as one human being among many, as dependent as the next person upon the recognition of others, comes about. Another question needs posing first, however, before we can describe *how* George comes, as it were, back to life: *Why* does George feel dead to the world in the first place? My answer is inspired by the following extended passage from Stanley Cavell's reading of Shakespeare's *Hamlet,* far and away the most famous ghost story in the history of Western culture, a story deeply haunted by thoughts of suicide and revenge and the deaths of various fathers, and one justly noted for its self-conscious study of the theatrical medium:

Figure 17. "I thought sure you'd remember me."

I see Hamlet's question whether to be or not, as asking first of all not why he stays alive, but first of all how he or anyone lets himself be born as the one he is. As if human birth, the birth of the human, proposes the question of birth. That human existence has two stages – call these birth and the acceptance of birth – is expressed in religion as baptism, in politics as consent, in what you may call psychology as what Freud calls the diphasic character of psychosexual development. In philosophy I take it to have been expressed in Descartes's *Cogito* argument, a point perfectly understood and deeply elaborated by Emerson, that to exist the human being has the burden of proving that he or she exists, and that this burden is discharged in *thinking* your existence, which comes in Descartes (though this is controversial) to finding how to say, "I am, I exist"; not of course to say it just once, but at every instant of your existence; to preserve your existence, originate it. To exist is to take your existence upon you, to enact it, as if the basis of human existence is theater, even melodrama. To refuse this burden is to condemn yourself to skepticism – to a denial of the existence, hence of the value, of the world.[14]

I run risks in turning again to Cavell and to Shakespeare; I have my reasons. One reason is to provide a sense of closure to the recitation of the ''skeptical problematic'' (as Cavell terms it), which I have repeatedly alluded to without much (or sufficient) elaboration. The wish underlying skepticism, recall, is ''a wish for the connection between my claims of knowledge and the objects upon which the claims are to fall to occur without my intervention, apart from my agreements.''[15] This desire for certain knowledge independent of human responsibilities, I have suggested, is closely akin to the ambition of melodrama for absolute expressiveness. Indeed, Cavell makes the generic connection here in his later work, and in terms that recall his earlier discussions of remarriage comedy:

> It stands to reason that if some image of human intimacy, call it marriage, or domestication, is the fictional equivalent of what the philosophers of ordinary language understand as the ordinary, call this the image of the everyday as the domestic, then the threat to the ordinary that philosophy names skepticism should show up in fiction's favorite threats to forms of marriage, namely, in forms of melodrama and tragedy.[16]

Crucial here, for allowing a political reading of ostensibly philosophical topics, is the way Cavell typically invokes a double logic or story, comparing the fate of the individual skeptic to the larger fate of philosophy and culture generally since the Renaissance, including most crucially ''the rise of the new science; the consequent and precedent attenuation or displacement of God; the attenuation of the concept of Divine Right; the preparation for the demand for political legitimation by individual consent.'' For philosophy as for the individual skeptic, doubt follows from the disruption of some prior state of certainty or assurance in the relation of self and society; Cavell calls it ''our old absorption in the world.''[17] In response to this doubt the skeptic, like Othello, seeks ''ocular proof,'' a certainty based on sense perception, chiefly on sight. Unfortunately, as the story goes, one never sees the entirety of an object, its front and back, say, a failure that allows the skeptic to claim that you never really *see,* and can therefore never really *know,* the object, hence the world. (Capra provides a marvellous allegory of this propensity for doubt, and of its overcoming through action, in *Mr. Smith Goes to Washington* when Jeff Smith, in the midst of his filibuster, whistles at the turned backs of his Senate colleagues, prompting them to turn around en masse: ''I just wanted to find out whether you still had faces.'') Moreover, the great irony of this attempt to stem tides of doubt by relying on sense perception alone, in preference to relying on the world and others in it, is its failure to provide human knowledge at all, a failure marked, for Cavell, by skepticism's destruction not only of the world but of the knower. (We might call this "inhuman" knowledge.) If knowledge is defined by the absence of the knower, then "in the case of my knowing myself, such self-defeat would be doubly exquisite: I must disappear in order that the search for myself be successful."[18] These matters are still (and will likely remain) somewhat murky. I cite them here, at the last minute, because *It's a Wonderful Life* strikes me as a virtual allegory of skeptical anxiety, a search for selfhood cast as a search for knowledge that culminates in something like the searcher's disappearance.

The risks I run by invoking Shakespeare are several. One involves the interpretive propriety of comparing Shakespeare and Capra *at all.* I take the question to be settled for *It's a Wonderful Life* during the graduation party, where Shakespeare is alluded to directly, and in ways that confirm the connections I have been exploring between Capra's fables of gender anxiety and Cavell's philosophical parables of epistemological doubt. Cavell frequently takes Othello's inexplicably violent antipathy to Desdemona as enacting the "skeptical problematic" in which "a self-consuming disappointment" seeks "world-consuming revenge."[19] It is exactly Othello's jealousy that is evoked when a high-school student, after his buddy loses out to George Bailey in the race for Mary Hatch's attentions, queries his despondent pal: "What's the matter, Othello, jealous?"

The likeliest result of posing *Othello* as an intertext for *It's a Wonderful Life* is the thought of taking George and Mary as Capra's equivalents for Othello and Desdemona. The man in each case woos by telling romantic tales of distant places; the woman in each case is associated with chastity and flowers. Othello commits suicide, George is "worth more dead than alive," and so forth. However, if the spurned high-school suitor is taken for Othello, as "jealous," then George might better be compared to Iago, whose general cynicism and discontent are a fit match for George Bailey's unhappiness in Bedford Falls. Or better yet, to Cassio, of whom Othello (thinks he) is *really* jealous, suspecting Cassio of adultery with Desdemona (as Potter accuses George of cheating with Violet Bick). Cassio, moreover, is reported dead but eventually returns, revived though wounded (like the split-lipped George); and he is compared, early on, to a "spinster," as being "bookish." At which point one can wonder whether *Mary* ought to be compared to Othello (Desdemona is described, after all, as her "general's general") and George to Desdemona. Indeed, Othello wishes at one point that *Desdemona* "hadst never been born."[20]

The implication that George and Mary are somehow equated via the *Othello* connection is confirmed in Cavell's description of Othello's dilemma: "The violence in masculine knowing, explicitly associated with jealousy, seems to interpret the ambition of knowledge as that of exclusive possession, call it private property. Othello's problem, following my suggestion that his problem is over success, not failure, is that Desdemona's acceptance, or satisfaction, or reward, of his ambition strikes him as being possessed, as if he is the woman."[21] Apart from the implication that the world of Bedford Falls is already a half-world, a split world, evidenced by the void that repeatedly opens up beneath the feet of the town's inhabitants, a void literally keyed open by jealousy in the graduation dance scene, there is an echo in this latter formulation of the tie that binds George Bailey and Henry F. Potter, each of whom seeks, one way or another, to "see," to "know," to "own," to "conquer" the world. Better that than be a woman.

In turning to the *Hamlet* intertext of *It's a Wonderful Life,* I run a deeper risk than that of an overly inflated estimate of Capra's cultural value based on an anxious "reading in" of Shakespearean detail. I am about to write a psychological history of George Bailey in the hope of explaining *why* he senses himself as already dead. Most Capra criticism avoids "character psychology" and for very good reason; most Capra characters, as we have seen, are psychological blank slates, characters in the making, often just barely "formed" by film's end if formed at all. No wonder critics like Silverman and Carney focus their attention chiefly on the culture that surrounds and "forms" these characters. I think it is the special brilliance of Carney's *American Vision: The Films of Frank Capra* that he sticks so closely and lovingly to the surface level of the films, showing how much detail other critics have had to ignore as the price for their populist interpretations. Yet even Carney makes an exception of sorts in the case of George Bailey, describing *It's a Wonderful Life* as a "psychodrama" with Sigmund Freud rather than Norman Rockwell as its guiding muse, and emphasizing the "interiority" of the film's basic dilemma: "The repressive language, the compromising system is everywhere, because it is inside us. George Bailey and everyone he loves has internalized the system of repression that, in the previous films, was located somewhere outside the main characters. There can now be no escape from it and no leverage over it. There is no imaginative space apart from it."[22] Despite the Freudian provenance of this insight, however, Carney sticks resolutely to the surface of the film, taking George's expressed desires, however powerfully repressed by social circumstance, at face value. I have already given my reason for taking George differently; it is far from clear what George wants. Moreover, what finally clinched this change of mind was the moment when I connected Hamlet and George – both of them notorious for delaying the execution of (somebody's) wishes – as equally "hard of hearing."

On the *Hamlet* side of the analogy, this claim depends on taking the dumb show Hamlet stages to catch the conscience of the king – which enacts the dispatching of a monarch by means of poison poured in his royal ear – as expressing in a displaced fashion Hamlet's personal conviction (confirmed by the fact that Hamlet bears his father's name) that he was *himself* poisoned, made a ghost, when his father's ghost poured into his heir-apparent ear the injunctions to remember and revenge the senior Hamlet's death. If accepting the human condition, one's birth as human, involves an acceptance of separation, then the Ghost's injunction, by asking Hamlet to "assume the burden of another's existence," denies that separateness, hence denies Hamlet's existence, haunting him.[23] A "hard" hearing indeed. George Bailey's case is strikingly similar in its outlines, though the deafness here is less a matter of things heard than of things *not* heard.

Like the younger Hamlet, George Bailey is haunted by the spirit of a dead father, whose place he is literally asked to take. But George's deafness or "deadness" precedes the death of his father, as if his father were already a ghost. Three incidents are crucial here, listed in reverse Story order to mark the interpretive priority of the latest one:

3. the last supper scene, in which Peter Bailey says to George, "I suppose you've decided what you want to do when you get out of college";
2. the scene in Gower's drugstore when the drunken Gower slaps George across the ear, for not doing what he was told to do; and
1. the scene at the Building and Loan in which the younger George, knowing that Gower has made up a poisoned prescription but uncertain what to do, interrupts his father's conversation with Potter over a question of indebtedness.

The line I have cited from the last supper scene, like Mary's asking George what he wished for in the "Buffalo Gals" scene, is usually taken as expository convention, a way of asserting the continuity of identity between the younger George (played by Bobby Anderson) and the older George (played by Jimmy Stewart). A more literal reading of the line, however, follows from George's reply: "Oh, well, you know what I've always talked about, build things, design new buildings, plan modern cities, all that stuff I was talking about." So how is it, if George has worked side by side with his father for the last four years while Harry finished high school and has talked the whole time about his future plans and ambitions, that his father can ask the question in tones that suggest either genuine ignorance or the hope of dissuading George from *his* hopes? Either way, I want to say that Peter Bailey has not *listened* to George, has not granted George a separate existence.

This deafness is confirmed in the earliest scene between them, when Peter Bailey refuses to listen to George's problem with Gower because he has problems of his own with Potter, a refusal that takes the form of a promise: "I'll talk to you tonight." However, the only night we see George and Peter share is that of the last supper scene, in which conversation is portrayed as being either "mistimed" (Peter: "I know it's soon to talk about it") or avoided altogether in George's decision to attend the graduation dance, despite his earlier contention that he would be bored to death. Gower's "hurting" of George's ear is thus a displaced version of what Peter Bailey has already been doing, from before the beginning. George's assertion, through a *megaphone,* designed to amplify sound, that Harry Bailey is a "scare-baby" is similarly a displacement of George's own view of himself as afraid, afraid of parental or paternal deafness, of not being heard. That being listened to can be a life-or-death matter is alluded to in George's "flying carpet" reference to the *Arabian Nights,* in which a female narrator named Scheherezade sustains her existence by telling romantic tales, 1,001 of them. However, like the water that ostensibly takes George's hearing, Peter Bailey is cold to his son's existence. No wonder George wants to leave town.

But leaving town is not exactly or entirely what George wants, or he would have left it. Something else George seems to want is to be depended on, as a means of denying his own unappeased or unacknowledged sense of dependency; he never misses a chance to go to someone's rescue. In Jessica Benjamin's terms, George is frozen into a form of infantile omnipotence by his father's inability to share and survive "destruction." George's fantasies of power and knowledge, which in developmental fact are driven by the pleasure that follows when limits are reached, when fantasy is revealed *as* fantasy, when intersubjective reality is accordingly discovered, are never acknowledged by George's father. As a result, George's fantasies acquire (contra Silverman) a sadistic aspect. Because the parent has withdrawn from or refused the child's fantasy, the child's aggression, lacking an external object, is "internalized." "When the parent fails to survive attack – to withstand the destruction without retaliating *or* retreating – the child turns its aggression inward and develops what we know as rage," a rage that in George Bailey's case is expressed in fantasies of death and dying and in his kinship to Henry F. Potter whose name, evoking the biblical Potter's Field, associates him with graves and gravediggers.[24]

The key to George Bailey, I now want to say, lies in recognizing the underlying *childishness* that drives his dreams and desires, childishness here understood *not* as a matter of simple regression to an early stage from a later one but as a matter, instead, of thwarted development that can ultimately be traced to the workings of capital in the person of Henry F. Potter. Even Uncle Billy knows that Potter killed Peter Bailey, had killed him long before the elder Bailey's heart ever stopped beating. George feels dead to the world because he was never, effectively, born; "born older," George never fully experienced the "mutual recognition" that allows a "real world" to come into being. Hence he feels ghostly, unreal, uncreated, a feeling expressed by his repeated assertions of omnipotence, figured alternately as wishing the whole world dead and (consequently, subsequently) by casting himself in the role of its rescuer. However, underlying the wish for omnipotence, according to Benjamin, is a deeper wish, a wish for embodiment, for birth. At which point all George's talk about leaving or departing can be matched with those moments when he casts or experiences himself as playing the female role, as "wet nurse," repeatedly associated with things that are "big" (or "biggest"), as someone set to "bust." George's ultimate fantasy is one of giving birth, to himself. George is less dead than unborn, in the sense that he has yet to accept separation and the mutual dependency on recognition that goes with it. In coming to recognize that need in the Dreamland sequence, George is finally empowered to wake up, to prove his own existence by accepting it, which means acknowledging as equally human those others whose recognition he requires.

Emphasizing the psychological over the theological aspects of George Bailey's spiritual quest solves one problem while raising another. The problem solved, or at least illuminated, is that of George's relation to Mary, seen by many, including George himself, especially toward the film's climax, as the primary institutional mechanism that traps George Bailey in Bedford Falls. Even critics who see George as internally riven by contesting imperatives – to leave, to stay – tend to see George's desires in either/or terms, as existing on the same psychic plane. A better picture of George's psychic geography, I have suggested, is less horizontal than vertical, multiple wishes, multiple desires, multiple fears, desires "covering" or "denying" fears, and vice versa, with the deepest wish being for embodiment or birthing. Hence the general aptness of the film's vertical symbolism of "descent" (George's various leaps into water) and "ascent" (his climbing the stairs to greet his children when he returns home). All of which complicates the place we ought to assign Mary in George's quest for (re)birth.

Of the film's (human) characters, Mary is the one most aware of the complexity of George's desires. Indeed, I would claim that Mary's wish to live in the old Granville place, and her subsequent impromptu inhabitation of the house as a honeymoon hotel, far from trapping George or belittling his desires or anxieties, amounts to her acknowledgment of them. Specifically, in finally telling George that living in the Granville place as his wife was the wish she wished the night of Harry's graduation party she effectively acknowledges his "ghostliness," which George had revealed to her the night she made the wish, and she acknowledges as well his hope to fill up that emptiness by encompassing the world, bringing it inside, like the moon George proposes to lasso for Mary, so she can "swallow it." Hence all the travel posters that adorn the walls of the house when George comes "home." That Mary is "mutually attuned" to George, as someone fit to share rather than thwart his wishes, is confirmed by the fact that she whispers her revelation in his deaf ear, and he *hears* her, declaring her "wonderful," that is, full of wonder.

Earlier I compared George and Mary to *Forbidden*'s Grover and Lulu for the sake of acknowledging the atypically domestic aspect of *It's a Wonderful Life* by contrast with Capra's other films, an element understood by many (e.g., Kaja Silverman) as marking the film's ideological complicity in a patriarchal status quo. The time has come to emphasize a more positive aspect of the comparison, the sense in which George and Mary, like Grover and Lulu, are alter egos, mirror images, soul mates, spiritual equals whose equality is marked by quiet suggestions of androgyny, Lulu twirling her "moustache" or leading Grover on a midnight ride along a moonlit beach in *Forbidden,* for instance. Similar hints of mutuality or androgyny are found in *It's a Wonderful Life*.

Spiritual mutuality is suggested, for example, after Potter offers George a job with his bank. George comes home late, to his and Mary's bedroom, accompanied by voice-over recollections of Potter's offer and of his own fantasy of seeing the world and building things. Into the sound mix come strains of Mary singing "Buffalo Gals," whether from off-frame or (as it were) from George's memory is unclear, as if the line between George's imagination and his real conditions, or between George's imagination and Mary's, were deeply uncertain. That this mutuality is linked to a measure of sexual uncertainty is confirmed when Mary reveals her pregnancy, and George asks "What is it, a boy or a girl?" to which Mary's enigmatic reply is "uh hunh." A similar gender ambiguity is apparent on the honeymoon night, when George and Mary embrace while Bert and Ernie sing "I Love You Truly" outside. Capra frames the action in such a way that George and Mary exist primarily as a two-headed Platonic shadow on a window shade in the background, while Bert and Ernie sing together in the foreground, posed facing each other, as if somehow *they* were casting the shadow on the window. As the song concludes, Ernie tilts Bert's wet-weather police cap back, like a bridal veil, and kisses Bert on the forehead, with predictably comic results. The implication that men can (want or fear to) be women should not be lost on us by now. All of which leads to the observation that pregnancy or birth is far more *George*'s fantasy than Mary's; she never mentions children until she announces her pregnancy. I want to say that her child-bearing enacts *George*'s desire more than her own, though the distinction here, like that of male and female, is (finally) difficult to make.

Granting that George and Mary are less conventional a couple than might first seem apparent does not, however, settle the question of the film's general complicity in the patriarchal status quo, not in light of the film's overtly Christian narrative framework, especially not when, at the film's conclusion, we hear George's family and neighbors sing the line "Glory to the newborn king" or hear Harry Bailey describe his older brother as "the richest man in town," not when either line puts us in mind of Henry F. Potter who is also described variously as a king and as the richest man in town. What *is* the difference between George Bailey and Old Man Potter and what *difference* does the difference make? The implication that without George Bailey Bedford Falls is really Pottersville, or that without Bedford Falls George Bailey is really Potter, makes the question of difference crucial indeed.

Questions of genre and narration intersect here. The standard view of *It's a Wonderful Life* hinges on the claim that the aesthetic and ideological worth of the film depends on the way the film's excessive style undercuts or qualifies the overt nostalgia and sentimentality associated with the genre of "small-town domestic comedy."[25] Whether the film's style is excessive, or whether its excessiveness works *against* the implications of its Story, are questions that cannot be answered until we are sure what the Story is, what *kind* of Story we are dealing with. I argued in *The Cinema of Frank Capra* that *It's a Wonderful Life* is better thought of as romance rather than as comedy. That claim is worth rewriting here in view of Stanley Cavell's repeated assertion that remarriage comedy owes its inspiration more to the Shakespeare of *The Winter's Tale* and *The Tempest* than to more conventional New Comedy models. Indeed, especially as described by Northrop Frye, Shakespearean romance shares much with what we have called, following Peter Brooks, melodrama.

Though romance and Romanticism cover between them huge portions of the map of literary and cultural history since the Greeks, I will follow Cavell along the path first marked by Northrop Frye with the observation that in his late romances Shakespeare located something Frye calls "the continuing primitive" in culture, which is closely associated with the archaic and the folkloric.[26] Simply put, the stories told by romance are profoundly mythic and fantastic; stories about children lost at birth or at sea, about parents falsely accused or imprisoned, about sea beasts who swallow their victims and vomit them forth, about heroes and heroines who journey down to hell or up to heaven, often accompanied by an angelic or a ghostly guide, about sexual disguise and confusion and metamorphosis, about returning to life, as if from death or a deathlike sleep, about the recovery of memory and identity via birth tokens or recognition talismans, a recovery often celebrated by a marriage feast or family reunion. All those things that "realistic" fiction feels compelled to "displace" into the realm of the probable or to scorn as sentimental or melodramatic. Romance, like melodrama, refuses the censorship or displacement. Indeed, especially in Shakespeare, the tendency is to emphasize the improbable, nowhere more openly or splendidly than in the revival of Hermione, a statue come literally (so it "seems") to life, at the conclusion of *The Winter's Tale*. The fact that the presiding deity in *The Winter's Tale* is Apollo rather than Yahweh or Christ marks the fact that nearly all of these narrative "units," or tropes, predate Christianity, however much Christianity has managed to make use of them. Two clauses of the romantic story bear especially on my current understanding of *It's a Wonderful Life*.

The first of these involves the vertical dimension of romance, invoking both a social and a cosmic "hierarchy" either of which can be taken as marking the basically conservative or regressive aspect of the genre. Hence the characters of romance tend to split fairly readily (as in melodrama) between heroes and villains, the former typically royalty of some sort, the latter only pretending to it. Moreover, these characters, as Frye elaborates in terms that echo *It's a Wonderful Life,*

> exist primarily to symbolize a contrast between two worlds, one above the level of ordinary experience, the other below it. There is, first, a world associated with happiness, security, and peace; the emphasis is often thrown on childhood or on an "innocent" or pre-genital period of youth, and the images are those of spring and summer, flowers and sunshine. I shall call this world the idyllic world. The other world is a world of exciting adventures, but adventures which involve separation, loneliness, humiliation, pain, and the threat of more pain. I shall call this world the demonic or night world.[27]

The general narrative principle that connects these two worlds, Frye remarks, is cyclical, a "movement of descent into a night world and a return to the idyllic world" so that "the higher up we are, the more clearly we can see the bottom of the action as a demonic parody of the top."[28]

It is hard to imagine a cosmology more comforting to the social status quo than this, in which social privilege is equated with innocence. Indeed, Kaja Silverman describes *It's a Wonderful Life* as doing something very similar in "transforming George's pain into pleasure, his lack into plenitude, and his debt into a gain."[29] In both cases, subjugation to the social status quo is paradoxically equated with salvation, with "happiness, security, and peace." It is the core of Frye's argument, however, that romance entails a proletarian and revolutionary potential, marked out most clearly by the fact that various cultural agencies, philosophers and literary critics since Plato chief among them, have labored mightily and with only minimal success to control romantic literature, either by kidnapping it into the service of the status quo or by ridiculing it as sentimental, false, nostalgic. Indeed, it is the fabulous and improbable elements of romance, always threatening to exceed the official mythology of a given culture, which indicate the "revolutionary" potential of romance, elements that no earthly city or kingdom can be taken to incorporate. Ultimately, on Frye's description, a kind of reversal is involved where all social authority is finally understood as pretense or illusion, however "real," and where true royalty accrues simply to the fact of birth. Here is Frye's climactic passage on these accounts:

> Revolutionary social ideals are traditionally those of liberty, equality, and fraternity, and the first two seem to be particularly the concern of comedy, whose tendency it is to gather all its characters together in the final scene and assign certain rights and functions to each one. After exhausting these images, romance's last vision seems to be that of fraternity, Kant's kingdom of ends where, as in fairy tales, we are all kings and princesses. The principle of the aristocracies of the past was respect for birth; the principle of fraternity in the ideal world of romance is respect rather for those who have been born, and because they have been born.[30]

Understanding *It's a Wonderful Life* as comedy entails a displacement of its fable in the direction of social allegory; the film's final gathering of neighbors is thus taken as emblematic of Capra's Norman Rockwell America while George Bailey stands as Capra's Andy Hardy Everyman. Any number of critics have pointed to the problems with this view. Potter's apparent success at extorting yet another $8,000 from the community remains more or less unaccounted for – none of the characters in view during George's homecoming even *knows* what happened – as is the fact that, in social terms, few of us can seriously claim the degree of social influence exercised by George Bailey in Bedford Falls; he is, after all, one of the town's two financial powers, however impoverished he is personally. Moreover, as we have seen, George's influence for good carries no rhetorical weight with George during the Pottersville sequence. Lined up horizontally, or "socially," these facts hardly yield or support the film's deeply utopian conclusion.

Arranged vertically or "romantically," however, they do make a certain sense, in part for allowing us (finally) to distinguish George Bailey from Henry F. Potter, despite all the pains taken in the film to imply their affinity. Briefly put, the America on view in *It's a Wonderful Life* is Pottersville from first to last. Potter is "the richest and meanest man in the county" from the very beginning, and what happens to George changes Potter's status not at all. Indeed, through the course of the film his power quietly grows, unabated. Potter thus instances the alienated and alienating omnipotence that George finally manages to escape. George may refuse Potter's offer of a job, but that same day Potter has no difficulty in telling a Congressman to cool his heels in an outer office; for that matter, apart from Bert the cop and George's stint as an Air Raid Warden, Potter, as chair of the draft board, is just about the only local government official we see. Money *is* social power in this film, and Potter has it.

So rather than see the Pottersville sequence chiefly as a matter of descent, into some kind of underworld, perhaps we should shift perspective and attend to the ascent side of things. Pottersville, shall we say, is the bottom line, even in Bedford Falls. Indeed, there are several characters who do not know George even *before* Clarence works his wish-granting magic, Mr. Welch in Martini's bar, the fellow whose tree George clips with his car. Moreover, George's sense of unreality, I have argued, can ultimately be traced to Potter's dispiriting influence on Peter Bailey. Accepting birth under the circumstances, *into* these circumstances, amounts to a genuinely revolutionary act, especially to the extent that accepting birth requires the abandonment of solitary omnipotence, requires the acknowledgment of otherness, our kinship in separation, something Potter never does ("They're not *my* children!"). Listen again to Frye on romance:

> Revolutionary attitudes are dialectical and polarizing attitudes, and this involves, in romance, the identifying of the demonic or regressive and its clear separation from whatever is progressive in the story. In romance it is much more frequently the individual, the hero or heroine, who has the vision of liberation, and the society they are involved with that wants to remain in a blind and gigantic darkness.[31]

I want to say that in repudiating his own Potter-like attributes, by acknowledging his life as *his,* as human, George ascends to that upper world, of innocence rewon, where he can look down and see Pottersville as a demonic parody of itself, which makes his wonderful life, shall we say, Pottersville's angelic counterpart, parody to a second or higher power. This gesture is ours to make as well, regardless of station or profession. George is a "newborn king" only in the sense that all newborns are, you and I among them. (Now *that*'s utopian!)

By way of conclusion I want to comment on one other clause of the romantic story as Capra has revised it in *It's a Wonderful Life.* Upon the heels of Frye's observation that Shakespeare never failed to include in his romances "some explicitly antirealistic feature," Cavell makes the claim that the comedies of remarriage, in their repeated inclusion of surrogate directors, take "responsibility for themselves" and in this self-consciousness "most deeply declare, and earn, their allegiance to Shakespearean romance."[32] Early on I questioned the degree to which *It's a Wonderful Life* exceeds in some special way the narrational self-consciousness on view in Capra's earlier films. I subsequently questioned the generic status of *It's a Wonderful Life.* In answering that the film is more akin to romance or to melodrama than to comedy I am effectively urging that the alleged "contradiction" of style and Story, which most critics use to justify their interest in the film, is more apparent than real.

Or better yet, *It's a Wonderful Life* is a case where *every* element of narration and narrative works to raise the question of self-consciousness – and the self-consciousness finally in question here is Frank Capra's. In *The Secular Scripture,* Frye distinguishes between the mere "projection" of romance, in which an idealized past is projected into the future, as something we can eventually and nostalgically "return" to, and romance understood as a matter of "recovery," in which the past is actively and continuously "recreated" in the mind of the poet and, subsequently, in that of the reader. The present is something we construct together, not something we merely suffer or live through. That is certainly the moral Cavell derives from Hamlet's predicament, that Hamlet must repeatedly and endlessly "originate" his life, by publicly enacting it. Attend again to Frye:

> As we make the first great move from projection to the recovery of myth, from return to recreation, the focus of interest shifts from heroes and other elements of narrative toward the process of creating them. The real hero becomes the poet. . . .In proportion as this happens, the inherently revolutionary quality in romance begins to emerge from all the nostalgia about a vanished past.[33]

In view of George Bailey's "revolutionary" acceptance of his own existence, his consent to himself as finite, as separate, as needing the recognition of others, I want to say that *It's a Wonderful Life* enacts Capra's version of the *cogito,* proving his own existence by enacting it, by producing and directing it.

A long-standing puzzle of the film, at least for me, is the logic behind George's decision to accept responsibility for Uncle Billy's lapse of memory in the matter of the $8,000, especially after he explicitly declares to Uncle Billy that George Bailey is not the one who is going to jail, especially after Potter explicitly questions George's subsequent claim that *he* lost the funds. This *can* be made credible – as an expression, deeply conflicted, of George's twin impulses for death and for martyrdom – but first and foremost it is a *fiction,* a story. Moreover, when George, having accepted his life, returns to the house to be confronted by his grateful neighbors, he never repudiates this story. Instead, he basks in the raw fact of family and

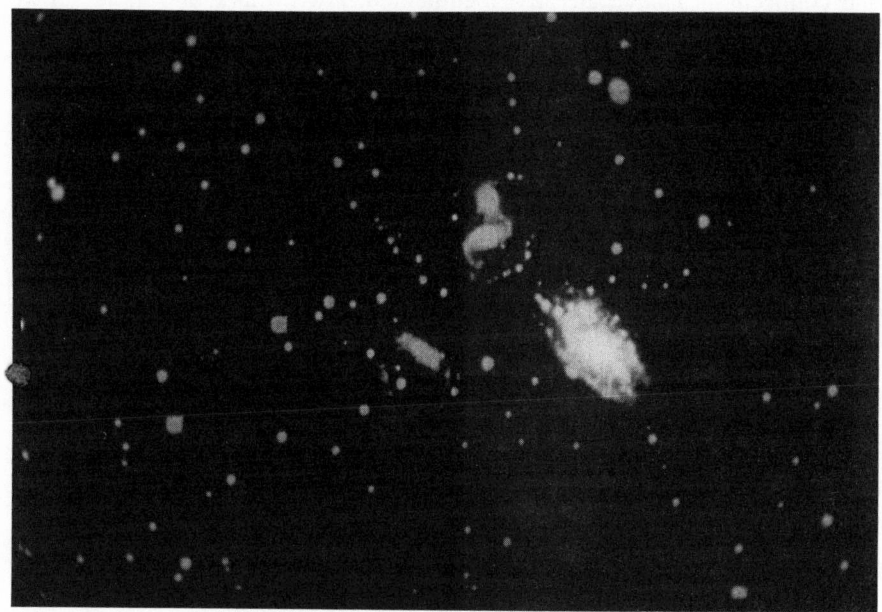

Figure 18. Awaiting deliverance: the universe as embryo in *It's a Wonderful Life*.

fraternity, becoming a screen upon which his friends and relatives can focus their own joyful acknowledgments of human existence. Like John Doe, George Bailey is nearly silent; he stares, he listens, while his neighbors, like moviegoers, pay admission and sing along with the sound track. He recognizes their existence by allowing their recognition of his. That the underlying fantasy is one of rebirth is confirmed by the fact that the centermost of Capra's "talking stars" looks for all the world like an embryo (Fig. 18), as if the entire cosmos were still in the process of birthing, say deliverance.

Another mute figure, who also stands aside to stare and to listen, all the better to solicit and acknowledge recognition, is Frank Capra. Of course, Capra does not inscribe his visage directly on film, in that sense cannot confront his audience as immediately as George confronts his friends and neighbors. Instead, like a guardian angel, Capra signs a text, a romantic fiction, which he offers as a gift, for our reading (Fig. 19). And he "signs" it, as any number of critics have noted, by a dense texture of cross references to other Capra films. A number of these intertextual connections I have already documented. I will mark one more set in closing.

In discussing *You Can't Take It with You* I observed the presence, on a table next to Grandpa Vanderhof's favorite chair, of an old-fashioned cigarette lighter, the same one upon which George repeatedly wishes for a million dollars in *It's a Wonderful Life*. Other details of *Wonderful Life* also recall *You Can't Take It with You*. Peter Bailey, for example, is played by the same actor (Samuel Hinds) who played Paul Sycamore in *You Can't Take It with You,* a connection confirmed by the motto inscribed under the photo of his father that George keeps in his Building and Loan office ("All you can take with you is what you have given away"); George and Mary's house is located at 320 *Sycamore* street. James Stewart is obviously present in both films, as the dreamy-faced son of a business-racked father, a connection confirmed when we learn that Sam Wainwright's scheme of turning soy beans into plastics, which echoes Tony Kirby's scheme to turn grass into energy, originated with George. There is also the obvious sense in which *Wonderful Life*'s conclusion, neighbors rallying round and taking up a collection to bail out their resident benefactor, is an echo of the night-court scene in *You Can't Take It with You.*

Often overlooked, however, is the casting of Lionel Barrymore, Grandpa Vanderhof in *You Can't Take It with You,* as Henry F. Potter. Few critics dwell on the connection, largely because Barrymore *looks* so different in the later role, not only for the makeup, but because he is never seen apart from his wheel chair. However, at least two features of *It's a Wonderful Life* make the connection of more than passing relevance. The more obscure of these is the fact that Henry Travers, who plays Clarence Oddbody, was the original Grandpa Vanderhof on Broadway; George's good and bad angels are, as it were, alternative versions of Grandpa Vanderhof's Emersonian sage.[34] The sense in which Bedford Falls is already a Capra nightmare, presided over by a demonic presence, is profoundly confirmed during the scene in which Peter Bailey, with young George interrupting, begs Potter for time, thirty days more on a loan. Potter asks Peter Bailey if he is running a charity ward, and before the elder Bailey can really reply he declares, "Not with my money!" We have heard that voice, speaking exactly that line, before, when Grandpa Vanderhof razzes the IRS agent in *You Can't Take It with You.* The "independence" of Grandpa Vanderhof's rejection of social pressure in *You Can't Take It with You* becomes, in *It's a Won-*

Figure 19. "Signing" the text.

derful Life, the assertion of social power, the claim that Henry F. Potter exists "independently" of the human connections that Grandpa Vanderhof so happily fostered. (Now *that*'s distopian.)

A last and most curious connection of *You Can't Take It with You* and *It's a Wonderful Life* involves Jimmy, the raven. We see Jimmy mostly as a denizen of the basement fireworks factory in the earlier film; in *It's a Wonderful Life* he appears in several of the scenes that take place in the offices of the Building and Loan.[35] I mention Jimmy last because I now understand him as offering an antidote to the false independence claimed by Henry F. Potter. He is a bird with a human name. Careful attention to the language of the film reveals that its human characters are repeatedly referred to as (or in connection with) birds; George as a canary, Potter as a buzzard, George and Mary (Mary *Hatch*) as ducks, not to mention that the high-school principal is named Mr. Partridge. Part of what Cavell and Frye invoke by the term "romance" is a world in which humanity "has become reconciled to nature," a hope both improbable and unappeasable, in that sense "romantic."[36] In *It's a Wonderful Life* being "reconciled to nature," to the Edenic cosmos, means "earning" your wings, becoming a first class angel, one result of which is sharper vision and the capacity to help others see more clearly. Vision can thus be *shared,* like a movie. It happens every day, every time a bell rings. The hymn George's neighbors sing to celebrate his return is "Hark, the Herald Angels Sing." I want to take that title literally. They are singing, they are heralds, they are angels. So too are we, each to the other. Attaboy, Frank. Thanks for the wings!

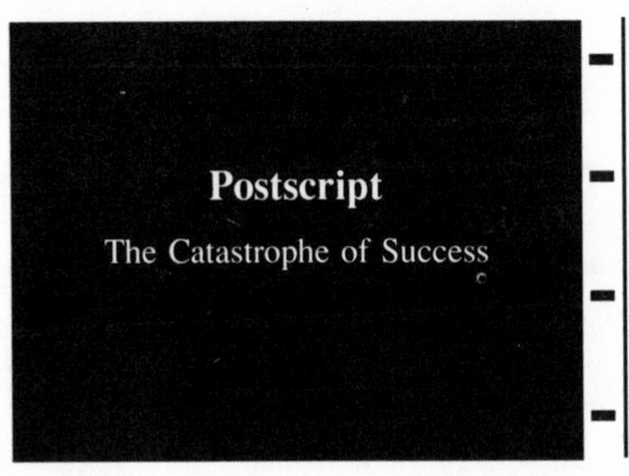

History is not merely or simply "the past." For most contemporary film scholars, history is, as Fredric Jameson reminds us, "what hurts."[1] Hence the return to "history" in contemporary film scholarship often functions as a gesture of solidarity with those who are hurting – whose voices are silenced, whose existence goes unacknowledged, whose pain goes unregistered. Another element of the current turn to historical scholarship is the greater prospect of certainty history seems to provide, by contrast, especially, with the practice of interpretation as the latter has been anatomized by those, like Jonathan Culler and David Bordwell, who advocate an explicitly historical poetics as a methodological alternative to hermeneutics.[2]

It can just as readily be the case, however, that the turn to history, far from "expressing" the past or explaining it, can express the wish to avoid it, transcend it, even deny it. Such is the case, I have argued, with any number of Capra critics, and especially so with those critics, like Nick Browne and Charles Maland, who explicate Capra's obviously ambiguous and elusive films by reference to their genetic context, chiefly thirties and forties Hollywood and the Depression. History here is "the known," the understood, which both causes and permits the explication of Capra's (otherwise) "unknown" or "misunderstood" films. The historical catch is that neither side of the epistemological equation of text and context is as certain as historically minded film scholars might wish.

The "text" side of the equation is always potentially unstable because the process of inference, by which viewers construct Story from Plot, say, or meaning from style, depends on generalized models or laws, akin to what Bordwell has called "semantic fields," which permit the projection of causality and motivation. Such "projections" are objectively "in" the text, are "parts" of the work, because they are public, are sharable, like "connotations"; but projection models obviously change – from Freud, say, to Lacan – and when they change the ''text'' changes with them.[3] Another kind of textual instability is evident in the concept of ''encrusted'' meanings as elaborated by Janet Staiger, Tony Bennett, and Pierre Macherey.[4] Though one might be skeptical about the claim that such accretions of meaning in the history of a text's reception have the effect of erasing (vs. ''moving'' or ''revising'') the border between text and context, it is hard to deny that some interpretations ''stick'' when they are attributed to a text, often in ways that make them very difficult to pry off. So texts ''grow'' and ''change'' over time, and it is therefore no easy or simple thing – though film critics sometimes think it is – to return to the text in its pristine form. Indeed, efforts to recover the interpretive or aesthetic experience of those audiences contemporary with a particular film – to see a given film through their eyes, as it were – almost always proceed through a kind of detailed historical reconstruction that *of itself* serves to distinguish latter-day experiences from contemporary ones. Though what a film has meant is always potentially a part of what it can mean, that potential always exists within ever-changing circumstances, within *history*.

The latter point bears on the motive for this postscript. I began writing the present study in the spring of 1989; I completed the first draft, which has survived an extended period of review and editorial tinkering largely intact, in April of 1991. In the meanwhile a number of significant contributions to the ''Capra context'' have appeared in print that in various ways confirm the picture I have offered of Capra as a nascently ''feminist'' director, or have at least confirmed my decision to risk that interpretation, chief among them Elizabeth Kendall's *The Runaway Bride: Hollywood Romantic Comedy of the 1930s,* Lee Lordeaux's *Italian and Irish Filmmakers in America: Ford, Capra, Coppola, and Scorsese,* and Joseph McBride's *Frank Capra: The Catastrophe of Success.* Together they raise any number of questions about Capra's historical stature or standing, especially in view of the fact that all three make decidedly *historical* claims.

One of these questions – involving the degree to which we can extrapolate from biography to interpretation, and the risks we run in doing so – is evident in the obvious clash between Lordeaux and McBride. Though I am heartened by Lordeaux's claims that Capra's heroes, like many of his heroines, instance ''the traditional Marian virtues of compassion, patience, and mediation,'' the basis of that claim – involving the assumption that ''Capra's positive religious vision was rooted in his childhood experience of family,'' which helps to explain ''the happy families and particularly the positive father figures in his films'' – is severely undercut by McBride's ''house of pain'' account of family relations among the Capra clan after their arrival in Los Angeles from Sicily.[5] What Lordeaux has taken as given, as ''known,'' largely on the basis of a single episode from Capra's already sketchy account of his childhood in *The Name above the Title,* is revealed by McBride as part of a sustained pattern of strategic misrepresentations that Capra employed over the years to ''print the legend.''[6]

McBride's *Frank Capra: The Catastrophe of Success* undertakes nothing less than a wholesale rewrite of the biographical context within which Capra's films can (on McBride's account: should) be located. It is a dazzling yet in many ways dispiriting performance. McBride's research is extensive and exemplary, yet the Frank Capra who emerges in McBride's account is not the Horatio Alger American hero many people remember from *The Name above the Title*. Though McBride began the book for the explicit purpose of explaining ''the most precipitous decline of any American filmmaker since D. W. Griffith,'' the explanation he eventually offers reaches far deeper in charting a moral decline attendant upon Capra's systematic efforts, culminating in *The Name above the Title* but dating from the early 1930s, to falsify the history of his relationships with collaborators, preeminently Robert Riskin.[7] Indeed, Capra was such a ''chest-thumping egomaniac,'' on McBride's account, that his tightly guarded decision to name names during the McCarthy era – to the Army–Navy–Air Force Personnel Security Board, to the FBI – appears as merely the flip side, in its mean-spirited anxiety over Capra's own ''good name,'' of his autobiographical ''erasure'' of the names of his collaborators, including the names of those who helped him write *The Name above the Title*.[8]

Must history *always* hurt? This history does. I share McBride's sense of promises betrayed. It was not a wonderful life after all. Then how do we explain all those wonderful films? Here is where I find McBride's book most dispiriting. Though his revelations could be taken to deepen the mystery of Capra's cinematic success, however catastrophic his guilt-ridden life may have been, McBride's basic tactic is to attribute that success to Capra's collaborators, which comes uncannily near to repeating the very sin of repression that McBride castigates when Capra is the sinner. Moreover, though he purports to demystify the Capra legend, the picture McBride offers of Capra's films is profoundly orthodox, especially so in light of Raymond Carney's deeply revisionary work on Capra, which McBride never once addresses, and which, in many ways, profoundly anticipates interpretive moves McBride himself would eventually make, not least in saying, as countless film critics have said over the years, that Capra's "official optimism" is an obvious cover for more excessive, more melodramatic surges of idealism and despair that are most profoundly eloquent in exactly those moments when the political logic of a particular script drives Capra into an expressively impossible corner.

Nothing sticks in McBride's biographical craw more than the image – indulged by few critics, in my experience, though by more than a few fans – that Capra was politically of the left, an image that Capra's strategically selective memory alternately encouraged, generally by denying creative credit to Riskin, and discouraged, by assigning credit on occasion to Sidney Buchman, "as if [Capra] were eager to disclaim responsibility" for the left-wing fervor of *Mr. Smith Goes to Washington.*[9] McBride hardly denies a left-wing tilt to many of the movies. On the contrary, what made those films of cultural moment was exactly their "passionately engaged social criticism."[10] However, that social conscience is attributable, in McBride's account, almost entirely to Capra's writers. In his private life, by contrast, and increasingly in his movies, among them "the essentially reactionary *It's a Wonderful Life,*" Capra was a thoroughgoing Darwinian whose commercial moxie told him that he needed to "say something" in his pictures, if he was going to successfully connect with Depression-era audiences, and who had brains enough to know a talented left-leaning writer when he saw one, among them Jo Swerling, Sidney Buchman, and especially Robert Riskin.[11] According to McBride, "Robert Riskin became the social conscience of Frank Capra's films in the 1930s."[12] Indeed, McBride describes Capra's career after *Meet John Doe,* the last film upon which Capra and Riskin actively collaborated, as "a flight from ideas" that "would leave [Capra] virtually bereft of his creative personality" by the end of World War II, as if Riskin *were* Capra's creative personality.[13]

I have no quarrel with the judgment that Capra's autobiographical pronouncements unjustly and self-servingly underplay, to the point of denigrating, the importance of his collaborators, or with the claim that "the sense of brotherhood and compassion that came from Riskin's writing and began to open up the narrow vision of Capra's work brought [Capra] into closer contact with his audience."[14] What I find problematic is the all but unbreakable film-critical habit of defining the political dimension or effectivity of a given movie almost entirely by reference to its narrative fable – what McBride, following Capra, calls a formula or a trademark – and to a very narrowly realistic appraisal of its import as either "reactionary" or "progressive." It is exactly this view of Capra that Raymond Carney inveighs against in *American Vision: The Films of Frank Capra* and that I have undertaken to refute, along somewhat different lines, in the present volume. Capra's films are certainly political, but the politics are far deeper and more nuanced than such course-grained political labels can possibly register.

Much that McBride has to say on the subject of collaboration is located by reference to debates over the auteur theory, of which Capra's famous one-man, one-film motto was a prototype and which Capra's autobiography does much to discredit. It is thus all the more ironic that McBride's curiously one-dimensional view of narrative politics – even when the claim follows that Capra's films at their best evidence a creative tension between progressive and conservative elements – effectively requires him to offer biographical or psychological explanations when the time comes to consider why Capra himself was an important contributor to the success of his movies. Partly this involves crediting Capra with a generalized capacity for responsiveness: "Capra in the prime of his career liked to surround himself with colleagues who were not yes men, and his ability to listen to and absorb such a range of viewpoints 'made him [in the words of Chester Sticht] an interesting guy,' contributing to the complexity of his films." Repeatedly, however, McBride falls back on more specific, and specifically autobiographical, connections between Capra's life story and his film stories in order to explain their energy and intensity. Thus *The Younger Generation* "has more emotional power than any of Capra's other pictures of the 1920s" because "Capra obviously felt a strong identification with the story of a Jewish immigrant (Ricardo Cortez) who grows up in the ghetto of New York's Delancey Street and feels he has to deny his ethnic origins to rise to success in America." Likewise, "What makes *Bitter Tea* such a rich and subtle film is the way that Capra manages to identify equally with the yearning, fatalistic general and with the ambivalent Megan" – the ambivalence reflecting his unrequited love for Stanwyck, Yen's suicidal fatalism allowing Capra "to exorcise those feelings by killing off the part of himself . . . that wanted her."[15]

Another tenet of orthodox Capra criticism that McBride is content to repeat, on Capra's authority no less, involves Capra's (astonishingly self-contradictory) claim that his "audience should never realize that a director has directed the picture," which McBride confirms – *not* by discussing, say, Capra's editing style, or his characteristic *mise-en-scène* – but chiefly by reference to Jimmy Stewart's observation that, during the shooting of *Mr. Smith Goes to Washington*'s filibuster scene, *he* was not distracted by moving cameras, to the point that he "forgot about the camera" altogether. True to form, when McBride *does* mention actual images – "the backlighting of actresses and the sculptural modeling of actors, the ability to transform minimal sets into dreamlike images" – he attributes them to a collaborator: "All of these elements were brought to Capra by [Joseph] Walker." Even in his discussion of *American Madness* – where Capra stepped in at the last minute and salvaged the picture after Allan Dwan, though working from the very same Riskin script that Capra inherited, fumbled the shoot, McBride still makes a point of crediting Riskin's script with "many of what usually are described as directorial 'touches' in *American Madness*."[16]

I hardly wish to deny due credit to Walker or Riskin. What I find most puzzling, in view of my running claim in the present volume that Capra was always a deeply self-conscious director who never hesitated to break with Hollywood's "invisibility" norms, often for the purpose of suggesting self-reflective analogies between on-screen and off-screen actions, is McBride's nearly complete acceptance of the cliché that Capra basically had no style beyond habitually repeating the narrative formula he developed with Riskin. Indeed, the only time McBride discusses a self-conscious reflexivity in Capra – he describes the narrative of *Meet John Doe* as "unusually self-reflective" in "that the plot revolves around a question of authorship" – he assigns that "reflection" chiefly to Riskin, as "Riskin's satirical take on his creative relationship with Capra," as if Capra's brand of self-consciousness was entirely subconscious, a matter of responding to similarities between his own life and the stories and characters he was handed by others.[17] The view I am advancing here amounts to a claim that Capra was simultaneously more *self*-conscious than McBride can imagine and more *un*-conscious, the two qualities being inextricably intertwined – certainly in the movies, just as probably in his life. If nothing else, McBride proves beyond all doubt that Capra was a master of repression. I want to say that his films express that mastery at every turn.

I imagine that McBride's response to Raymond Carney's book was largely a matter of incredulity generated by an assumption of consistency and coherence, hence his total repression of Carney's expansive attempt to read Capra, and especially Capra's visual tropes, by reference to the history of American literature and painting. Capra was a political simpleton and must therefore have been a cinematic simpleton as well. Claims to the contrary, like Stanley Cavell's, like Carney's, like mine, are simply another version of that early "auteurist" rush to judgment that resurrected Capra, on McBride's account, at the expense of Capra's colleagues and the truth. In the process, however, McBride retreats to an even more archaic critical position, though it is represented in his book by Elliott Stein, Capra's most eloquent latter-day detractor. Despite the fact that Stein is the critic McBride most loves to quote in his campaign to credit Riskin with Capra's social consciousness, it is Stein's more general position that "the dry rot of quack benignity was setting in fast" even before *Mr. Deeds Goes to Town.* Like many of Capra's late 1930s critics – like Alistair Cooke who feared that Capra was "on his way out" with *Mr. Deeds* because "he's started to make movies about themes instead of about people" – Stein takes the general position that Capra was at his best in his early movies: "After *Deeds,* he would never again be capable of a film as funny as *Long Pants,* as charming as *Rain or Shine,* as sensibly erotic as *Bitter Tea*. . . , as simply exciting as *Dirigible.*"[18]

I detail these historical and critical ironies partly because McBride does not. Given McBride's own record as a sensitive and accomplished film critic, given the engagement with film-critical issues he undertakes in disputing auteurist film scholarship, he should have. A greater sense of irony, or of history, might have helped McBride to see that imputations of expressivity or meaning are *not* identical to statements imputing an exclusive originality – as my discussion of *Meet John Doe,* I hope, makes clear. I do not doubt that Capra was a success because of his extraordinary responsiveness to others, Walker and Riskin chief among them. However, my claims to the effect that *Forbidden* represents Capra's attempt to speak the feminine in himself do not entail that he alone was the speaker or the only one "spoken." Indeed, the film is literally about the overlap and interplay of authorships, about *mutuality.*

Likewise, arguments premised on the view that Capra was too simpleminded to do something ought, on historical grounds, to yield precedence to arguments that claim that it was done. Of course, some sense of probability is unavoidable in so intensely collaborative an art as filmmaking. I am more than satisfied – given the significance and depth of the narrative and stylistic continuities that bind Capra's canon together – that Capra's was the agency that brought all the many contributions into harmonious accord and in ways that augmented them all. However, the interpretive issue really comes first, or else the attribution question is beside the point. If *Mr. Deeds Goes to Town* is (something like) the film I claim it is, there is more than credit enough to go around; if *Mr. Smith Goes to Washington* is as different from *Mr. Deeds* as I claim it to be, not simply a formulaic remake of its predecessor, there is more credit yet to be accorded. To insist on reading Capra's populist trilogy at the level of shorthand political labels, as McBride largely does, risks painting Riskin with the brush of simple-mindedness usually used to tar and feather Frank Capra. Indeed, if Riskin is "responsible" for the social consciousness of *Mr. Deeds Goes to Town,* then Elliott Stein has an eloquent ally in Elizabeth Kendall, who reads the conflicted quality of *Mr. Deeds* rather differently and less flatteringly than McBride:

> It's a peculiarly bifurcated movie to watch. The romantic scenes display some of the qualities of Capra's earlier movies – warmth, wit, tolerance, and real respect for the achievement of intimacy. The political scenes betray Capra's [and Riskin's?] coarser side – his self-consciousness, his sentimentality, his desire to please which get funneled, for the parable's effectiveness, into a treacly patriotism with religious overtones.[19]

McBride's extremely orthodox view of Capra's films is especially painful to contemplate, in light of his own work and Raymond Carney's, given the opportunity McBride had (and missed) to move in the direction of a genuinely "thick" history of Capra's Hollywood career by incorporating both historical and interpretive insights. For example, an important element of the Capra myth was the status he claimed as an almost divinely inspired cinematic neophyte whose ignorance had the happy effect of setting him somewhat apart from his more conventionally apprenticed studio peers. As Capra tells the tale in *The Name above the Title,* he had hardly even *seen* a film, much less had his hands on celluloid, before the day he walked into a San Francisco gymnasium and bluffed his way into the job of directing *Fulta Fisher's Boarding House* in 1921. What McBride uncovers, by contrast, is a long history of theatrical, literary, and cinematic experience on Capra's part stretching back to his high-school days – not to mention his working as an extra in an early John Ford film; working as a gagman for the Christie Film Company; as scriptwriter, secretary-treasurer, and actor for the fly-by-night Tri-State Motion Picture Company of Reno, Nevada;

directing or assisting in directing the *Screen Snapshots* series for C.B.C. pictures, all of which preceded his move to San Francisco in 1920. Capra's apprenticeship was long and laborious, involving him in nearly every aspect of filmmaking, including lab work and editing. So he *probably* knew what he was doing when he walked on to a movie set or took his seat at an editing table. Moreover, the evidence of what he did is voluminous, reel after amazing reel unwinding before our very eyes and ears. It is profoundly ironic that, of all the evidence he had at hand, McBride finds the films themselves the least credible part of the record, when he could as readily have written a very different study, of the studiously pragmatic intelligence that brought those contributions and images together into those richly dense and vibrant movies.[20]

The kind of scholarship I have in mind is splendidly evident in Elizabeth Kendall's *The Runaway Bride.* Like the present study, Kendall's is focused on questions of gender and genre. Thus she traces the emergence of romantic comedy to a set of historical and institutional circumstances:

1. the Depression, which made conventional Hollywood representations of class and gender propriety less than credible, so that "male actors could no longer stand, as they had in twenties comedies, for some kind of decency at the heart of American life," a role that subsequently "devolved upon the actresses";
2. the coming of sound, which gave new voice to women in the genre of fallen-woman melodrama; and
3. a crop of young one-man, one-film directors (Stevens, La Cava, McCarey, Sturges, and Capra) whose positioning "on the margins of the movie industry" and whose backgrounds in silent comedy allowed them to escape the "pattern of sameness" pressures experienced by directors at more major studios.

Most important, because "these were men who didn't shrink from imagining what it might feel like to be a woman," these directors genuinely collaborated with their actresses, treating them "not as icons of femininity but as companions." Furthermore, the first movie wherein these possibilities were realized, according to Kendall, was not *It Happened One Night,* as the genre story is more usually told, but rather Capra's *Ladies of Leisure,* starring Barbara Stanwyck.[21]

The deftness with which Kendall moves back and forth from social history to biographical background to cinematic specifics is hard to capture in summary, though it is nicely exemplified in her reading of *Ladies of Leisure*'s opening shots, of inebriated young women tossing liquor bottles off a penthouse balcony to the streets below, as a "visual allegory" (sonic allegory too!) of "The Crash"; "something dangerous was falling on the ordinary people in the street, something that came from the careless doings of the idle rich above them."[22] However, crucial to Kendall's elaboration of what transformed *Ladies of Leisure* from a fallen-woman melodrama into the very prototype of "Depression romantic comedy" is the connection she makes, via Capra, with silent comedy.

Partly this is a matter of directorial style, as referring, in McBride's sense, to Capra's on-set handling of actors, though Kendall also employs the notion to account for specific shots and framings in a manner McBride generally eschews. *Ladies of Leisure* instituted a generic revolution, that is, because Capra, like many silent-comedy directors, went after character rather than story, and did so by trial and error, in such a way as to match performer and persona. In "responding" to Stanwyck's slowly building performance in *Ladies of Leisure,* as evidenced on screen and in Capra's working copy of the script where his revisions of Swerling's dialogue are documented, Capra "endowed her with something more complex than the Shavian spunk that Swerling put into her vocabulary; he has allowed her a private, thoughtful core of *self* that relates more to the movies than to the stage." Indeed, in "her longing, her resentment, and her improvised dignity" Stanwyck and Capra's Kay Arnold infuses into melodrama "the [emotional and class] dynamic of silent comedies, but with the genders reversed," a reversal which, crucially, "allowed Capra to encounter the subject of sexuality, which the silents had excluded."[23]

I find these echoes of my own view of Capra deeply gratifying, as confirming my claims about Capra's generic complexity and his interest in the human female as embodying the human as such. Indeed, here too one can enlist McBride's exemplary historical scholarship to fill out the picture of Capra's expansive gender loyalties in ways that point to further research. I cannot help but wonder what Kendall would make of early Capra efforts like *His First Flame* (1925), the "first feature-length screenplay of Capra's to be filmed in Hollywood," in which Harry Langdon tangles with "WOMAN – the eternal question" and winds up, before the film is over, wearing a dress and on the run from lustful men; or of Capra's unproduced 1927 screenplay *Hold Your Husband,* which features a young wife teaching her wandering spouse a lesson in marital fidelity "by masquerading as a suave, mustachioed French aviator'' who not only woos the husband's dancer girlfriend but who also convinces her husband that *she* is being wooed by her French fly-boy self.[24] Though the Capra McBride gives us is something less than the Capra of popular legend, there is a lot *more* of Capra to consider now that McBride has helped to expand the canon!

Where Kendall and McBride most obviously part company is *not* on the question of gender per se. Indeed, part of what McBride means in calling *It's a Wonderful Life* a ''reactionary'' film involves the apparently conventional sexual standing of Donna Reed's Mary Hatch Bailey by contrast, say, with the sexually progressive interest Capra took in such strong-minded female characters as Jean Arthur's Babe Bennett in *Mr. Deeds* and Clarissa Saunders in *Mr. Smith*.[25] For that matter, Kendall and McBride agree that Capra underwent a sea change at some point that saw him leave behind whatever quality it was that made his films socially significant. However, they disagree in their location of the moment. For McBride, it was Capra's departure from Robert Riskin after *Meet John Doe*. For Kendall, as for James Harvey, it was Capra's growing involvement with Robert Riskin culminating in *Mr. Deeds Goes to Town* in which Capra, as Kendall describes it, ''brings that quality of trust [in humankind] right back to the persona of the baby-man Stanwyck had herself displaced,'' as if to make us ''forget, for a moment, that the Stanwyck movies were ever made,'' thus reversing the very revolution he had started with *Ladies of Leisure*.[26]

By way of conclusion, let me extend the conversation on these latter two points, involving what Capra lost and when he lost it, by reference to the feature films Capra made after the relative commercial failure of *It's a Wonderful Life*. What Capra *never* lost, I am moved to say, is his (always problematic) identification with women, which I have already traced in detail through the films of Capra's populist trilogy and *It's a Wonderful Life*. I have described the latter, indeed, as enacting George Bailey's desire to give birth to himself – a wish that simultaneously expresses his longing for female identity and power as well as a fear of female rejection, as if he *had* to mother himself for fearing that his real mother would not, a fear harrowingly pictured during the ''unborn sequence'' when a frantic George confronts an embittered ''Ma Bailey'' at her boardinghouse, only to have the door slammed shut in his face. George Bailey's problematically feminine identification here is confirmed, in ways that also echo my linking of Capra and Shakespeare via *Hamlet,* by Elaine Showalter's discussion of Ophelia's (reported) suicide-by-drowning in Shakespeare's version of the story. Drowning, Showalter declares, drawing on the work of Gaston Bachelard, is "the truly feminine death," a "beautiful immersion and submersion in the female element. . . . A man contemplating this feminine suicide understands it by reaching for what is feminine in himself."[27] Maybe it is *that* self George effectively acknowledges when he leans on the bridge rail above a surging river and asks to be reborn. No wonder water figures so prominently in Capra's iconography!

One way of observing this feminist element in Capra's later films is by attending to their continuing reenactment of the Cinderella narrative, which can be traced as far back in Capra as *That Certain Thing* and which obviously plays a central role in Capra's populist fables of nobility (more of soul than class standing) disinherited. As often as not it is a man who plays the Cinderella role. Sometimes it is a woman who is the fairy godmother – Ann Schuyler, then Gallagher, in *Platinum Blonde;* Susan Paine, then Clarissa, in *Mr. Smith Goes to Washington* – hence a stand in for Capra's magical brand of cinematic authorship. In the later films this identification of authorship and motherhood is made explicit via male characters, like newspaper reporter Peter Garvey in *Here Comes the Groom,* the very title of which rings the role-reversal theme; it is Pete who "delivers" the children in this movie, and Pete who tutors Winifred Stanley in the finer points of feminine deportment. Likewise, Dave the Dude, in *Pocketful of Miracles,* though he shares the authorial function with Queenie Martin far more than his *Lady for a Day* predecessor did with Missouri Martin, is implicitly likened to Mother Goose, in telling a "Mother Goose story" to the powers that be. Indeed, all but one of Capra's films after *It's a Wonderful Life* focus on what we might call "male mothers," including *A Hole in the Head,* and most of them are rife with throwaway gags about gender reversal, as in the latter film's running quiz-show routine. Twice (once early, once late) Tony asks Ally who was the last light heavyweight to hold three crowns, to which Ally (who "looks like" his mother) always replies "Greta Garbo." Furthermore, a similar exchange in the middle of the film finds Mrs. Rogers (who looks like Ally) coming up with the right fight-fan answer to another of Tony's quiz-show questions, much to the latter's (gender-based) surprise.

These observations should *not* be taken as implying that Capra's female identification is untroubled or untroubling in his later years. On the contrary, several of these films also invoke, as if defensively, a decidedly traditional picture of marriage that counterbalances the feminist subtext. A relatively benign picture of this involves Queenie Martin's attempts to lure Dave the Dude out of the rackets and into marriage, the ceremony to be conducted in Silver Springs, Maryland, no less, by the very minister who married her mother and father. A far more distasteful version of marriage is on view in *Riding High,* where even the role-reversal gags are infected by a weirdly despairing animus. Thus when Douglass Dumbrille's Eddie Howard bails Bing Crosby's Dan Brooks out of jail – in order to make sure that Broadway Bill runs in the race Eddie (without Dan's knowledge) is rigging – Dan proposes marriage and asks Eddie when they should go on their honeymoon. The gag seems another throwaway – until it is connected to the cynicism of Professor Pettigrew's financially motivated promise to marry Margaret Hamilton's "Vinegar Puss" if Broadway Bill loses, and to the general practice of marrying for money, to get it, to keep it, that typifies the marriages of all the Higgins daughters but one. *Riding High* is a dispiriting and dispirited film in any number of dimensions; it is positively heartbreaking to see the difference between footage originally shot for *Broadway Bill* and the newly taken footage that Capra tries, without success, to match it with; the former material is crisp and alive, the latter is all too often dead from the get go. However, cynicism about marriage is also a part of what makes *Riding High* a great blot on Capra's record, as if he were revenging himself on himself for ever "marrying the harlot," as he often described his addiction to filmmaking. It is almost as if he wanted simply to sell out and quit, like J. L. Higgins does in *Riding High*'s conclusion, as in some sense Capra already had when he sold Liberty Films to Paramount, as if *he* were the harlot.

Capra never abandoned, I am claiming, the habit of identifying authorship with femininity. What he lost was something that often went with that identification, a volatile equation of the erotic and the political whereby each alternately expressed and energized the other. Furthermore, he lost it when he made *State of the Union,* the very title of which, in seeking to link eros and politics, betokens a quality of anxiety only hinted at in *Frank Capra: The Catastrophe of Success,* though I am now in agreement with at least some of McBride's reasons for seeing the film as Capra's "elegy for his abandonment of socially conscious filmmaking."[28] That is, though I disagree with McBride's claim that the film's explicit political vantage point is "a nonsensical jumble of contradictory political opinions" – Grant Matthews, even when cutting distasteful political deals, makes far more coherent political sense than Jeff Smith ever did, if explicit sense-making is the issue – I am willing to grant that Capra's political caution in all probability reflected personal anxiety in the midst of the House Un-American Activities Committee (HUAC) scandals, an anxiety fed by Capra's long-standing association with left-wing writers and the difficulties he experienced obtaining security clearances even as early as 1942 when the lack of clearance prevented him, for a time, from viewing *Triumph of the Will* in connection with making the *Why We Fight* series.[29] Put another way, if Capra's greatest creative asset was his capacity for responsiveness, then we might say that in *State of the Union* he responded to the national mood yet again by closing himself off from his own better instincts. However, he did so by making politics, of a sort, more explicit than ever.

We can glimpse the strangeness of *State of the Union* by comparing it to *Forbidden,* a film that *State of the Union* can be almost literally described as "overwriting," to the point of erasure. Again we have a man of substance, curiously estranged from his wife, whose political career is manipulated, to the point of being stage managed, by a female journalist, Stanwyck's Lulu Smith in *Forbidden,* Angela Lansbury's Kay Thorndyke in *State of the Union.* Again there is an intriguing play with gender stereotypes. Kay Thorndyke is first seen in a trench coat and a mannish hat, and is described by her father as having "a woman's body with a man's brains"; during the Detroit hotel sequence a barber comes to the door of Grant's hotel room and asks if someone needs a shave: Katharine Hepburn's Mary Matthews feels her chin and answers in the negative, in a gesture recalling Lulu's twirling of her "moustache" in the Havana sequence of *Forbidden.* Again there is a specter of sexual scandal haunting a political campaign; again we see a political speech being given by a man who at some level would prefer to come clean and have done with it. *State of the Union* almost literally begins where *Forbidden* ends, with reporters gathered in a deathwatch while a woman has a last few words with a dying man who embodies her identity. However, what all the similarities boil down to is a matter of profound difference, a difference hard to miss when we observe Adolphe Menjou, once the guilt-plagued politician in *Forbidden* who tried but failed to bail out of a political campaign, standing on the *State of the Union* sidelines, now in the role of political operative Jim Conover (Fig. 20), while Spencer Tracy's Grant Matthews goes right ahead and quits over a nationwide radio–television hookup.

But what, exactly, is Grant quitting? He is resigning from a political campaign in which various politically active and powerful individuals have

Figure 20. On the political sidelines: Adolph Menjou and Angela Lansbury in *State of the Union*. (Copyright © by Universal City Studios, Inc. Courtesy of MCA Publishing Rights, a division of MCA, Inc.)

negotiated their differences for the sake of acquiring more political power through the standing procedures of the Republican Party. The most emphatic ''sin'' we see committed, political or otherwise, is when Grant and Kay conspire to excuse Mary's absence from the radio broadcast by cooking up the ''sick child'' story, though it is of a piece with Kay's instructions to her editors to cook up damaging news stories that will set various Republican candidates at odds in such a way as to deadlock the Republican convention, though we never see those orders carried out. (Whether or not there is an illicit sexual affair going on between Grant and Kay that needs denying, denials of which would count as blatant falsehoods, is a question repeatedly raised but never exactly settled.) What we decidedly do *not* have in *State of the Union* is a fascist ''What the American people need is an iron hand'' plot akin to D. B. Norton's in *Meet John Doe,* nor, for that matter, is there any garden-variety political graft in train like that on view in *Mr. Smith Goes to Washington.* Indeed, Conover simply wants to get back to political work after years of forced inaction, and when he asks Kay her motive, her reply amounts to nothing more than a desire to avenge the slights her father suffered at the hands of certain Republican Party pols (''heads'' will ''roll''). So we see *lots* of politics at work in *State of the Union,* especially by contrast with the curious political blankness that characterizes *Forbidden,* but it does not generate anywhere near so much heat or passion as was typical of Capra's earlier political fables, for all of their political indirection.

Something else we see considerably less of in *State of the Union,* especially by contrast with *Forbidden,* is anything even vaguely akin to the transcendental eroticism of the earlier movie. Though Kay declares her love for Grant, in urging him to get into the political race, her declaration is nearly indistinguishable in tone from any of her other rhetorical gestures, including her politically canted assurance to Conover that Grant loves her. Even those moments when Kay and Grant briefly touch are decidedly lacking in sexual energy. Moreover, the moment when Kay assures Grant that his being in the White House will mean her being there, at least in spirit, despite its echoes of Lulu Smith's similar assurance to Bob Grover that his success is hers, is colored by her dying father's prediction that she will make the White House where he could not, ''one way or another.'' Grant is the means, not the end. In sum, it is hard to see any reason why Grant should ever have been attracted to her, or Kay to him, in the first place, apart from political expediency itself. Indeed, Kay *wants* Mary to be jealous, on the (mistaken) premise that a jealous Mary will push all the harder on behalf of Grant's candidacy; and after Grant finally quits Kay quickly shifts her (political) interest to the fellow on the cover of *Newsweek* (Grant had been on *Time*). One way of marking the difference of the Kay–Grant relationship in *State of the Union* from that of Lulu and Grover in *Forbidden* is that the worm of ambition, which in the earlier film had been depicted as a positive, and positively erotic, goad to shared worldly action, becomes in the later film the soul-destroying ''worm'' of political ''compromise'' that Mary denounces to Conover while Kay, who has slipped into an adjoining room without Mary's knowledge, convinces Grant (apparently) to tone down any attack on big business in his upcoming speech.

Such eroticism as remains in *State of the Union* is entirely a matter of the relationship between Grant and Mary Matthews. Here is where the film's only moment of real sexual intimacy is on view, as we watch Grant watch Mary's shadow on the bathroom door while she undresses for bed (Fig. 21). Yet here is where the film's real complications and incoherences

Figure 21. The erotic gaze in *State of the Union.* (Copyright © by Universal City Studios, Inc. Courtesy of MCA Publishing Rights, a division of MCA, Inc.)

are most evident. Despite Mary's claim that the "state of [her] union" with Grant is "entirely political," despite, that is, her agreeing with Conover to dissemble her estrangement from Grant by accompanying him on a speaking tour for the sake of Grant's ideals, Mary's chief "passion" in the movie is a vision of political honesty – of a Grant Matthews "drunk on sincerity" – that stands directly opposed to the political tactics, of avoiding controversy and cutting deals for convention delegates, practiced by the likes of Conover and Kay Thorndyke. Mary would rather see Grant honest than president. And in the world of the film that means her every gesture in the direction of encouraging Grant's more honest instincts is a gesture in the direction of sabotaging his campaign. There is the interpretive rub. Though Mary's emotional stance seems opposed at every juncture to the "show" that Kay and Conover are staging – a show scheduled to culminate in the broadcast from the Matthews's living room, a show that, with its cast of wife and kids, leads Spike MacManus to declare that "no one will top this for Corn" – her method of opposition is to stage a countershow. That she *seems,* all the while, merely to be going along with the show they are staging, against her better judgment, a mere bystander, only complicates the matter, as if her strategy were an unconscious one, expressed by repression.

In other words, like Grandpa Vanderhof in *You Can't Take It with You,* Mary Matthews can be taken as a figure for Capra's authorship, engaged in a battle of authorships (Fig. 22), a kinship confirmed, to my mind, by the extravagant framing and lighting effects by which Capra manages to center the broadcast drama around Mary, though its ostensible center or prime mover seems to be Kay. Indeed, Mary's shadow on the bathroom door recalls our first glimpse of Robert Conway in *Lost Horizon,* also a cinematic shadow very precisely and emphatically framed in a doorway; Mary is the one, Grant tells us, who first read to Grant the line, attributed in McBride to the poet Alfred Noyes, one of Capra's Throop College English professors, attributed in *Lost Horizon* to Robert Conway, about those "moments in every man's life when he glimpses the eternal."[30] Mary's supposed affair with an unnamed major is a blatantly fictionalized attempt to arouse Grant's jealousy (as, I am suggesting, Kay's "affair" with Grant is designed to arouse Mary's). Mary's "drunk" act during the radio broadcast, moreover, like so many other similar drunk scenes in Capra, seems as much a matter of role playing as inebriation; Mary wants Grant "drunk on sincerity" and she "shows" him how to do it. I have no doubts that Capra tried, at some level, to make a film about politics. However, the film he made is most energized and most interesting when politics and show business collapse in on one another.

The Platonic catch, however, is that the charge of dishonesty and insincerity that Mary is constantly leveling at Conover and Kay is equally as applicable to her – as in the moment when she accuses Grant of being "a ghost, a shadow, a stooge, mouthing words not your own." Apart from the fact that Hepburn at that moment, as a movie actress, is *herself* "a ghost, a shadow, mouthing words not her own," Mary Matthews, as we have already learned, is not averse to passing words along to Grant herself, say, by reading to him. Indeed, it is by reading from a prepared script that Mary induces Grant to scrap his own prepared text and withdraw from the political race. Grant sees his own dishonesty mirrored in Mary's and the sight is literally unbearable. What is equally unbearable, at least in historical retrospect, is the extent to which this shared identification – of Capra with Mary, of Grant with Mary – has as its literal and figurative outcome an emphatic rejection of the political *tout court,* which risks bidding farewell

Figure 22. The contest of authorships: Mary Matthews (Katharine Hepburn) vs. Kay Thorndyke (Angela Lansbury) in *State of the Union.* (Copyright © by Universal City Studios, Inc. Courtesy of MCA Publishing Rights, a division of MCA, Inc.)

to popular culture altogether, as a responsibility too burdensome to bear. The sense in which Kay Thorndyke is an echo of Lulu Smith (or Kay Arnold) only confirms the painful sense of rejection here; in rejecting Kay, Capra is also rejecting the shadow of an earlier and better self.

In films like *Forbidden, It Happened One Night,* and *Mr. Deeds Goes to Town* Capra had managed to suggest that erotic union was both a precondition and a prefigurement of political recovery, of new birth, of human hope, especially to the extent that it permitted men, like Robert Grover, like Peter Warne, like Longfellow Deeds, like Frank Capra, to voice their own femininity, and in so doing to accept vulnerability and responsiveness to others as qualities fully equivalent to power and authority as tokens of human existence, hopes and qualities without which one's existence is not (yet) fully human. In *It's a Wonderful Life* this vision reached something like perfection in showing how we give birth to the world, to each other, by acts of mutual acknowledgment. That the film was not acknowledged by his contemporaries as a new birth for Capra must have been personally devastating.[31] Or perhaps the HUAC hearings, which were in full swing while Capra was shooting *State of the Union,* provided too clear a reminder of a political vulnerability that Capra would spend the rest of his lifetime seeking to disguise or deny. However it happened, in *State of the Union* Capra cuts the link between eroticism and politics, between the fate of the feminine and the fate of the nation. Identification with the Katharine Hepburn character in *State of the Union* expresses a wish to withdraw from the public world, a wish Grant's afterthought pledge to attend the nominating conventions only underscores in the act of denying it.

That the choice smacked of wormwood and gall is evident in one of the film's strangest passages, though it links Capra's status as an outsider, ineligible for election as president for not being native born, with Hepburn's status as a woman. I have already noted the moment when Mary tells the hotel barber she does not need a shave. As the barber gets set to work on Grant the latter tries to respond to Mary's proposal that they repeat the campaign trip, though her phrasing (''Let's do it all over again'') as readily applies to their marriage. Grant remarks that the trip has agreed with her, and mentions the sight of Mary at the Denver airport, the prop-wash blowing her dress in the moonlight. However, the intimacy implicit in the moment is never allowed to develop as various handlers and hotel employees, the barber among them, interrupt. After Spike tells Grant to get ready for the radio broadcast, the (Italian) barber tells Grant that the latter's candidacy ''is a no solution,'' which the barber explains by repeating his wife's claim that male politicians have proven that ''roosters'' are brainless, are always fighting; the time has come for ''hens'' to run the show (''Your wife – ah – that's a solution''), a claim he repeats when Mary refers to a dozing Grant Matthews as ''Mr. President.'' To which Mary replies that ''no woman could ever run for President'' because she'd ''have to admit she was over 35'' – the other constitutional requirement, along with native birth, of eligibility for election, as we are reminded by Conover very early in the film. That the barber is expressly represented as Italian, and as agreeing with his wife's explicitly feminist take on politics, confirms the Capra–Hepburn connection – as does the barber's odd (silent comedy) gesture of lathering his own face rather than Grant's by mistake, which humorously equates him with Mary: Neither one needs a shave.[32]

In light of Hepburn's career and persona, even circa 1948, asking her to speak such stereotypically antifeminist lines could not have been easy, nor her speaking them. However, they capture the sense, evident throughout the film, that Capra is looking for a way out, a matter of not admitting something, which he manages, like Grant Matthews, by admitting to something else under the pressure of Mary's theatrical example. It is heartbreakingly ironic that what once had been the most interesting and progressive element of Capra's career – his equation of authorship and femininity – could be so quickly and decisively turned to that purpose. The woman Capra now longs to be, astonishingly enough, is a ''small potatoes,'' though financially well-fixed, Republican matron. That he succeeded was indeed catastrophic for his subsequent career as a filmmaker. However, I believe the terms I have elaborated or developed for describing that catastrophe are significantly different from those that have generally been employed by Capra's critics; they are certainly different from McBride's. In that difference resides a hope that the career of Capra's wonderful films is far from over, is just beginning. ''It'll be honest this time,'' as Capra-surrogate Ann Mitchell once avows to her fictionalized alter ego in *Meet John Doe,* and honest largely because Capra, like John Doe himself, left a message for posterity, all of his personal papers – scripts, correspondence, even undergraduate essays on Whitman and Emerson! – which he donated to Wesleyan University in 1980, and which McBride, as it were, has forwarded in *Frank Capra: The Catastrophe of Success.* And McBride accuses Capra of using a ghostwriter! (The accusation, under the circumstances, haunts itself.) Mille grazie, Francesco!

Notes

Sources listed in the bibliography are generally cited here in abbreviated form. Where the bibliography lists more than one publication venue for a particular article or chapter, the note citation is to the most recent instance unless otherwise indicated. The following abbreviations will be used for sources most frequently cited:

AV Carney, *American Vision: The Films of Frank Capra*
MJD Wolfe, ed., *Meet John Doe*
NAT Capra, *The Name above the Title*
PH Cavell, *Pursuits of Happiness*

Preface

1. *NAT,* p. 3.

2. Joseph McBride reports in *Frank Capra: The Catastrophe of Success* (pp. 91–2) that Capra received a ''general'' Bachelor of Science degree from Throop, having failed to complete the course of study specific to chemical engineering. Nevertheless, Capra did seek employment *as* a chemical engineer, without success, after World War I. ''Pattern of sameness'' alludes to Capra's 1946 *New York Times Magazine* article.

3. I borrow phrasing from Jeanine Basinger's *American Film* article ''America's Love Affair with Frank Capra.''

4. Otis Ferguson, ''Worth Seeing,'' *New Republic 78* (9 May 1934), 364–5; reprinted as ''It Happened One Night,'' *American Film Criticism: From the Beginnings to* Citizen Kane, ed. Stanley Kauffmann (New York: Liveright, 1972), p. 299.

5. William Troy, ''On a Classic,'' *Nation* 140 (10 Apr. 1935), 426–7; reprinted as ''It Happened One Night,'' in Kauffmann, *American Film Criticism,* pp. 300–1.

6. See Cobbett S. Steinberg, *Film Facts* (New York: Facts on File, 1980) and Paul Michael et al., eds., *The American Movies: The History, Films, Awards* (New York: Garland, 1969). The only discrepancy between the two involves *Pocketful* *of Miracles,* listed by Michael et al. as among the top twenty-five grossing films of 1961–2, though missing from the 1962 list (of the top twenty) in *Film Facts.*

7. Charles J. Maland, *Frank Capra,* p. 161.

8. Ibid., p. 180.

9. Jean-Louis Comolli and Jean Narboni, "Cinéma/idéologie/critique," *Cahiers du cinéma* no. 216 (Oct. 1969); reprinted as "Cinema/Ideology/Criticism," trans. Susan Bennett, *Movies and Methods,* ed. Bill Nichols (Berkeley: Univ. California Press, 1976), p. 24.

10. An exemplary instance of the rejection of "subtextual" features in favor of the "surface text which contemporary audiences related to" is found in Jeffrey Richards's oddly bifurcated review of Ray Carney's *American Vision.* Richards takes it as axiomatic that the contemporaneous reading, however superficial, is always to be maintained or privileged, no matter how convincingly better the alternative picture might be. Whether Richards's own view as detailed in "Frank Capra and the Cinema of Populism" is more accurate, for being more clearly "contemporary," is far less self-evident than he assumes it to be.

11. Maland, *Frank Capra,* p. 186.

12. Nick Browne, "System of Production/System of Representation," *MJD,* pp. 270, 273–4.

13. Ibid., pp. 270, 284, 274.

14. See especially David Bordwell's *Narration in the Fiction Film* and Kristin Thompson's *Breaking the Glass Armour: Neoformalist Film Analysis* (Princeton: Princeton Univ. Press, 1988).

1. Picturing Capra

1. Nick Browne, "System of Production/System of Representation," *MJD;* see especially p. 288.

2. See Capra's "A Sick Dog Tells Where It Hurts," "Sacred Cows to the Slaughter," and "Breaking Hollywood's Pattern of Sameness."

3. *NAT,* p. 297.

4. Ibid., p. 303.

5. Richard Glatzer, "*Meet John Doe:* An End to Social Mythmaking," *MJD,* pp. 251–2. On the "mythmaking" theme as it is elaborated in *Meet John Doe* see also Pascal Bonitzer, "Frank Capra: La machine à influencer."

6. Charles J. Maland, *Frank Capra,* p. 113.

7. See, for example, Jeanine Basinger's "America's Love Affair with Frank Capra" in *American Film* where the *Time* cover is reprinted in color; Capra reprints a black-and-white version in his autobiography. The cover photo (by itself) is also frequently used in advertisements for the paperback version of *The Name above the Title;* see the Spring and Summer 1989 catalogs for the mail-order book service "A Common Reader."

8. "Columbia's Gem," *Time* (8 Aug. 1938), 35–8.
9. Dudley Andrew, "Productive Discord in the System," *MJD,* pp. 260, 262.
10. Ibid., p. 260.
11. *AV,* p. 350.
12. Ibid., p. 361.
13. Ibid., p. 354
14. Ibid., p. 372
15. Andrew, pp. 264, 266.
16. *AV,* p. 370.
17. Ibid., p. 368.
18. Andrew, p. 267.
19. Luce Irigaray, *Spéculum de l'autre femme* (Paris: Minuit, 1974), p. 249; quoted (in English) in Toril Moi, *Sexual/Textual Politics: Feminist Literary Theory* (London: Methuen, 1985), p. 137.
20. Charles Wolfe (*MJD,* p. 25) reports that the "John Doe" letter Capra cites in his autobiography as providing the inspiration for the ultimate conclusion to the film is not to be found among Capra's papers in the Wesleyan University Capra Collection. That Capra in "reconstructing" the letter in question for *The Name above the Title* might have employed "a story-telling license not unrelated to the one assumed by Ann in the film" is one more reason for equating the two; each uses "John Doe" as a nom de plume.
21. It is worth noting how history gets "reversed" in the matter of these magazine covers, at least as their sequence bears on possible interpretations of *Meet John Doe.* Capra's cover preceded John Doe's, which preceded Gary Cooper's. Still, many viewers at the time would have seen the Cooper cover before seeing the film, at which point they might have been alerted to catch the "Doe" cover, which in turn might have prompted recollection of the Capra cover. Circular hermeneutics indeed!
22. Kenneth Burke, "*Coriolanus* and the Delights of Faction," in *Language as Symbolic Action* (Berkeley: Univ. California Press, 1966), p. 81.
23. Raymond Durgnat, "Genre: Populism and Social Realism," *Film Comment* 11(4) (July–Aug. 1975), 23. My citation drops a footnote number from the original passage.
24. Jeffrey Richards, "Frank Capra and the Cinema of Populism," p. 66.
25. Ibid., p. 67. Richard Griffith's "fantasy of goodwill" formula originally appeared in his 1949 "The Film Since Then" addition to Paul Rotha's *The Film Till Now* (1930; rev. 1949 and 1960; Middlesex: Spring Books/The Hamlyn Publishing Group, 1967), pp. 449–54; my reference is to the version reprinted in Griffith's subsequent *Frank Capra,* New Index Series 3 (London: British Film Institute, 1951), p. 3.
26. Richards, pp. 68, 67.
27. Ibid., p. 73.

28. Duncan Webster, *Looka Yonder!: The Imaginary America of Populist Culture* (London: Comedia/Routledge, 1988), p. 17.

29. Ibid., pp. 17–18.

30. Ibid., p. 16.

31. Leonard Quart, ''A Populist in Hollywood: Frank Capra's Politics,'' p. 73. See also Quart, ''Frank Capra and the Popular Front,'' and Glenn Alan Phelps, ''The 'Populist' Films of Frank Capra,'' *Journal of American Studies* 13(3) (Dec. 1979), 377–92.

32. Robin Wood, ''Ideology, Genre, Auteur,'' p. 60.

33. Ibid., pp. 60–2.

34. Durgnat, p. 21.

35. Andrew Bergman, ''Frank Capra and Screwball Comedy, 1931–1941,'' *We're in the Money: Depression America and Its Films* (New York: New York Univ. Press, 1971), pp. 132–48; citations are to the version reprinted in *Film Theory and Criticism: Introductory Readings,* ed. Gerald Mast and Marshall Cohen, 2nd ed. (New York: Oxford Univ. Press, 1979), pp. 761–77; see p. 762.

36. Ibid., p. 766.

37. See Wes D. Gehring, ''Screwball Comedy,'' *Handbook of American Film Genres,* pp. 105–24.

38. *PH* (''Knowledge as Transgression''), p. 105.

39. *PH,* p. 85.

40. Stanley Cavell, ''A Capra Moment,'' p. 3.

41. *PH,* p. 85.

42. Ibid., p. 80.

43. Ibid., p. 101.

44. Ibid., p. 79.

45. Rick Altman, *The American Film Musical* (Bloomington: Indiana Univ. Press, 1987), p. 95. For an Altmanesque reading of Capra in particular see ''The Screwball Comedy'' chapter of Thomas Schatz, *Hollywood Genres: Formulas, Filmmaking, and the Studio System* (New York: Random House, 1981), pp. 150–85.

46. Altman, p. 96.

47. Ibid., pp. 331, 336.

48. Ibid., p. 336.

49. Sam Rhodie, ''Totems and Movies,'' *Movies and Methods,* ed. Bill Nichols (Berkeley: Univ. California Press, 1976), p. 480.

50. Altman, pp. 331, 336.

51. Claude Lévi-Strauss, ''The Structural Study of Myth,'' *The Structuralists from Marx to Lévi-Strauss,* ed. Richard and Fernande DeGeorge (Garden City, N.Y.: Doubleday, 1972), p. 181.

52. *PH,* p. 28.

53. Stanley Cavell, ''The Fact of Television,'' p. 242.

54. Cavell, ''Fact,'' p. 243.
55. *PH,* p. 28.
56. *PH,* p. 31.
57. Cavell, ''Fact,'' p. 247.
58. *PH,* p. 37.
59. Claude Lévi-Strauss, ''Le Triangle culinaire''; quoted in Edmund Leach, *Claude Lévi-Strauss,* rev. ed. (Harmondsworth: Penguin, 1976), pp. 31–2.
60. Stanley Cavell, *The Claim of Reason,* p. 5.
61. Charles Wolfe, *Frank Capra,* p. 22.
62. Robert Sklar, ''The Imagination of Stability: The Depression Films of Frank Capra,'' Glatzer and Raeburn, p. 127.
63. André Bazin, ''The Evolution of the Language of Cinema,'' *What Is Cinema?,* trans. Hugh Gray (Berkeley: Univ. California Press, 1967), pp. 23–40. A better translation, by Peter Graham, to which all my citations refer, is included as ''The Evolution of Film Language,'' *The New Wave,* ed. Graham (Garden City, N.Y.: Doubleday, 1968), pp. 25–50; see (here) p. 35.
64. Bazin, ''Film Language,'' p. 26.
65. Bordwell's story/plot distinction is elaborated in a series of texts, among them David Bordwell, Janet Staiger, and Kristin Thompson, *The Classical Hollywood Cinema: Film Style & Mode of Production to 1960* and David Bordwell, *Narration in the Fiction Film.* In the *Narration* book Bordwell substitutes the Russian formalist terms *fabula* and *syuzhet* for ''story'' and ''plot.'' Given the currency Bordwell has granted the ordinary English usage in *The Classical Hollywood Cinema,* yet wanting to honor his reasons for switching to the Russian terminology, I have substituted ''Story'' and ''Plot'' for *fabula* and *syuzhet* in all citations; my use of capital letters on these terms is designed to mark this special usage, though where Bordwell himself is cited using the English terminology I have not tinkered with the cited matter. The reference noted here is to *Narration,* p. 49.
66. Bordwell, *Narration,* p. 49.
67. Ibid., p. 50.
68. Bordwell et al., *The Classical Hollywood Cinema,* p. 12.
69. Bordwell, *Narration,* p. 50.
70. Ibid., p. 52.
71. Ibid., p. 157.
72. Ibid., p. 163.
73. Ibid., p. 165.
74. Peter Brooks, *The Melodramatic Imagination,* pp. 35–6.
75. Stephen Handzo, ''Under Capracorn,'' p. 161.
76. Bordwell et al., *The Classical Hollywood Cinema,* p. 14.
77. On the 30-degree rule see David Bordwell and Kristin Thompson, *Film Art: An Introduction,* 4th ed. (New York: McGraw-Hill, 1993), p. 281.

78. Ibid., p. 290.
79. William Pechter, "American Madness," pp. 130–2. On this quality of desperation in Capra I recommend the George Toles essay on *It's a Wonderful Life* in *North Dakota Quarterly*. Toles describes "the prevailing impression one receives of Capra's method" as that of someone "always risking total failure" in that "he allows himself no sure way of getting from one moment or scene to the next," an impression he specifies as following from Capra's insistently retrospective and revisionary "look – now look again" method of scene construction in which conventional reading expectations "rapidly drop away," as if Capra were seeking "an unmediated primary recognition" beyond the conventional (see pp. 47–8, 54). Though I wrote my description of Capra's stylistic difference before encountering the Toles essay, I am heartened that his discussion of *Wonderful Life* confirms my larger Pechter-inspired claims on these accounts.
80. I allude here to Alva Johnston's "Capra Shoots as He Pleases," *Saturday Evening Post* (14 May 1938), 8–9, 67–74.
81. *NAT,* pp. 277–8.
82. "You Can't Take It with You," *Newsweek* (12 Sept. 1938), 22.
83. "Movie of the Week: *You Can't Take It with You,*" *Life* (19 Sept. 1938), 42–7.
84. Char., "You Can't Take It with You," *Variety* (7 Sept. 1948), 12.
85. Among articles already cited, those by Quart and Phelps on Capra's "populism" mention *You Can't Take It with You* only in passing if at all, while neither Sklar nor Bergman devotes more than two paragraphs of sustained commentary to the movie, as if it had not been available for viewing, though no mention is made of that possibility.
86. Maland, p. 104.
87. James Dugan, "Movies," *New Masses* (13 Sept. 1938), 28.
88. I have consulted the first edition of the play: Moss Hart and George S. Kaufman, *You Can't Take It with You* (New York: Farrar & Rinehart, 1937).
89. James Harvey, *Romantic Comedy,* p. 161.
90. Ibid., p. 146.
91. Ibid., p. 160.
92. Otis Ferguson, "Boys of All Ages," *New Republic* 96 (21 Sept. 1938), 188; reprinted in *The Film Criticism of Otis Ferguson* (Philadelphia: Temple Univ. Press, 1971), p. 236.

2. Melodrama and the Unknown Woman

1. Mary Anne Doane, *The Desire to Desire,* pp. 20–1.
2. Geoffrey Nowell-Smith, "Minnelli and Melodrama," *Screen* 18(2) (Summer 1977), 113–19. Citations refer to the version reprinted in *Home Is Where the Heart*

Is: Studies in Melodrama and the Woman's Film, ed. Christine Gledhill (London: BFI, 1987); here pp. 73–4.

3. Peter Brooks, *The Melodramatic Imagination,* p. 41.

4. Ibid., p. 49.

5. Charles J. Maland, *Frank Capra,* p. 58.

6. *AV,* pp. 182–3.

7. On the topic of "working women" see Viviani, "Who Is Without Sin?"; in Gledhill (cited), pp. 91–2.

8. I adduce here the odd fact that Charles Maland refers to Grover throughout his discussion of *Forbidden* in *Frank Capra* as "Conover," the name of the sleazy political operative played by Adolph Menjou in Capra's 1948 film *State of the Union.*

9. Holland's habitual complaint about burning desk lamps is taken, according to Capra, from the gesture-repertoire of Harry Cohn, who ruled Columbia Pictures in a similarly high-handed manner. See *NAT,* p. 82.

10. My willingness to risk the Rembrandt allusion follows Capra's own habit of alluding to Rembrandt – literally in *The Name above the Title,* where he avers he copied Rembrandt's visual style in making *Fulta Fisher's Boarding House,* more "figuratively" in *American Madness,* where the bank boardroom is dominated by a framed portrait reminiscent of Rembrandt's *Man Standing in a Doorway* or his *Man in a Wide-Brimmed Hat.*

11. Brooks, pp. 35–6.

12. Stanley Cavell, *The Claim of Reason,* pp. 351–2.

13. Stanley Cavell, "Two Cheers for Romance," p. 89.

14. *PH,* pp. 207–10.

15. Stanley Cavell, "Psychoanalysis and Cinema," p. 232.

16. Stanley Cavell, "Naughty Orators," p. 343.

17. Stanley Cavell, "Ugly Duckling, Funny Butterfly," p. 217.

18. Brooks, p. 43.

19. *NAT,* p. 134.

3. Questions of Difference

1. Morris Dickstein, "It's a Wonderful Life, But . . . ," *American Film* 5(7) (May 1980), 44.

2. To be precise, Dugan's *New Masses* piece on "Movies" (13 Sept. 1938) alludes to the "invasion of the farmers" as evincing a "feeling for the underdog" (p. 28). See as well the left-leaning *New Theatre* review ("Mr. Capra Goes to Town") by Robert Stebbins [Sidney Meyers] (Glatzer and Raeburn, *Man and His Films,* pp. 117–20), which quotes at length from the script version of the specific "farmer" scene alluded to by Dickstein.

3. Gerald Weales, *Canned Goods as Caviar,* p. 165.

4. *NAT,* p. 185.

5. In *Frank Capra: The Catastrophe of Success,* Joseph McBride reconfigures the chronology of these events, placing the onset of Capra's illness *before* the Oscar ceremony. While acknowledging that Capra was sick if not guilt-ridden for a period of some six months from November of 1934 to April of 1935, McBride sees Capra's "little man" scenario as a literary device, borrowed in part from *Mr. Deeds,* which enabled Capra to express growing doubts about his vocation and celebrity while simultaneously denying Robert Riskin due credit for the political elements of their films. See McBride, pp. 317–24; also see the Postscript.

6. Wes D. Gehring, *Handbook of American Film Genres,* p. 113.

7. James Harvey, *Romantic Comedy,* p. 81.

8. Ibid., p. 115.

9. Ibid., pp. 159, 149–50, 141, respectively.

10. On the Grant's Tomb sequence see Patrick Gerster, "The Ideological Project of 'Mr. Deeds Goes to Town,' " *Film Criticism* 5(2) (Winter 1981), 35–48.

11. Raymond Durgnat, *The Crazy Mirror: Hollywood Comedy and the American Image* (New York: Horizon Press, 1970), p. 124.

12. Ibid., p. 125.

13. Glenn Alan Phelps, "The 'Populist' Films of Frank Capra," *Journal of American Studies* 13(3) (Dec. 1979), 384.

14. Harvey, p. 113.

15. According to Capra, the legless beggar is played by an old acquaintance from Capra's days as a newspaper boy in Los Angeles (*NAT,* p. 152).

16. Harvey, p. 163.

17. *AV,* pp. 263, 279, 228.

18. Ibid., pp. 289–90.

19. Stanley Cavell, *The Claim of Reason,* p. 31.

20. Ibid., p. 32.

21. Harvey, p. 141.

22. My phrasing alludes to Stanley Cavell's "What Photography Calls Thinking" and "Two Cheers for Romance."

23. Stanley Cavell, *The World Viewed,* pp. 188–9.

24. Cavell, *Disowning Knowledge,* p. 6.

25. Stanley Cavell, *In Quest of the Ordinary* ("The Skeptical and the Metaphorical"), p. 147, and ("Texts of Recovery"), p. 60.

26. On the skeptic's haunting the world see Stanley Cavell's "Being Odd, Getting Even," p. 108; on the haunting in remarriage comedy see his "Psychoanalysis and Cinema," p. 232; on the haunting in melodrama see Cavell's "Naughty Orators," p. 371.

27. *PH,* p. 28.

28. See Cavell's "Psychoanalysis and Cinema," p. 233; and "A Capra Moment," p. 3.
29. Cavell, "Being Odd, Getting Even," pp. 113–4.
30. *PH,* pp. 14, 18.
31. *PH,* p. 88.
32. *PH,* pp. 11–12.
33. Cavell, "Two Cheers for Romance," p. 88.
34. *PH,* p. 15.
35. Cavell, "Two Cheers for Romance," p. 89.
36. Cavell, *Disowning Knowledge,* p. 28.
37. My references to *Antony and Cleopatra* are to G. Blakemore Evans, ed., *The Riverside Shakespeare* (Boston: Houghton Mifflin, 1974) I.iv.5–7. See also Cleopatra's report of mutual cross dressing (II.v.22–23).
38. *PH,* p. 82.
39. Ibid., p. 123.
40. Luce Irigaray, *Spéculum de l'autre femme* (Paris: Minuit, 1974), p. 249; quoted (in English) in Toril Moi, *Sexual/Textual Politics: Feminist Literary Theory* (London: Methuen, 1985), p. 137.
41. Stebbins (cited; note 2), p. 119.
42. My own contribution to this male-typical "deafness" is the publication in *The Cinema of Frank Capra* of a production still that leaves the false impression that Babe fully participates in the celebration of Longfellow's victory – when it is her *exclusion* Capra clearly emphasizes.
43. Cavell, "Two Cheers," p. 95.

4. Glimpsing the Eternal

1. *NAT*, p. 200.
2. Ibid., p. 201.
3. For details of *Lost Horizon*'s restoration, see the essays by Rudy Behlmer and Sam Frank and McBride's Chapter 12 ("The doghouse").
4. *NAT*, p. 201.
5. Charles J. Maland, *Frank Capra,* p. 101.
6. Ellen Draper, "Lost Horizon (1937)," *Cinema Texas Program Notes* 18(2) (26 Feb. 1980), 18–19.
7. Elliott Stein, "Frank Capra," p. 187.
8. The *Life* magazine photo feature on the film (14 Dec. 1936: 30–3) was entitled "$2,000,000 Worth of Scenes from *Lost Horizon*."
9. My general indebtedness to Raymond Carney's *American Vision* is more than usually explicit in the paragraph to which this note is appended. Indeed, *because* his entire book stands behind these claims, I feel free to state them in the

briefest of summary forms. That said, I cannot help but remark on their applicability to *Mr. Smith* (where the "palatial house" is the U.S. Senate) and to *Meet John Doe* (where the "house" is the baseball stadium that is literally made to stand, via the signs denoting state delegations, for the entire country, though a country John now sees through new eyes). For that matter, this "Capra story" also applies with uncanny precision, at least in view of the film's middling reputation, to *State of the Union.*

10. "Lost Horizon," *Time* (8 Mar. 1937), 54.

11. James Hilton, *Lost Horizon,* "Author's Edition" (New York: Morrow, 1933, 1936), pp. 137–8.

12. Ibid., p. 143.

13. Ibid., p. 142.

14. Ibid., pp. 196–7.

15. *NAT,* p. 201.

16. Hilton, p. 49.

17. See Hilton, pp. 177, 180.

5. "This Is a Man's World"

1. Jeffrey Richards, "Frank Capra and the Cinema of Populism," pp. 68, 70.

2. Charles J. Maland, *Frank Capra,* p. 22.

3. *AV,* p. 228.

4. See, respectively, Charles Affron, *Cinema and Sentiment,* p. 118, and Nick Browne, "The Politics of Narrative Form," p. 5.

5. Brian Gallagher, "Speech, Identity, and Ideology in 'Mr. Smith Goes to Washington,' " *Film Criticism* 5(2) (Winter 1981), 12.

6. Browne, I should be clear, though employing generically Freudian vocabulary, never mentions Lacan directly; Gallagher's essay *does* refer to Browne's and cites that version of psychoanalysis employed by Laura Mulvey and Jean-Louis Baudry, but he (likewise) avoids explicit reference to Lacan or to speech-act theory – though his terminology too is deeply indebted to both. I take it that nearly all latter-day film-study references to psychoanalysis are (by default) to Lacan's Saussurean rewrite of Freud. The most explicit application of Lacan to Capra is Kaja Silverman's "Male Subjectivity and the Celestial Suture," which I discuss in Chapter 6.

7. Summary explications of Lacan are easy to come by and hard to judge against Lacan's own writings, which are anything but summary. A place to start is the "Hitchcock and Film Theory" section of Marshall Deutelbaum and Leland Poague, eds., *A Hitchcock Reader* (Ames: Iowa State Univ. Press, 1986).

8. See J. L. Austin, *How To Do Things with Words,* 2nd ed. (Cambridge: Harvard Univ. Press, 1975). On the application of speech-act theory to film study see Dana Polan's "The Felicity of Ideology."

9. *AV*, pp. 315, 301.
10. Ibid., p. 309.
11. Ibid., p. 310.
12. The implausibility here is curiously confirmed by the fact that Capra misremembers the details of the Paine-Smith relationship in *The Name above the Title*. Paine's argument on behalf of Jeff's appointment, Capra there recounts, hinges on Paine's claim that "Jeff's a fine boy. His father was an old law partner" (*NAT*, p. 257).
13. The script's Jeff is well aware that Taylor is a publisher. See Sidney Buchman, *Mr. Smith Goes to Washington, Twenty Best Film Plays*, ed. John Gassner and Dudley Nichols (New York: Crown, 1943), p. 624.
14. Buchman, p. 619.
15. Browne (cited), p. 10.
16. Ibid., p. 10.
17. Affron, p. 123.
18. Ibid., p. 125.
19. Gallagher (cited), pp. 20–1.
20. Ibid., p. 16.
21. In the screenplay Jeff knows that Willet Creek is "dry four months out of the [year]" and is therefore a poor site choice for a dam. In the film Jeff merely notes that other places in the state need the water just as much before asking who Taylor is. What drives the film's Jeff is clearly the graft issue and not the site question. See Buchman (cited), p. 624.
22. The concept of transitional realms or objects, like my subsequent remarks on "mutual attunement," derives from the theory of "intersubjectivity" elaborated by Jessica Benjamin in *The Bonds of Love*.
23. On the political aspects of the film's production circumstances see Charles Wolfe's "*Mr. Smith Goes to Washington:* Democratic Forums and Representational Forms."
24. This description is accurate for all 16mm prints I have seen. A slight flaw in the print negative has tempted the manufacturers of videotapes of *Mr. Smith* to "restore" the scene by inserting process-shot close-ups of Taylor and Paine, *against* conversation, to cover the glitch, thus obscuring Capra's stylistic program.
25. See Peter Brooks, *The Melodramatic Imagination*, pp. 15, 21, 44, 16, 38 respectively.
26. Ibid., p. 20.
27. Ibid., p. 44.
28. Ibid., p. 32.
29. *PH*, pp. 54–5.
30. Ibid., p. 123.
31. Ibid., p. 209.
32. Ibid., p. 109.

33. Benjamin, p. 12.

34. Ibid., pp. 32, 33, 36, respectively.

35. Ibid., pp. 179–80.

36. Ibid., p. 38. On the applicability of Winnicott's theories of development to discussion of romantic comedy and its insistent childishness or playfulness, see Wendy Lesser's analysis of *The Lady Eve* in the ''Stanwyck'' chapter of *His Other Half.*

37. *PH,* p. 60.

6. ''To Be or Not to Be''

1. On this retrospective aspect of the film see George Toles, '' 'No Bigger than Zuzu's Petals': Dream-Messages, Epiphanies, and the Undoing of Conventions in *It's a Wonderful Life.*'' For that matter, compare my claim about George's ''acknowledging'' his life *as* his with the following (lovely) passage from Toles: ''It is Capra's intention to show that the present only becomes real – real enough so that we can genuinely 'hear the urgent ring of its presentness' – when one accepts the *enormousness* of what one is in one's achieved relation to things'' (p. 46).

2. Kaja Silverman, ''Male Subjectivity and the Celestial Suture: *It's a Wonderful Life,*'' *Framework* no. 14 (1981), 17.

3. Ibid., p. 22.

4. Robin Wood, ''Ideology, Genre, Auteur,'' p. 63.

5. Robert B. Ray, *A Certain Tendency of the Hollywood Cinema, 1930–1980,* p. 200.

6. Wood, p. 65.

7. Ray, pp. 203–4.

8. Ibid., pp. 213, 179, 34.

9. *AV,* p. 429.

10. Ibid., p. 410.

11. Silverman, p. 16.

12. Barbara Deming, *Running Away from Myself: A Dream Portrait of America Drawn from the Films of the Forties* (New York: Grossman, 1969), p. 115.

13. On the links between *Lost Horizon* and *It's a Wonderful Life* see Christian Viviani's chapter on the two films (''Les deux visages de Shangri-La'') in *Frank Capra.*

14. Stanley Cavell, *Disowning Knowledge,* p. 187.

15. Stanley Cavell, *The Claim of Reason,* pp. 351–2.

16. Stanley Cavell, ''The Uncanniness of the Ordinary,'' p. 176.

17. Cavell, *Disowning Knowledge,* pp. 21, 94.

18. Cavell, *The Claim of Reason,* p. 352.

19. Cavell, *Disowning Knowledge,* p. 6.

20. *Othello,* IV.ii.69, per G. Blakemore Evans, ed., *The Riverside Shakespeare* (Boston: Houghton Mifflin Company, 1974).

21. Cavell, *Disowning Knowledge,* p. 10.

22. *AV,* p. 380.

23. Stanley Cavell, "Being Odd, Getting Even," p. 128.

24. Jessica Benjamin, *The Bonds of Love,* p. 70.

25. Wood, p. 63.

26. Northrop Frye, *A Natural Perspective,* p. 53.

27. Northrop Frye, *The Secular Scripture,* p. 53.

28. Ibid., pp. 54, 52.

29. Silverman, p. 21.

30. Frye, *The Secular Scripture,* p. 173.

31. Ibid., p. 139.

32. Frye, *A Natural Perspective,* p. 18; *PH*, pp. 66–7.

33. Frye, *The Secular Scripture,* p. 178.

34. The observation that Henry Travers was the original Grandpa Vanderhof I owe to Stephen Handzo, "Under Capracorn," p. 170; confirmation comes from checking the first published edition of the play, where Travers is cited in the cast list and pictured in a photograph of one of the supper scenes: Moss Hart and George S. Kaufman, *You Can't Take It with You* (New York: Farrar & Rinehart, 1937).

35. Samuel Hinds refers to the bird as "Jim" in *You Can't Take It with You.* Stewart says, less distinctly, "Come on, Jimmy" as he swings (or flies) over the Building and Loan counter to speak with Uncle Billy in *It's a Wonderful Life.* That they are referring to the same bird is confirmed in Jeanine Basinger, *The It's a Wonderful Life Book,* p. 17.

36. Frye, *The Secular Scripture,* p. 172.

Postscript: The Catastrophe of Success

1. Fredric Jameson, *The Political Unconscious: Narrative as a Social Symbolic Act* (Ithaca, N.Y.: Cornell Univ. Press, 1981), p. 102.

2. See Jonathan Culler, *The Pursuit of Signs: Semiotics, Literature, Deconstruction* (Ithaca, N.Y.: Cornell Univ. Press, 1981), and David Bordwell, *Making Meaning: Inference and Rhetoric in the Interpretation of Cinema* (Cambridge: Harvard Univ. Press, 1989).

3. My language evokes, derives from, Monroe Beardsley's *Aesthetics: Problems in the Philosophy of Criticism* (New York: Harcourt, 1958); see p. 279 especially.

4. See Janet Staiger, *Interpreting Films: Studies in the Historical Reception of American Cinema* (Princeton: Princeton Univ. Press, 1992), p. 46. Staiger cites

Bennett citing Macherey. My own closest engagement with Bennett and Macherey, of some relevance in the present context, is ''History/Cinema/Criticism (2).''

5. Lee Lordeaux, *Italian and Irish Filmmakers,* pp. 139, 134, 133, respectively; Joseph McBride, *Frank Capra,* p. 39.

6. The sketchiness of Capra's recollections of his childhood is indicated by the fact that he graduates from ''Caltech'' (*sic*) on p. 9 of *The Name above the Title.* That event does not surface in McBride's account until p. 100.

7. McBride, p. 657.

8. On Capra's egomania see McBride, p. 271.

9. Ibid., p. 412.

10. Ibid., p. 522.

11. Ibid., pp. 522, 77, 606, respectively.

12. Ibid., p. 238.

13. Ibid., p. 469.

14. Ibid., p. 238.

15. Ibid., pp. 260, 202, 280, respectively.

16. Ibid., pp. 214, 215, 252, respectively.

17. Ibid., pp. 432–3.

18. Elliott Stein, ''Frank Capra,'' p. 186.

19. Elizabeth Kendall, *The Runaway Bride,* p. 122.

20. For a more film-centered analysis of Capra's style, I heartily recommend Richard T. Jameson's ''The Lighthouse.''

21. Kendall, pp. xiv–xvi.

22. Ibid., p. 14.

23. Ibid, pp. 19, 20.

24. McBride, pp. 153, 184. It is worth noting here that McBride's description of *His First Flame* does not correspond at every point to the film as described in Hanson. Also worth noting is Joyce Rheuban's claim that Arthur Ripley rather than Capra was responsible for the ''dark side'' of Langdon's comedies, including an element of the ''perverse'' that Rheuban associates explicitly with ''the bizarre eroticism'' latent in Langdon's ''amorphous sexual identity.'' Although Rheuban is correct in claiming that such elements ''do not conform to Capra's view of the [Langdon] character as an elf whose only ally was God,'' those elements *do* correspond to the view of gender relations in Capra set forth in the present study. See Rheuban's ''Footnote: Arthur Ripley and the Dark Side of Langdon's Comedies'' in *Harry Langdon,* especially pp. 205–7.

25. McBride, pp. 416, 522.

26. Kendall, p. 131.

27. Elaine Showalter, ''Representing Ophelia: Women, Madness, and the Responsibilities of Feminist Criticism,'' *Shakespeare and the Question of Theory,* ed. Patricia Parker and Geoffrey Hartman (New York; Methuen, 1985), pp. 77–94; see p. 81. Showalter, I should point out, reads this ''immersion,'' in the case of Laertes's ''surrender to his own fluidity – that is, his tears,'' as ''temporary.'' He ''becomes a man again in becoming once more dry.'' I am moved to wonder whether George ever really ''dries out'' in *It's a Wonderful Life* – especially in view of the film's notorious capacity to evoke tears at its conclusion.

28. McBride, p. 535.

29. Ibid., pp. 540, 466.

30. Ibid., p. 77.

31. See Jimmy Stewart, ''Frank Capra's Merry Christmas to All.''

32. For a different reading of the barber scene in *State of the Union* see Andrew Britton's *Katharine Hepburn*.

Selected Bibliography

The indispensable bibliographies for Capra scholars are Charles Wolfe's *Frank Capra: A Guide to References and Resources* and the scholarly apparatus appended to Joseph McBride's *Frank Capra: The Catastrophe of Success.*

The bibliography that follows, while providing documentation of those (mostly post-1980) sources that proved most crucial to the present study, is also designed to supplement Wolfe and McBride – hence the general *exclusion* of sources already listed in Wolfe and, similarly, the *inclusion* of foreign-language materials, few of which had any sustained effect on my thinking. Pre-1980 sources that did *not* play a central role in the drama of my writing are documented in my notes. (Though the claims I make were inspired by and addressed to "domestic" Anglo–American film study debates, I especially regret not having had earlier access to Christian Viviani's insightful study of Capra.)

The advent of home-video and cable has occasioned many cursory "second-generation" reviews of Capra's films; most of these I have not listed, nor have I included brief "book note" reviews of recent books *about* Capra.

A number of items pertain more to critical debates surrounding Stanley Cavell's theories of film genre than to Capra per se, though I (obviously) take those debates to be crucial to the task of interpreting Capra's contribution to American culture and cinema. A more extensive Cavell bibliography is appended to Fleming and Payne's *The Senses of Stanley Cavell.*

Where an essay has been repeatedly reprinted, I have generally limited my entry to the initial publication and to the source cited in my notes. In most cases, more complete publication histories are available in Wolfe.

Affron, Charles. *Cinema and Sentiment.* Chicago: Univ. Chicago Press, 1982.

Alix, Yves. "*Les Horizons perdus* et *M. Smith au Sénat.*" *Positif* no. 321 (Nov. 1987): 63–7.

Amengual, Barthélemy. "Les bonnes fées de Frank Capra, ou 'Dire merci à l'Amérique.' " *Positif* nos. 317–18 (July–Aug. 1987): 4–10.

Amiel, Vincent. "La raison des justes: Sur *l'Enjeu* et *Vous ne l'importerez pas avec vous*." *Positif* nos. 317–18 (July–Aug. 1987): 17–18.

Andrew, Dudley. "Meet John Doe." *Enclitic* nos. 10–11 (Fall 1981–Spring 1982): 111–19. Reprinted as "Productive Discord in the System: Hollywood *Meets John Doe*." *Film in the Aura of Art*. Princeton: Princeton Univ. Press, 1984, pp. 78–97. Reprinted as "Productive Discord in the System: Hollywood *Meets John Doe*." Wolfe, *Meet John Doe*, pp. 253–68.

Babington, Bruce, and Peter William Evans. *Affairs to Remember: Comedy of the Sexes*. Manchester: Manchester Univ. Press, 1989.

Basinger, Jeanine. "America's Love Affair with Frank Capra." *American Film* 7(5) (Mar. 1982): 46–51, 81.

——"Collector's Choice: Meet Frank Capra." *American Film* 13(3) (Dec. 1987): 59–62.

——*The It's a Wonderful Life Book*. New York: Knopf, 1986.

Behlmer, Rudy. "A Dream and a Vision: *Lost Horizon*." *America's Favorite Movies: Behind the Scenes*. New York: Ungar, 1982, pp. 22–39.

Bellicha, Amit. "Capra en prise sur l'air du temps: Le plaisir du cinéma." *Jeune Cinéma* no. 179 (Feb.–Mar. 1987): 23–9.

Belton, John. "James Stewart: Homegrown." *Close-Ups: The Movie Star Book*. Ed. Danny Peary. New York: Workman, 1978, pp. 537–42. Reprinted as "James Stewart." *Cinema Stylists*. By Belton. Filmmakers 2. Metuchen, N.J.: Scarecrow, 1983, pp. 330–9.

Benjamin, Jessica. *The Bonds of Love: Psychoanalysis, Feminism, and the Problem of Domination*. New York: Pantheon, 1988.

Blake, Richard A. "The Screwball Comedy: *It Happened One Night*." *Screening America: Reflections on Five Classic Films*. New York: Paulist Press, 1991, pp. 103–27.

Blakefield, William J. "A War Within: The Making of *Know Your Enemy – Japan*." *Sight & Sound* 52(2) (Spring 1983): 128–33.

Bonitzer, Pascal. "Frank Capra: La machine à influencer." *Cahiers du cinéma* no. 357 (Mar. 1984): 36–9.

Bordwell, David. *Narration in the Fiction Film*. Madison: Univ. Wisconsin Press, 1985.

Bordwell, David, Janet Staiger, and Kristin Thompson. *The Classical Hollywood Cinema: Film Style & Mode of Production to 1960*. New York: Columbia Univ. Press, 1985.

Bourget, Jean-Loup. "Un livre." *Positif* nos. 317–18 (July–Aug. 1987): 44.

Bowman, Barbara. *Master Space: Film Images of Capra, Lubitsch, Sternberg, and Wyler*. Contributions to the Study of Popular Culture 31. New York: Greenwood, 1992.

Britton, Andrew. ''Appendix: State of the Union and The Desk Set.'' *Katharine Hepburn: The Thirties and After*. Newcastle upon Tyne: Tynside Cinema, 1984, pp. 111–13.

Brooks, Peter. *The Melodramatic Imagination: Balzac, Henry James, Melodrama, and the Mode of Excess*. New Haven: Yale Univ. Press, 1976.

Browne, Nick. ''The Politics of Narrative Form: Capra's *Mr. Smith Goes to Washington*.'' *Wide Angle* 3(4) (1979): 4–11.

——Review of *American Vision: The Films of Frank Capra,* by Raymond Carney. *Wide Angle* 10(3) (1988): 63–4.

——''Sistem di produzione/sistema di rappresentazione: *Meet John Doe*.'' *Hollywood in Progress: Itinerari cinema televisione*. Ed. Vito Zagarrio. Venice: Marsilio, 1984, pp. 53–72. Reprinted as ''System of Production/System of Representation: Industry Context and Ideological Form in Capra's *Meet John Doe*.'' Wolfe, *Meet John Doe,* pp. 269–88.

Capra, Frank. ''Breaking Hollywood's 'Pattern of Sameness.' '' *New York Times Magazine* (5 May 1946): 18, 57. Reprinted as ''Briser l'uniformité de la production: Telle est la tâche que se sont fixée les producteurs indépendants.'' Trans. Pierre Véronneau. *Positif* nos. 317–18 (July–Aug. 1987): 28–30.

——*The Name above the Title*. New York: Macmillan, 1971. Reprinted as *Hollywood Story: Autobiographie*. Trans. Ronald Blunden. Paris: Stock, 1976. Ramsay Poche Cinéma. Paris: Ramsay, 1985. Reprinted as *Autobiographie*. Trans. Sylvia Höfer. Zurich: Diogenes, 1992.

——''The Name above the Title.'' With Richard Schickel et al. Introduction by Michel Cieutat. *Positif* nos. 317–18 (July–Aug. 1987): 32–45.

——''Sacred Cows to the Slaughter.'' *Stage* 13(10) (July 1936): 40–41.

——''A Sick Dog Tells Where It Hurts.'' *Esquire* (Jan. 1936): 87, 130.

Carlson, Susan. *Women and Comedy: Rewriting the British Theatrical Tradition*. Ann Arbor: Univ. Michigan Press, 1991.

Carney, Raymond. *American Vision: The Films of Frank Capra*. Cambridge: Cambridge Univ. Press, 1986.

——''Dreams, Deeds, Words, Gasps, and Glances–Frank Capra's *Mr. Deeds Goes to Town*.'' *Notebooks in Cultural Analysis,* vol. 3. Ed. Norman F. Cantor. Durham: Duke Univ. Press, 1986, pp. 221–47.

——''Frank Capra and American Modernism–Notes Towards the Reevaluation of a Cliché.'' *Art & Artist* 16(1) (Jan. 1987): 8–14.

——''Life Achievement Award: Frank Capra.'' *Magill's Cinema Annual, 1983: A Survey of 1982 Films*. Ed. Frank N. Magill and Patricia King Hanson. Englewood Cliffs, N.J.: Salem Press, 1983, pp. 1–15.

——''My Capra.'' *The Boston Phoenix* (20 Sept. 1991): Sec. 3, p. 8.

Caron, Alain. ''De *Vous ne l'importerez avec vous* à *L'enjeu:* naissance du scepticisme.'' *Jeune Cinéma* no. 179 (Feb.–Mar. 1987): 29–30.

——''Seuls les téméraires devraient faire des films: L'autobiographie de Capra.'' *Jeune Cinéma* no. 179 (Feb.–Mar. 1987): 31–2.

Cavell. Stanley. ''Being Odd, Getting Even: Threats to Individuality.'' *Salmagundi* no. 67 (Summer 1985): 97–128. Reprinted as ''Being Odd, Getting Even (*Descartes, Emerson, Poe*).'' Cavell, *In Quest of the Ordinary,* pp. 105–30.

——''A Capra Moment.'' *Humanities* 6(4) (1985): 3–7.

——*The Claim of Reason: Wittgenstein, Skepticism, Morality, and Tragedy.* New York: Oxford Univ. Press, 1979.

——*Conditions Handsome and Unhandsome: The Constitution of Emersonian Perfectionism.* Chicago: Univ. Chicago Press, 1990.

——*Disowning Knowledge: In Six Plays of Shakespeare.* Cambridge: Cambridge Univ. Press, 1987.

——''The Fact of Television.'' *Daedalus* 111(4) (Fall 1982): 75–96. Reprinted in Cavell, *Themes Out of School,* pp. 235–68.

——*In Quest of the Ordinary: Lines of Skepticism and Romanticism.* Chicago: Univ. Chicago Press, 1988.

——''In Quest of the Ordinary: Texts of Recovery.'' *Romanticism and Contemporary Criticism.* Ed. Morris Eaves and Michael Fischer. Ithaca: Cornell Univ. Press, 1986, pp. 183–214. Reprinted as ''Texts of Recovery (*Coleridge, Wordsworth, Heidegger. . .*).'' Cavell, *In Quest of the Ordinary,* pp. 50–75.

——''Knowledge as Transgression: Mostly a Reading of *It Happened One Night.*'' *Daedalus* 109(2) (Spring 1980): 147–75. Reprinted as ''Knowledge as Transgression: *It Happened One Night.*'' Cavell, *Pursuits of Happiness,* pp. 71–109.

——''Naughty Orators: Negation of Voice in *Gaslight.*'' *Languages of the Unsayable: The Play of Negativity in Literature and Literary Theory.* Ed. Sanford Budick and Wolfgang Iser. New York: Columbia Univ. Press, 1989, pp. 340–77.

——''Postscript (1989): To Whom It May Concern.'' *Critical Inquiry* 16(2) (Winter 1990): 248–89.

——''Psychoanalysis and Cinema: The Melodrama of the Unknown Woman.'' *Images in Our Souls: Cavell, Psychoanalysis, and Cinema.* Psychiatry and the Humanities, vol. 10. Ed. Joseph H. Smith and William Kerrigan. Baltimore: Johns Hopkins Univ. Press, 1987, pp. 11–43. Reprinted in *The Trial(s) of Psychoanalysis.* Ed. Françoise Meltzer. Chicago: Univ. Chicago Press, 1988, pp. 227–58.

——*Pursuits of Happiness: The Hollywood Comedy of Remarriage.* Cambridge: Harvard Univ. Press, 1981.

——"A Response to Robert Mankin." *Salmagundi* no. 67 (Summer 1985): 90–6. Reprinted as "The Skeptical and the Metaphorical." Cavell, *In Quest of the Ordinary,* pp. 144–9.

——*Themes Out of School: Effects and Causes.* San Francisco: North Point, 1984; Chicago: Univ. Chicago Press, 1988.

——"Two Cheers for Romance." *Passionate Attachments: Thinking About Love.* Ed. Willard Gaylin and Ethel Person. New York: Free Press; London: Collier Macmillan, 1988, pp. 85–100.

——"Ugly Duckling, Funny Butterfly: Bette Davis and *Now, Voyager.*" *Critical Inquiry* 16(2) (Winter 1990): 213–47.

—— "The Uncanniness of the Ordinary." *The Tanner Lectures on Human Values,* vol. 8. Ed. Sterling M. McMurrin. Salt Lake City: Univ. Utah Press; Cambridge: Cambridge Univ. Press, 1988, pp. 81–117. Reprinted in Cavell, *In Quest of the Ordinary,* pp. 153–78.

——"What Becomes of Things on Film?" *Philosophy and Literature* 2(2) (Fall 1978): 249–57. Reprinted in Cavell, *Themes Out of School,* pp. 173–83.

——"What Photography Calls Thinking." *Raritan* 4(4) (Spring 1985): 1–21. Reprinted in *Raritan Reading.* Ed. Richard Poirier. New Brunswick: Rutgers Univ. Press, 1990, pp. 47–65.

——*The World Viewed: Reflections on the Ontology of Film.* Enlarged edition. Cambridge: Harvard Univ. Press, 1979.

Ching, Barbara, and Rita Barnard. "From Screwballs to Cheeseballs: Comic Narrative and Ideology in Capra and Reiner." *New Orleans Review* 17(3) (Fall 1990): 52–9.

Christensen, Terry. " 'We're the People': Reel Politics in the Late Thirties." *Reel Politics: American Political Movies from* Birth of a Nation *to* Platoon. Oxford: Blackwell, 1987, pp. 43–53.

Cieutat, Michel. *Frank Capra.* Paris: Rivages, 1988.

Ciment, Michel. "Capra revisité." *Positif* no. 338 (Apr. 1989): 74–5.

Comuzio, E. Review of *Accade una notte: Frank Capra (1928–1934) e la Columbia (1934–1945). Cineforum* no. 291 (Jan.–Feb. 1990): 92–3.

Cook, Pam, ed. *The Cinema Book.* London: British Film Institute; New York: Pantheon, 1985.

Corliss, Richard. "Our Town: George Bailey Meets 'True,' 'Blue,' and 'Peggy Sue.' " *Film Comment* 22(6) (Dec. 1986): 9–17.

——"Still Talking." *Film Comment* 28(6) (Nov.–Dec. 1992): 11–23.

Coursodon, Jean-Pierre, with Pierre Sauvage. "Frank Capra (1897)." *American Directors,* 2 vols. New York: McGraw-Hill, 1983, vol. 1, pp. 41–9.

Culbert, David. " 'Why We Fight': Social Engineering for a Democratic Society at War." *Film & Radio Propaganda in World War II*. Ed. K. R. M. Short. London: Croom Helm, 1983. Knoxville: Univ. Tennesee Press, 1983, pp. 173–91.

Dawidoff, Heidi G. "Endings." *Between the Frames: Thinking about Movies*. Hamden, Conn.: Archon, 1989, pp. 178–92.

Denby, David. "It's a Wonderful War." *Premiere* (Jan. 1990): 33–4.

Dervin, Daniel. "Conditions into Conventions: The Genres of Comedy and Science Fiction." *Through a Freudian Lens Deeply: A Psychoanalysis of Cinema*. Hillsdale, N.J.: Analytic Press/Lawrence Erlbaum Associates, 1985, pp. 153–97.

Dick, Bernard F. *The Merchant Prince of Poverty Row: Harry Cohn of Columbia Pictures*. Lexington: Univ. Kentucky Press, 1993.

Dickstein, Morris. "It's a Wonderful Life, But. . . ." *American Film* 5(7) (May 1980): 42–57. Reprinted (expanded) as "Frank Capra: Politics and Film." *The Artist and Political Vision*. Ed. Benjamin R. Barber and Michael J. Gargas McGrath. New Brunswick: Transaction Books, 1982, pp. 317–33. Reprinted (expanded) as "The People Vs. Frank Capra: Populism in Popular Culture." *CUNY English Forum*, vol. 1. Ed. Saul N. Brody and Harold Schechter. New York: AMS, 1985, pp. 23–44.

Doane, Mary Anne. *The Desire to Desire: The Woman's Film of the 1940s*. Bloomington: Indiana Univ. Press, 1987.

Edgerton, Gary. "Capra and Altman: Mythmaker and Mythologist." *Literature/Film Quarterly* 11(1) (1983): 28–35.

El Guedj, Fédéric. "*L'homme de la rue*." *Cinématographe* no. 97 (Feb. 1984): 61–2.

Estrin, Allen. *The Hollywood Professionals, Volume 6: Capra, Cukor, Brown*. South Brunswick: A. S. Barnes; London: Tantivy, 1980.

Eyquem, Olivier. "Quelques éclairs dans la nuit." *Positif* no. 267 (May 1983): 36–9.

Fischer, Lucy. "Mr. Dummar Goes to Town: An Analysis of *Melvin and Howard*." *Film Quarterly* 36(1) (Fall 1982): 32–40.

Fischer, Michael. *Stanley Cavell and Literary Skepticism*. Chicago: Univ. Chicago Press, 1989.

Fleming, Richard, and Michael Payne. *The Senses of Stanley Cavell*. *Bucknell Review* 32(1). Lewisburg: Bucknell Univ. Press, 1989.

Frank, Sam. "*Lost Horizon* Losses Restored." *American Cinematographer* 68(7) (July 1987): 46–54.

——"*Lost Horizon* – A Timeless Journey." *American Cinematographer* 67(4) (Apr. 1986): 30–9.

Frye, Northrop. *A Natural Perspective: The Development of Shakespearean Comedy and Romance*. New York: Columbia Univ. Press, 1961.

——*The Secular Scripture: A Study of the Structure of Romance*. Cambridge: Harvard Univ. Press, 1976.

Garis, Robert. "Hollywood Romantic Comedy." *Raritan* 7(3) (1988): 130–48.

Garrett, Greg. "Muffling the Bell of Liberty: Censorship and the World War II Documentary." *Journal of the American Studies Association of Texas* 22 (Oct. 1991): 63–73.

Gehring, Wes. " 'The Electric Horseman': A Contemporary 'Capra' Film." *Journal of Popular Film* 10(4) (Winter 1983): 175–82.

——*Handbook of American Film Genres*. New York: Greenwood, 1988.

——*Screwball Comedy: A Genre of Madcap Romance*. New York: Greenwood, 1986.

——"Screwball Comedy: An Overview." *Journal of Popular Film and Television* 13(4) (Winter 1985): 178–85.

——*Screwball Comedy: Defining a Film Genre*. Muncie, Ind.: Ball State Univ. Press, 1983.

Gewen, Barry. "It Wasn't Such a Wonderful Life." *New York Times Book Review* (3 May 1992): 3, 37.

Glatzer, Richard, and John Raeburn, eds. *Frank Capra: The Man and His Films*. Ann Arbor: Univ. Michigan Press, 1975.

Gordon, Andrew. "You'll Never Get Out of Bedford Falls: The Inescapable Family in American Science Fiction and Fantasy Films." *Journal of Popular Film and Television* 20(2) (Summer 1992): 2–8.

Gottlieb, Sidney. "From Heroine to Brat: Frank Capra's Adaptation of *Night Bus* (*It Happened One Night*)." *Literature/Film Quarterly* 16(2) (1988): 129–36.

Handzo, Stephen. "Under Capracorn." *Film Comment* 8(4) (Nov.–Dec. 1972): 8–14. Reprinted in *Great Film Directors: A Critical Anthology*. Ed. Leo Braudy and Morris Dickstein. New York: Oxford Univ. Press, 1978, pp. 160–72.

Hanson, Patricia King, and Alan Gevinson, eds. *Meet Frank Capra: A Catalog of His Work*. Palo Alto: The Stanford Theatre Foundation; Los Angeles: The National Center for Film and Video Preservation, 1990.

Harvey, James. *Romantic Comedy in Hollywood, from Lubitsch to Sturges*. New York: Knopf, 1987.

Harvey, Stephen. "The Strange Fate of Barbara Stanwyck." *Film Comment* 17(2) (Mar.–Apr. 1981): 34–6.

Henderson, Brian. "Harvard Film Studies: A Review." *Film Quarterly* 35(4) (Summer 1982): 22–34.

——"A Musical Comedy of Empire." *Film Quarterly* 35(2) (Winter 1981–2): 2–16.

Henry, Michael. "Capra." *Dictionnaire du cinéma*. Paris: Larousse, 1986, p. 101.

Hill, Steven P. "Le confessioni del 'filibustiere' Frank Capra." *Banco e Nero* 23(5) (May 1962): 49–57. Reprinted as "Confessions of a 'Swindler.' " *Focus Magazine* 2(2) (June 1982): 6–9.

Hurley, Neil P. "The Divine Comedies of Frank Capra." *America* (New York) (20 Apr. 1985): 322–4.

——"Joe Walker: The Cameraman." *New Orleans Review* 12(4) (Winter 1985): 71–81.

Jameson, Richard T. "The Lighthouse." *Film Comment* 28(1) (Jan.–Feb. 1992): 24–7.

——"Stanwyck & Capra." *Film Comment* 17(2) (Mar.–Apr. 1981): 37–9.

Jarvie, Ian. "The Burma Campaign on Film: 'Objective Burma' (1945), 'The Stilwell Road' (1945) and 'Burma Victory' (1945)." *Historical Journal of Film, Radio and Television* 8(1) (1988): 55–73.

——*Philosophy of the Film: Epistemology, Ontology, Aesthetics*. New York: Routledge and Kegan Paul, 1987.

Kapsis, Robert E. "Beyond Hitchcock." *Hitchcock: The Making of a Reputation*. Chicago: Univ. Chicago Press, 1992. pp. 216–46.

Katsahnias, Iannis. "Les nouvelles jeunesses situationnistes." *Cahiers du cinéma* no. 435 (Sept. 1990): 34–7.

Kauffmann, Stanley. "Double Features." *New Republic* 206 (8 June 1992): 44–50.

Keane, Marian. "The Authority of Connection in Stanley Cavell's *Pursuits of Happiness*." *Journal of Popular Film and Television* 13(3) (Fall 1985): 139–50.

Kendall, Elizabeth. *The Runaway Bride: Hollywood Romantic Comedy of the 1930s*. New York: Knopf, 1990.

Lambert, Gavin. "The World Outside the Pictures." *Los Angeles Times Book Review* (17 May 1992): 2, 13.

Larvor, Mariette. "Capra et James Stewart: Le marriage de l'Europe et du rêve américain." *Positif* nos. 317–18 (July–Aug. 1987): 25–7.

Leff, Leonard. Review of *American Vision: The Films of Frank Capra*, by Raymond Carney. *Georgia Review* 42(1) (1988): 211.

Lesser, Wendy. *His Other Half: Men Looking at Women Through Art*. Cambridge: Harvard Univ. Press, 1991.

Levine, Lawrence W. "Hollywood's Washington: Film Images of National Politics During the Great Depression." *Prospects: An Annual of American Cultural Stud-*

ies, vol. 10. Ed. Jack Salzman. New York: Cambridge Univ. Press, 1985, pp. 169–95.

Lordeaux, Lee. *Italian and Irish Filmmakers in America.* Philadelphia: Temple Univ. Press, 1990.

Luke, Timothy W. ''Xmas Ideology: Unwrapping the American Welfare State Under the Christmas Tree.'' *Sexual Politics and Popular Culture.* Ed. Diane Raymond. Bowling Green, Ohio: Bowling Green State Univ. Popular Press, 1990, pp. 219–30.

Magny, Joël. ''Frank Capra: Le réalisme de l'utopie.'' *Cahiers du cinéma* no. 405 (Mar. 1988): xv.

Maland, Charles J. *Frank Capra.* Boston: Twayne, 1980.

——''Frank Capra at Columbia: Necessity and Invention.'' *Columbia Pictures: Portrait of a Studio.* Ed. Bernard F. Dick. Lexington: Univ. Press of Kentucky, 1992, pp. 70–88.

Marchetti, Gina. ''The Threat of Captivity: Hollywood and the Sexualization of Race Relations in *The Girls of the White Orchid* and *The Bitter Tea of General Yen.*'' *Journal of Communication Inquiry* 11(1) (Winter 1987): 29–42.

Masson, Alain. ''Une démonstration et une critique: Sur *La Vie est belle* et *l'Homme de la rue.*'' *Positif* nos. 317–18 (July–Aug. 1987): 13–16.

McBride, Joseph. *Frank Capra: The Catastrophe of Success.* New York: Simon & Schuster, 1992.

Modleski, Tania. *Feminism Without Women: Culture and Criticism in a ''Postfeminist'' Age.* New York: Routledge, 1991.

Murray, Tom. ''Aren't Capra and Life Still Wonderful.'' *Classic Images* no. 92 (Feb. 1983): 68–9.

Neale, Steve, and Frank Krutnik. ''The Comedy of the Sexes.'' *Popular Film and Television Comedy.* London: Routledge, 1990, pp. 132–73.

Neill, Alex. ''Kinship and Separation in Cavell's *Pursuits of Happiness.*'' *Philosophy and Literature* 11(1) (Apr. 1987): 136–47.

Neve, Brian. ''Hollow Man.'' *Sight & Sound* 3(2) (Feb. 1993): 35–6.

——''Populism, Romanticism and Frank Capra.'' *Film and Politics in America: A Social Tradition.* London: Routledge, 1992, pp. 28–55.

Palmer, James W., and Michael M. Riley. ''America's Conspiracy Syndrome: From Capra to Pakula.'' *Studies in the Humanities* 8(2) (Mar. 1981): 21–7.

Pearce, Frederick William. *An Analysis of Frank Capra's 'Why We Fight' Films (1942–1945) as Documentary Film Rhetoric.* Ph.D. dissertation, Univ. Pittsburgh, 1990.

Pechter, William. ''American Madness.'' *Kulchur* 3(12) (Winter 1962): 64–77. Reprinted in *Twenty-four Times a Second: Film and Film-makers*. New York: Harper & Row, 1971, pp. 123–32.

Pinciroli, Gianmarco. ''1 – Gesti, atti, azioni in *Accadde una notte*.'' *Cineforum* no. 279 (Nov. 1988): 56–62.

Poague, Leland. ''Cavell and the Fantasy of Criticism: Shakespearean Comedy and *Ball of Fire*.'' *CineAction!* no. 9 (Summer 1987): 47–55.

——*The Cinema of Frank Capra: An Approach to Film Comedy*. South Brunswick: A.S. Barnes; London: Tantivy, 1975.

——''Engendering *Vertigo*,'' *Hitchcock Annual* (forthcoming 1994).

——''History/Cinema/Criticism (2).'' *Film Studies: Proceedings of the Purdue University Sixth Annual Conference on Film*. West Lafayette, Ind., 1982, pp. 214–19.

——''Pursuits of Happiness: Cavell and Film Criticism,'' *Film Criticism* 7(2) (1983): 53–62.

——Review of *American Vision: The Films of Frank Capra*, by Raymond Carney. *Film Quarterly* 40(4) (Summer 1987): 25–7.

——Review of *A Certain Tendency of the Hollywood Cinema, 1930–1980*, by Robert B. Ray. *Film Criticism* 10(2) (1986): 39–47.

——Review of *The Hollywood Professionals, Volume 6: Capra, Cukor, Brown*, by Allen Estrin. *Film Criticism* 5(2) (1981): 70–4.

Polan, Dana. ''The Felicity of Ideology: Speech Acts and the 'Happy Ending' in American Films of the 1940's.'' *Iris* 3(1) (1985): 35–45.

——''The Light Side of Genius: Hitchcock's *Mr. and Mrs. Smith* in the Screwball Tradition.'' *Comedy/Cinema/Theory*. Ed. Andrew Horton. Berkeley: Univ. California Press, 1991, pp. 131–52.

Quart, Leonard. ''Frank Capra and the Popular Front.'' *Cineaste* 8(1) (1977): 4–7. Reprinted in *American Media and Mass Culture: Left Perspectives*. Ed. Donald Lazere. Berkeley: Univ. California Press, 1987, pp. 178–83.

——''A Populist in Hollywood: Frank Capra's Politics.'' *Socialist Review* 13(2) (Mar.–Apr. 1983): 58–74.

Ray, Robert B. *A Certain Tendency of the Hollywood Cinema, 1930–1980*. Princeton: Princeton Univ. Press, 1985.

Rheuban, Joyce. *Harry Langdon: The Comedian as Metteur-en-Scène*. Rutherford: Fairleigh Dickinson Univ. Press; London: Associated Univ. Press, 1983.

Richards, Jeffrey. ''Frank Capra and the Cinema of Populism.'' *Cinema* (London) no. 5 (Feb. 1970): 22–8. Reprinted in *Movies and Methods: An Anthology*. Ed. Bill Nichols. Berkeley: Univ. California Press, 1976, pp. 65–77.

——Review of *American Vision: The Films of Frank Capra,* by Raymond Carney. *Journal of American Studies* 21(3) (Dec. 1987): 450–1.

Rimoldi, Oscar A. "Frank Capra: A Great Director with a Great Heart!" *Hollywood Studio Magazine* 18(12) (1985): 36–9.

Roth, Marty. "Slap-Happiness: The Erotic Contract of *His Girl Friday*." *Screen* 30(1–2) (Winter–Spring 1989): 160–75.

Rothman, William. "Hollywood Reconsidered: Reflections on the Classical American Cinema." *East–West Film Journal* 1(1) (Dec. 1986): 36–47. Reprinted in *The "I" of the Camera: Essays in Film Criticism, History, and Aesthetics.* By Rothman. Cambridge: Cambridge Univ. Press, 1988, pp. 1–10. Reprinted in Fleming and Payne, *The Senses of Stanley Cavell,* pp. 175–85.

——"Hollywood and the Rise of Suburbia." *East–West Film Journal* 3(2) (June 1989): 96–105.

——"Overview: What Is American about Film Study in America?" *Melodrama and Asian Cinema.* Ed. Wimal Dissanayake. Cambridge: Cambridge Univ. Press, 1993, pp. 254–77.

Rubenstein, Elliot. "The Home Fires: Aspects of Sturges's Wartime Comedy." *Quarterly Review of Film Studies* 7(2) (Spring 1982): 131–41.

Saada, Nicolas. "Reine d'un jour." *Cahiers du cinéma* no. 446 (July–Aug. 1991): 58–9.

Sainderichin, Guy-Patrick. "Rétrospective Capra: Capra, c'est pas fini!" *Cahiers du cinéma* no. 353 (Nov. 1983): vii.

Sante, Luc. "American Pie." *New York Review of Books* (28 Jan. 1993): 17–19.

Sarris, Andrew. "Footage Fetish: Recovering 'Lost Horizon.' " *Village Voice* (23 Sept. 1986): 55, 66.

Scheer, Ronald. "Doublevision: TV Remakes Frank Capra." *Journal of Popular Film and Television* 8(2) (Summer 1980): 28–33.

Schelly, William. *Harry Langdon.* Metuchen, N.J.: Scarecrow, 1982.

Scheman, Naomi. "Missing Mothers/Desiring Daughters: Framing the Sight of Women." *Critical Inquiry* 15(1) (Autumn 1988): 62–89.

——"Othello's Doubt/Desdemona's Death: The Engendering of Skepticism." *Power, Gender, Values.* Ed. Judith Genova. Edmonton, Alberta: Academic Printing & Publishing, 1987, pp. 113–33.

Scherle, Victor, and William Turney Levy. *The Complete Films of Frank Capra,* 1977. New York: Citadel Press–Carol Publishing Group, 1992.

Schultz, Robert. "Celluloid History: Postwar Society in Postwar Popular Culture." *American Studies* 31(1) (Spring 1990): 41–63.

Shiner, Roger A. ''Getting to Know You.'' *Philosophy and Literature* 9(1) (Apr. 1985): 80–94.

——''Masculinizing the Problem of Skepticism.'' *Power, Gender, Values*. Ed. Judith Genova. Edmonton, Alberta: Academic Printing & Publishing, 1987, pp. 134–42.

Shumway, David R. ''Screwball Comedies: Constructing Romance, Mystifying Marriage.'' *Cinema Journal* 30(4) (Summer 1991): 7–23.

Sikov, Ed. *Screwball: Hollywood's Madcap Romantic Comedies*. New York: Crown, 1989.

Silverman, Kaja. ''Male Subjectivity and the Celestial Suture: *It's a Wonderful Life*.'' *Framework* no. 14 (1981): 16–22. Reprinted (excerpts) in ''Historical Trauma and Male Subjectivity.'' *Male Subjectivity at the Margins*. By Silverman. New York: Routledge, 1992, pp. 52–121.

Sklar, Robert. ''American Sadness.'' *Village Voice* (10 May 1986): 70.

——''God and Man in Bedford Falls: Frank Capra's *It's a Wonderful Life*.'' *The American Self: Myth, Ideology, and Popular Culture*. Ed. Sam B. Girgus. Albuquerque: Univ. New Mexico Press, 1981, pp. 211–20.

Springer, Claudia. ''Military Propaganda: Defense Department Films about World War II and Vietnam.'' *Cultural Critique* no. 3 (Spring 1986): 151–67.

Stanbrook, Alan. ''As It Was in the Beginning.'' *Sight & Sound* 59(1) (Winter 1989–90): 28–32.

Steele, Richard W. '' 'The Greatest Gangster Movie Ever Filmed': *Prelude to War*.'' *Prologue* 11(4) (Winter 1979): 220–35.

Stein, Elliott. ''Frank Capra.'' *Cinema: A Critical Dictionary: The Major Film-Makers*. 2 vols. Ed. Richard Roud. London: Secker & Warburg, 1980, vol. 1, pp. 181–8.

Stewart, Jimmy. ''Frank Capra's Merry Christmas to All.'' *Reader's Digest* (Dec. 1991): 81–5.

—— ''The Many-Splendored Actor: An Interview with Jimmy Stewart.'' With Neil P. Hurley. *New Orleans Review* 10(2–3) (Summer–Fall 1983): 5–14. Reprinted as ''Entretien avec James Stewart.'' *Cahiers du cinéma* no. 358 (Apr. 1984): 18–25.

Thompson, David. ''Falling in Love Again: Divorce and Remarriage in the Movies.'' *Film Comment* 18(2) (Mar.–Apr. 1982): 9–17.

Thompson, Robert. ''American Politics on Film.'' *Journal of Popular Culture* 20(1) (Summer 1986): 27–47.

Tobin, Yann. ''Capra et ses acteurs.'' *Positif* nos. 317–18 (July–Aug. 1987): 19.

——''Le Cinema Retrouvé: *New York–Miami* et *Lady Eve:* Transports (amoureux) en commun.'' *Positif* no. 310 (Dec. 1986): 64–6.

Toles, George. '' 'No Bigger than Zuzu's Petals': Dream-Messages, Epiphanies, and the Undoing of Conventions in *It's a Wonderful Life.*'' *North Dakota Quarterly* 52(3) (Summer 1984): 43–66.

Tomasulo, Frank P. ''Colonel North Goes to Washington: Observations on the Intertextual Re-presentation of History.'' *Journal of Popular Film and Television* 17(2) (Summer 1989): 82–8.

Vecchi, Paolo. ''*La vita è meravigliosa* di Frank Capra.'' *Cineforum* no. 271 (Jan.–Feb. 1988): 50–4.

Veillon, Olivier-René. ''Frank Capra.'' *Le Cinéma américain, Les années trente, 1929–1945.* Collection ''Point-Virgule.'' Paris: Seuil, 1986, pp. 36–49.

Véronneau, Pierre. ''Le contexte.'' *Positif* nos. 317–18 (July–Aug. 1987): 30–1.

Vineberg, Steve. ''Master of Manipulation.'' *Threepenny Review* no. 54 (Summer 1993): 28–31.

Viviani, Christian. ''Capraland: Sur *L'Extravagant Monsieur Deeds.*'' *Positif* nos. 317–18 (July–Aug. 1987): 11–12.

——*Frank Capra.* Collection Spectacle/Poche 2. Paris: Lherminier-Éditions des Quatre-vents, 1988.

——''Qui est sans péché: Le mélo maternal dans le cinéma américain, 1930–39.'' *Les Cahiers de la Cinémathèque* no. 28 (July 1979): 73–87. Reprinted as ''Who Is Without Sin?: The Maternal Melodrama in American Film, 1930–39.'' Trans. Dolores Burdick. *Wide Angle* 4(2) (1980): 4–17. Reprinted as ''Who Is Without Sin?: The Maternal Melodrama in American Film, 1930–39.'' Trans. Dolores Burdick. *Home Is Where the Heart Is: Studies in Melodrama and the Woman's Film.* Ed. Christine Gledhill. London: BFI, 1987, pp. 83–99. Reprinted as ''Who Is Without Sin?: The Maternal Melodrama in American Film, 1930–39.'' Trans. Dolores Burdick. *Imitations of Life: A Reader of Film & Television Melodrama.* Ed. Marcia Landy. Detroit: Wayne State Univ. Press, 1991, pp. 168–82.

Viviani, Christian, and Yann Tobin. ''Capra et Barbara Stanwyck: éclat et éclatment du mélo.'' *Positif* nos. 317–18 (July–Aug. 1987): 20–4.

Warren, Paul. ''Imitation et récupération d'Eisenstein.'' *Études-Littéraires* (Quebec) 20(3) (Winter 1987–88): 27–49.

Weales, Gerald. *Canned Goods as Caviar: American Film Comedy of the 1930s.* Chicago: Univ. Chicago Press, 1985.

Willett, Cynthia. ''Hollywood Comedy and Aristotelian Ethics: Reconciling Differences.'' *Sexual Politics and Popular Culture.* Ed. Diane Raymond. Bowling Green, Ohio: Bowling Green State Univ. Popular Press, 1990, pp. 15–24.

Willis, Ellen. "Sins of the Fathers." *Village Voice* (15 Dec. 1987): 85–6.

Wolfe, Charles. *Frank Capra: A Guide to References and Resources.* Boston: G. K. Hall, 1987.

——ed. *Meet John Doe.* New Brunswick: Rutgers Univ. Press, 1989.

——"*Mr. Smith Goes to Washington:* Democratic Forums and Representational Forms." *Close Viewings: An Anthology of New Film Criticism.* Ed. Peter Lehman. Tallahassee: Florida State Univ. Press, 1990, pp. 300–32.

——"The Return of Jimmy Stewart: The Publicity Photograph as Text." *Wide Angle* 6(4) (1985): 44–52.

——Review of *An Examination of Narrative Structure in Four Films of Frank Capra,* by Brian Rose. *Post Script* 1(2) (Winter 1982): 75–8.

Wood, Robin. "Ideology, Genre, Auteur." *Film Comment* 13(1) (Jan.–Feb. 1977): 46–51. Reprinted in *Film Genre Reader.* Ed. Barry Keith Grant. Austin: Univ. Texas Press, 1986, pp. 59–73.

Zagarrio, Vito. *Accade Una Notte: Frank Capra (1928–1934) e la Columbia (1934–1945).* Rome: Di Giacomo, 1989.

——*Frank Capra.* Il Castoro Cinema 112. Florence: La Nuova Italia, 1985.

Zucker, Carole. "On 'Over-Reading' and 'Under-Reading' Films." *Canadian Review of American Studies* 17(1) (Summer 1986): 251–5.

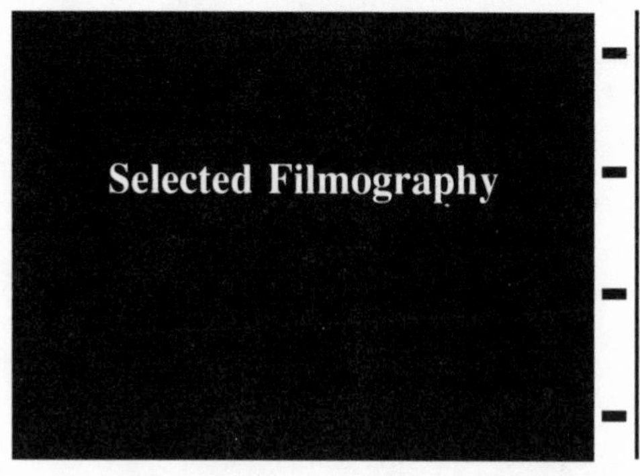

Selected Filmography

Many Capra filmographies are in print and readily available, the two most definitive being that included in Charles Wolfe's *Frank Capra: A Guide to References and Resources* and *Meet Frank Capra: A Catalog of His Work,* produced by the staff of the American Film Institute Catalog under the executive editorship of Patricia King Hanson. The filmography appended to Joseph McBride's *Frank Capra: The Catastrophe of Success* is more recent (and recently researched) than the first two sources cited, though McBride provides far less complete cast lists and production credits. The filmographic entries that follow are limited primarily to those films treated at some length in the present volume and to those credits most pertinent to the interpretive approach I have taken. Because standard Capra filmographies vary remarkably in regards to running times, I have whenever possible listed the running time of the best available video issue of the film in question. For readers who may not have immediate access to more comprehensive filmographies, I have appended, as prologue to the more extended entries, a list of feature-length theatrical and documentary films written, directed, produced, and/or supervised by Capra, keyed to release dates. Finally, less extensive credits are supplied for those non-Capra films referred to with some frequency in the present study.

The Films of Frank Capra

1926 – *Tramp, Tramp, Tramp*
The Strong Man
1927 – *Long Pants*
His First Flame
For The Love of Mike
1928 – *That Certain Thing*
So This Is Love
The Matinee Idol
The Way of the Strong
Say It with Sables
Submarine
The Power of the Press
1929 – *The Younger Generation*
The Donovan Affair
Flight
1930 – *Ladies of Leisure*
Rain or Shine
1931 – *Dirigible*
The Miracle Woman
Platinum Blonde
1932 – *Forbidden*
American Madness

1933 – *The Bitter Tea of General Yen*
Lady for a Day
1934 – *It Happened One Night*
Broadway Bill
1936 – *Mr. Deeds Goes to Town*
1937 – *Lost Horizon*
1938 – *You Can't Take It with You*
1939 – *Mr. Smith Goes to Washington*
1941 – *Meet John Doe*
1943 – *Prelude to War*
The Nazis Strike
Divide and Conquer
The Battle of Britain
Know Your Ally: Britain
The Battle of Russia
1944 – *The Negro Soldier*
Tunisian Victory
The Battle of China
Arsenic and Old Lace
1945 – *War Comes to America*
The Stilwell Road
Know Your Enemy: Japan
Here Is Germany
1946 – *It's a Wonderful Life*
1948 – *State of the Union*
1950 – *Riding High*
1951 – *Here Comes the Groom*
1952 – *Westward the Women*
1956 – *Our Mr. Sun*
1957 – *Hemo the Magnificent*
The Strange Case of the Cosmic Rays
1958 – *The Unchained Goddess*
1959 – *A Hole in the Head*
1961 – *Pocketful of Miracles*

Capra Fims Discussed in Depth

Ladies of Leisure (1930). Columbia Pictures/A Frank R. Capra Production. Producer: Harry Cohn. Director: Frank R. Capra. Screenplay: Jo Swerling, from the play *Ladies of the Evening* by Milton Herbert Gropper. Photography: Joseph Walker. Music: Bakaleinikoff. Editing: Maurice Wright. Art direction: Harrison Wiley. Cast: Barbara Stanwyck (Kay Arnold), Ralph Graves (Jerry Strong), Lowell Sherman (Bill Standish), Marie Prevost (Dot Lamar), Nance O'Neil (Mrs. Strong), George Fawcett (Mr. Strong), Johnnie Walker (Charlie), Juliette Compton (Claire Collins). 98 or 102 minutes. (A silent version with titles by Dudley Early was released for theaters unequipped for sound; the longer version is probably the silent print.)

Platinum Blonde (1931). Columbia Pictures/A Frank R. Capra Production. Producer: Harry Cohn. Director: Frank R. Capra. Story: Harry E. Chandlee, Douglas W. Churchill. Adaptation: Jo Swerling. Dialogue: Robert Riskin. Continuity: Dorothy Howell. Photography: Joseph Walker. Editing: Gene Milford. Cast: Loretta Young (Gallagher), Robert Williams (Stew Smith), Jean Harlow (Anny Schuyler), Halliwell Hobbes (Smythe), Reginald Owen (Dexter Grayson), Walter Catlett (Bingy Baker), Louise Closser Hale (Mrs. Schuyler), Edmund Breese (Conroy), Donald Dillaway (Michael Schuyler), Claude Allister (Dawson). 89 minutes.

Forbidden (1932). Columbia Pictures/A Frank R. Capra Production. Producer: Harry Cohn. Director: Frank R. Capra. Story: Frank Capra. Adaptation and dialogue: Jo Swerling. Photography: Joseph Walker. Editing: Maurice Wright. Cast: Barbara Stanwyck (Lulu Smith), Adolphe Menjou (Bob Grover), Ralph Bellamy

(Al Holland), Dorothy Peterson (Helen Grover), Myrna Fresholt (Roberta, baby), Charlotte V. Henry (Roberta, 18), Harry Holman ("Mary Sunshine"). 85 minutes.

American Madness (1932). Columbia Pictures/A Frank Capra Production. Producer: Harry Cohn. Director: Frank R. Capra. Screenplay: Robert Riskin. Photography: Joseph Walker. Editing: Maurice Wright. Cast: Walter Huston (Thomas Dickson), Pat O'Brien (Matt Brown), Kay Johnson (Phyllis Dickson), Constance Cummings (Helen), Gavin Gordon (Cyril Cluett), Arthur Hoyt (Ives), Edwin Maxwell (Clark), Robert E. O'Connor (Inspector). 76 minutes.

The Bitter Tea of General Yen (1933). Columbia Pictures/A Frank Capra Production. Director: Frank R. Capra. Screenplay: Edward Paramore, from the novel by Grace Zaring Stone. Photography: Joseph Walker. Music: W. Frank Harling. Editing: Edward Curtis. Cast: Barbara Stanwyck (Megan Davis), Nils Asther (General Yen), Toshia Mori (Mah-Li), Walter Connolly (Jones), Gavin Gordon (Robert Strike), Richard Loo (Captain Li). 87 minutes.

It Happened One Night (1934). Columbia Pictures/A Frank Capra Production. Director: Frank Capra. Screenplay: Robert Riskin, from the story "Night Bus" by Samuel Hopkins Adams. Photography: Joseph Walker. Music: Louis Silvers. Editing: Gene Havlick. Cast: Clark Gable (Peter Warne), Claudette Colbert (Ellie Andrews), Walter Connolly (Alexander Andrews), Roscoe Karns (Oscar Shapely), Jameson Thomas (King Westley). 105 minutes.

Mr. Deeds Goes to Town (1936). Columbia Pictures/A Frank Capra Production. Director: Frank Capra. Screenplay: Robert Riskin, from the story "Opera Hat" by Clarence Budington Kelland. Photography: Joseph Walker. Art direction: Stephen Goosson. Music: Howard Jackson. Editing: Gene Havlick. Cast: Gary Cooper (Longfellow Deeds), Jean Arthur (Louise "Babe" Bennett), George Bancroft (MacWade), Lionel Stander (Cornelius Cobb), Douglass Dumbrille (John Cedar), Raymond Walburn (Walter), H. B. Warner (Presiding Judge), Ruth Donnelly (Mabel Dawson), Walter Catlett (Morrow), John Wray (Farmer), Warren Hymer (Bodyguard), Wryley Birch (Psychiatrist), Arthur Hoyt (Budington), Jameson Thomas (Mr. Semple), Mayo Methot (Mrs. Semple), Charles Lane (Hallor), Margaret Seddon (Jane Faulkner), Margaret McWade (Amy Faulkner), Edwin Maxwell (Douglas). 115 minutes.

Lost Horizon (1937). Columbia Pictures/A Frank Capra Production. Director: Frank Capra. Screenplay: Robert Riskin, from the novel by James Hilton. Photography: Joseph Walker. Aerial photography: Elmer Dyer. Special camera effects: E. Roy Davidson, Ganahl Carson. Art direction: Stephen Goosson. Music: Dimitri Tiomkin, Max Steiner. Editing: Gene Havlick, Gene Milford. Costumes: Ernst Dryden. Cast: Ronald Colman (Robert Conway), Jane Wyatt (Sondra Bizet), Edward Everett Horton (Alexander P. Lovett), John Howard (George Conway), Thomas Mitchell (Henry Barnard), Margo (Maria), Isabel Jewell (Gloria Stone), H. B.

Warner (Chang), Sam Jaffe (High Lama), Hugh Buckler (Lord Gainsford). 132 minutes.

You Can't Take It with You (1938). Columbia Pictures. Director: Frank Capra. Screenplay: Robert Riskin, from the play by George S. Kaufman and Moss Hart. Photography: Joseph Walker. Art direction: Stephen Goosson, Lionel Banks. Music: Dimitri Tiomkin, Morris Stoloff. Editing: Gene Havlick. Cast: Jean Arthur (Alice Sycamore), Lionel Barrymore (Grandpa Vanderhof), James Stewart (Tony Kirby), Edward Arnold (Anthony P. Kirby), Misha Aueur (Boris Kolenkhov), Ann Miller (Essie Carmichael), Spring Byington (Penny Sycamore), Samuel S. Hinds (Paul Sycamore), Donald Meek (Mr. Poppins), H. B. Warner (Ramsey), Halliwell Hobbes (Mr. DePinna), Dub Taylor (Ed Carmichael), Mary Forbes (Mrs. Kirby), Lillian Yarbo (Rheba), Eddie Anderson (Donald), Clarence Wilson (John Blakely), Charles Lane (Wilbur G. Henderson), Harry Davenport (Judge), Robert Greig (Lord Melville). 127 minutes.

Mr. Smith Goes to Washington (1939). Columbia Pictures. Director: Frank Capra. Screenplay: Sidney Buchman, from the story "The Gentleman from Montana" by Lewis R. Foster. Art direction: Lionel Banks. Music: Dimitri Tiomkin, M. W. Stoloff. Editing: Gene Havlick, Al Clark. Montage: Slavko Vorkapich. Cast: Jean Arthur (Clarissa Saunders), James Stewart (Jefferson Smith), Claude Rains (Senator Joseph Paine), Edward Arnold (Jim Taylor), Guy Kibbee (Governor Hubert Hopper), Thomas Mitchell (Diz Moore), Eugene Pallette (Chick McGann), Beulah Bondi (Ma Smith), H. B. Warner (Senate majority leader), Harry Carey (President of the Senate), Astrid Allwyn (Susan Paine), Ruth Donnelly (Mrs. Emma Hopper), Grant Mitchell (Senator MacPherson), Porter Hall (Senator Monroe), Pierre Watkin (Senate minority leader), Charles Lane (Nosey), William Demarest (Bill Griffith), Billy Watson, Delmar Watson, John Russell, Harry Watson, Gary Watson, Baby Dumpling (The Hopper boys), H. V. Kaltenborn (himself). 129 minutes.

Meet John Doe (1941). Frank Capra Productions. Distributed by Warner Bros. Pictures. Director: Frank Capra. Screenplay: Robert Riskin, from the story "A Reputation" by Richard Connell. Photography: George Barnes. Special effects: Jack Cosgrove. Art direction: Stephen Goosson. Music: Dimitri Tiomkin, Leo F. Forbstein. Editing: Daniel Mandell. Montage effects: Slavko Vorkapich. Cast: Gary Cooper (Long John Willoughby), Barbara Stanwyck (Ann Mitchell), Edward Arnold (D. B. Norton), Walter Brennan (The "Colonel"), Spring Byington (Mrs. Mitchell), James Gleason (Connell), Gene Lockhart (Mayor Lovett), Rod La Rocque (Ted Sheldon), Irving Bacon (Beany), Regis Toomey (Bert Hansen), Ann Doran (Mrs. Hansen), J. Farrell MacDonald ("Sourpuss" Smithers). 123 minutes.

It's a Wonderful Life (1946). Liberty Films. Distributed by RKO Radio Pictures. Producer: Frank Capra. Director: Frank Capra. Screenplay: Frances Goodrich, Albert Hackett, Frank Capra, from the story "The Greatest Gift" by Philip Van Doren

Stern. Photography: Joseph Walker, Joseph Biroc. Photographic effects: Russell A. Culley. Art direction: Jack Okey. Set decoration: Emile Kuri. Music: Dimitri Tiomkin. Editing: William Hornbeck. Cast: James Stewart (George Bailey), Donna Reed (Mary Hatch), Lionel Barrymore (Mr. Potter), Henry Travers (Clarence Oddbody), Thomas Mitchell (Uncle Billy), Beulah Bondi (Mrs. Bailey), Frank Faylen (Ernie), Ward Bond (Bert), Gloria Grahame (Violet Bick), H. B. Warner (Mr. Gower), Todd Karns (Harry Bailey), Samuel S. Hinds (Peter Bailey), Mary Treen (Cousin Tilly), Frank Albertson (Sam Wainwright), Virginia Patton (Ruth Dakin), Clarence Williams (Cousin Eustace), Sarah Edwards (Mrs. Hatch), William Edmunds (Mr. Martini), Lillian Randolph (Annie), Argentina Brunetti (Mrs. Martini), Bobby Anderson (Little George), Jean Gale (Little Mary), Jeanine Anne Roose (Little Violet), Georgie Nokes (Little Harry Bailey), Sheldon Leonard (Nick), Karolyn Grimes (Zuzu), Harry Holman (Mr. Partridge), J. Farrell MacDonald (house owner), Stanley Andrews (Mr. Welsh). 130 minutes.

State of the Union (1948). Liberty Films. Distributed by Loew's Inc. (MGM). Producer: Frank Capra. Associate Producer: Anthony Veiller. Director: Frank Capra. Screenplay: Anthony Veiller, Myles Connolly, from the play by Howard Lindsay and Russel Crouse. Photography: George J. Folsey. Special effects: A. Arnold Gillespie. Art direction: Cedric Gibbons, Urie McCleary. Music: Victor Young. Editing: William Hornbeck. Cast: Spencer Tracy (Grant Matthews), Katharine Hepburn (Mary Matthews), Van Johnson (''Spike'' MacManus), Angela Lansbury (Kay Thorndyke), Adolphe Menjou (Jim Conover), Tom Pedi (Barber). 124 min.

Additional Films Cited

1925 – *The Gold Rush* (Chaplin Studio/United Artists, dir. Charles Chaplin)
1931 – *The Front Page* (Caddo Company/United Artists, dir. Lewis Milestone)
1932 – *Scarface* (Atlantic Pictures/United Artists, dir. Howard Hawks)
1937 – *The Awful Truth* (Columbia Pictures, dir. Leo McCarey)
Stella Dallas (Goldwyn/United Artists, dir. King Vidor)
1938 – *Bringing Up Baby* (RKO, dir. Howard Hawks)
1940 – *His Girl Friday* (Columbia Pictures, dir. Howard Hawks)
1941 – *The Lady Eve* (Paramount, dir. Preston Sturges)
1942 – *Now, Voyager* (Warner Bros., dir. Irving Rapper)
1948 – *Letter from an Unknown Woman* (Rampart Production/Universal International, dir. Max Ophuls)
1949 – *Adam's Rib* (MGM, dir. George Cukor)

Index